# Agustín Lara

## A Cultural Biography

ANDREW GRANT WOOD

OXFORD
UNIVERSITY PRESS

# OXFORD
### UNIVERSITY PRESS

Oxford University Press is a department of the University of Oxford.
It furthers the University's objective of excellence in research,
scholarship, and education by publishing worldwide.

Oxford   New York

Auckland   Cape Town   Dar es Salaam   Hong Kong   Karachi
Kuala Lumpur   Madrid   Melbourne   Mexico City   Nairobi
New Delhi   Shanghai   Taipei   Toronto

With offices in

Argentina   Austria   Brazil   Chile   Czech Republic   France   Greece
Guatemala   Hungary   Italy   Japan   Poland   Portugal   Singapore
South Korea   Switzerland   Thailand   Turkey   Ukraine   Vietnam

Oxford is a registered trade mark of Oxford University Press
in the UK and certain other countries.

Published in the United States of America by
Oxford University Press
198 Madison Avenue, New York, NY 10016

Library of Congress Cataloging-in-Publication Data
Wood, Andrew Grant, 1958-author.
Agustín Lara: A Cultural Biography / Andrew Grant Wood.
pages cm
Includes bibliographical references, filmography, and index.
ISBN 978-0-19-989245-7
1. Lara, Agustín, 1897–1970. 2. Composers—Mexico—Biography. I. Title.
ML410.L284W66   2014
780.92—dc23
[B]
2012029552

Publication of this book was supported by the Gustave Reese Endowment of the American Musicological Society.

1 3 5 7 9 8 6 4 2

Printed in the United States of America
on acid-free paper

Lara exalts the Lost Woman, in whose eyes are seen sun-drunk palm trees; he beseeches love from the Decadent One, in whose pupils boredom spreads like a peacock's tail; he dreams of the sumptuous bed of the silky-skinned Courtesan; with sublime ecstasy he deposits roses at the feet of the Sinful One, and covers the Shameful Whore with incense and jewels in exchange for the honey of her mouth.

—Eduardo Galeano

# CONTENTS

See also the Lara discography online at www.oup.com/us/agustinlara

# LIST OF ILLUSTRATIONS

# ACKNOWLEDGMENTS

Studying Agustín Lara has allowed me to pursue my passion for Latin American musical history, literature, film, and urban popular culture. For what has been a fascinating, decade-long journey, I first would like to acknowledge support from the University of California Institute for Mexico and the United States (UC MEXUS). Support from the University of Tulsa Office of Research, Center for Global Education, Department of History, and the Arts and Sciences Dean's Office also proved invaluable.

In Mexico, staff at the Universidadad Nacional Autonónoma de México (UNAM) Filmoteca, UNAM Hermeroteca, Archivo General de la Nación, Biblioteca Lerdo de Tejada, Archivo General del Estado de Veracruz (Xalapa), Archivo Municipal de Veracruz (Port of Veracruz), Casa Cultural de Agustín Lara (Tlacotalpan), and the Casita Blanca (Boca del Río) patiently responded to my questions and many requests for material. Curators at the Juan Antonio Pérez Simon private collection in Mexico City were also generous in granting me access to Lara materials. I am grateful to all for their professionalism and warm hospitality. In the United States, librarians at the Nettie Lee Benson Collection at the University of Texas, Austin, UC Berkeley's Bancroft Library, and the McFarlin Library at the University of Tulsa all provided helpful assistance.

Monica Barczak, Thomas Buoye, Jeffrey Pilcher, and Elissa Rashkin reviewed earlier drafts and made helpful suggestions. Arnold Bauer, Rob Katz, Bryan McCann, Alejandro Madrid, and Mark Pedelty read various versions of the entire manuscript and provided many insightful comments. Cheryl Clay offered her perfect pitch in sounding out certain portions of the Lara songbook. Pável Granados, Pablo Dueñas, and Jesús Flores y Escalante generously provided information on Lara's recordings. Mónica Barrón Echauri helpfully shared biographical details for some of the musician-poet's closest friends. María de los Ángeles Magdaleno Cárdenas greatly assisted me in gaining access to the Juan Antonio Pérez Simón collection. Bruce Dean Willis generously lent his considerable talent in helping polish song lyric translations, while Alicia Chesser and Arley Ward greatly improved the manuscript's overall presentation. Michael Boyd, Mark Brewin, Olivia Domínguez Pérez, Miguel Fematt, Juan Antonio Flores Martos, Tammy Lewellen, Pepe Ochoa, Ariel Rodríguez Kuri, María del Rosario del Ochoa, Jeffrey Pilcher, Terry Rugeley, Margarita Peraza-Rugeley, Amy Nicole Salvaggio, and Minerva Saldivar, among many others, have provided helpful encouragement along the way. More recently, Celeste McNeal has helped sustain me with her joyful spirit.

Musicologist John Koegel deserves special mention for stepping forward after reviewing the manuscript and unflinchingly supporting the project by sharing sheet music, reference materials, and publications. His painstaking commentary on several drafts, attention to detail, and guidance has greatly contributed to this study.

This book is lovingly dedicated to my parents Mary A. Wood (Wendy) and Grant R. Wood, who provided a home environment where an appreciation for music was encouraged. Having just recently discovered a Canadian edition of "Canciones del Corazón" (Songs of the Heart) by the popular Trío Los Panchos in a crate of old family records. I am pleased to learn that the allure of Golden Age Mexican music reached as far north as the beautiful city of Montreal, where Grant and Wendy spent their halcyon days.

# PRELUDE: SELL YOUR LOVE DEARLY

*[Music] cannot be defined as having merely a mathematical, a poetic, or a sensual element . . . it is all these things and much more.*

—Daniel Barenboim[1]

With his chiseled face and long, thin fingers gently dancing on the keyboard, Agustín Lara plays an introductory vamp consisting of a descending cluster of notes before launching into an opening verse with violin, timbales, and his own piano accompaniment. Following the opening bars, he softly sings:

> *Vende caro tu amor aventurera,*
> *da el precio del dolor a tu pasado,*
> *y aquél que de tu boca la miel quiera*
> *que pague con brillantes tu pecado,*
> *que pague con brillantes tu pecado.*

> Sell your love dearly, adventuress,
> Charge for the pains of your past,
> And he who wants the honey from your lips
> Let him pay for your sin with jewels,
> Let him pay for your sin with jewels.[2]

A two-measure instrumental transition moves the song into the chorus, which takes on a determined tone:

> *Ya que la infamia de tu ruin destino*
> *marchitó tu admirable primavera,*
> *haz menos escabroso tu camino*
> *vende caro tu amor . . . aventurera.*

Since the infamy of your sad fate
has forever stained your once-promising spring,
at least make the best of it
sell your love dearly, adventuress.[3]

Lara then makes his way through an instrumental verse with some light improvising on the melody before turning once again to the chorus and ending with the refrain "vende caro tu amor . . . aventurera." As the last notes of the song fade, the audience politely applauds. The popular composer acknowledges their appreciation and takes a long drag on his cigarette before launching into the next number.[4]

This performance on an early television broadcast—from sometime in the late 1950s or early 1960s—features one of Lara's most famous *boleros*: his 1930 composition "Aventurera" (Adventuress). Here, as in many of his songs, Lara celebrates love, romance, sensuality, and female beauty. In "Aventurera" Lara honors a prostitute. She is thought to be an attractive, youthful figure, yet compromised and subsequently corrupted, if not altogether doomed, by society. Unable to remedy her situation, Lara acknowledges through his lyrics the need for beauty to confront the commercial and material world. Hence the advice, "make them pay dearly for [your] charms."

A musician-composer whose career would extend over four decades of the mid-twentieth century and eventually gain legendary status, Lara serves as a critical link to what the entertainment industry—and the work of some cultural historians—identifies as the Golden Age of Mexican entertainment: the *época de oro*. Running roughly from 1935 to 1960, this now "classic" period is considered as such because it was a time when Mexico developed its radio and film industries. Engendered in this often state-sponsored process designed to influence the hearts and minds of the public at large was an accompanying celebrity star system, archetypical narrative structures, and standard song repertoire. In the context of modernizing Mexico after the Revolution of 1910–1920, Lara's music as broadcast far and wide significantly sparked the nation's imagination.

It is believed that Mexicans at the time still identified with the expectations of the national political elite and that mass media largely conformed to a prescribed set of limitations. As historian John Mraz writes, "The president was the untouchable core of the nation; the wealthy and powerful were to be emulated, the underdogs made picturesque or ignored completely or demonized if they did not follow the rules; [and] the nation was one, indivisible and homogeneous."[5] Postrevolutionary Mexico, in other words, saw the rise of a powerful new political elite who skillfully used cultural programming as a way to bolster their hegemony. My interest in Lara is to connect him to this complex undertaking in Mexico as well as the larger articulations of modernity and the developing global consumer culture in the Americas more generally.[6]

## Global Connections

By the turn of the twentieth century, most of Western society found itself in the throes of major economic, technological, and social change. By no means a universal process, the manner in which a new paradigm took shape—what one can loosely characterize as "modernity"—varied significantly by time and place.

The definitions of "modern," "modernity," and "modernism" vary depending on one's particular focus, time, and place, yet scholars generally agree that the term signifies a processes emanating initially from Europe and further extending with the spread of industrial capitalism. Driven by changes not only in production but also in politics, philosophy, and the arts, this long period of accelerating change began with the Enlightenment, came of age during the second half of the nineteenth century, and extended well into the twentieth. During this period as various metropolitan urban cultures and spaces were significantly reshaped, communications and emerging media acknowledged and sought to influence a mass public that—increasingly found ways to enjoy leisure time pursuits. These and other related historic developments produced an unprecedented array of new sensory impressions, signs, and social interactions across a vast range of different geographies.[7]

In Mexico during the mid- to late nineteenth century, growing secularization and capitalist growth, along with expanding railroad, steamship, and telegraph connections, reshaped the nation and connected it to the world. Advances in finance, medicine, agriculture, industry, administration, law, and a host of other endeavors grew rapidly. Although years of intraelite conflict had produced a general social instability that hampered Mexico's development, Presidents Benito Juárez (1806–1872) and, perhaps even more significantly, Porfirio Díaz (1830–1915) eventually gained the upper hand and brought relative peace to the nation. Still, uneven progress in this regard in addition to a lack of any real democracy brought further challenges to the political and economic order. In 1910, Mexican society erupted in civil war—a process that would further divide the nation for another decade before a new set of political leaders managed to restore law and order by imposing their own disciplinary designs on the body politic.[8]

Lara came of age in this larger international context of political and economic transformation. Emblematic of the new age in Mexico and elsewhere, pathbreaking technological and cultural innovation paralleled political and social change.[9] Photography gained popular acceptance along with a number of other new communications media such as the telephone, typewriter, phonograph, radio, and film. Many sensed an exhilarating feeling of increased social mobility and human potential as countless individuals created fresh opportunities and developed dynamic forms of expression—often across previously impermeable national, regional, ethnic, class, and gendered boundaries. Millions would take part in what can be characterized as the rise of an emerging middle class.

Artists, writers, and creative types of all kinds participated in this epochal transformation across the Americas. A variety of popular music genres and dances won favor. Ragtime, for example, flourished in New Orleans, St. Louis, and New York, *milonga* in Buenos Aires, *maxixe* in Rio de Janeiro, danzón in Havana, and *bambuco* in Bogotá, just to name a few. In rapidly urbanizing Mexico, many eagerly patronized a growing number of entertainment venues where these and other international musical styles could be heard and danced to.

Lara's career is notable—although certainly not unique—in this historic and cultural context in that it depended heavily on the stuff of early- and mid-twentieth-century modernity: cabarets, clubs, movie houses, theaters, concert halls, music publishing, newspapers, sound recording, radio, film, advertising, airplanes, automobiles, and so on.[10] Lara cashed in on the new wave of technological innovation that swept Mexico, the Americas, and Europe in the early-to-mid-twentieth century as his music reached millions of listeners.[11]

His artistic work also critically engaged an emerging modernity in Mexico. Like other artists of the age, the composer's lyrics reflect upon the changing times. He was not an intellectual or an artistic/political vanguardist purportedly seeking to liberate "the masses" like some of his high-minded compatriots. Yet in some of his hugely popular compositions, Lara expressed ambivalence about the kind of fast-paced, capitalist-led initiatives. His songs seduce the listener as they speak of finding a respite from the ordinary, seemingly loveless modern world through romance and idealized beauty.

Lara drew on the innovations and generalized tone of the turn-of-the-century Latin American *modernista* writers—however directly or indirectly—in crafting a melancholic commentary on the condition of social life and a possible temporary escape from that life in the ideal.[12] As his popularity grew in the 1930s and subsequently took on the trappings of legend, his songs were believed to be encoded with an aesthetic message that audiences interpreted as tacitly discounting the material in favor of romanticized notions of love and beauty.[13] To quote the late cultural critic and essayist Carlos Monsiváis (1938–2010), Lara issued a kind of "*modernismo* for the masses."[14]

Lara did not so much intentionally take part in artistic revolt as simply try to make a living for himself as a twentieth-century popular musician, songwriter, and entertainer.[15] He embraced no radical political beliefs and rose to fame in large measure because of his close affiliation with powerful business and political interests associated with the entertainment industry in the Mexican capital.

His popular—often sentimental—promotions of love and romance were some-what ironically made possible by an ever-expanding capitalist communications infrastructure that stretched across much of the American hemisphere and Europe.

Lara did not engage much with either the *corrido* (narrative folk ballad) or *canción ranchera* (rural popular song) forms as these genres increasingly became identified with essentialist identifications of *lo mexicano* (Mexicanness).[16] Rather than constructing a public image as a typical rural *charro* (Mexican cow-boy), which would have been quite difficult for him given his slight build and somewhat underwhelming appearance, he developed a different, more urban-based archetypal role: that of the romantic musician-poet. With this celebrity persona (later to be supplemented by that of the regional Veracruz jarocho), Lara addressed his sonic love poems to the growing ranks of the urban middle class and helped forge a new popular culture that complemented rather than challenged the official discourse of the Mexican state. In so doing, he joined with other artistic producers and celebrities who benefited either directly or indi-rectly from revolutionary elite largesse.[17]

Lara's music provided his audiences with a sentimental education. Writer Sal-vador Novo (1904–1974) commented on the composer's importance in Mex-ico during the formative decades of the twentieth century by observing that "he sang to the nation and his music became an essential spiritual force with which several generations have nourished themselves."[18] Mexican composer and critic Daniel Casteñeda Soriano (1899–1957) noted that Lara produced music that ordinary people could understand as he developed fairly simple yet elegant mel-odies for lyrics that commented on the joys as well as the difficulties of love.[19] Pável Granados has suggested that the composer's music became "a fundamental part of our education [in that] he has been a model for lovers from many dif-ferent sectors of Mexican society."[20] Sociologist María del Carmen de la Peza Casares has noted that his "bolero[s] reflected the multiple articulation of romantic practices and the instrument of transmission of these traditions to the subsequent generation."[21] Each of these writers speaks to the relevance of Lara's music for his listeners in Mexico.[22] But this influence was not limited to Mexican audiences; it extended throughout the Americas, Europe, and beyond thanks to his constant touring, recording, appearances on radio, and work in film and, later, television. His songs were interpreted by countless instrumentalists and singers, thus further extending his influence.

As one of the most recognized composers of popular song, Lara ranks with other important twentieth-century popular musical greats elsewhere in North America such as Irving Berlin (1888–1989), George Gershwin (1898–1937), and Cole Porter (1891–1964), whose compositions could be heard in the in-creasingly transnational entertainment worlds of popular song, musical theater, recording, radio, and film. Like them, Lara was a product of his age. Similarly, his songs reflected events in his own life as well as the anxieties and larger character of the time.[23]

Much of the musician's history remains tangled in the myths he advanced and his admirers subsequently perpetuated. Most of what has been published amounts to historical chronicle, memorabilia, and assorted reflections. To my knowledge, no comprehensive historical archive of Lara material exists, although portions of his extensive work can be found in various collections and libraries in Mexico and the United States.[24] My sources make very little comment about specific recordings. Given the disparate nature of the information, I have nevertheless sought to make the most of assorted personal effects, later recordings, song lyrics, sheet music, films, photographs, media coverage, and previous studies of Lara and his contemporaries. I note explicitly the specific recordings I comment on; however, because of the significant lack of available earlier material, many of these are from the mid- to late 1950s and were released by RCA Victor.

Lara's life and art is here considered in the larger context of twentieth-century Mexico—and to some extent, the Western world. I have attempted to address his music and lyrics in relatively plain language. Song titles have been left in the original Spanish, along with the occasional non-English language phrase whose meaning will be reasonably self-evident.[25]

In Chapter 1, I describe the historical geography of turn-of-the-twentieth-century Mexico City as well as some of the major social and cultural influences taking shape at that time. This overview includes a short history of the Cuban danzón and bolero and how they were taken up and adapted by Mexican musicians. This is followed by a brief discussion of the influence of the modernista poets in Mexico around the turn of the century and the ensuing popular craze for romantic poetry during the Revolution.

Chapter 2 focuses on Lara's early years before, during, and immediately after the Revolution. As a teenager said to have wandered the streets of Mexico City playing piano in bordellos, and later, in cinemas and cafes, this proved a formative time. The young Lara learned the popular styles of the day and slowly gained recognition as a member of a new generation of composers. Here, I argue that Lara did not seek to explicitly redefine Mexican popular song, but rather worked to establish his own style as he borrowed from available international genres. This he did while entertaining for long hours at a stretch in some of Mexico City's most notorious pleasure palaces before moving on to more "legitimate" venues.

Chapter 3 begins with a look at Lara's participation in a variety of musical revues (*teatro de revista*) in Mexico City during the first half of the 1930s. Running parallel to similarly styled Broadway shows, Mexico City stages also featured a host of young, attractive performers sporting the latest

fashions, dances, comedy, and music packaged in lightly scripted, often satirical, productions for nightly consumption. These revues not only provided timely entertainment for audiences, but also served as a proving
ground for a new generation of performing artists—some of whom would
find their way into the soon burgeoning popular media of radio and film.

Chapter 4 follows Lara to Los Angeles, where he worked on the film *Tropic
Holiday*. Subsequently he would tour in France, England, New York, and South
America. This was an especially prolific time, and Lara penned a number of songs
including "Palmeras" (Palms, also known as "Palmera"), "Amor de mis amores"
(Love of My Loves), "Veracruz," "Farolito" (Little Lighthouse), "Noche de
ronda" (Night Moves), "Naufragio" (Shipwreck), "Cada noche un amor" (Every
Night a Love), and "Solamente una vez" (Only Once), as well as a group of songs
about various Spanish cities including the classic "Granada." These works
ensured Lara's immortal status as a composer of popular music.

Chapter 5 considers Lara's life during the mid-1940s, when he courted the
young starlet María Félix and subsequently enjoyed increased public attention
until the two parted ways in the fall of 1947. While it lasted, the Lara–Félix
romance captured the imagination of the nation. Lara's 1946 waltz "María
bonita" forever memorialized their union with its tribute to the film star relaxing
on the beach in Acapulco. Set in the larger context of World War II, the chapter
also details collaboration between the US Office of the Coordinator of Inter-
American Affairs (CIAA) Latin American Division and Mexican broadcasters—
particularly the Azcárraga Group headed by Lara's *patrón* and media mogul
Emilio Azcárraga Vidaurreta.

Chapter 6 looks at Lara's further participation in the film industry, specifically
a series of *cabaretera* (cabaret or dance hall) genre films during the second half of
the 1940s when a Mexican economic boom encouraged the entertainment
industry to grow significantly. Lara benefitted from postwar prosperity as he
toured fairly extensively both inside and outside of Mexico, performing in several South American countries as well as at venues in Central America and Cuba.
By the end of the 1940s, he had begun appearing in films loosely based on his
own life story. Not surprisingly, some of these productions would fare better
with critics and audiences than others.

Chapter 7 completes the Lara story. From the early 1950s up to his death in
the fall of 1970, he continued to participate in film and to tour and compose,
although not at the prolific rate he had earlier in his career. He also took part in a
number of early television broadcasts, providing somewhat nostalgic entertainment for an aging generation being eclipsed by the new, youthful sounds of rock
and roll. Realizing a lifelong goal, Lara was able to travel to Spain twice during
his last years. He also enjoyed frequent visits to Veracruz, where he had a second
home thanks to a generous gift from the state governor.

Since Lara's death, Mexico has experienced many difficult years: continued boom and bust economic cycles, rampant corruption, civil conflict, emigration, femicide, pandemics, and drug wars. Perhaps such a bleak present is why nostalgia for Mexico's mid-twentieth century cultural Golden Age continues to run high. My hope, however, is that readers will find cause in Lara's story to muster renewed optimism in forging new social and cultural practices.

# Agustín Lara

# Music and Mexican Modernity

*Lara is "modernismo" for the masses.*
—Carlos Monsiváis[1]

As a young man coming of age in turn-of-the-century Mexico City, Agustín Lara lived between two worlds. Raised a doctor's son in the fashionable suburb of Coyoacán, he and his family were associated with members of the national elite. Yet during the tumultuous years of the 1910–1917 Revolution, Lara ventured forth as a rebellious young teenager, finding his way in the heart of the growing metropolis where he frequented many of the capital's popular theaters, *tivolis* (recreation gardens), dance halls, restaurants, cafés, cabarets, cinemas, and bordellos.[2] Lara's subsequent work combined lyrical content that spoke of romantic desire in the larger context of social uncertainty and loss drawn from elite literary circles with incipient urban-based rhythms that mixed new, more international styles such as the Argentine tango and Cuban bolero.[3] The resulting Mexican urban sound proved hugely successful in both artistic and commercial terms.

## Mexico City

Late nineteenth-century modernizing Mexico was a society in transition, and Mexico City its showcase. At the heart of this great metropolis lay the Zócalo or main plaza, adjacent to the site where the ruins of the Aztec Templo Mayor can still be seen. In the sixteenth century, Spanish colonizers had appropriated this area and subsequently constructed an immense cathedral and series of government and ecclesiastical buildings around the plaza's perimeter. The late nineteenth century saw a number of dramatic changes to the city's built environment, including the appearance of department stores, banks, boutiques, pharmacies, clothing retailers, millineries, toy shops, book sellers, and furniture outlets. Growth heralded the dawning of a modern urbanism predicated on export-led development, foreign investment, and accelerated consumerism.[4]

Profiling the busy downtown Plateros Street (now Madero) as representative of this bustling era, one guidebook described a colorful cast of characters who graced the city center:

> [The avenue] and the contiguous streets awaken memories of Paris, Naples and Madrid; they are among the liveliest in the city, and one will rarely see a more pleasing spectacle than they offer on a Sunday or holiday... At certain hours in the forenoon, and just before twilight on any day, they are usually thronged with handsome women, gay equipages, hurrying messengers, merchants, priests, American promoters, bull-baiters, *cargadores*, dawdling *lagartijos* (dandies) and groups of animated men who talk business, dodge automobiles, smoke cigarettes, suck caneheads, deplore the high prices of rents, discuss the phenomenal rise in city realty, question the stability of the gold-standard and the fluctuations of silver, and pass the sunny hours with true Latin *insouciance.*[5]

Lara's youthful experience included this and other dynamic Mexico central city scenes framed on the east by the San Lázaro railway station, north by the Peralvillo gate, west by the Alameda Park (Figure 1.1), and running south to Tlaxcoaque Plaza. Beyond these informal boundaries stretched an assortment of neighboring *colonias* (neighborhoods), villages, and small towns that would

*Figure 1.1* The Alemeda. Courtesy of the Agrasanchez Film Archive.

eventually be incorporated into the rapidly expanding urban conglomeration.[6] Commercial elites headquartered in Mexico City directed the national economy and an attendant central state bureaucracy.[7] Resulting wealth generated during this time came largely through the exportation of silver, copper, rubber, coffee, and henequen.

Considerable portions of the federal budget went toward projects in the capital. Advances such as electric lighting, the telegraph, telephone, electric tramlines, and well-paved roads in central areas (Figure 1.2) symbolized Mexico's entry into the modern age.[8] In time, many well-to-do residents in Mexico City moved to new suburbs such as the *colonias* Santa María and San Rafael to the northwest, as well as Juárez and Roma to the southwest, investing in new homes and picturesque gardens. Further to the south, developers created fashionable areas including the Lomas de Chapultepec, Polanco, and Hipódromo Condesa. Other new settlements such as Industrial, Vallejo, Lindavista, Rastro, and Michoacán rose up and offered more affordable homes.[9]

The blossoming of Mexico City into a modern metropolis reflected a larger national process that powerful commercial and state agents had envisioned years earlier. Like elites in Europe and across the Americas, urban reformers sought a rational, open environment that could better facilitate

*Figure 1.2* Avenida Mayo. Courtesy of the Agrasanchez Film Archive.

Economic exchange, social stability, and political order. With internal migration from elsewhere in the Republic and an increasing number of foreigners making their way to the nation's capital, the city's population grew rapidly. The number of inhabitants rose from approximately 329,774 in 1895 to 368,898 in 1900, to 471,066 in 1910, 661,708 in 1921, and 1,048,970 in 1930. In the postrevolutionary decades, population in the capital soared from 1,559,782 in 1940 to 2,872,334 in 1950 and 4,909,961 in 1960.[10]

In contrast to developments to be found in the city core, older areas to the north, east, and south of the Zócalo housed tens of thousands of workers whose labor helped create the many brilliant achievements of Mexico's modern age. Packed into small homes, apartments, tenement houses, adobe huts, and other makeshift constructions, these people populated neighborhoods that played host to a vast cross-section of Mexican society. Less fortunate souls roamed the streets by day and slept at night in alleyways, parks, and flea-bitten flophouses.[11] During the late nineteenth and early twentieth centuries, nearly everyone was made to march to the beat of the new, industrial rhythm.[12]

Elites in Europe and the United States led the way as time–work discipline in accord with the ideology of developmentalism called for a constant drive to bring an ever-expanding range of resources, territories, and populations under capitalist control.[13] "Order" and "progress" became the motto as production and consumption rapidly gained momentum.[14]

The advancing machine age dramatically changed how life was experienced. Railroads, trolleys, telegraph, and telephones all became instrumental in the creation of a modern consciousness.[15] Reflecting the growing influence of capitalist-associated technology and work discipline in Mexico, many mixed a range of new entertainments such as baseball, bicycling, tennis, golf, rowing, and cricket with more traditional pastimes of bullfights, *charreadas* (rodeos), cockfights, gambling, itinerant theater, circuses, acrobats, traveling puppet shows, wrestling, boxing, and jai alai, among other pursuits. Nearly all were accompanied by regular feasting and drinking scheduled to fit with the annual cycle of religious and patriotic holidays.[16]

Elites spent Sundays promenading in the latest European fashions or sitting in the shade at the horse races or bullfights after a midday meal that featured the finest in imported—usually French—cuisine. "Respectable" people (*gente decente*) increasingly expressed their sophistication (i.e., distinction from the popular classes) through consumption and articulations of "taste."[17]

Mass circulation newspapers (i.e., *El Nacional*, *El Tiempo*, *El Globo*, and *El Universal*) marketed the new consumer culture. As well as reporting on current events, each promoted an array of new products.[18] Newspaper editors packed their pages with advertisements for concerts, theater productions, movies, and other cultural events. Extending from the late nineteenth century well into the twentieth, picture postcards and other photographic articulations featured risqué shots of young, attractive women such as Celia Montalván (1900–1958), Esperanza Iris (1888–1962), Mimí Derba (1893–1953), Lupe Rivas Cacho (1894–1975), and Lupe Vélez (1908–1944).[19]

Mexicans marveled at the sights of the first movies when, in August 1896, Frenchman Gabriel Vayre (1871–1936) arranged to have the Lumière brothers' *cinématographe* brought to the capital for a series of public screenings at 9 Plateros Street.[20] Reports at the time told that the new invention had impressed audiences with its "spectacular style" and "scientific promise."[21] Shortly thereafter, Salvador Toscano Barragán (1872–1947) would initiate Mexico's own national cinema with his 1898 film version of the play "Don Juan Tenorio." Enthusiasm for the new medium grew and by the end of 1906, officials registered a total of sixteen new movie houses in the city.[22] Suggesting the advent of an exciting new age, many sported names such as Moderno, Lux, Majestic, Parisiana, and Progreso Mundial.[23]

The capital's entertainment district extended from the Arcos de Belén in the north, south to 5 de Febrero Street, and west to Bucareli and Reforma. Santa María la Redonda and San Juan de Letrán streets (today Eje Lázaro Cárdenas) served as the main north–south axis along which could be found a dizzying array of business and pleasure establishments (Figure 1.3).[24]

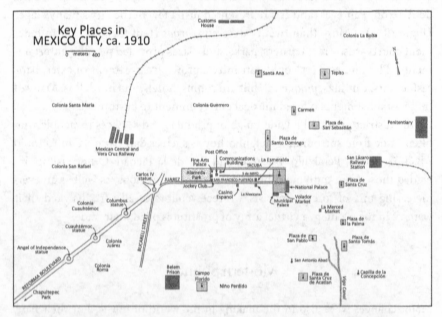

*Figure 1.3* Mexico City, ca. 1910. Cherie Semans, 1997. Courtesy of Michael Johns.

*Figure 1.4* Insurgentes Theater ca. 1960. Courtesy of the Agrasanchez Film Archive.

Within this zone stood prominent establishments such as the Teatro Principal and Teatro Arbeu. Nearby, theaters such as the Apolo, Lírico, Juan Ruíz de Alarcón, Fábregas, and Iris represented just a few of the city's many stages (Figure 1.4).[25] More than twenty different *carpas* (tent theaters) set in tenement courtyards, street corners, parks, and plazas provided popular entertainment.[26] Pleasure-seekers could patronize a growing assortment of cafés, bars, restaurants, cantinas, *pulquerías*, billiard rooms, hotels, and bordellos. Many of these establishments offered musical entertainment to customers.

The district provided a wide range of products and services to people who often came from surrounding neighborhoods such as San Lázaro, San Antonio Abad, Guerrero, Peralvillo, Bucareli, and Río de la Piedad. Other visitors included those from outlying suburbs and provincial regions, as well as an ever-increasing mix of foreign tourists.[27] Street vendors of all sorts hawked their wares.[28] In the evening, a virtual army of prostitutes plied their trade.

## Modern Sounds

Major changes were also in the making in the world of music. For their part, Mexican elites had for some time defined themselves by listening to Italian opera, the music of composers such as Chopin, Granados, Grieg, and Albéniz, and Spanish *zarzuelas*. Salon life featured the sounds of French piano scores as well as mazurkas, polkas, and schottisches. By the end of the nineteenth century the waltz, along with the *danza habanera*—both introduced sometime earlier to Mexico—had become extremely popular.[29]

Into this mix gradually came an infusion of new music developed by a handful of lesser-known artists toiling in the Mexico City shadows. Over the next few years, young composers and players would increasingly incorporate elements of popular Argentine, Cuban, and Colombian music. In the capital, demand for live music surged and soon led to the opening of the Sylvain—Mexico City's first nightclub—in 1908. Scores of similar establishments including dance halls such as the Salón Rojo and the California Dancing Club would open their doors to an entertainment-hungry public.[30] The Salón México, where visitors could enjoy a wide range of performers in three separate ballrooms, was perhaps the most famous of these urban haunts.[31]

In addition to direct contact with other musicians and performers, famil-iarity with these different styles came from increased access gained through the proliferation of various reproduction devices. As a handful of pioneers devel-oped recording technology during the late nineteenth century, music and music appreciation entered a revolutionary era. The new age began with a handful of innovators such as Alexander Graham Bell (1847–1922), Emile Berliner (1851–1929), and Thomas Edison (1847–1931), each working on various sound reproduction devices that would eventually emerge as telephones and phonographs.[32] Edison's first prototypical tinfoil phonograph apparatus ap-peared in 1877. Soon others, such as the North American Phonograph Com-pany, took to the idea and in 1888 came out with what they called "automatic phonographs." For a nickel, one could listen to a two-minute offering through a set of ear tubes. As one scholar writes, "the ear tubes gave the listener the im-pression that the music and entertainment he or she heard was inside his or her own head, thereby deepening the social and psychological impact of their intro-duction to recorded sound."[33]

Meantime, court recorders Edward D. Easton and Roland F. Cromelin founded the Colombia Phonograph Company. Their coin-operated machines could be found in an assortment of public places such as cafes, restaurants, fairs, carnivals, train stations, shopping areas, and a growing number of amusement arcades during the 1890s. Sometimes referred to as "the machine with a soul," new devices represented the advance guard in what would eventually amount to a total technological transformation in the way music was performed and lis-tened to during the twentieth century.[34]

Emile Berliner had established the Berliner Gramophone Company after inventing a hand-driven flat disk to record and play back sound. He then teamed up with inventor and businessman Eldridge Johnson and soon invented a spring-driven motor with the capacity to maintain constant speed on a

turntable. Johnson then improved and subsequently patented the new technology and soon teamed up with Berliner to form the "the Victor Talking
Machine" in 1901. Effective advertising by the two included introduction of
the famous dog "Nipper" logo.[35]

In Brazil, Zonophone had begun operations in 1902. While Brunswick and
Odeon tapped the incipient Latin American market around the same time. At
the same time firms such as Berliner, Edison, and Zonophone similarly marketed early recordings of Latin American music to growing audiences in the
United States.[36] In 1924, the fledgling industry improved the quality of its recordings greatly when engineers managed to incorporate electricity into the
process.

The advent of recording technology made an important difference in the reception of music. No doubt major changes came about in performance as well,
but most significant was the fact that with the availability of phonograph records,
listeners could experience music played and recorded in other places. Enthusiasts gained access to the work of any number of composers and recording artists. From his home in the US Virgin Islands, for example, bandleader Alton
Adams (1889–1987) marveled at the creative potential engendered in the
record listening experience. "How well do I recall," Adams later testified, "the
many hours spent in rhapsodic ecstasy, listening outside the residence of a dev-
otee of the art to the recordings of beautiful music—orchestral and band selections, operatic arias, and so forth, but particularly . . . the marches of Sousa."[37]
For Adams, hearing these discs allowed him to imagine further his own work as
a composer.[38]

## Musical Mexico

With a repertoire of polkas, waltzes, marches, and *danzas*, prominent Italian
American, Mexico-based bandleader and composer Carlos Curti (1859–1926)
realized a series of recordings for the Columbia label in 1904 while on tour in the
United States.[39] That same year, representatives of the American Victor Company produced the first documented sound recordings in Mexico by capturing
two male vocal duos. Soon thereafter, band director and composer Miguel Lerdo
de Tejada's (1869–1941) *Orquesta Típica* recorded for the Edison Company in
Mexico City for the first time.[40]

Eagerly joining in this burgeoning revolution in sound, a handful of public
forums featuring Thomas Edison's cylinder system provided ordinary Mexicans
with their first exposure to recorded sound. One such occasion took place in
January 1913 at Mexico City's Salon Mérida, when sponsors organized an

exhibit of the Victor Phonograph.[41] Soon thereafter, "records" made their way into Mexican life, sparking interest in the imported sounds of Argentine tango, Cuban danzón, and later, American jazz.

The proliferation of recorded music in the early twentieth century led to an unprecedented sharing of musical ideas worldwide. Sound recordings invited listeners to cross temporal, geographic, cultural, and class boundaries in profound new ways. Yet this situation benefited not just consumers but also producers of music for, as George Gershwin remarked, "the composer . . . has been helped a great deal by the mechanical reproduction of music [because] music is written to be heard and any instrument that tends to help it be heard more frequently and by great numbers is advantageous to the person who writes it."[42]

In tracing the emergence of the modern popular music in Mexico, it is essential that the influence of Cuban sound be acknowledged. Danzón was—and still is—a hybrid genre comprised of both European and African traditions, combining contradance with the syncopated rhythm of the *cinquillo*.[43]

Below, the top line shows the sixteenth, eighth, sixteenth, and eighth note values of the 2/4 measure. The line below it is written in orthographic notation and gives a sense of the syncopated feel of the figure. When then expanded to a two-measure sequence so that a three-side/two-side (cross rhythm syncopated/unsyncopated) tension is established, the feel of what would later become known as the Latin *clave* can be heard (Figure 1.5).

While already somewhat popular among Cuban *orquestas*, the first documented danzónes originated in Matanzas in June 1877 with Miguel Faílde Pérez's (1852–1921) compositions "El delirio," "La ingratitude," and "Las quejas," along with his most famous song, "Las Alturas de Simpson" (Simpson Heights).[44]

Born in late 1853 of a Spanish father and a free black (*parda libre*) mother, Faílde lived as a man of color (classified as mulatto) at a time of harsh racial

*Example 1.1* The cinquillo.

*Figure 1.5* Chinos Ramírez danzón orchestra. Courtesy of the Archivo General del Estado de Veracruz.

discrimination. His family was active musically. Miguel mastered the cornet while his brothers Eduardo and Cándido played clarinet and trombone respectively. All three performed in the firefighters' band in Matanzas, which Miguel directed.

The earliest ensembles consisted of one or two violins, a cornet, valve trombone, clarinet, *figle* (similar to a bugle), string bass, timbales, and Afro-Cuban *güiro*.[45] A composition would contain four or more distinct sections, each with its own melody. Often danzón would quote melodic lines from other genres such as opera to satisfy this demand. The resulting blend offered listeners a satisfying variety of sounds despite occasional protestations from some who objected to such open borrowing of musical ideas.[46]

When "Los Alturas de Simpson" was first performed in 1877 it provoked a strong negative reaction from white audiences. Faílde subsequently revised the piece (to soften the African rhythmic influence, one would suspect) and successfully played it as part of a New Year's celebration held at the Club de Matanzas on January 1, 1879.[47] As musicologist Peter Manuel writes,

> In several ways . . . the danzón was novel, and its rapid ascent to popularity was dramatic. The collective figures were forgotten and the bastonero (master of ceremonies) banished, as intimate couple dancing reigned supreme. The jaunty cinquillo (in its creole two-bar form) now emerged as a ubiquitous recurring ostinato. In general, the Afro-Caribbean tinge that had subtly enlivened the danza now became unmistakable and

overwhelming, in the insistent cinquillos, the obstreperous percussion, and the sensually swaying of hips of the dancers. Traditionalists fulminated, either denouncing the rowdy music or, like musicologist and composer Eduardo Sánchez de Fuentes, insisting that it had no African influence. However, their battle was soon lost, and the danzón, as played primarily by black and mulatto musicians, became the new focus of dancers and listeners of all classes and races.[48]

The danzón gained widespread popularity—particularly among the island's middle class and elite after 1880—and soon became known as "the national dance of Cuba." After the turn of the century, composer-musicians Jorge Ankermann (1877–1941), Antonio María Romeu (1876–1955), and Luis Casas Romero (1882–1950) further developed the style.[49]

In the meantime, waves of Cubans had migrated to Mexico during the second half of the nineteenth century. As the expatriates made their way via the Yucatán, Campeche, and the Veracruz coast, they brought the danzón with them. According to Veracruz local chronicler and poet Francisco Rivera Ávila (aka "Paco Pildora," 1908–1998), Cuban migrants came with their "habaneras and *criollas*, *guarachas*, *yambus* and rumbas, claves and *puntos guajiros*."[50] Of course, it was not long before Mexicans took to the new rhythms.

On the mainland, musicians adapted and subsequently performed danzón in a variety of social contexts. In the Port of Veracruz, for example, the popular classes gathered for dances in open-air settings and learned a new, more intimate step which required maneuvering within a small space they termed the *ladrillo*— allegedly defined by the size of a sixty-bottle case of regionally produced Moctezuma beer.[51] Meanwhile, elites frequented salons where they danced the waltz, *contradanza*, and habanera, as well as their own "respectable" interpretation of the danzón.[52] One of the first performances of this music in the Mexican capital took place when Miguel Salas's Compañía de Bufos Habaneros gave a concert at the Teatro Principal on June 28, 1884.[53]

Some of the earliest danzón orchestras (danzoneras) in Mexico included those led by Juan Cumbá, Severiano Pacheco, brothers Joseíto and Tomás Vueltiflor, Alberto Gómez, and Los Chinos Ramírez, while the Veracruz-based Orquesta de Severiano y Albertico proved one of the most popular. Together, they made the genre the musical centerpiece of an emerging popular culture as they performed on festival days and on weekends in a multitude of dance spots, as well as at the Veracruz seaside Villa del Mar resort.[54] By the late 1920s, Veracruz musicians such as Pío García and Feliciano "Chano" Montero, along with other talented players, had made their way to Mexico City where they added their own sound to the expanding cosmopolitan musical mix there. In the meantime, however, an equally dynamic music had taken shape in the Yucatán peninsula: the bolero.[55]

The Cuban bolero—much like the danzón—developed out of a transcultural mix of European and African musical influences.[56] Although the claim is difficult to document, some charge that the bolero has European roots in operatic arias, French romantic music, and Neopolitan song, which were then combined in the Caribbean context with rhythmic traditions of the African diaspora.[57]

For many observers, danzón is the father of the bolero.[58] As was the case in the evolution of danzón, conditions that would later lead to the development of the bolero in the twentieth century began to take shape in conjunction with the growing assertiveness of the Cuban middle class—particularly in the central-eastern part of the island—beginning around the time of the first independence wars against Spain (late 1860s). In addition to adopting notions regarding national sovereignty circulating at the time, many individuals also began to invest in new, romantic ideas during the latter part of the nineteenth century which they articulated in works of poetry, literature, and, increasingly, music. When musicians in Santiago de Cuba subsequently adapted different guitar strumming styles to fit the syncopated cinquillo and accented it with triplets played in a two-beat moderato pattern, the beginnings of what would become the modern bolero were established.[59]

The tailor and guitarist Pepe Sánchez (1856–1918) is credited with the first documented Cuban bolero—"Tristezas" (Sadness)—which he premiered in Havana in 1883. The song would provide a hint of what the new genre would emphasize. Following the first line of "Tristezas," one can note that Sánchez establishes a definite bittersweet, melancholic tone: "Tristezas me dan tus quejas, mujer" (Your complaints bring me sadness, woman).[60] The subject is failed romance—a theme that would remain at the center of the bolero genre as other artists such as Sindo Garay (1867–1968), Alberto Villalón (1882–1955), Manuel Corona (1880–1950), and Rosendo Ruiz (1885–1983) also began writing in a similar vein. The music gained popularity with a number of players in cities such as Camagüey, Matanzas, and, of course, Havana.[61] Musicians soon introduced the new style to audiences abroad.

Improvements in communication and transport paved the way for greater exchange between Cuba and her Caribbean neighbors, including Mexico.[62] Yucatecan musicians, poets, and singers responded favorably to the new music. Mixing a variety of regional and foreign strains found in tango, bambuco, and Foxtrot, they developed a softer style of 4/4 bolero with accents on the one, three, and four beats.[63]

A bolero watershed of sorts began when Spanish poet Pedro Mata teamed up with Campeche native Emilio Pacheco to create the 1924 composition "Presentimiento" (Premonition). Musically, Pacheco set a standard that others would follow: a 32-measure composition split into two 16-measure parts, with the first being played in a major key and the second in a minor key.

It was not long before Monterrey-based composer Armando Villareal Lozano (1903–1976) achieved popularity with another bolero titled "Morena mía" (My brown skinned girl). Indicating the still relatively unknown genre, he recorded the work in 1924 under the classification of "Colombian song." Taken along with Alfonzo Esparza Oteo's (1898–1950) "Su mamá tuvo la culpa" (Your mama's fault) and Domingo Casanova and Osvaldo Basil's 1925 composition "Ella," among others, "Morena mía" helped lead the way in establishing the new bolero in Mexico.[64] Added to the critical work achieved by these popular composers was a young Yucatecan guitarist, singer, and composer who would go on to become one of the most important figures in this history: Augusto "Guty" Cárdenas Pinelo (1905–1932).

Cárdenas was born in the Santa Lucía neighborhood of Mérida, Yucatán on December 12, 1905. Following in the tradition of the *trova yucateca* articulated by such greats as Ricardo Palmerín (1887–1944), Enrique Galaz Chacón, and Pedro Baqueiro, he learned guitar as a teenager and soon began writing songs, including "Por la mañana" (In the morning) (also known as "Un rayito de sol," "Ray of Sunlight") which he composed at the age of fifteen (Figure 1.6).

*Figure 1.6* Guty Cardenas. Courtesy of Agrasanchez Film Archive.

Over the next few years, the young Yucatecan musician crafted a number of boleros: "No me olvides" (Don't Forget Me), "Era" (It Was), "Aquellos besos" (Those Kisses), and "Pasión" (Passion) while also maintaining a repertoire that included a cosmopolitan array of *corridos*, tangos, danzones, waltzes, and Foxtrots, as well as other Mexican, and more general Latin American songs.[65]

In his early twenties Cárdenas moved to Mexico City where, on August 19, 1927, he entered a new composition titled "Nunca" (Never) with lyrics by Ricardo López Méndez (1903–1989) in a citywide *concurso* (contest) called "La Feria de la Canción" organized by Pepe Campillo and held at the Teatro Lírico (1900–1970).[66] With much of the capital's music elite present, including fellow participants Tata Nacho, Ignacio Fernández Esperón, Alfonso Esparza Oteo, Luis Martínez Serrano, and the Trío Garnica Ascencio, "Nunca" was well received by an enthusiastic crowd.[67] Cárdenas incorporated a variety of musical influences in his repertoire. He adapted regional sounds from his native Yucatán as well as other popular styles such as the *huapango* while also playing waltzes, tangos, boleros, and other compositions, fashioning a uniquely Mexican urban style. Winning a prize for his effort, Guty subsequently gained sufficient recognition to begin a recording career that would eventually win him lasting fame throughout the hemisphere.[68]

Cárdenas first recorded for Mexican labels Huici, Olympia, and Artex in 1927. The next year he traveled to New York, where a growing number of Mexican and other Latin American artists at the time made their earliest recordings. After being turned down by Victor's Spanish-language artistic director Eduardo Vigil y Robles (1873–1945), he succeeded in being named to the important post of Latin music artistic director for Columbia.[69] He then collaborated with young Cuban singers Conchita Utrera and Tomasita Núñez, Puerto Rican composer Rafael Hernández, Colombian singer and composer Jorge Añez, Mexican composer Lorenzo Barcelata, and singer Nancy Torres for a series of recording sessions with Brunswick and Columbia.[70] Subsequently he appeared on radio, toured the United States (including a performance at the White House for President Herbert Hoover), and appeared in two Hollywood films: *The King of Jazz* (1930) and *La dama atrevida* (1931). Produced by Warner Brothers and First National Bank of Burbank, the seven-minute melodrama was initially titled *The Lady Who Dared* before a decision was rendered by director William McGann and others to make the film in Spanish.[71] That same year, Cárdenas also participated in a Los Angeles revue along with actress Virginia Fábregas (1870–1950) and singer José "Che" Bohr.

## Literary Roots of the Modern Bolero

Steeped in a sentimentality that artfully combined feelings of hope and despair, deceit and desire, the bolero became an essential unifying element for what constituted romantic discourse during the first half of the twentieth century.[72]

According to one observer, the bolero offered "a catalogue of affective ways of being" and borrowed from the high culture worlds of opera and late nineteenth-century modernist poetry.[73] Contrasting the bolero with other musical genres of the time, yet another observer comments that "while the idea of the bolero as an encoded plea for sex should not be discounted, the corporeal locus of the bolero's discourse is not *la pinga* (penis) . . . but rather, *el corazón* (heart)." Indeed, the modern bolero is a musical genre given, in most general and inclusive terms, to romance.[74]

Understanding the bolero requires an appreciation of the late nineteenth-century writers from which many composers would draw lyrical inspiration. Generally representing a romantic movement both in Europe and the Americas, in Latin America these writers were collectively known as the modernistas.

Following Mexican writer Antonio Plaza Llamas (1832–1882), who was one of the first to honor not only the virgin but the prostitute (see his poem "Á una ramera"/"To a Whore"), the modernists' poetic musings would similarly be dedicated to the adoration of women. But here, as is evident from Plaza's work, these writers made irreverent use of the dedicational language of the church for their own secular aesthetic purposes. In this regard, another influential Mexican poet would do much the same around the turn of the century.[75]

Amado Nervo (1870–1919) was born in Tepic, Nayarit and got his literary start with Mazatlán newspaper *El Correo de La Tarde* in 1894. Shortly thereafter, he moved to Mexico City to work on the *Revista Moderna* with Manuel Gutiérrez Nájera and others. Nervo subsequently traveled to Paris and saw parts of Europe in 1900 before returning to Mexico to teach literature at the *Escuela Nacional Preparatoria* (National Preparatory School). In 1906 he returned to Europe to serve as a member of Mexico's diplomatic corps in Spain. This experience qualified him to work as an ambassador in Argentina and Uruguay during the year before his death.

Nervo began publishing his own poetry in 1898 with the release of *Perlas negras*. This was followed by *Místicas* (1898), *Poemas* (1901), *El éxodo y las flores del camino* (1902), *Lírica heroica* (1902), *Los jardines interiores* (1905), *En voz baja* (1909), *Serenidad* (1914), *Elevación* (1917), *El estanque de los lotos* (1919), *El arquero divino* (1919), and the posthumous *La amada inmóvil* (1920).[76] Taken together, Nervo's work qualified him as one of Mexico's—if not Latin America's—most important poets.

Nervo and his colleagues generally acknowledged Nicaraguan Ruben Darío (1867–1916) as the writer who helped consolidate the Latin American modernist literary movement. Darío, beginning with his *Abrojos* in 1887 and well-received *Azul* the following year, crafted an eclectic poetic style. He traveled widely in the Americas and Europe. Writing for the Argentinian newspaper *La Nación*, Darío reported on conditions in Spain during the Spanish-American War. Appointed Nicaraguan ambassador to France in 1903, Darío then lived in

Paris, where he gained a familiarity with avant-garde writers Paul Verlaine, Arthur Rimbaud, Stéphane Mallarmé, and Charles Baudelaire.[77] While there, Darío "poeticized, with incomparable elegance, the joy of living and the terror of dying."[78]

More generally, Darío and the modernistas absorbed the tremendous changes taking shape in society around the turn of the century. They spoke of crossing geographic and cultural boundaries. In doing so, these writers produced a more concise form of lyrical poetry, prose poems, short stories, and a hybrid literary form that mixed reportage, autobiography, art criticism, and narrative known as the *crónica*.[79]

Nervo wrote short stories and novels along with a large number of articles on a variety of subjects. Inspired by Darío as well as the European symbolists, he sought out ideal "beauty" and "love." Nervo believed that poetry had the power to bring one in contact with the eternal. For him, the poet served as a kind of spiritual go-between, uniting male and female through poetry, ultimately connecting one with the transcendent.[80] Many critics, using the harsh words of the members of the postrevolutionary *Contemporaneos* group, have accused Nervo of crude sentimentalism and "trite mysticism" aimed at cultivating an audience with middle-class female readers.[81] In retrospect, these charges seem overblown.

For his part, Agustín Lara would similarly fill his artistic universe with archetypal beauties made of "crystal, mother of pearl, alabaster, silk, light, flowers, morning stars, poisons, felts, liquors, desirous tastes and smells."[82] Like the modernistas, he objectifies his women from afar, casting them as goddesses, queens, princesses, and other royalty. Lara's image of women in his songs would owe much to Nervo's alleged "subversion of sacramental codes."[83] Like the poetry of *modernista* writers during the late nineteenth century, themes of desire and romance became central in Lara's and much of the new popular music of the time. As Carlos Monsiváis comments:

> During the Revolution, romantic song [became] central to the language of the community, in which Lyric, Love and Metaphor become irrefutable values. To die for love. Die? Yes, die. It was not a question of really dying, like the desperate Romantics of previous generations, but, rather, of popularizing the "culturescape" of the nineteenth century, the mythologies of passionate frenzy.[84]

The revolutionary years gave rise to much popular testimony about the power of love.

As a musical counterpart to romantic poetry, the urban bolero made its way into the mainstream as it provided the public with a new emotional language.[85] In a sense, the bolero functioned as a "lovers' discourse" as "[it] reflected the multiple articulations of romantic practices for [the postrevolutionary society] and the instrument of transmission of these traditions to the subsequent generation."[86]

The bolero stands in contrast to the corrido genre. Corridos are ballads generally authored by anonymous agents. They tell of real social historical events, places, and people. Boleros tend to be works composed by named artists, whose lyrics often describe character types who are often morally challenged,—most often in the ways of love. Corridos lend themselves more to epic situations, while boleros portray more nuanced, often ambivalent predicaments. With Lara and many other practitioners, bolero music and lyrics express a variety of emotions (desire, anxiety, jealousy, adoration) in any number of archetypal romantic situations (encounter, separation, union, isolation). In contrast to the corrido, which often features a heroic protagonist, the bolero's principal subject is nameless or has only a one-word, archetypical identity. Some—as would prove the case with Lara—used the genre to imagine an idealized state of affairs, one where the often dramatic cycles of love and loss ruled supreme. Perhaps not surprisingly, this reimagined romantic perspective took hold just as the pace of life in Mexico and other major modern urban centers in the Western world accelerated to an unprecedented degree.[87]

Intoxicated by turn of the century change, some observers compared Mexico City to Paris and claimed that "the same glare and glitter of a pleasure-loving metropolis" could be found on both sides of the Atlantic.[88] Whether the Mexican capital's scene should be ranked alongside that of Paris can be debated. Nevertheless, demolition, renovation, new construction, and public works projects transformed the city significantly.

Architects reshaped the city not only vertically, but horizontally. Several new residential areas opened up in every direction.[89] At the same time, residents found themselves confronted by an advancing array of technological and cultural innovations: telephones, gramophones, dance halls, movie houses, and advertisements painted on building façades and electric signs calling out from rooftops.[90] It was into this social and cultural environment that Agustín Lara was born in the fall of 1897.

# 2

# From Bordello Pianist to Tropical Troubadour: 1897–1930

*I am as Mexican as epazote or tequila.*[1]
—Agustín Lara

*El divino flaco era el mitómano más grande del mundo* (the glorious *flaco*
[skinny] was the biggest mythmaker in the world).
—Francisco Rivera Ávila[2]

Civil registry records verify that Agustín Lara, officially named Ángel Agustín
María Carlos Fausto Mariano Alfonso del Sagrado Corazón de Jesús Lara Aguirre, was born on October 30, 1897 in Mexico City.[3] Lara's then thirty-eight-
year-old father, Joaquín Lara Aparicio, hailed from Tlatlauqui, Puebla and
worked as a doctor. Six years younger than her husband, María Aguirre del Pino
originally came from the town of Tlalnepantla in the state of Mexico. Soon nicknamed "Ticón," Agustín lived with his parents and older sister María Teresa
(1901–1984) at 16 Puente (or Callejón) del Cuervo (now República de Colombia) just a few blocks northeast of the Plaza Santo Domingo. Approximately two
years after Agustín was born, his mother gave birth to a boy named Joaquín.
Sadly, Joaquín—nicknamed "Pipo" by his older brother and sister—died a few
years later at the age of seven after being hit in the head with a baseball.[4]

When he turned six, Agustín went to live with his mother's sister Refugio
("Maquencita") in the Mexico City suburb of Coyoacán. Lara began primary
school in the Hospicio de Coyoacán, an orphanage where his aunt worked as
director. Refugio soon sent the young boy to take piano lessons with a woman
named Luz Torres Torija. The *maestra* eventually ended the sessions after becoming frustrated with Agustín's determination to pound out little tunes by ear
rather than follow her instruction. His stubborn persistence, however, would
later prove an asset in his teenage years.

Sometime thereafter, it is said that Dr. Lara arranged for his son to begin
taking instruction with the esteemed composer Ricardo Castro (1864–1907).

Considered the last in a line of romantic Mexican composers and pianists of the late nineteenth century, Castro is known for his waltzes, some of which demonstrated his talent for complex progressions and nuanced chromaticism. He composed five operas and is perhaps most famous for his 1901 work *Atzimba*, about the Spanish conquest of Michoacán.[5]

Despite the tremendous potential for learning from such an accomplished artist, legend has it that the young Lara chafed under the disciplinary demands of his mentor. He once again abandoned the piano lessons, but—if it is true that he did work briefly with Castro—not before gaining at least a basic exposure to some of the prevailing musical literature.[6] Over the next few years, Lara finished his primary school education at the Colegio de los Hermanos Maristas (Marist Brothers School) and then attended the distinguished French Fournier School located in the San Rafael neighborhood. Proving himself a capable but average student, Lara made friends both at school and in his neighborhood. For the first time, he also began to develop an interest in girls, as well as a self-consciousness about his looks. "My father told me straight out that I was born ugly and would remain so for my entire life," Agustín later commented.[7] Self-doubt notwithstanding, Lara nevertheless set about expressing his feelings of affection for several girls whom he allegedly courted by sending some of his first love letters.[8]

The young Lara soon took to spending more and more time wandering the city. The story goes that on one occasion he returned home past his nine o'clock curfew after he had attended a Sunday bullfight with a few friends. Not allowing his son to enter the house, Dr. Lara forced twelve-year-old Agustín to spend a cold night outside. The next morning he ended up at the house of his aunt Refugio, who provided him with breakfast and 20 pesos. Determined to test the limits of his newfound freedom, Lara did not return home but instead boarded a trolley for the working-class La Lagunilla district just north of the central plaza. There, a pickpocket took his money and first communion cross. The near-desperate Lara found a friend in a transient named El Erizo, who let the runaway share his flophouse hotel room. Lara then made the acquaintance of a vendor named doña Arcadita, who helped him earn enough money to survive. From there, it is said he maintained himself in La Lagunilla by selling papers, performing odd jobs, and relying on the kindness of strangers.[9] Like his contemporaries Diego Rivera (1886–1957) and Frida Kahlo (1907–1954), the specifics of Lara's early years are largely lost to us, thus leaving much room for subsequent self-invention and strategic mythmaking.

It is said that Agustín soon got word from a former schoolmate that his father had gone to work in Europe. Lara rushed home to his mother and sister María Teresa. He discovered that they had moved to a smaller house in Coyoacán and taken in two boarders to help make ends meet. Hearing Lara play the piano at an

afternoon party, one of the men staying with the family suggested that he try
to find a job as an entertainer. Legend has it that this man, named Tomás,
subsequently introduced Lara to doña Carolina—the madam of a downtown
bordello.[10]

Mexico City had long played host to a thriving sex trade, and in 1904 officials
registered more than 10,000 prostitutes out of a total urban population of
368,000. Not surprisingly, the city had earned a reputation in certain circles as a
"city of pleasure" because of its many whorehouses, many of which took their
name after the madam in charge—"Margarita," "Lola," "Francis," and so on.[11]

Renowned social hygienist Dr. Luis Lara y Pardo shocked many when he
figured that between 15 and 30 percent of Mexico City's female population
participated in the sex trade. In his 1908 book *La prostitución en México,* Lara
y Pardo claimed that a majority of these women represented a generation of
poor, largely uneducated rural migrants who had come to the capital and
crowded into a variety of working-class neighborhoods. The area centered
around the narrow Cuauhtemoctzín Street in Colonia Obrera (southwest of
the Zócalo) represented one of the leading centers for sexual commerce.[12]
Lara y Pardo determined that many who faced the dismal prospect of working
as domestic servants, laundresses, seamstresses, factory workers, or at some
other low-paying job that did not provide a living wage ended up selling
themselves on the street in order to supplement their otherwise meager
income. Of course, not all of those who engaged in sexual commerce—and
its many variations—came from the lowest depths of society. Mexico City
played host to a wide range of cash-for-pleasure possibilities depending on
one's ability to pay.[13]

For his part, Lara is believed to have managed to convince the tough, cigarette-
smoking madam of his performing talents by playing various popular styles such
as the Foxtrot, waltz, tango, and danzón. Before long, he reportedly delighted the
mix of politicians, businessmen, artists, intellectuals, and military men who frequented doña Carolina's with his melodies. Many seem to have been quite
impressed with the young musician.[14]

Agustín concealed his newfound position from his family by telling his
mother that he had found a job working nights at a telegraph office, and he
played night after night until a wave of violence hit the capital in early February
1913.[15] Called "the Ten Tragic Days" (*La decena trágica*), the city became a
battlefield as reactionary generals Bernardo Reyes (1850–1913) and Porfirio
Díaz's nephew Félix Díaz (1868–1945) led an insurrection against the recently
established democratic administration of revolutionary president Francisco
Madero (1873–1913).[16]

When the fighting subsided in the capital, Lara returned to work. His prac-
tical training as a pianist continued as he entertained for hours on end. One day,

however, his father returned home after spending nearly eighteen months in Europe. Unable to account for Agustín's long periods away from home, the elder Lara eventually tracked his son down. Enraged, he dragged him out into the street and subjected him to a thorough interrogation. Dr. Lara then enrolled his son at a military academy named Teipan in the Tlatelolco district of Mexico City—presumably to "set him straight."[17]

Lara's superiors at Teipan eventually judged their recruit "highly irresponsible," and dismissed him after twelve months.[18] Agustín's father then made arrangements to have his son sent north to work as a paymaster at the Cañitas encampment along the railway line to Durango. What Agustín did next is not exactly clear. Years later, Lara told an interviewer that he had attained the rank of captain second class while allegedly serving under a close friend of Francisco "Pancho" Villa (1877–1923) in the División del Norte (Northern division).[19] Subsequent retelling of the composer's early life were included in a comic book series from the 1960s titled *Vida de Agustín Lara* (Figure 2.1).

The civil war phase of the Revolution (ca. 1914–1916) eventually ran its course and the Constitutionalist faction under the former governor of Coahuila, Venustiano Carranza (1859–1920), emerged victorious. Drafting a Constitution in 1917, the new political elite presented themselves to the nation as advocates of social democracy and economic development. In the ensuing decade, presidents Álvaro Obregón (1880–1928) and Plutarco Elías Calles (1877–1945) would head federal programs that undertook bold measures intended to combat illiteracy, disease, and poverty. State initiatives encouraged thousands to join labor unions, participate in agrarian reform, and take part in educational efforts. Beginning in the early 1920s, enthusiastic and hopeful Mexicans set out to transform their nation into a dynamic, modern society proud of its culture and newfound place in the world.[20] Overall, the number of those occupying a middle position in the Mexican class structure increased significantly between 1895 and 1940.[21] More specifically, Mexico's rapidly growing urban population experienced a "gradual blurring of sharp economic and social class lines" after the Revolution.[22]

By 1921, Mexico City hosted a growing population of young people with approximately one-third between the ages of ten and twenty-four.[23] The burgeoning urban youth culture and ensuing cultural changes spurred on by a new generation of Mexicans coming of age produced many exciting opportunities. Young women and men distinguished themselves from their parents' generation as they ventured out beyond the confines of traditional family life to partake in what was then an emerging consumer culture.

With a strong emphasis on Mexican nationalism during the first decades of the Revolutionary Era, many worried about the influence of foreign products and ideas. Perhaps not surprisingly, music became an area of contention as

*Figure 2.1  Vida de Agustín Lara* #18, "Mi primera musa." Collection of the author.

postrevolutionary elites endeavored to define "Mexicanness" not only in political but also in cultural terms.[24]

For his part, composer Manuel M. Ponce (1882–1948) had published an essay in 1913 titled "Music and [the] Mexican [traditional] Song" (*La música y la canción mexicana*), in which he set out to define a national standard.[25] Along with his arrangements for piano and guitar of certain standard folk songs such as "El abandonado" (The Abandoned One), "Mañanitas mexicanas" (The Little Mornings),

"Cielito lindo" (Heavenly one/Pretty darling), and "La Valentina" (revolutionary female fighter), Ponce added original compositions rooted in this same tradition such as "Estrellita" (Little Star) and "Por tí mi corazón" (For you my love).

In this important article, Ponce determined two primary song types as typically "Mexican." The first reflected the music of the central Bajío region (Jalisco, Guanajuato, Michoacán, Querétaro, and Aguascalientes) with their lighter, lengthier, almost mid-nineteenth-century Italian phrasing. The other main tendency according to Ponce came from northern Mexico with its more muscular, rapid, and essentially rural sound.

Yet the composer's project of classifying traditional music in a quest to determine Mexico's "popular soul" coincided with the prevailing sentimentality of the Revolutionary Era. In this context Ponce's endeavor gradually turned from an effort that initially sought out more anonymous, traditional songs in a quest for essential Mexican music to one that increasingly understood national musical culture as being better represented by middle-class, romantic compositions.[26]

When he assumed his post as Minister of Education in the Obregón administration in late 1920, José Vasconcelos (1882–1959) borrowed from Ponce a set of allegedly hispanicist parameters in trying to determine a "truly national" music. Although not as a direct response per se, a group of popular composers nevertheless set out to cultivate a repertoire of Mexican popular music. Sentimental songs such as Mario Talavera's (1885–1960) "Arrullo" (Whisper), Alfonso Esparza Oteo's "La rondalla" (Carousing) and "Un viejo amor" (An Old Love), Tata Nacho's "Nunca, nunca, nunca" (Never, Never, Never), Ricardo Palmerín's "Peregrina" (Pilgrim), and "María Elena" by Lorenzo Barcelata (1898–1943) would be considered representative "Mexican" compositions. Works by up-and-coming composers such as Gonzalo Curiel's (1904–1958) "Son tus ojos verde mar" (Your eyes are like the green sea) and "María del mar," (Maria of the sea) as well as Alberto Domínguez's (1913–1975) "Frenesí" (Delirium) and "Perfidia" (Perfidy), added to this general effort.[27]

Initially mythologized as a site of "collective creation" where many in postrevolutionary society partook in the writing of poetry and romantic lyrics, the Mexican romantic song gained in stature.[28] Lara himself later commented on the period as a "sad and impoverished era when the fruits of the Revolution had yet to be realized . . . nevertheless there was a certain romance in the air and song lyrics had a unique language that on some occasions achieved a truly exquisite quality."[29] In the coming years, work undertaken by a new generation of romantic song composers, including Guty Cárdenas and Agustín Lara, would elevate Mexican popular music to unprecedented heights.

## Back in Town

By early 1917, the nineteen-year-old Lara had returned to Mexico City. On February 16 he married a twenty-one-year-old woman named Esther Rivas Elorriaga. Little is known about their relationship, how long they may have lived together, or to what extent Lara's family knew Esther. Allegedly, the couple produced a son, Armando Lara Rivas, who died of unknown causes only a few months after his birth.[30] Public records show that on June 11, 1920, the couple filed for divorce.[31] Shaken by the experience, Lara sought out his mother and sister for solace. Free of his father's control after his short stint in the military, he decided once again to begin looking for work playing piano.

Documentation of Lara's life during the early 1920s is scant. Following his divorce, we can assume, however, that he ingratiated himself anew to downtown madams and took up playing for the nighttime set. He told a story of how he met a woman named doña Martina one day. When he learned that she had lost her husband (supposedly a general during the Revolution), the two became friends. Martina then asked Agustín if he would be interested in playing in the evening at a brothel called La Marquesa. Eager to pick up additional work, Lara visited the establishment that same night and soon signed on as house pianist.[32]

The job of entertaining clients at La Marquesa lasted about four months and produced some legendary tales. During this time Lara is said to have made friends with several of the sex workers, including one named Frances, who supposedly had lost her eyesight and was eventually forced to retire to a convent. Another story has it that one day Martina's long-lost, top-ranking military husband returned to Mexico City. Searching for his wife, he made his way to their former home. Arriving at the address to find the bordello in full swing, he saw her at the center of an exotic social scene. With Lara playing the piano in a corner, Martina's husband pulled out a pistol and shot his wife dead. Agustín and the others stood in disbelief as police removed the body and closed the business. This and other stories from this period in Lara's life stand as some of the most dramatic examples of the popular composer's soon-to-be legendary sympathy for Mexico City's "fallen women"[33]

Perhaps the most fantastic of Lara's bordello experiences came when his face was slashed shortly after the pianist found work performing at an establishment located at 61 Libertad Street. Exactly when the attack occurred is unclear. Some suggest that it took place sometime in late 1922 or early 1923. Others believe it was later, between 1924 and 1926.[34] The story goes that Lara's music gained the attention of a young woman named Marucha (also referred to as "Estrella" and "Maruxa"), who endeavored to make Lara her own. Some say the young pianist welcomed her advances, and that he was subsequently caught in bed with her by a jealous husband or boyfriend. Another version that clearly favors Lara suggests that he did not respond favorably to Marucha because she had a reputation for being extremely possessive and prone to fits of rage. One fateful day, he is said to have inadvertently provoked the volatile woman.[35] Assaulting the pianist in a violent fury, she broke the end off a liquor bottle and slashed the pianist on his left cheek. With blood everywhere, Lara covered the gash with a towel and scurried off to a nearby medical clinic where his colleague—both a medical doctor and a talented singer—Alfonso Ortiz Tirado (1893–1960) tended to the wound.[36] One of the leading male voices of the era, Ortiz Tirado would go on to perform and record several of Lara's compositions.[37]

Treatment after the attack allegedly involved mercury, which seriously burned the left side of his mouth and ultimately forced Lara to wear a partial set of false teeth—badly fitting, as it turns out—on that side.[38] Fearing himself scarred for life at a young age, Agustín slipped into a deep depression.[39] He soon remembered this incident and the pain it caused in a bolero appropriately titled "Marucha" (also known as "Ingrata" or "Maruxa").[40] Although it was never recorded, the song nevertheless registered Lara's bitter response to the event:

> *Tú no sabes el mal que me has hecho*
> *ni comprendes mi duro penar,*
> *me dejaste un puñal en el pecho*
> *y en el alma continuo llorar.*

> You don't what evil you have done to me
> nor understand the lasting torment I suffer
> you left me with a dagger in the chest
> and in my soul I still cry.[41]

The incident would indeed leave the musician's face scarred for life. Yet in time, it would also provide Lara with a trademark as he crafted his identity as a bohemian composer of romantic song and unlikely conqueror of beautiful women (Figure 2.2).

Following the attack, Lara is said to have left Mexico City and traveled to Puebla looking for work. After landing a job in a high-class bordello where he worked thanklessly for hours on end, Agustín soon offended his boss, doña Julia. She conspired with local police and politicians to have the pianist arrested and thrown in jail. Lara remained locked up by day, and local authorities escorted him to the cabaret to perform each night. Little is known of this particular episode in Lara's life. Somehow, however, he managed to break free and return to the capital after learning of his mother's death in 1923 in the small-town of Teziutlán, Puebla. Given his great admiration and love for his mother, he must have grieved deeply.[42]

*Figure 2.2* Agustín Lara. Courtesy of Archivo General del Estado de Veracruz.

Lara made the acquaintance of popular Veracruz musician Rodolfo "El Garbanzo" Rangel sometime in early 1924.[43] Their meeting allegedly took place
when Agustín walked into what most likely was a downtown bordello overseen
by Madame Irene Inclán, located at 173 Moctezuma, one day for a drink after
hearing the sound of Rangel's piano playing from outside. At the time Rangel
was considered one of the foremost danzón players in the city, and the two struck
up a conversation in which Rangel eventually asked Lara if he would be interested in occasionally taking his place as house pianist for an upcoming three-
week period. Agustín eagerly agreed and before long the entertainers began not
only trading shifts but also starting up an alliance along with fellow musicians
Mario Ruiz Suárez and Manuel Sereijo who, with Lara, came to represent a new
generation of Mexico City musicians and some of the most important danzón-
styled pianists based in the capital at the time.[44] Lara seriously took to El Garbanzo's informal mentorship, which included a significant amount of musical
borrowing from abroad—not only Cuban danzón, but also Colombian bambuco and the very popular Argentine tango. Their adaptations prompted other
Mexicans to redefine their own musical approach as well. Lara was already quite

capable of playing romantic melodies with his right hand, but Rangel encouraged him to develop his left hand technique by teaching him syncopated rhythms.[45]

Rangel displayed considerable talent as an instrumentalist and was well connected in entertainment circles. Taking the young pianist under his wing, El Garbanzo essentially versed Lara in the popular music of the day.[46] This training later proved invaluable in the years to come, as Lara's familiarity with the tango and danzón would later serve as a solid foundation for his own bolero style.

Although many of the details are lost, Lara continued to work assorted jobs playing piano in cinemas, cafes, and bordellos during the mid-1920s. Among the many places he found employment was the Pedro Portillo Dance Academy at 11 Tacuba Street.[47] As part of this job, Agustín entertained for as many as eight or nine hours per session. This experience provided him with a heightened sense of musical confidence. Lara later commented that "this was the time when I developed my sense of improvisation that then helped me to sketch out melodies to go with different rhythms."[48] Describing how he sat at the piano for hours at a time, the young artist recalled that he "specialized in writing singing parts for songs whose refrains I would improvise."[49] This practice set an important pattern in Lara's approach to music, and many of his interpreters later commented that he never played a song the same way twice but was always making modifications and changing arrangements to suit the moment.[50]

Lara became friends with popular entertainers Celia Montalván and Aurora Walker (1904–64), who took him to several American-styled "dancings," often held at local movie houses.[51] Montalván and Walker knew well the Mexico City scene. Since debuting at the Teatro Lírico in 1920 as "Las Walkirias" (perhaps a tongue-in-cheek reference to Wagner's opera *Die Walküre*), the two collaborated for a time. Montalván later went out on her own and scored with a hit Foxtrot titled "Mi querido capitán" (My dear captain) by José Antonio Palacios, which appeared in a 1920 revue on interim President Adolfo de la Huerta playfully titled *La huerta de Don Adolfo* (Don Adolfo's Orchard).[52] With this and several ensuing projects, Montalván went on to establish her reputation as an attractive young variety performer (then termed *vedette*) and woman about town.[53]

In the company of his female friends, Lara learned that these dancings featured the music of a small tropical or danzón orchestra as well as a variety of singers and comedians. As with the earliest cabarets elsewhere in the Americas, they represented a somewhat daring, active entertainment environment where men and women could mingle freely despite misgivings by often self-appointed guardians of morality. Dancings epitomized the youth culture taking shape in Mexico City as they reflected a more casual, open attitude regarding sex, marriage, and the changing roles of women and men in society.

Weighing in at barely more than 110 pounds, Lara possessed little in the way of macho appeal. Nevertheless, he began to cultivate the image of a *conquistador de mujeres*—a ladies' man—by developing a penchant for romantic language, gift-giving, and other chivalric strategies. In a series of interviews with Lara in Mexico, visiting North American journalist June Kay remarked that he "has the expression and style of an eighteenth-century *hidalgo*."[54] She suggested that some would even go so far as to refer to him as "our Rudolph Valentino" (1895–1926).[55] Writing a profile of the aspiring musician sometime later, Oscar LeBlanc referred to Agustín as a "Don Juan without the sword or Casanova without malice."[56]

It is not surprising that in Lara's recollections of his coming of age in the Mexico City entertainment scene in the mid-1920s he would insinuate that he and Celia Montalván indulged in a bit of free-spirited behavior themselves. The pianist later boasted, "There have been dozens of women in my life whom I have adorned with thousands of kisses [and] over the years my 'rough complexion' (*cara dura*) has touched the most beautiful faces of the century beginning with Celia Montalván."[57] Never one to shy away from beautiful young women, Agustín's desire for Montalván was an unremarkable passion, as thousands of other men no doubt felt the same way about the young actress.

As Lara began to associate with one of the most sought-after female entertainers of the early postrevolutionary period, he also paid close attention to musical trends, noting that the popularity of the dancings came at a time when "a new wave of jazz and improvisation created a craze in the city."[58] Unspecific in his reference to jazz, he probably was referring to a host of early white dance band recordings from the late 1920s in combination with live performances by groups such as the México Jazz Band, the Jazz Band León, as well as US-based touring bands such as the one led by Paul Whiteman (1890–1967).[59] He told an interviewer that "jazz had invaded and its influence could be felt not only in the dance academies but also in several of the higher-class salons where the rhythmic sounds of banjos and saxophones were heard."[60] Indeed, jazz was a pioneering musical force to be reckoned with.

Some of Lara's colleagues also found the early jazz bands irritating.[61] For example, Miguel Lerdo de Tejada had earlier complained—not perhaps without some demeaning undertones about African Americans—that the new sound was "overpowering," sometimes even "horrible."[62] Still, it seems that Lara did not take such criticisms all that seriously. "I was an essentially romantic composer, preferring waltzes," he later commented, "but the excitement transformed me so that my music began to take a different structure."[63] Tenor and early Lara collaborator Juan Arvizu later commented that the young Agustín's music may indeed have taken some inspiration from the deceivingly simple arrangements, lyrics, and vocalizing of the blues. Jazz, we might presume, provided him a certain artistic license to assume a more relaxed and inventive attitude and to improvise on occasion.[64]

It was not only US influences that caused some to be wary. Aspects of imported Argentine music also came under scrutiny despite its wide appeal. Lara once said that tango provided appealing music but also "[often] hard-to-sing melodies and corny lyrics."[65] Colombian and Cuban styles, as Lara commented, made "a more diplomatic entrance" into the Mexican music scene. These sounds, as Lara put it, "[had] arrived on our southeastern shores in Veracruz and Yucatán and easily won over the hearts of the people who then made them their own."[66]

Criticisms of nonnative influences notwithstanding, Lara nonetheless made use of the new international styles. Arvizu later described what he heard as the main ingredients in Agustín's early music by saying it blended "the rhythm of the bolero, melody of the blues, sentiment of the tango, and soul of the Mexican song." To this Arvizu added that Lara produced a type of popular music that appropriately reflected the "cosmopolitan commotion" of the times.[67]

Many years later singer Chavela Vargas (1919–2012) similarly suggested that Lara, along with other composers of his generation, had taken the "sweet poetry" of the Cuban bolero and combined it with a "certain rough Mexican sentimentality" to create something new and unique.[68] Success in the postrevolutionary music scene clearly required a suitable balance among musical influences, both national and international.

In the midst of these rapidly shifting musical currents, Lara had grown tired of the dance academy's long sessions and found work at a different cabaret called the Agua Azul in 1928. He may have also played at a dancing spot located nearby on Isabel la Católica Street. When President Plutarco Elías Calles closed many Mexico City nightspots—seen as centers of vice—in a renewed attempt at moral reform that summer, these establishments shut their doors, leaving the young musician without a job. Luckily, a friend named Luis Fuentes helped Lara become acquainted with members of the Bruschetta family, whose widowed mother Sofía and attractive twenty-two-year-old divorcée daughter Angelina (with a two-year-old son at the time) co-owned a modest English-styled tea house named Café Salambó on the corner of Bolívar and 5 de Mayo.[69] The meeting would provide Agustín not only a meager income, but also critical creative inspiration over the next decade.[70]

Lara and Fuentes arrived at the Café Salambó one September afternoon in 1928. Well dressed, the two ordered coffee and then quietly observed the scene as the few remaining customers finished their mid-day meals. After smoking one of his favored El Buen Tono No.13 cigarettes, Agustín walked over to a beautiful new pianola (player piano) that stood in the center of the dining room. Taking a handkerchief out of his pocket, the pianist carefully wiped off the keyboard as he prepared to play. The informal audition consisted of a tango and a danzón. When Lara finished, the few remaining clients and café staff offered a warm response. Agustín's unassuming demeanor won the support of the tall, green-eyed Bruschetta, who convinced her mother and business partner that live music in the afternoon would help attract customers.[71] The twenty-two-year-old (nicknamed "güera" in reference to her light skin, and then later "Bibi") offered to pay Lara a salary of four pesos a day and a midday meal for two three-hour sessions, one during the afternoon from one to four and then again in the evening from nine to midnight. With Fuentes's encouragement, Agustín agreed and began the next day with a repertoire of understated, often melancholy compositions. He also sang, performing a bolero that would be titled "Imposible." The lyrics reveal a man's desire for more than just a casual affair with a woman.

> *Yo sé que es imposible que me quieras,*
> *que tu amor para mí fue pasajero*
> *y que cambias tus besos por dinero,*
> *envenenando así mi corazón.*

> I know that it is impossible that you'd love me
> For you only wanted me for a fling
> To exchange a kiss for money and nothing more
> And that is how you poisoned my heart.[72]

Drawn no doubt from Lara's long-running downtown work experience, the song explores the tension between the male lover's allegedly pure, romantic intentions and the apparent motivations of an attractive yet corrupted prostitute. It is not so much the fact that she is a hooker but rather the protagonist's own unrequited love that causes the singer pain. "Imposible" has a tango feel throughout the verse. Initially set a minor key, it then transitions into major key with the phrase "I know that it is impossible. . . ." Lara would use this modulation between the minor and major modes, common in Mexican popular songs, in many future compositions.[73]

After Lara had settled in to a routine at the Café Salambó, Angelina's mother Sofía began to take pity on him and soon invited him to live with her family in a spare room in their apartment on Matamoros Street in the La Lagunilla district.[74] Deeply touched by their offer, the struggling musician happily left his downtown boarding house and moved in with Angelina, her mother, Angelina's young son Jorge, and her brother Alfonso. Agustín would not enjoy the comfort of his new circumstance for long, however, as his bordello-playing past soon caught up with him.

One day two plainclothes police arrived at the Café Salambó looking for Lara. Finding him at the piano, they declared that the shady cabaret owner in Puebla who previously employed the pianist was now charging him with robbery. The agents allowed the musician a quick trip home to pick up some clothes. On the way out the door, Lara is said to have handed Sofía some folded pieces of paper, claiming they contained the music and lyrics to his latest song. When Angelina read them she found a confession of his love for her in the lyrics to a bolero titled "Orgullo" (Pride).

*Entre tus labios jugará la brisa,*
*cuando te diga yo lo que te quiero,*
*cuando pueda decirte lo que lloro,*
*cuando pueda decirte que me muero.*

Between your lips the breeze will play,
when I tell you how much I love you,
in the moment when I can tell you how much I cry,
when I can tell you that for you I die.[75]

With its melodramatic statement of enduring love in the face of otherwise difficult and depressing circumstances, Lara's lyrics seemed to anticipate his being chased down by the avenging *poblano* bordello owner.[76]

In a panic, Bruschetta contacted a friend of Agustín's in Puebla named José Galindo and asked him for help. Lara's captors kept him sequestered for a week or so, forcing him to perform nights at the cabaret while locking him up during the day. Eventually, however, Galindo found his friend and greased a few palms to secure his release. The two then caught a late-night ride to Mexico City in the back of a newspaper truck.[77]

Lara arrived home in a bad state. After a visiting doctor diagnosed him with bronchial pneumonia, his condition worsened rapidly and he became delirious. Fearing the worst, Sofía called for a priest, who granted what at the time seemed to be a last request from the ailing musician. The clergyman improvised an emergency civil marriage ceremony (*matrimonio in artículo mortis*) for the young couple on the night of November 19, 1928.

It took weeks of intensive care on the part of Angelina and her family to bring Lara back to life. Medicine and doctors did not come cheap, and neither Agustín nor Angelina had much money. To make ends meet, Bruschetta sold her share of the Café Salambó. Circumstances then forced her to sell various household items at the downtown Monte de Piedad pawnshop, including a Victrola player and a modest record collection.[78] Luckily, Lara eventually regained his strength and began to reconnect with a number of young performers. One important contact that would lead to a profitable collaboration was with Juan Arvizu.

Known at that time as the *tenor de la voz de seda* (the tenor with the silken voice), Arvizu, like so many of his generation, had begun his musical training in his hometown of Querétaro by singing both opera and popular song. Moving to Mexico City, he took classes at the Conservatorio Nacional de Música de México (National Conservatory of Music) before studying privately with the renowned voice teacher José Pierson (1861–1957).[79] Arvizu had traveled abroad with the Consuelo Escobar de Castro Opera Company performing in a production of the *bel canto* work *La Sonnambula* by Vincenzo Bellini (1801–35). He had also been in New York City developing a wide-ranging repertoire that included Argentine tangos as well as recently penned songs by Mexican composers Alfonso Esparza Oteo and María Grever (born María Joaquina de la Portilla Torres, 1885–1951), before returning to Mexico where he appeared in Giacomo Meyerbeer's opera *Dinorah* in 1927 at the Teatro Iris.[80]

Arvizu was finding it difficult to secure a living despite having earned a considerable reputation as a vocalist.[81] Setting out to market himself in more of a popular music vein, he added tango (among other styles) to his repertoire and began entertaining in movie houses and cafes.[82] Looking for an accompanist, Arvizu happened to hear Lara while visiting the Café Salambó one day. They agreed to team up and soon found work playing downtown cinemas between features.[83]

It is said that when Arvizu had the chance to play one of Lara's own compositions in those days he would proclaim, "It gives me great pleasure to sing for you a song written by my pianist—a composer who will soon earn tremendous praise for himself and all of Mexico."[84] For his part, Lara remembered that Arvizu "liked how I played piano and he became my official interpreter . . . those were happy times when I had a kind of complete freedom."[85]

The two collaborators would occasionally visit Café Principal—a popular place where young writers, journalists, poets, lyricists, musicians, and other artists gathered. One day Lara and Arvizu met lyricist and arranger Rodolfo "El Chamaco" Sandoval (1910–1965).[86] Sandoval had migrated to the capital from the southern state of Oaxaca in 1926 and subsequently landed a job at the Teatro Lírico.[87] Around this time, Lara also became acquainted with Chilean poet, pianist, and impresario Raúl G. Rodríguez ("Raulito"), who played regularly at another popular artists' café called El Retiro, located on the corner of Oaxaca and Valladolid streets in the northern section of Colonia Roma.

It was Rodríguez who provided Lara with his first professional work in the recording industry when he persuaded the popular female Trío Garnica Ascencio (Julia Garnica and Blanca and Ofelia Ascensio) to include the young composer's bolero "Imposible" in their repertoire. In the fall of 1928 they traveled to New York and then Camden, New Jersey for a session at the Victor recording studios. On October 2, 1928, the singers recorded "Imposible" with Rodríguez providing musical accompaniment and direction. The effort proved a creative success as other Mexico City musicians began to perform the composition. Thought by some to be the first bolero actually written in Mexico City, "Imposible" soon became available for purchase in different versions.[88] At the time, Lara did not benefit from growing artistic interest in his music and soon financial pressures forced him to sell "Imposible." As fate would have it, it was Emilio Azcárraga Vidaurreta (1895–1973) who purchased the copyright.[89]

Born on March 2, 1895 in Tampico, Tamaulipas, Emilio Azcárraga initially lived in the northern Mexican city of Piedras Negras, Coahuila. His father Mariano worked for a time as a customs agent on the US–Texas border and so the family made their home in San Antonio and, later, Austin, Texas, where young Emilio attended school. Azcárraga learned English and is said to have gained an appreciation for a certain "American" way of doing business.[90]

At age seventeen, Azcárraga traveled south and took a job as a shoe salesman in the Port of Veracruz and later in Tampico. His subsequent success as an itinerant salesperson traveling south through the Isthmus of Tehuantepec attracted the attention of a Boston footwear manufacturer, who hired him to serve as a representative in Mexico during the last years of the Revolution. The ambitious entrepreneur reportedly not only sold shoes but also engaged in trading black market gold, currency, jewels, and other precious metals on the side. Later basing himself in Monterrey, Azcárraga gained business savvy as well as important contacts with the local business elite and their many connections in the United States.[91]

By the end of the 1910s, Azcárraga had begun selling automobiles, first opening a dealership in Mexico City on Juárez Avenue, In 1919 he expanded to the city of Puebla, and in 1920 to Guanajuato.[92] He then turned his attention turned to radio, as he had gained a fascination with the new medium through his brother Raúl, who had studied for a while as a radio technician under a US colonel named Sandal S. Hodges. By the end of 1923, Azcárraga obtained a license to distribute Victor phonographs in Mexico. Two years later, he married Laura Milmo Hickman, daughter of banker Patricio Milmo. With this, Azcárraga gained a modicum of social capital and greater access to financial backing.

## First Collaborations

In early 1929, Lara and Arvizu began performing with a diminutive young singer named Maruca Pérez (1907–1937), who had been entertaining audiences with an assorted, largely Argentine-styled repertoire of tangos.[93] She appeared on

Sunday afternoons at the El Retiro.[94] As the story goes, Maruca's boyfriend Vicente Godínez casually knew Agustín and asked him to join her there for a couple of songs. One of the selections included a bolero that he would call "Clavelito" (Small Carnation).[95] The composition is said to have been inspired by Angelina.

> Como divina floración de perlas
> en rojo marco de suaves corales,
> como una ensoñación de madrigales
> que sus mieles me dé para beberlas.

> Like the divine brilliance of pearls
> Your smooth corals are marked in red,
> Like a sounding of madrigals
> Oh, what sweetness it would bring me in kissing them.[96]

With a title inspiring an image of an attractive young woman with a flower in her mouth, the bolero expressed in sensual terms Lara's desire for his new lover. Like "Imposible," the song spoke yearningly of a potential—perhaps unattainable— love still yet to be consummated. References to a woman's mouth, eyes, and overall feminine charms would prove lasting in the composer's repertoire.

The next day, Godínez and Pérez, as well as librettist José F. Elizondo (1880–1943) and journalist José Elguero, followed up on the previous evening's encounter and visited Café Salambó. Finding Lara there, Pérez proposed that the composer accompany her in an upcoming show. Lara later remembered, "It was the tango epoch and Arvizu and Pérez—nicknamed after a favored tango, 'La mocosita'—sang things like 'Mano a mano' (Hand to hand), 'A media luz' (Half-light), 'Cierra esa puerta' (Close this Door), and 'Adiós muchachos' (Goodbye Boys), among others. Before long, we were performing three times daily in movie houses . . . and on Sundays we would play five *salones*."[97]

On one occasion, Godínez hired Lara to serenade Maruca. Renting an upright piano for the occasion, he provided the couple with an evening of entertainment and then took the piano home for the remainder of the month. Excited by the prospect of uninterrupted time for composing, Lara dedicated himself to an intense period of creative work that produced a number of new songs, including the tango "Poco a poco" (Little by Little).[98] Angelina later wrote that when she heard this song she realized Lara had fallen in love with her.[99]

Throughout 1929, audiences filled El Retiro to hear Arvizu, Lara, and Pérez. One night, two representatives from the El Buen Tono cigarette company invited the duo to appear in a half-hour show on Mexico City radio station XEB.

Maruca and Agustín arrived at the station full of nervous excitement before playing a short selection of songs. In the wings, Angelina and Vicente watched as the show was broadcast live. After the program, the Buen Tono artistic director gave them a complimentary pack of cigarettes as their pay but apparently mentioned nothing in regard to future engagements. Little came of the appearance and the two, somewhat embarrassed, swore to mention nothing of the experience to their friends. Perhaps a more profitable opportunity would come along soon.

In the meantime, Agustín had met a young, relatively unknown tango singer and composer named Manuel Álvarez, known as "Maciste" (1892–1960) who played evenings at another popular entertainment venue called the Broadway Café.[100] Despite his fledgling status, Maciste had managed to make a few connections in the music business and soon introduced Lara to representatives of the Brunswick Record Company during an informal audition. Maciste sang a couple of Lara's songs with guitar accompaniment, but the Brunswick men apparently showed little interest. Undeterred, the two musicians contacted agents for Victor Records in Mexico City. In response, the company agreed to a meeting at Lara's apartment. For the occasion, Agustín and Maruca performed accompanied by Álvarez as well as members of the visiting Trío Argentina (made up of singers Agustín Irusta and Roberto Fugazot along with pianist Lucio Demare), who had appeared recently with Maruca. According to Angelina, the Victor talent scouts were impressed and offered Lara a ten-year contract. Determined to align himself with Victor without, perhaps, sufficient concern for his musical colleagues, he eagerly signed.[101] Wasting no time, he subsequently teamed up with Álvarez to record the pianist's first effort for the company, a tango called "Más tarde" (Later).

*No me mientas, no mi digas*
*que no me quieres*
*porque yo sé bien que tú eres*
*manejada por un truhán,*
*instrumento de placeres*
*como todas las mujeres*
*que la crápula se dan.*

Don't lie to me or tell me what I don't want to hear
because I know well that you are
manipulated by a scoundrel
[you are a] fool for pleasure
like all women
who are given to lewdness.[102]

Aside from that fact that this was his label debut, the brief collaboration was not especially memorable for Agustín, perhaps because of Álvarez's largely unappealing lyrics.[103] Nevertheless, Lara's new commercial affiliation soon led to a tour of eastern Mexico with performances scheduled in the cities of Toluca, Pachuca, Orizaba, Xalapa, and the Port of Veracruz. Impresario-agent Dagoberto Campos ("Campitos") served as manager for a newly constituted ensemble that included Agustín on piano along with vocalists Arvizu, Pérez, and another promising young singer named Ana María Fernández (1905–1993).[104]

Fernández had grown up in Mexico City and worked for a time as a dancer in Roberto "El Panzón" Soto's (1896–1960) troupe.[105] She began singing with the Hermanas Martínez as part of a trio that performed at the Teatro Politeama. When each of the sisters married, Ana María continued as a soloist. She then went on tour, singing alongside a number of artists associated with the Politeama in late 1928.[106] The following October, the vocalist made her Mexico City debut at the Teatro María Guerrero (aka María Tempache) under writer, comic actor, and satirist Leopoldo "El Cuatezón" Beristáin (1875–1948).[107]

After hearing her sing one night late in 1929, Lara invited Fernández to appear with him at the Teatro Iris (Figure 2.3).[108] Agustín's first impressions paid off as their ensuing stint attracted enthusiastic crowds. Before long, Fernández would craft her own distinctive sound, becoming one of the first in a long line of so-called torch singers who eschewed the large, more Italian operatic approach—then popular with male singers—in favor of a more stylized, softer interpretation that used the microphone to great effect. Over the next few years, she would develop into one of Mexico's premier bolero singers as she gained valuable experience working with Lara.

Under the aegis of Victor Records, Arvizu, Pérez, Fernández, and Lara boarded the Interoceanic Railway in Mexico City and traveled east to perform in the states of Puebla and Veracruz. The program each night featured Arvizu with the others filling out the bill. While affording Lara and company important early exposure, the endeavor did not end up paying the performers much for their efforts as recording companies at the time did not compensate artists to any degree for either their studio or touring performances.[109] For his part, Lara treated the outing as a kind of belated honeymoon since the tour represented the first time he and Angelina had traveled out of Mexico City together.

Arriving in the Port of Veracruz, the ensemble enjoyed a four-night run at the Teatro Eslava beginning Saturday, November 9, 1929. They followed on the heels of the popular 1929 film *The Broadway Melody,* a musical that boasted on-screen performances by Charles King, Anita King, and Bessie Love transmitted by "vitaphonic equipment as good as anything in the capital."[110] Announcing the four young artists, the local daily *El Dictamen* printed a photo of Juan Arvizu along with the following description:

*Figure 2.3* Lara and Ana María Fernández. Collection of the author.

A notable group of stars will appear tonight at the Teatro Eslava headed by well-known tenor Juan Arvizu. Accompanying the Mexican singer will be the popular soprano Ana María Fernández, the famous tango singer Maruca Pérez and the inspired composer and pianist Agustín Lara whose work will be interpreted by the ensemble.[111]

Saturday's show began with Lara playing the waltz "De mi vida" (Of My Life) and another piece simply called "Short Spanish Study." Maruca then joined him to sing two of his tangos ("Canalla" (Rotten) and "Adiós tango" (Goodbye Tango)). Next, Ana María performed "Ultimo beso" (Last Kiss) by H. Aznar (not to be confused with Lara's 1934 composition of the same name) and "Oriente soñador" by Mario Ruiz before Juan Arvizu took the stage to perform melodies (unidentified) composed by Lara and Mexican composer Jorge del Moral (1900–1941), as well as a few traditional numbers.[112]

Favorable notice of the concerts is said to have spread quickly despite the fact that *El Dictamen* appears to have offered no published review. Enjoying their first visit to the legendary port as a couple, Agustín and Angelina took a short bit of time to soak up the city's tropical ambiance.[113] The storied seaside site enchanted them both and Lara promised Bruschetta that he would someday write a song about Veracruz.[114] Indeed, the visit to the port would soon prove propitious, for shortly after returning to Mexico City Lara began to claim Veracruz—with its associated jarocho regional identity—as his native home in interviews and other testimonials.[115] Like other twentieth-century stars who took pleasure in fabricating certain aspects of their autobiography, the young composer's story would be crafted with contradictions and half-truths.[116]

## Tropical Troubadour

The early association between Veracruz and Lara had, in fact, begun a year earlier in January 1929 when, while performing at the El Retiro, Maruca Pérez referred to Agustín as "the inspired Veracruz composer."[117] Further constructing this fictive identity, Lara began telling interviewers in the early 1930s that he had been born in the charming tropical town of Tlacotalpan, located on the banks of the Papaloapan River ("Río de Mariposas" or River of Butterflies). Over time, the connection would stick.[118]

With a European connection through certain French and Spanish resident families as well as a reputation as a fashionable destination for elite and middle-class Mexicans around the turn of the century, Tlacotalpan afforded the *capitalino* (Mexico City) artist a certain provincial respectability.[119] Clean streets, colorfully painted houses, and Tlacotalpan's charming historic center served as an idyllic setting for Mexicans nostalgic for a small-town past.[120] As one's place of birth and regional identity is fundamental in all national cultures, Lara's fictive testimony provided the rationale for his claim to the regional Veracruz tradition. With this came an important cultural connection that tied him to the region's longstanding association with Cuba, the Caribbean, and the Atlantic world at large.

Lara's emerging public persona as a gifted young composer "from Veracruz" came at the same time officials in Mexico City endeavored to reconstruct national identity through a mythic characterizing of specific regional "types." Among a wide array of these traditional "personalities" (including *poblanos* from Puebla, *tehuanas* from the Isthmus of Tehuantepec, and so on), Veracruz-area jarochos were attributed a certain lowland essence thought to be made manifest in all areas of social and cultural expression: an open, friendly attitude; relaxed comportment; ripe sexuality; flavorful food; ample drink and expressive music; visual art, literature, and the like.[121] With Mexican elites working to reinvent a vision of the nation that made use of romanticized images from each of the many regional cultures, Lara's taking on a jarocho identity fit nicely with this larger program, adding to his growing reputation as an artist by providing him a specific regional and cultural locus.[122]

Lara's association with Veracruz also provided him with an important set of nationalist credentials. Known for its "four times heroic" defense against foreign invasion during the nineteenth and early twentieth centuries (most recently against the US invasion and occupation of 1914), a spirit of popular resistance circulated among those gathered in the union halls, neighborhoods, parks, plazas, and *portales* (archways that ring the central square in Veracruz where cafes, restaurants, hotel entrances, and storefronts are located).[123]

Lara's newfound jarocho identity also tapped Mexico's postrevolutionary desire for personal pleasure. In the mid to late 1920s many sought to regain time they had lost during the violent years of the Revolution by embracing an assortment of leisure time activities with a special exuberance. Mexicans began to travel for fun, and Veracruz represented a popular destination for national tourists who came to enjoy the tropical sun, ocean breezes, beaches, rum, food, cigars, gambling, dancing, festivals, and the all-around seductive nightlife of the port.[124]

These cultural and geographic identifications with Veracruz proved critical in the making of Lara's emerging celebrity identity. He would crystallize this connection in his 1936 composition "Veracruz." Thought to have been "born under the silvery moon, a jarocho troubador with the soul of a pirate," Lara would indeed take seriously his role as a hopeless romantic always desiring the company of a beautiful woman and an eventual return to his beloved Veracruz:

> *Yo nací con la luna de plata,*
> *y nací con alma de pirata,*
> *yo he nacido rumbero y, jarocho*
> *trovador de veras*
> *y me fui lejos de Veracruz*

I was born under the silvery moon
I was born with the soul of a pirate
And I was born a rumbero and jarocho
A real troubadour,
And I fled, far from Veracruz.[125]

A 1951 RCA Victor recording of "Veracruz" opens with a dramatic piano introduction in a minor key with Lara playing arpeggiated tonic and dominant chords
followed by ascending ii, iii, iv chords before concluding on the tonic.[126] In this,
Lara takes certain liberties in holding the notes for dramatic effect. The introduction creates a somewhat dark storytelling mood due to the minor key and the
percussive sustaineo, manner in which he sounds out the chords. The verse continues in the minor key and takes on a tango feel as violin and percussion join in.
Moving toward the chorus, Lara plays a transitional part while singing "I was
born rumbero . . .," leading to the "Veracruz" chorus that switches to the major
key followed by a solo and final refrain of the chorus.

> Veracruz, rinconcito donde hacen su nido las olas del mar.
> Veracruz, pedacito de patria que sabe sufrir y cantar,
> Veracruz son tus noches diluvio de estrellas, palmera y mujer.
> Veracruz, vibra en mi ser, algún día hasta tus playas lejanas tendré que volver.

Veracruz, little corner where the ocean waves make their nest.
Veracruz, little piece of the country that knows suffering and song,
Veracruz, with your nights filled with stars, palms, and woman.
Veracruz, resonates in my being, one day I will have to return to your
     distant beaches.[127]

The composition would prove one of the composer's most enduring, as it
created not only an important association between Lara and Veracruz but
also a compelling melodic and lyrical combination for jarocho enthusiasts
more generally.

One of the first associations between Lara and Tlacotalpan to appear in print
can be found in a 1931 newspaper article titled "La tierra de Agustín Lara" (The
Homeland of Agustín Lara).[128] An alleged testimony describing his boyhood
past, this short piece included three photos of Tlacotalpan, including one of the
house where Lara was supposedly born. A month later, while on tour in northern Mexico, Lara tempered his story somewhat by telling an interviewer that he
came "originally from Tlacotalpan but had spent many of his early years in Mexico City."[129] Subsequent tales of Lara's youth, however, did not shy away from
full-blown mythmaking about his origins.

Illustrated magazine coverage of radio personalities did much to keep Lara in the public spotlight during the early 1930s. A regular feature in *El Ilustrado* often published photos of Lara with short captions.[130] Building on the musician's growing popularity, the magazine then launched a biographical series titled "La vida íntima de Agustín Lara" (The Intimate Life of Agustín Lara) that characterized the musician as a sensitive, decent man. The Writer Jorge Loyo praised Lara's ability to compose love poems dedicated to the honor of some of the "poorest, most tormented women while also stirring desire in the hearts of restless virgins."[131] Effusive in his retelling of Agustín's life story, the journalist's series began with a narrative of Lara's childhood and included lengthy "testimony" from the artist himself. This and other press coverage both created the desire for—and then in turn provided—information Lara's fans wanted in their eagerness to learn more about the celebrity that the popular composer was becoming.

Early childhood memories naturally provided background material for explaining the composer's love for music and singing. Because his uncle took him to a bullfight, Lara was said to have decided to become a matador himself. At the age of nine, the composer claimed he had his first girlfriend. According to Agustín, he also had graduated from the Fournier School with honors. Given this and other embellishments, however large or small, Lara was to be appreciated as talented, romantic, and duly educated in the way any respectable middle-class Mexican man should be.

Tellingly, perhaps, the musician often noted that the memories of his early days were somewhat clouded.[132] Despite this, interlocutors such as Jorge Loyo did not pressure him, but allowed Lara to develop his own mythic constructions. In subsequent interviews, Agustín continued to refine his public persona as he provided "testimony" regarding his family's alleged move to Coyoacán as well as stories about his first piano lessons.[133]

"La vida íntima de Agustín Lara" featured many photos of Lara in following his rise to stardom. It included commentary from his friends as well as curious tie-ins to postrevolutionary political life such as snapshots of Lara and Pancho Villa's widow, who was said to be a great admirer. The series continued through the spring and summer of 1934 and represented the first biographical treatment of Agustín in print. Shortly thereafter, writers turned the musician's story into a syndicated radio show.[134]

The reportage established the blueprint for future stories told in the service of Lara's Veracruz connection. As his close friend Francisco Rivera Ávila[135] would comment, "the divine el flaco was the world's greatest mythmaker," and no doubt this was true.[136] *Vida de Agustín Lara*, published toward the end of his life, capitalized most elaborately on this fabled history in chronicling the musician's life.[137]

In the first of a lengthy 135 weekly issues that began in early September 1964, Lara offers his readers the following explanation regarding his alleged birth in Tlacotalpan:

> My father was working as a doctor in Veracruz when one day a mes-
> senger came and told him that Señor Malpica in Tlacotalpan needed his
> help because his wife was going to have a baby. My mother, who was
> also expecting, said she was going to go too. Then, almost by accident,
> my mother gave birth there in Tlacotalpan. When they hoisted me up to
> take a look, they said, "How ugly." Still for me, Tlacotalpan was the most
> beautiful town you could ever imagine.[138]

Associating the natural beauty of Tlacotalpan with his later development as a professional musician, Lara then tells his readers:

> My first memories are of swimming in the [Papaloapan] river when I was
> four. It was at that time that I first became aware of the musical rhythms
> being born in me. [Commenting to a childhood friend while swimming]
> "Listen, do you hear that? There's music in the river!"[139]

Establishing the town of Tlacotalpan as a fountainhead for his creative en-
ergies, Lara's tale also touched upon another essential mythic element: his mother María. Laying the basis for what would become a legendary commitment to his female muse, Agustín takes time to share his first impression of her:

> When I opened my eyes, I saw the face of my mother . . . and saw that
> she had the face of a queen; very tall, very straight with long and beau-
> tiful hair. With a mother so attractive, I knew that I could not be all that
> bad looking. In her love for me, maybe my mother knew something:
> that I would have sensitivity to the natural beauty all around. Indeed,
> some nights when everyone was asleep, I would open the window
> and listen to the sounds of the night . . . I realize now it was that little
> Veracruz river town that nurtured my musical talents.[140]

Forging a mythic link between his mother, his adopted hometown, and the in-
spiration behind his professional career, Lara's presumed boyhood testimonials consolidated his status as a national icon. With credentials as a jarocho artist with a creative power deeply rooted in maternal love, Lara's celebrity identity promoted a nostalgic embrace of the home and family. The legend eventually proved so compelling that it prompted the mayor of Tlacotalpan to issue a fictive birth certificate for Lara in April of 1941 that claimed he had been born in the city in

1900.[141] In the end, publications such as "La vida íntima de Agustín Lara" and *Vida de Agustín Lara* proved critical not only in telling Lara's fictive biography but also in identifying his upbringing as a decent, respectable one. Reassuring audiences in print, the artist was said to honor his mother, family, hometown, and regional traditions. Because of this, listeners could enjoy fully the pleasure of Lara's songs—even when the artist sang lovingly about fallen women.[142]

## Back on Tour

Victor Records sent Lara, along with Raulito and the Trío Garnica Ascencio, on a national tour in late November 1929. The company paid Agustín a modest salary of twenty-five pesos daily and a share of his expenses. In Guadalajara the entourage helped popularize Lara's song "Solo tu" (Only you). Before long, the young composer penned what would be his second major hit: a bolero titled "Rosa." Lara premiered his new piece in the Teatro Degollado with vocalist Julia Garnica singing the lead.[143]

Lara's own 1958 RCA Victor recording of the song begins with his piano in a minor mode as he foreshadows the verse melody with a syncopated, upbeat feeling accompanied by light percussion (maracas and bongo) during the first half of the introduction. The pizzicato (plucked) violin anticipates the turn toward the first vocal verse. Agustín continues in a minor mode as he vocalizes "Mi vida, triste jardín . . ." (My life, sad garden . . .) while the violin adds melodic accents to his phrasing. The "Rosa" chorus then shifts to a major mode as he declares his admiration and love for the young woman.[144]

Over the years, Lara provided different accounts as to the origins of "Rosa." Probably the most credible explains that he named the song after an attractive dancer named "Rosa" Téllez Wood, whom he had seen at the Teatro Lírico. Lara's own explanation suggested that "Rosa" paid tribute to his mother, but the fairly erotic lyrics seem largely to confound that interpretation:

> *Mi vida, triste jardín,*
> *tuvo el encanto*
> *de tus perfumes y tu carmín,*
> *brotaste de la ilusión*
> *y perfumaste con tus*
> *recuerdos mi corazón.*

> My life [was] a sad garden
> Until I was enchanted

By your perfume and carmine,
Giving flower to a dream
Beautifully scented with
memories of you my love.

*Rosa, deslumbrante,*
*divina rosa*
*que encendió mi amor,*
*eres en mi vida*
*remedio de la herida*
*que otro amor dejó*

Dazzling Rosa,
Divine Rosa
Who has lit up my love,
You are in my life
Remedy of the hurt
Another lover caused me.[145]

Whatever the exact inspiration, Lara's "Rosa" added another romantic composition to his growing repertoire of original songs. He obviously felt confident the song would appeal to listeners, and is said to have sent Angelina Bruschetta a copy in Mexico City with instructions to show it to Emilio Azcárraga. Dutifully, she followed up on his request and offered "Rosa" to the Monterrey businessman, who offered her 70 pesos.[146] Agustín later recorded it for the Mexico City-based Peerless Records, apparently feeling little need to work exclusively for the Victor Company.[147] Details regarding this and other matters such as income from his performances, music recordings, publishing, and other related contractual obligations throughout his career are scant.[148]

Following tour dates in northeastern Mexico, Lara remained on the road during late 1929. During this time he added boleros "Reliquia" (Relic), "No te perdonaré" (I Will Not Forgive You), "Boca chiquita" (Little Mouth), and a danzón "Monísima" (Monistic), which Juan Arvizu would record.[149] Lara wrote to Angelina that their separation had inspired him to dedicate himself to his music like never before. "Every song," he told her, "is filled with the memory of you."[150] Clearly sensing an opportunity to advance his career, Agustín wrote several other new songs during this time away including "Si yo pudiera" (If I Could, also known as "Anhelos," Yearnings,) and "Cabellera rubia" (Red Hair), among others.

Back home for the holidays, Lara paid romantic tribute to Angelina in early January 1930 in the bolero "Mujer" (Woman).[151] The song was soon to become one of the composer's favorites. Angelina claimed Agustín composed it as a gift to her on the popular Mexican holiday night of *El Dia de los Reyes* (Three Kings Day) on January 6:

> *Mujer, mujer divina*
> *tienes el veneno que fascina*
> *en tu mirar.*

> Woman, divine woman
> You have a strange allure that shines
> In your gaze.

> *Mujer alabastrina*
> *tienes vibración*
> *de sonatina pasional.*

> Alabaster woman
> You vibrate
> Like a passionate little sonata.[152]

"Mujer" (not to be confused with a later recitation of the same name) contains many of the classic elements of the romantic style. Borrowing from the modernistas, the lyrics idealized the feminine through mention of alabaster, perfume, divinity, and so on. It was an approach that observers felt "constituted an incredibly elegant and stylish effect; not something derived from the common classes."[153] The song proved appealing to executives at Peerless Records in Mexico City, where Agustín recorded it along with "Rosa." Unfortunately, the company released only three hundred copies of the disc and paid Lara a paltry sum.[154] Despite this, Agustín's fortune would soon increase significantly when Emilio Azcárraga invited him to be part of the inaugural broadcast of Mexico City radio station XEW.[155]

By mid-1930 Lara had emerged as one of the most important young composers of Mexican-styled urban bolero. To his credit, he had developed a solid collection of original songs and an assemblage of talented interpreters. Increasingly, his compositions were being incorporated into the repertoire of popular touring groups such as the Trío Garnica Ascencio. Recording artists such as Guty Cárdenas and Alfonso Ortiz Tirado had begun to have success with his songs as well. Developing his own romantic style, his work over the next few years would further position him as a leading figure on the burgeoning Mexican entertainment scene. Yet Lara did more than just become a new star; he also helped establish a popular music that was rooted in the urban experience. As his friend Renato Leduc (1897–1986) would later comment, "Mexican music before Lara was rural, largely *ranchera*."[156] After him, as Leduc implies, popular song took on a more cosmopolitan character. The young composer's ensuing association with the powerful new popular media of radio and film would add significantly to this growing cultural trend.

# 3

# Musical Revue, Radio, and Film: 1931–1934

*Without Emilio Azcárraga there would have existed neither Mexican radio nor television.*

—Alfredo Jiménez R.[1]

Economic and political troubles contributed to a renewed period of social crisis in Mexico during the late 1920s. Longstanding conflict over the status of the Catholic Church led to a heated struggle that broke out across much of west central Mexico beginning in the summer of 1926. The ensuing Cristero War—as the ensuing violence was termed—left many dead and thousands seeking refuge.

In early 1928, President Calles selected former President Álvaro Obregón as his successor. They managed to convince members of Congress to revise constitutional provisions prohibiting such a move. Outside the legislature, anti-Calles groups saw the effort for what it was: undemocratic. Thousands responded by staging a series of protests in the lead-up to the elections that year. A handful of military revolts broke out in the provinces. The army responded by wiping out the resistance, and Obregón eventually won the election.

Celebrating his victory in Mexico City, Obregón fell victim to an assassin's bullet while attending a dinner in suburban San Ángel on July 17, 1928. In the shock and confusion that followed, Calles appointed General Emilio Portes Gil (1890–1978) as interim president, then engineered the election of General Pascual Ortiz Rubio (1877–1963).

In the midst of much unnerving political conflict, the New York Stock Exchange crashed in late October 1929.[2] The ensuing worldwide economic downturn hit Mexico hard, and over the next few years, the rural economy crumbled. The depression had the effect of displacing thousands of people to urban areas across the country. Many of the new arrivals crowded into working-class neighborhoods both in the historic center and on the margins of Mexico City.[3]

While some within the capital's artistic community responded to the larger social and economic changes taking shape during this period by creating works that called for greater support of Mexico's rural and urban working class, residents also witnessed the further proliferation of lighter, entertainment-oriented musical theater productions known as revues (*teatro de revista*). Created late in the previous century, these shows featured attractive female dancers, comedians, and specialty acts, as well as a rising cohort of young singers and composers—including a young Agustín Lara.

## Musical Revue

Mexico City's early twentieth-century musical revue paralleled the rise of the Broadway theatrical establishment in the United States, where the New York productions of Florenz Ziegfeld (1867–1932), among others, dazzled audiences in the late teens and roaring twenties.[4] Most representative and perhaps the best of his annual *Follies*, Ziegfeld's 1919 show boasted songs by Irving Berlin (including the famous "A Pretty Girl Is Like a Melody"), vocals by operatic tenor John Steel, the comic minstrelsy of Bert Williams and Eddie Cantor, specialty singers Van and Schenk, and the exquisitely costumed Follies girls. Ziegfeld redefined the female aesthetic by accentuating the face, rounded eyes, neck, back, shoulders, legs, and, above all, the proportionate figure of these women. Coming at the end of the First World War, the *1919 Follies*, along with other similar shows, engendered "a compelling blend of old-fashioned showbiz traditions confronting the uncertainty of changing times."[5]

Mexico's modern musical revue, or *teatro de revista*, was adapted from the Spanish *zarzuela* musical theater genre. Early productions in Mexico after the turn of the century included *La Cuarta Plana* (1899) and *La Marcha de Cadíz* (1901), as well as (soon-to-be-renowned writer of revues) José F. Elizondo's, with *La Gran Avenida* (1902). By the end of 1904, the hugely popular *zarzuela Chin-chun-chan* was well on its way to a run of nearly one thousand performances.[6] With humorous dialogue, contemporary dancing (including a performance of the Cakewalk), and a variety of dramatic situations (many satirical, eccentric, and at times impudent), the show marked the dawning of a new entertainment era.[7]

With only the most basic—if any—plot stitching the acts together, revues proliferated in the early postrevolutionary period as peacetime afforded a larger number of shows the chance to open in venues such as the Principal, Politeama, Apolo, Fábregas, Arbeu, Princesa, Lírico, Regis, and Iris theaters.[8] These paralleled another related genre, the *teatro sicalíptico* (sexually suggestive theater), where attractive female performers (*vedettes*) such as Spanish-born María Conesa (1892?–1978) often stole the show with their sensuous—at times, scandalous—mix of drama, song, and dance.[9]

If earlier Mexican shows had not already done so, the success of scantily clad Berthe Rossiní in the 1925 French production "Voilá le Ba-ta-clán" raised eyebrows as well as male-dominated audience expectations for more overtly erotic themes.[10] Not to be outdone, homegrown divas such as Celia Montalván, Mimí Derba, Lupe Vélez, Lupe Rivas Cacho, and María Tubau countered with their own tantalizing mixture of humor, song, and sex appeal. Productions often featured chorus girls with modern, bobbed hairstyles and alluring figures.[11] Postcards and illustrated magazines such as *Revista de Revistas* (Magazine of Magazines) supported the change by featuring stylish portrayals of young women (later to be dubbed *chicas modernas* or modern girls) sometimes with automobiles, radios, and other modern accessories.[12] Along with a wide assortment of actors, comedians, writers, composers, directors, and musicians, this new generation provided the talent for Mexico's rapidly expanding entertainment industry.[13]

As the 1930s began, Lara had attracted sufficient attention to land himself steady work at three of the capital's most popular theaters: the Politeama, Principal, and Lírico. It was at the Lírico that impresario Roberto Soto invited Lara to appear in a show titled "Cachitos de México" (Little Pieces of Mexico).[14] The early 1930 production starred Celia Montalván interpreting Lara's tune "Rosa," with Spaniard Eugenia "la Negra" Galindo featured in a new composition titled "Rosa Castellana" (Castilian Rosa).[15] Issa Marcué (Montalván's sister), Soto, Joaquin Pardavé (1900–1955), and others also played leading roles. Juan Díaz de Moral (1893–1944) did the main writing and scene-making, which translated some of Lara's lyric content into a stunning visual montage for the stage.[16] Kept just out of sight in the wings, Lara found himself at first somewhat put off by the whole affair. Yet when journalists began to pay attention to him after shows, his attitude changed. Years later, he remembered the production in favorable terms, recalling it as "perhaps, the first glorious touch of fame that God had helped me to realize . . . for it was then that I came to know the divine *gordo* (fatty) Roberto Soto."[17] The production ran for a total of one hundred performances. Its success prompted Soto to commission another revue structured around Lara's music. In line with Lara's penchant for female subject material, he titled it "Mujeres y canciones" (Women and Songs), and it opened in late May, 1930. This offering featured dancers Issa Marcué, Eva Beltri, Juanita Barceló, and Carmen Godoy along with singers Juan José Martínez Casado and Ramón Armengod (1909–1976). Reviews for the show considered it a "triumph."[18]

Impresario Dagoberto Campos then contracted Lara both to write for and perform in shows at the Teatro Iris. After the success of "Cachitos de México" and "Mujeres y canciones," the composer would participate in close to twenty revues during the first half of the 1930s including "La señorita emociones" (Miss Emotions, 1930), "Alma cancionera" (Musical Soul, 1931), "Brujería" (Witch-craft, 1931), "La cancionera de Lara" (Lara Songbook, 1931), "Talismán" (1932), "Nuestro México" (Our Mexico, 1932), "Su amado" (Your Lover, 1932), "Sea como sea" (It Will Be As It Will Be, 1933), "Bambú" (Bamboo, 1933), "Aquí estamos" (Here we are, 1933), "Maravilla" (Marvelous, 1934), "Carnaval" (Carnival, 1933), "Amor de mis amores" (Love of my Loves, 1935), "Calles y más calles" (Streets and More Streets, 1935), "El robador de estrellas" (Stealer of Stars, 1935), "Rival" (Rival, 1935), and "Estos hombres" (These Men, 1936).[19]

As journalist Walter Winchell (1897–1972) had written in 1928 in regard to the burgeoning New York entertainment scene: "song, laughter, wine, beauty, color and life—always life—these are the good things of Broadway [while] the bitterness, the failures, the tragedies—these are for the side streets into which are crowded those whose steps have grown heavy in the swift dance."[20] This can also be said in regard to musical revue in the Mexican capital. As on Broadway, this form represented something exciting, seemingly altogether new.

Musical revue was modern, and differentiated itself from Mexico's rural re-alities. The fashionable costumes, scenery, bobbed female hairstyles, and more provocatively clad dancers complemented the men's stylish tuxedos (dubbed *smokings*). Promoted by a young generation of impresarios, theater managers, and talent scouts, revues were advertised in nearly every major daily newspa-per as well as a host of illustrated magazines. In short, the *revista* led the way for a time in remaking the Mexican capital as the nation's most culturally modern city.[21] Yet as the dynamism of urban life continued to gather momentum, countless new places and possibilities arose. Before long, several new opportu-nities came Lara's way, including an offer to appear on the opening broadcast of what would become Latin America's most powerful commercial radio sta-tion: XEW.[22]

# Radio

The very first radio broadcasts in central Mexico took place in Mexico City and in Monterrey in the fall of 1921.[23] Two years later, Raúl and Luis Azcárraga Vid-aurreta, along with *El Universal* journalist Carlos Noriega Hope (1896–1934), convinced managers of the Mexico City newspaper to establish a radio station. Their ensuing effort would pave the way for the Founding of XEW, under the management of Luis and Raul's younger brother Emilio Azcárraga. It would be Azcárraga (Figure 3.1) who would provide Lara the patronage needed to help him rise to new heights as an international star.[24]

*Figure 3.1* Emilio Azcárraga Vidaurreta. Courtesy of (left) Agrasanchez Film Archive.

At eight o'clock on the night of May 8, 1923, the *El Universal Ilustrado–La Casa del Radio* program went on the air. Avant-garde poet Manuel Maples Arce (1898–1981) read his poem "Oda a la radiofonía" (aka T.S.H.—short for "telefonia sin hilos" or wireless telephonics), written especially for the broadcast.[25] Following him, Raúl Azcárraga took the microphone to proclaim the importance of radio for the material and intellectual progress of the nation. Visiting Spanish guitarist Andrés Segovia (1893–1987) then performed, as did a handful of Mexican musicians, including composer Manuel M. Ponce and Celia Montalván, who sang two tangos. Julia Wilson de Chávez and pianist Manuel Barajas also played requests. Despite fears that inclement weather might interfere with the transmission, diffusion to an eager, yet relatively small Mexico City audience proved successful. Going forward with the call letters CYL, the station continued to broadcast Tuesday and Friday nights, albeit with a limited range.[26]

In mid-June 1923, industry promoters organized Mexico's first Radio Fair (*Feria de Radio*), in the Palacio de Minería. Producers brought an array of equipment, including Hubbard De Forest and Westinghouse kits. Mexican radio maker J. M. Velasco also exhibited his wares. Raúl Azcárraga had a special soda bottled with the brand "Radio," while El Buen Tono marketed special "El Radio" cigarettes.[27] Hundreds attended, including President Álvaro Obregón, who opened the event.

Obregón's presence represented a key moment in the history of radio in Mexico as government and commercial interests collaborated in backing the new medium. Years earlier, framers of the 1917 Constitution had anticipated such a relationship when they gave the government total control over radio and telegraph communications with the option to grant concessions for commercial initiatives.[28]

Following the 1923 exposition, a group of broadcasters formed the Mexican Radio League and subsequently called for a standard set of regulations to govern the fledgling industry. This led to the 1924 Inter-American Conference on Electrical Communications in Mexico City and subsequent passage of Mexico's Law of Electric Communications in 1926. The measure decreed that the Ministry of Communications and Public Works would oversee all radio broadcasting. Despite efforts by US industry agents who had served as delegates to the conference, the ensuing legislation (and subsequent revisions made in 1931 and 1932) successfully registered radio as a national resource to be strictly owned or operated by Mexican citizens as consistent with other actions taken by the Mexican state to advance national economic development.[29]

Before long, a couple of private stations (CYA, CYZ) as well as two government radio facilities (CZA and CZZ) began broadcasting at a limited capacity. Most promising during the early years of radio, however, was the establishment of the El Buen Tono sponsored enterprise station CYB or XEB, as it and all Mexican stations were identified by an "X" following a 1923 US Federal Communications Commission ruling. Headed by businessman José J. Reynoso, the El Buen Tono outfit produced programs of high quality involving musicians, actors, comedians, announcers, and commentators.[30] Others followed in the capital, including stations XEG, XEO, XEX, and XETA.[31] Yet while XEB and other facilities competed for listeners, no facility in the city or any of the new regional stations, including XEJ in Ciudad Juárez, XET in Monterrey, XES in Tampico, or XEV in Veracruz, yet had the capacity to transmit at the national level.

Mexican retailers promoted the purchase of home sets and reports suggest that radio ownership skyrocketed. In 1926, approximately 26,000 were in operation. Reflecting a huge increase in demand, by 1940 the total number of radios had grown to 450,000 and would rise sharply during the war years to one million in 1945, and then double again by 1950.[32] Given these changes, radio developed a massive audience eager for information, education, entertainment, and commercial advertisement, as it promoted an array of new ideas, consumer goods, and lifestyles.

The new medium greatly interested government officials working to promote the image of Mexico as having an autonomous national culture. To many, it seemed as if radio could embody the promise of a Mexican postrevolutionary "imagined community."[33] Breaking down seemingly impermeable geographic, social, and cultural barriers, many figured that radio could truly bring the nation together. Interestingly, official national discourse promoting the postrevolutionary state and civil society through radio—as would also prove the

case with Mexican cinema in the coming years—relied significantly on support from the United States.

During the late 1920s, Emilio Azcárraga had come to believe that a powerful
station could in fact "unify the great Mexican family."[34] His vision developed from
his growing number of contacts with the burgeoning commercial radio industry in
both Mexico and the United States. When Victor merged with the rapidly expanding RCA radio network in late 1929, Azcárraga assumed the position of general
manager for RCA Victor's Mexican division: the Mexican Music Company. Over-
seeing the recruitment and promotion of recording artists, Azcárraga and his employees Walter Rademann and Francisco de Paula Yáñez became acquainted with
a dynamic group of musicians associated with Victor including the Trío Garnica
Ascencio, Juan Arvizu, Carlos Mejía, Mario Talavera (1885–1960), and Margarita
Cueto, among others.[35] In the years to come, Azcárraga would bring together a
wide range of young Mexican talent in realizing radio's vast potential.

One night, Rademann arranged for an informal concert to be held in the luxurious Paseo de la Reforma home of General Rafael Manzo. Lara, pianist Ofelia
Euroza de Yáñez, tenor Paco Santillana, singer Ana María Fernández, Yucatecan
poet Ricardo López Méndez, and tenors Juan Arvizu and Alfonso Ortiz Tirado
all performed for Emilio Azcárraga, the guest of honor. While the evening program offered many highlights, Lara apparently stole the show. It endeared him to
the then thirty-five-year-old impresario, who in future years would serve as
Lara's prime entertainment industry *patrón*. Not uncoincidentally, a majority of
those gathered that night—along with a host of other performers soon to be associated with the Mexican Music Company—turned out to be among a fortunate group that broadcast frequently on commercial radio during the medium's
early years.[36] Azcárraga's invitation to participate in the inaugural broadcast of
XEW and his ensuing steadfast promotion of Lara would prove critical.[37]

With great anticipation, Emilio Azcárraga and his staff finalized preparations
for the first broadcast of XEW during the summer of 1930. A stunning Art
Deco-styled full-page ad in *El Universal* on September 18, 1930 announced
the opening of the station and its first evening program (Figure 3.2). Promotional copy for the event read:

> Today at eight o'clock the powerful radio station XEW will officially be on
> the air with its inaugural concert. XEW will begin a completely new and
> advanced era in the history of radio in Mexico as from a technical point of
> view there are few stations in the world that can equal it. Artistically, we
> can assure you that XEW will be of the highest quality, earning your
> respect and full attention. The station will be a revelation with its clarity,
> range and perfection. XEW's well-managed operations and constantly
> updated programming will no doubt make it your preferred station.[38]

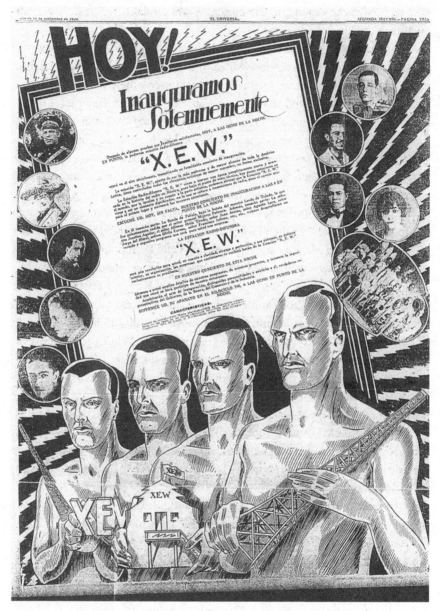

*Figure 3.2* Advertisement for inaugural XEW broadcast. Collection of the author.

That night, from the XEW studio located above the Teatro Olimpia on 16 September Street, announcer Leopoldo de Samaniego opened the event and then introduced Minister of Education Aarón Sáenz, who offered a short statement.[39] Following this, producers shepherded a range of performers to the microphone, including Miguel Lerdo de Tejada and his Orquesta Típica playing

"La marcha de la alegría (The march of good feeling)." Tenors Alfonso Ortiz Tirado, Juan Arvizu, and Juan Santillana sang, as did the popular contralto Josefina "La Chacha" Aguilar (1904–1968). The event featured the music of composers such as Alfonso Esparza Oteo, Jorge del Moral, Manuel M. Ponce, and Lorenzo Barcelata (1898–1943), as well as Lara. Although recently historians have cast doubt as to whether the musican-poet actually made the date, recollections of the event by Lara himself—perhaps not surprisingly—allege that he was there.[40] For her part, Angelina Bruschetta recounts that she, singer Manuel Bernal, and Azcárraga's mother Emilia watched Agustín from the wings, and that Emilia had commented to Angelina that Lara held great potential for the upstart radio station. Others claim that he did not show.[41]

Either way, there is no doubt that Lara's music, performed by talented tenors Ortiz Tirado and Arvizu, made a very favorable impression that night. Early in the program, Ortiz Tirado sang Agustín's 1929 composition "Campanitas de mi tierra" (Little Bells of My Homeland). Contrasting with the other, more serious musical selections, "Campanitas" offered a more popular perspective.[42] A while later, Arvizu provided the listening audience a bit more from the growing Lara songbook as he delivered renditions of the tango "Sintiendo una pena" (Feeling a Sorrow, also composed in 1929) and the relatively new song titled "Aventurera" (Adventuress).[43] In this and countless radio programs to follow, Lara's career entered a new era in which his music would reach a vast number of listeners.

With an initial power of 5,000 watts, XEW's transmission extended well beyond the greater Mexico City area, but not the entire country. Like broadcasters in the United States at this time, Azcárraga and his team used telephone connections to relay their product to provincial cities such as Veracruz (XEU), Monterrey (XET), Tampico (XES), and Guadalajara (XED). Because this method proved limited and was fraught with technical problems, however, station executives decided to abandon it in favor of efforts that would lead to increasing XEW's power.

While conforming to Mexican national communication regulations, Azcárraga affiliated his station with the NBC network and regularly visited the United States for industry meetings, tours, and training. He also implemented important technical improvements. On April 7, 1934, Mexican public officials and radio heads hosted an assortment of guests from the United States, Spain, France, Cuba, and Great Britain on hand to mark the station's increase to 20,000 watts.[44] XEW soon expanded to 50,000 and then to 100,000 watts in 1938. Working to resolve far-reaching reception inconsistencies, XEW technicians would double this again in August 1940.[45]

Because of close binational technical affiliations, Mexican broadcasters also adopted commercial approaches pioneered in the United States. Advertisements for both Mexican and US-produced consumer goods could be heard. Companies such as Coca-Cola and Colgate Palmolive sponsored programming.[46] Newspaper and magazine promotions proliferated not only for health aids and soft drinks but also processed foods, beer, clothing, and household furnishings. Similarly, enticements to buy home radio sets produced by Westinghouse, Radios 80-RCA-Corporación Radio Mexicana S.A., Brunswick, and Atwater-Kent were also regularly broadcast. This is not to say, however, that US–Mexican radio relations necessarily played out peacefully. Often, both US government and industry heads grumbled about the powerful control Azcárraga exercised over Mexican radio. Attempts to make an end-run around the communications mogul—especially in the early 1940s—would not prove especially successful, however.[47]

## Promotion

Just as XEW launched its inaugural broadcast, the newspaper *La Prensa*, in cooperation with Pathé Films, invited composers to participate in a waltz competition organized around the production of North American actress Ann Harding's (1901–1981) newest film.[48] Promoters announced a prize of 5,000 pesos, a week's engagement at the Cine Balmori, and four programs to be broadcast on XEW.[49] Just two days after the station's initial broadcast, more than twenty composers arrived at the "Teatro Imperial" (Imperial Theater) on September 20, 1930, including Lara, Jorge del Moral, Alfonso Esparza Oteo, Fernando López Vargas, and Carlos Espinosa de los Monteros (1902–1972), each with their own singer in tow.[50] XEW staffers prepared to broadcast the contest live.

Contestants provided a spectacular evening program played before a packed house. First place went to Espinosa de los Monteros with a slow waltz titled "Noche Azul" (Blue Night), sung by tenor Pedro Vargas (1906–1989).[51] Néstor Mesta Chayres (1908–1971) performed Jorge del Moral's "Divina mujer" (Woman Divine), winning second place.[52] Alfonso Ortiz Tirado interpreted Lara's 1930 waltz "Cortesana" (Courtesan, also sometimes known as "Abanico," or Fan):

> *En el espejo de tu mirada*
> *puse mi corazón,*
> *Y por el brillo de tu alborada*
> *vino la decepción.*
> *Tu figurita de porcelana*
> *de pronto se animó,*
> *Y con andares de cortesana*
> *hasta mi se acercó.*

In the reflection of your gaze
I put my heart,
And in the brilliance of your dawn
Deception came.
Your porcelain figure
Suddenly came to life,
And with the gait of a courtesan
Came closer to me.[53]

"Cortesana" uses an array of romantic images in idolizing the female. As in much of his work, Lara focuses on particular aspects of the body, eyes, lips, and skin. He speaks of a seductive walk, attractive scent, and urbane sophistication of the figure to create tension between the idealized object and his own desire. Lara and Ortiz Tirado's third-place finish caused quite a commotion, as many felt they deserved to win the first prize. A photo taken of Lara on stage just after their performance with dozens of roses at his feet and a somber look on his face suggests an apparent frustration with the contest results.[54]

Miguel Lerdo de Tejada nevertheless acknowledged the growing talent and contemporary appeal of his younger colleague a few days later during a live radio broadcast on XEW: "Lara is the most inspired and prolific Mexican composer today and his lyrics reveal that he is a true poet as well. He knows the sadness and melancholy as well as optimism and bravery of people. Moreover, his music has the flavor of the modern city."[55] The popular bandleader's praise affirmed Lara's growing importance in the Mexican music world.[56] In part, Agustín's breakthrough came from his teaming up with the talented singer Pedro Vargas, who, in the wake of their meeting during the Ann Harding contest, agreed to join Lara for some upcoming dates. When the tenor accepted, the two immediately set to work (Figure 3.3).[57]

Vargas was born on in San Miguel de Allende, Guanajuato. Singing in his parish choir as a boy, he developed his talent and eventually left San Miguel for Mexico City. He met singer and composer Mario Talavera, who helped him begin formal training at the Conservatorio Nacional (National Conservatory).[58] By the early 1920s, Vargas had begun taking private classes with the famed voice teacher José Pierson. He then expanded his operatic training with Alejandro Cuevas. The young tenor became acquainted during this time with many of the leading figures in the Mexico City music scene, including Manuel M. Ponce, Tata Nacho, Alfonso Esparza Oteo, and Miguel Lerdo de Tejada.[59]

At the age of twenty-two, Vargas made his singing debut during a recital on January 22, 1927, at the Teatro Iris. In the company of María Romero and other members of his opera troupe, Vargas impressed his listeners as he sang selections from the opera *Cavalleria Rusticana* by Pietro Mascagni (1863–1945). Among

*Figure* 3.3  Pedro Vargas. Collection of the author.

those who formed a sympathetic audience and congratulated Vargas immediately after the performance were Mario Talavera, Alfonso Esparza Oteo, the Spanish soprano Ángeles Ottein (1895–1981), and Miguel Lerdo de Tejada.[60]

Celebrating at Café Tacuba, Lerdo de Tejada offered Vargas a job performing in the United States and Canada with his Orquesta Típica. The ensuing one-year tour, which departed on January 26, 1928, afforded the singer a tremendous professional experience. They performed in Chicago and then New York, where Vargas recorded two songs for Columbia as a soloist with Lerdo de Tejada's ensemble: "Canción del primer amor" (Song of a First Love) and "Ya va cayendo" (Falling in Love).[61] Before long, he would earn much respect for his vocal talents, becoming known as the "Samauri de la canción" (Samurai of the Song) and also sometimes "El tenor continental" (The Continental Tenor).[62]

Lara and Vargas began playing in the Rialto and Monumental theaters. They then moved to the Teatro María Guerrero. From there, the two joined Roberto

*Figure 3.4*  Lara, Raulito, Vargas, and Pérez. Collection of the author.

Soto in a new production titled *Rayando el sol* (Reaching for the Sun) at the Teatro Iris.[63] Lara's first song written especially for the tenor was the 1931 composition titled "Romance." Soto soon arranged for Lara and Guty Cárdenas to compete in a number of afternoon songwriters performances (*tardeadas*) at the theatre. In what would turn out to be an encounter between the most important young Mexican bolero composers of their time, Vargas sang Lara's compositions while Cárdenas played his own material, accompanying himself on guitar. Each engagement at the Iris proved a huge success as eager fans clamored for a glimpse. On more than one occasion police had to be called in to calm cheering crowds.[64] Along with Cárdenas, Lara's fresh sound and modern compositions caused reviewers to lavish much praise. In so doing, they expressed astonishment that a young artist, "without ever formally studying piano, [could] compose [such] amazingly romantic, emotional songs."[65]

Lara worked diligently to expand his repertoire (Figure 3.4). Often, ideas for new tunes would come to him while relaxing with his musical colleagues Juan Arvizu, Maruca Pérez, Manuel Álvarez ("Maciste"), and Julieta Flores during a midday meal at the Broadway restaurant (near the Alameda) or the Hollywood restaurant on Colón Street.[66] When an interviewer in late 1930 asked him how he could be so prolific, Lara remained somewhat aloof about the creative process:

> I don't know, sometimes I feel like playing when there is a piano in a house I am visiting. Then, if I sit down for a time new ideas come out. The words come later. The songs are my work, my life, and if they are either good or bad—this must be decided by the public—the only thing that counts is that they are sincere.[67]

Whatever the circumstance, Agustín worked closely with arrangers such as Ernesto Belloc and, later, a young Roberto "El Chamaco" Sandoval, who wrote down the music as Lara finalized the melodies and lyrics.[68] Since Lara did not in fact know how to read music, rumors spread that he might not be the actual author of his songs. On occasion, critics went so far as to speculate that others, including Sandoval, might actually be doing the writing. Journalist Pedro Centellas refused, however, to believe that "some secretary" could have realized Lara's hugely popular work. "If writing music and lyrics is so easy," he suggested, "then why haven't others managed to accomplish what Lara has?" Further defending the composer, Centellas baited readers by saying, "Señores detractors . . . go ahead and write your songs and I'll see if you can sing them."[69] Apparently few, if any, mustered much of a response.

Lara's steady output continued to impress.[70] Among a number of songs written in 1930 were Mexican songs "Adiós Nicanor" (Goodbye Nicanor), claves "Como dos puñales" (Like Two Daggers), and "Despierta" (Awake), as well as a variety of boleros such as "Aventurera," "Contraste" (Contrast), "Gotas de amor" (Drops of Love), "Loca tentación" (Crazy Temptation), "Paginas rotas" (Torn Pages), "Pervertida" (Pervertress), "Silencio" (Silence), "Talismán" (Talisman), and "Tu ventana" (Your Window). The 1930 bolero "Mi novia" (My Sweetheart), like many other Lara tunes, offers a variation on the melancholic lover theme:

> Mi novia es la tristeza,
> mi canto lamento de amor,
> mi orgullo tu rubia cabeza,
> y tus brazos cruz de mi dolor.

> My lover is sadness,
> my song of a love lament,
> my pride your blond hair,
> and your arms the cross of my suffering.[71]

In this relatively compact work, Lara effectively combined key romantic elements of desire, despair, and hope.[72] The 1960 RCA Victor recording of "Mi novia" may be quite typical of earlier recordings with its upbeat and lively feel. As Lara's piano opens the tune with a light, almost tango, touch foreshadowing the verse melody, accompanist Carlos Águila's violin along with syncopated percussion move the song along at a moderately quick tempo. Interestingly, the combination of music and lyrics creates a certain irony: Lara's words speak of love's sorrows while the music portrays a happy, carefree mood.[73]

Written around this same time, "Como dos puñales" resonates with related themes of betrayal and loneliness.

*Como dos puñales de hoja damasquina,*
*tus ojitos negros ojos de acerina,*
*clavaron en mi alma su mirar de hielo,*
*regaron mi vida con su [sic] desconsuelo.*

Like two fine sterling daggers,
Your black steely eyes,
and your icy gaze stabs my soul,
they fill my life with your disaffection.[74]

Accompanied only by his piano, Lara later recorded this 1930 composition for the Anfión label in 1948 when a labor dispute undertaken by the American Federation of Musicians affected his relationship with the RCA Victor Company.[75] In this rendition, Lara, following an introductory segment, launches into the verse with his vocalizing "Como dos puñales" over a mild rumba beat. His voice sways into the second two lines of the verse with greater passion and a slight tremolo while singing:

*Tus ojos bonitos,*
*tus ojos sensuales,*
*tus negros ojitos,*
*como dos puñales.*

Your pretty eyes,
your sensual eyes,
your dark eyes,
are like two daggers.[76]

Lara then repeats the introductory piano figure in a higher register before continuing into the second part of the song, which is slightly different as it sings of sadness. In the lyrics, Lara professes his desire for his lover to rid him of his sadness with her piercing eyes—literally stabbing his melancholy with them.[77]

The 1930 bolero "Contraste" falls into Lara's assortment of tango-influenced compositions. Guty Cárdenas would in fact be the first to record the song, soon followed by singers Juan Arvizu and Ramón Armengod, both in 1931.[78] The opening lyrics tell of rejection as well as the protagonist's desire to win back lost love despite the odds.

*Después de haber jurado aborrecerte,*
*cuando tanto sufrí para olvidarte,*
*he vuelto por mi mal a recordarte,*
*nació mi corazón para quererte.*

After having sworn to detest you,
When I had suffered so much to forget you,
I have again dangerously begun to remember you,
My heart was born to love you.

*Acaso mi secreto sorprendiste,*
*y para ver mi amor sacrificado,*
*cuando yo te engañé, tú me quisiste,*
*y hoy que sufro por tí me has olvidado.*

Perhaps you discovered my secret,
And to see my love sacrificed,
When I betrayed you, you wanted me,
And now that I long for you, you have forgotten me.[79]

With a lilting, piano introduction containing low register left hand chords, the tune picks up with a light, tango-style swing.[80] Taken together, these compositions added to a growing repertoire of material that was rapidly gaining much popularity.

## Critical Acclaim

When *Revista de Revistas* critic Oliverio Toro attended a Lara show in late 1930 with two of his colleagues, he subsequently waxed poetic about how "inspired" the music had been. Although Toro called Lara "untrained," the reviewer nevertheless marveled at how "spontaneous" the musician appeared.[81] Ensuing live performances as well as a growing number of radio broadcasts evoked similar praise. One commentator asked, "Who has not felt a desire to know him, see him perform, and applaud him in person?" Referring to a recent concert given at the Teatro Olimpia, this same reporter observed that "the management of the venue proudly sought to satisfy the very real and popular demand for this exceptional artist and present him to the public with the proper degree of importance he truly deserves."[82] Another writer considered Lara's place in the history of Mexican music by arguing that the musician's inspired lyrics and melodies had surpassed those of all other national composers.[83]

Articles published in 1931 again praised the musician-poet and his expanding repertoire of romantic songs. Critic Rafael de la Cerda described Lara's music as "powerfully seductive . . . almost like he is telling you a secret" and Agustín's voice as "sounding as though he has suffered greatly."[84] The same writer also found Lara's piano accompaniment mesmerizing, adding, "It is not monotonous, as some have charged, but extremely moving when combined with the poetry of his lyrics."[85]

Agustín's penchant for romantic drama entranced audiences. In the 1931 bolero "Cautiva" (Captive), for example, Lara portrays himself—and by extension his audience—as a prisoner of love:

> *Yo fui la encantadora mariposa,*
> *que vino a los jardines de tu vida,*
> *yo fui la princesita candorosa,*
> *que iluminó tu senda obscurecida.*

> I was the enchanting butterfly,
> who came into the garden of your life,
> I was the innocent little princess
> who illuminated your darkened path.

> *Yo fui de tus quereres la sultana,*
> *la divina mujer sensual y altiva,*
> *la majestad radiante y soberana,*
> *que en tus hilos de amor quedó cautiva.*

> I was the sultan of your desires,
> the divine woman sensual and proud,
> the radiant and sovereign majesty,
> who in your web of love fell captive.

> *Si tus besos pudieron lograr,*
> *que de mi se alejara el dolor,*
> *nunca, nunca te podré olvidar,*
> *aunque muera cautiva de amor.*

> If your kisses could work wonders,
> and separate me from my suffering,
> never, never would I be able to forget you,
> even if I die a prisoner of love.[86]

What could be more romantic than an enduring alienation and even death for one's soulmate? Harking back to his *modernista* predecessors, if not to the older tradition of medieval troubadours, Lara had clearly touched a nerve. In a version of "Cautiva" from the mid-1950s, the composer uses a technique in which he briefly slows the tempo halfway through the song, as if to bring the listener closer, before moving to a short second part that restates his being in a "helpless state" because of his consuming love.[87]

Summing up the musician's rapidly growing reputation during this time, another reviewer remarked that, although Lara had received virtually no formal training, he had nevertheless successfully forged a unique sound by incorporating the influences of jazz, Argentine tango, and Colombian song, as well as the imagery of "mountains, forests, gardens, and beaches of tropical Veracruz."[88]

While certainly gaining significant momentum, the "Lara phenomenon"—as it soon became known—did not necessarily conquer all. Some who did not take to the musician-poet's romantic ways observed that Lara's music "could be heard on every radio and nearly every street corner," and that the seeming omnipresence of his songs represented "a virtual plague that has infested Mexico."[89] Yet even Agustín's detractors might have been willing to acknowledge that the young composer was, if nothing else, helping to defend against "invading" foreign music—especially American jazz and blues. At a time of fervent nationalism it was Mexican culture, however vaguely defined at times, that was supposed to reign supreme. This nationalist agenda also played an important part in the making of Mexico's film industry.

## Lara on Film

In 1930, Lara wrote a bolero commissioned by the Spanish-born silent Hollywood film star turned director Antonio Moreno (1887–1967), for the film *Santa*.[90] The movie was based on one of the first modern literary attempts to deal with prostitution in Mexico, Federico Gamboa's (1864–1939) 1903 novel of the same name. In subsequent years, *Santa* would capture the imagination of readers and play no small part in the articulation of sexual ideology and gendered archetypes.[91] No doubt Moreno had contacted Lara not only because of his compositional skills, but also because of his growing reputation for honoring the fallen woman (Figure 3.5).

The film called for a song that assumed the point of view of a blind musician, "Hipólito," in love with an unfortunate young woman recently arrived in the big city. Preparing for the project, Agustín drew upon the notion that Hipólito possessed exceptional insight and sensitivity. Angelina even claimed that he composed the tune with his eyes closed as she wrote down the lyrics on paper.[92]

*En la eterna noche,*
*de mi desconsuelo,*
*tú has sido la estrella,*
*que alumbra mi cielo.*

In the eternal night,
Of my loneliness,
You have been the star,
That has illuminated my sky.[93]

*Figure 3.5* Promotion for *Santa*. Collection of the author.

Lara's 1953 RCA Victor version opens with a piano introduction that leads to a slow first verse in which he gradually builds to a lead-in to the chorus—"Y yo he adivinado, tu rara hermosura, y has illumidado toda mi negrura" (and I have divined, your rare beauty [that] has lightened all my darkness)—and then the more upbeat chorus: "Santa, Santa mía, mujer que brilla en mi existencia, Santa, sé mi guía, en el triste calvario del vivir" (Santa, my Santa, woman that shines in my life, Santa, I know you are my guide in the sad march of existence).[94] The second verse is played staccato, building tension as it leads to the chorus. Lara's piano playing offers a number of lush chord voicings and light-touch embellishments as he moves from section to section and in opening and ending what is otherwise a relatively simple tune.[95]

When he played this new song for Moreno and Gamboa, both wholeheartedly approved.[96] Yet Lara's composition soon caused a stir because, like the film and the novel, it cast an archetypal couple in a melodramatic setting in which traditional values were thought to be under attack. Agustín's singing about the lost woman, created a powerful tension because he used words usually reserved for more honorable individuals.[97] Santa's plight resonated with audiences. After all, she, like so many others, was a relatively young and vulnerable person in the midst of a society swept up in a wave of rapid cultural and technological change.

As postrevolutionary Mexico sought to redefine itself through an often tumultuous process of political and cultural debate, Lara's musical melodrama represented a parallel universe. His artistic world was one populated with figures who sometimes, despite appearances, personified clear moral qualities and choices. At the center of this discourse was the fallen woman. In Lara's songs, she is often a "good" person who has been victimized by the "evils" of the city, and by extension, the modern industrial age.

As Agustín would tell interviewer Oscar LeBlanc, his time working alongside prostitutes allowed him to "know their soul" and "put into verse many of the tragic details of their human pain."[98] Not only did Lara draw upon his past experience in the urban underworld, however; his work also romanticized seemingly marginalized figures by attributing to them a "pure" love that surpassed social judgment. In his songs, love, above all, triumphed. Melodramatic works such as Lara's allowed audiences both to acknowledge the dizzying array of social change going on around them and also to imagine the reestablishment of moral standards and, quite possibly, a "happy ending."[99]

In taking prostitution as a reccurring subject in his art, Lara certainly did not stand alone. Numerous Argentine tangos told of similarly unfortunate women in Buenos Aires. Cuban "boleros de bayú" (of the bordello) did much the same. But in contrast to the tango with its varied cast of seductresses, opportunists, and treacherous urban types, Lara's music took a more positive perspective, looking on the scene with a transcendent eye. Insightfully intuitive, he could see past the complicated circumstances that allegedly corrupted the prostitute to appreciate her inner beauty. "Good or bad," as one critic has written about Lara, "these women [were] beautiful and attractive to him."[100]

Although a silent film of *Santa* had been produced in 1918, Moreno's 1932 cinematic version pioneered a new sound era in Mexican film (Figure 3.6).[101] It featured actress Lupita Tovar (1911–) in the title role and Carlos Orellana (1900–1960) as Hipólito. As her name suggests, Santa is an innocent country girl who happily lives with her family in a small village (Chimalistac) just outside the capital. Soon, however, she is seduced and subsequently abandoned by a soldier named Marcelino. Learning of their sister's relationship, Santa's brothers insist she leave town. Their rejection pushes her to Mexico City, where she soon finds herself in the parlor of a brothel surrounded by attractive young women and watched carefully by the cigar-smoking madam Doña Elvira (played by Mimí Derba). Santa joins them at a large dinner table. The madam shows her how to eat soup properly while the other women giggle and ask if she has a boyfriend. They suggest that she will soon have "lots of boyfriends" and drink a toast in her honor.

One of the women then takes Santa to the brothel entrance, where a number of men arrive. The men and women then pair up, laughing and joking,

*Figure 3.6* Promotion for *Santa*. Courtesy of the Agrasanchez Film Archive.

while Santa looks on in shock. Realizing her predicament, Santa goes into the parlor where people are dancing to the music provided by the blind musician Hipólito. The madam watches Santa dance and is pleased with her new "catch." As the scene ends, Hipólito affectionately says Santa's name to himself. Santa's situation soon goes from bad to worse and the audience realizes her only friend is the piano man. Hipólito's disability gives him a special quality, one that suggests he is a man who profoundly "sees" despite the fact that he is physically blind. Further, it becomes clear that Hipólito possesses a moral authority in an otherwise corrupt society. Idle hours at the bordello allow time for Hipólito and Santa to develop their friendship. When other people are present, Hipólito plays his piano and smokes cigarettes. He stops at one point and asks his young companion Genaro what Santa looks like. Listening to the boy's response, he plays the piano gently while Genaro describes her hair, face, and figure while admiringly telling Hipólito that "she seems like the virgin in the church."

Santa asks Hipólito to play for her. He agrees and sings the title song "Santa." His passionate ode renders a heartfelt confession with lyrics that idolize the fallen woman. Hipólito gives himself over to his female muse saying that she is a beautiful "star who has shed her light on him." Yet as he performs, other counter-vailing forces are at work. Women at the bordello laugh and make fun of him. The next day his composition is ostracized by drunks who sing it in the street while an indifferent newsboy shouts "Santa sheet music for sale!" By now it seems as if Hipólito and Santa are truly the only decent people left in an other-wise cruel and cynical world. Viewers identify with the odd couple and sympa-thize with their hard luck story. Hipólito eventually invites Santa to live with him. The two go to church and pray. Santa thanks him for his kindness. The blind man asks God to protect her.

We learn that Santa is sick as the next scene shows her in the hospital with Hipólito and Genaro waiting outside. She is operated on for cancer (or perhaps syphilis) but dies during the surgery. Hipólito mournfully places his ring on Santa's hand and caresses her before walking off. The film's tragic ending en-courages audiences to identify not only with the sad loss of the female protag-onist but also with her leading man Hipólito, for he embodied a love and respect for women that other men seemingly no longer possess. In death, Santa, Hipólito, and their stand-in son Genaro are meant to represent a makeshift holy family in a society in the throes of rapid change. The story of Santa is a modern melodramatic parable.

Under the musical direction of Miguel Lerdo de Tejada, Lara created compo-sitions for the film that included not only the title song but also an unidentified danzón (danced in the film by Lupita Tovar and a partner), as well as another piece that the character Santa enjoys alone in her room. According to film histo-rian Emilio García Riera, Agustín also provided some vaguely "Andalusian" sounding background music for a party scene.[102]

Lara's cinematic collaboration gained him critical public exposure. Curiously, Agustín later portrayed Hipólito in a series of short sketches at the Teatro Polite-ama with actress Andrea Palma (1903–1987). Reflecting Lara's growing associ-ation with the character, a cartoon that appeared in a Mexican magazine during the mid-1930s pictured a blind musician begging on a street corner. Asked why he was in such a condition, the man replied, "because señor Lara did not pay me to use my songs."[103]

Following the Mexico City debut of *Santa* on March 30, 1932 at the Cine Palacio, an increasing number of films during the 1930s (including a significant number of imported Hollywood productions) would invite growing numbers into the new social/cultural practice of moviegoing.[104] A host of film theaters sported elegant designs and lavish decorations meant to signify Mexico's entrance into the modern world. Taken together, the occasion reflected major changes in popular behavior and consciousness.[105] As Carlos Monsiváis writes:

> In the cinema, they learned some of the keys to modern life. The mod-
> ernization presented in films was superficial, but what was seen helped
> the audience to understand the changes that affected them; the de-
> struction or abandonment of agricultural life, the decline of customs
> once considered eternal, the oppressions that come with industrializa-
> tion. Imagine a worker from Celaya, a peasant in the Oaxaca Hills, a
> waitress in Chihuahua, a woman worker in Mexico City. Repressed in
> every sense, they never identified their daily life with emotion. In the
> urban conglomeration, in the solitude of the rural world, in the weari-
> ness of the endless hours of work, people did not live out "the intimate
> life" day in and day out; but it was what they would have liked to live,
> the flow of dreams that are most personal the more collective they are.
> Each melodrama was an encounter with identity, each comedy the
> proof that we do not live our lives in vain.[106]

Postrevolutionary audiences, in other words, identified with what they saw, heard, and felt when watching films. Going to the movies allowed one to view representations of modern society as well as occasional glimpses of life outside the republic. This new experience also exposed one to scripts that often pre-sented "cautionary tales" for those seemingly adrift from the core values and controls of more traditional culture.[107] The sad fate of Santa turned out to be not unlike that of other young women and men in Mexican cities whose new freedoms had led them to become embroiled in a degenerate tangle of lost op-portunity.[108] Most, however, experienced the filmed narrative as entertainment as they took in the movie house atmosphere and enjoyed being part of a ci-nema crowd.[109] *Santa* would also serve in years to come as a prototype for a distinct genre of Golden Age films called the cabaretera. These dance hall-centered movies presented a melodramatic formula that cast characters in a stark moral universe. Cabaretera plots often turned on a young female charac-ter's fall from grace after migrating to the city. As narratives developed, audi-ences were usually provided commentary on the dangers that awaited those who dared to deviate from traditional social values, while at the same time being thrilled by a series of film noir plot twists and turns. The first sound film in

Mexican cinematic history, *Santa* also marked the dawning of a new era as critics favorably compared the technical production to the prevailing Hollywood standard despite the fact that they generally panned the drama.[110]

## A Brush with Death

Lara's contributions to *Santa* served as an important precedent for future collaboration in Mexico's incipient film industry.[111]Meanwhile, new difficulties arose when early one morning during Easter week 1931, Angelina opened the door of their apartment to find a delirious Lara being carried by friends Ernesto García Cabral, José Elizondo, and José Elguero. After calling a doctor and a priest, Agustín was diagnosed with an acute case of appendicitis. He was rushed to the Hospital Juárez, where Dr. José Rojo de la Vega performed an emergency surgery and hoped for the best given that he had determined the musician's defenses to be quite weak. The next day, newspaper accounts announced that Lara had taken ill and remained in somewhat critical condition. It would not be long, however, before Agustín had the opportunity to provide his own version of the story to reporters and explain to them that he was on the mend.[112]

In the meantime, Angelina's son Jorge had come down with typhoid fever and had to be hospitalized. Upon hearing the news, however, Agustín selfishly demanded that she stay with him rather than attend to Jorge. Fortunately Angelina's mother was largely able to care for the boy. About this same time Angelina returned home one afternoon to find Lara visiting with his aunt Refugio, his sister María Teresa, and his cousin Magdalena. At first Agustín had not wanted to receive them but when they apologized for having neglected their beloved "Ticón," he obliged them. Indeed, family relations had not been especially happy in recent years and so, perhaps fearful of what exactly motiviated their visit now that he was gaining in notoreity, Agustín tended to keep his aunt, cousin, and even his sister at a safe distance.

Lara was not so standoffish with everyone. One afternoon, impresario Dagoberto Campos stopped by for a visit to ask Lara if he would like him to work as his agent. Having gained the trust of Juan Arvizu and Ana María Fernández, "Campitos" easily won Lara over and subsequently encouraged the pianist to return to work as soon as possible. To help facilitate this process he helped secure a new apartment for Agustín and Angelina at 78 Morelia in Colonia Roma. Before long, Lara was again composing new songs, including the bolero "A tus pies" (At Your Feet) and a Spanish-themed piece, "Sevilla."[113]

Lara soon also played at the Teatro Iris in an extravaganza Campos dubbed *Mujer*, and then at the Teatro Principal where he shared the bill with Miguel

Lerdo de Tejada, Guty Cárdenas, Jorge del Moral, Roberto Soto, and others.[114] Testifying to Lara's artistic status, the editors at *Excélsior* sponsored a contest with young female singers interpreting Agustín's songs at the Teatro Lírico. No doubt the composer enjoyed being the center of attention.[115]

Campos then organized a series of benefit shows honoring Lara. The tribute (*homenaje*) at the Teatro Iris took place over four nights in mid-May 1931 and enlisted the services of many of Mexico City's most sought-after entertainers. Topping the bill were Lara's three most regular collaborators: Ana María Fernández, Alfonso Ortiz Tirado, and Pedro Vargas. Esperanza Iris, María Teresa Santillán, María Conesa, María Tubau, Enrique Ramos, Miguel Lerdo de Tejada, Aurelio L. Campos, Horacio G. Meza, and Jesús Camacho Vega also participated. The event proved an enormous success and provided Agustín with needed financial support as well as a renewed sense of confidence.[116]

Lara now had enough money to afford a rented piano once again.[117] With this, he dedicated himself to composing a number of new songs, including the boleros "Besa" (Kiss), "Caballera negra" (Black Hair), "Chamaquita" (Little Girl), "Decepción" (Deception), "Dos rosales" (Two Roses), "Mi querer" (My Wish), "Morena" (Brown-Skinned Girl), Señora tentación" (Tempting Woman), and "Tengo mucho miedo" (I Am Very Afraid, also known as "Miedo," or Fear), as well as the Foxtrots "Ella dijo así" (She Said So, also known as "Nunca digas," Don't Ever Say) and "Tus pupilas" (Two Pupils).

Lara soon prepared for travel to Northern Mexico and Texas where he toured with Pedro Vargas, Ana María Fernández, and tenor Jorge Martagón, as well as a small orchestra directed by Raul C. Rodríguez and an assortment of dancers during the spring and summer of 1931.[118] In San Luis Potosí, a throng of admirers, including members of the local symphony orchestra, children from the Escuela Normal, and several young women carrying flowers greeted Lara at the train station. Interviewed by a reporter from the local paper, Agustín said he felt proud to be part of a new generation of Mexican composers.[119] That July, performances mesmerized audiences in Querétaro, Durango, Torreón, and Monterrey.[120] Then in San Antonio, Texas, Lara confidently told one journalist that he looked forward to serving as an "ambassador of Mexican art."[121] Reviews during this time rhapsodized about the musician's talent for creating "human, passionate and beautiful" songs.[122] Noting Lara's cosmopolitan perspective, a writer for Torreón's *El Siglo* commented:

> He is not one to romanticize the countryside, rather the composer embodies more refined emotions, those of the city. And while in the music one can note here the influence of Cuban melody, tango, Colombian song, and jazz, these do not take away from the fact that Lara's songs are eminently Mexican. In contrast to our familiar rancheras,

these powerful songs are created in the city about modern, sensual, and often down on their luck women.[123]

Recalling Agustín's stage presence, the writer described him as "almost timid" with a voice that was so soft it seemed as if he was "mumbling his songs."[124] This perceived practice would later be added to the Mexican lexicon by Lara observers as *ladraba*—meaning to have engaged in the practice of half-speaking/singing like Lara. Interestingly, Agustín's singing style somewhat paralleled two of the first electronic age pop idols in the United States: that of male vocalists Rudy Vallée (1901–1986) and Bing Crosby (1903–1977).[125]

Indeed, Lara's soft, quiet, and rather thin voice as transmitted through the microphone and broadcast by powerful radio stations contrasted with that of his trained male interpreters Juan Arvizu and Pedro Vargas. Although neither a strong singer nor technically a crooner, Lara's tone as registered through the use of a microphone was similar to that of the US-based singers and their seemingly "disembodied" sound.[126] As one historian writes, Vallée and his appeal to radio audiences "offered a disturbingly disembodied, artificially amplified male presence, one that competed with traditional patriarchal authority for the attention of the family. The fact that it was largely female listeners who supported crooners . . . revealed the power of [the new] domestic [radio] audience."[127] Like the others, Lara's music took advantage of new recording and broadcasting technologies while also provoking similar reactions among radio audiences who, along with Vallée and Crosby, now numbered in the millions.[128]

The winter of 1932 saw Lara back in Mexico City joining a number of entertainers for a new revue titled *Su amado* (Your Lover) at the Teatro Iris.[129] Although the plot was largely incidental, the program for the show nevertheless offered printed lyrics to "Como dos puñales" and "Pervertida" and listed Mario Talavera as master of ceremonies along with the Lerdo de Tejada orchestra, María Teresa Santillán singing "Cortesana," Maria Tubau performing a new song titled "Alguna vez," Ana María Fernández interpreting yet another fresh Lara composition named "Vencida" (Triumphant), Pedro Vargas delivering "Romance," Esperanza Iris doing "Su amado," and María Conesa performing the 1929 composition "Tardecita" (Dusk).[130] Another portion of the show included more brand new pieces by Agustín: "Aprenderé a olivdar" (I'll Learn to Forget), "Todavía" (Still), and "Tu mirar" (Your Look)—a love song filled with references to seeing and light:[131]

*Me sorprendió la luz de tu mirar*
*y fue un amanecer en mi canción,*
*por eso tiene luz este cantar;*
*este cantar, por eso tiene luz*
*mi corazón.*

The light of your gaze surprised me
and was the dawn in my song;
because of this it shines,
this song has light, my heart.[132]

Listed as a "canción-criolla," the unrecorded "Tu mirar" is a bolero. Much like other Lara creations, it speaks of a powerful desire awoken by the gaze of another. It is a look, perhaps not surprisingly, that inspires not only love but musical song as well.

Just as Lara was on the verge of capturing national attention, premier *bolerista* Guty Cárdenas died tragically in a senseless late afternoon barroom fight.[133] Juan Arvizu later remembered the events of April 5, 1932:

> Guty [Cárdenas] and I were working together on a show named "Picot" and had just gotten paid.[134] To celebrate and prepare for our next performance we planned to meet up at a bar later that day. Before I arrived [at the Salon Bach], Guty and some others at the bar, including two Spanish brothers who owned a shop across the street, engaged in a game of "vencidas." Apparently, the game had gotten quite heated and the bartender needed to break it up. When I walked in, I saw Guty lying in a pool of blood. I was told that Cárdenas had said something to the Spaniard as he was on the way to the bathroom [and the Spaniard] in turn hit him over the head with a bottle. Injured, Guty pulled a pistol and shot his attacker—injuring him. Seeing this, the Spaniard's brother, who was also in the bar, fired back at Guty and killed him.[135]

Cárdenas was only twenty-seven. During his short career, he recorded more than 190 songs. Had Guty lived, no doubt he would have enjoyed much greater success. With Cárdenas suddenly gone, Lara now stood as one of the most important young Mexican exponents of bolero.[136]

## Cuba and Beyond

In a somewhat strange coincidence, Lara, Pedro Vargas, and Ana María Fernández performed a series of concerts in Campeche, Tabasco, as well as Guty's hometown of Mérida, Yucatán. Perhaps aiming to honor their fallen colleague, the company impressed Mérida audiences to such a degree that they demanded the performers extend their stay.[137] Things turned sour, however, in Villahermosa, Tabasco, when the group encountered poor accommodations and then endured a white-knuckle flight to Veracruz aboard a rented plane. Furious, Lara

fired manager Dagoberto Campos and then found a new agent named Gonzalo
de la Gala, who traveled with them to Havana in mid-June 1932 aboard the
steamer "Sierra Ventana."

To welcome the Mexicans, Cuban President Gerardo Machado (1871–1939)
took a brief time-out from grappling with a floundering economy and growing
civil unrest. Lara rented an apartment at the América building on Havana's Calle
Ocho, where he had use of a piano while enjoying a spectacular view of Havana
Bay. Vargas and Fernández stayed at the nearby Hotel Saratoga.[138]

Performing for several nights at the Teatro Encanto, Lara and his colleagues
received a warm, although not overwhelming, response.[139] On occasion, they
joined popular Cuban bandleader Ernesto Lecuona on a double bill in the hopes
of sparking further interest.[140] Perhaps the fact that Mexican tenors Alfonso Ortiz
Tirado and José Mojica (1896–1974), and actor Ramón Novarro (1899–1968)
were also in Havana at the same time may have distracted Cuban audiences from
Lara and his interpreters.[141] Nevertheless, Cuban critics praised him, claiming
that his music represented a new sophisticated sound. One writer declared:

> Sure, he sings of love, but more than that he is creating a totally new
> school of music, his smooth sound inspired by his original muse. He
> represents not just modernism but futurism. Much has been made of
> his triumphs, productivity, and so on, but we want to emphasize here
> his originality in creating his repertoire. What we admire about this
> young composer is that he offers us romantic inspiration at a time when
> there is little available elsewhere.[142]

For this critic, Lara offered not just romantic music but a new, smooth sound
that blended several key influences including Cuban bolero.

Agustín wrote to Angelina at the end of June expressing frustration with local
promoters.[143] He then became quite sick. Managing to speak briefly with Angelina back in Mexico City by telephone, Lara told her, "come quickly however you
can, I don't want to die alone here in a foreign country."[144] Desperate, Bruschetta
asked friends Raúl G. Rodríguez and Miguel Lerdo de Tejada for help. With connections to President Abelardo Rodríguez Luján (1889–1967), the two managed to get a ticket and the proper diplomatic permissions for Angelina, who
took a Pan American plane on July 3 from Mexico on to Mérida and then on to
Havana.[145]

Word of Lara's critical condition caused a sensation back home. Would another of Mexico's brightest young musical talents be lost in the prime of life?
United Press reports from Cuba published in Mexico City's *El Universal* went as
far as to say that Lara had died.[146] Indeed, when Angelina read a newspaper
headline while en route to the island that declared "Agustín Lara passed away

yesterday in Havana," she collapsed. With the aid of the other passengers and airline staff, Bruschetta endured the remainder of the journey. Then, after the plane touched down on a military airfield outside Havana, Angelina breathed a sigh of relief when she saw a relatively healthy Lara riding in an expensive automobile with a dozen roses for her. Next to him stood their mutual friend Alfonso Ortiz Tirado who, as it turned out, had diagnosed Agustín with a hernia a day or so earlier.[147]

With his beloved Bibí now at his side, Lara soldiered on. He soon dispelled rumors of his death by scheduling three additional performances at the Teatro Encanto.[148] Meanwhile, popular resistance to Machado increased. Businesses closed as sporadic fighting spread throughout the capital. Unavoidably caught up in the turmoil, Lara and his collaborators ran out of money. Desperate, Ana María and Pedro borrowed some cash and sent urgent word back home for help, to no avail. Stuck in Havana, the four still did not have enough to pay for their return until the Mexican ambassador arranged to have them travel aboard an Italian cargo ship called the "Recca Triste."[149]

Following a no-frills journey home on the Italian vessel, Lara and his weary companions came ashore in Veracruz to the sounds of a cheering crowd in early March 1933. Agustín and Angelina stayed in the port for a short while for three concerts in the Teatro Díaz Mirón as well as a performance on the local XEU radio station.[150] Reporters covering Lara related that the musician's trip had been a huge success.[151]

Accepting an invitation to visit the neighboring town of Tlacotalpan, Lara and Bruschetta enjoyed the tropical environs and hospitality offered there. Showing his appreciation, Lara performed a free show at a small theater where audiences treated the young couple with characteristic local charm.[152] Newspapers in the capital related the good news to an anxious public: "[Agustín Lara] has not died."[153] Lara's trip paid off, and his music gained considerable attention in Cuba during the 1930s as musicians such as Antonín Machín (1904–1977) and his quartet (with the incomparable Mario Bauza (1911–1993) on trumpet), the Cuarteto Caney (famous for "La Cumbancha"), and singer Rita Montaner (1900–1958) performed his compositions.[154]

Nevertheless, Lara must have breathed a great sigh of relief to be home when he finally arrived in Mexico City. Fresh from his Cuban sojourn, he eagerly agreed to interviews and soon contracted for a series of recitals at the Teatro Regis.[155] Although photos of Agustín at his studio desk suggested that he regularly corresponded with his admirers, it was Angelina who did much of the behind-the-scenes work in this regard.[156]

Reviews of Lara's endeavors that summer and fall claimed that the musician-poet had surpassed his cabaret/bordello days and had reached a new "purified," "elevated" creative level following his "conquest of Cuba."[157] With audiences apparently wanting more, Lara arranged for future appearances at a number of Mexico City clubs including the El Retiro and the art deco-Aztec revival-styled Teocalli on Insurgentes Boulevard.[158]

The entourage soon hit the road to perform shows in Puebla and San Luis Potosí.[159] Back in Mexico City by early September, Agustín played with Pedro Vargas and Lauro Uranga (on the violin) at the Teatro Regis. Critics praised his work and claimed that the composer had "cleaned up his act by abandoning muses found in seedy dives" to achieve a new, more sophisticated sound.[160] The ensemble then traveled to Ciudad Juárez later that month, where Lara again won audiences over. In Juárez, the city's mayor even felt so moved as to voice his concern that students in local schools had (quite naturally) begun to study Lara's songs.[161]

Shortly thereafter, Emilo Azcárraga presented the popular composer with a golden opportunity—his own radio program on XEW. To be titled "La hora íntima de Agustín Lara," the program would allow for the unprecedented dissemination of Lara's music to hundreds of thousands of listeners across Mexico as well as north to portions of the US Southwest, east into the Caribbean, and south to Guatemala.[162] Beginning in 1933 and continuing an amazing run until 1960, the one-hour feature aired three times a week starting at 10:00 p.m.[163] It was produced by Azcárraga along with members of his team including Ricardo López, Méndez, and Enrique Contel.[164]

By design, the format of "La hora íntima" had the composer perform live in the studio while talking to a small assembled audience between songs.[165] In practice Lara's concept proved a little different, as he preferred singing in his soft, spoken-word style rather than formally stopping to talk.[166] Pursuing this strategy, Agustín's presentation soon enchanted listeners thrilled to be hearing him in the comfort and privacy of their homes. On occasion, announcers such as Manuel Bernal, Ricardo López Méndez, and Álvaro Gálvez y Fuentes would engage Lara in between songs to ask him questions about his music and life. Aside from the popular composer's live performances, various guests included Juan Arvizu, Luis G. Roldán, Chamaco Sandoval, Raulito Rodríguez, Lucha Guzmán Tabú, Elvira Ríos (1913–1987), the Trío Garnica Ascencio, Chucho Martínez Gil (1918–1988), Pedro Varsas and Ana María Fernández, among others. Trumpeter José Nicolás "Chino" Ibarra and Lauro Uranga often provided accompaniment along with an assortment of percussionists, clarinetists, and guitarists. Several nonmusicians also appeared on the show, including journalists Manuel Horta and Renato Leduc, cartoonist Ernesto García Cabral, and other denizens of the *capitalino* entertainment world.

Emilio Azcárraga paid Agustín a handsome 3,000 pesos per month when the program began. He also offered incentives for new musical material premiered on the show. Making the most of the situation, Lara wrote a number of songs. After the considerable exposure generated by "La hora íntima," journalists continued to write about Lara in glowing terms.[167] When XEW moved to 54 Ayuntamiento in 1933 (off Eje Lázaro Cárdenas), Azcárraga gave Lara his own studio equipped with a grand piano, the latest microphones, exquisite furniture, carpet, velvet curtains, and other amenities. Clearly, business was good—while behind the scenes, word had it that producers required invited guests to perform Lara's material almost exclusively.[168]

Testifying to the growing allure of those early radio broadcasts, singer Amparo Montes (1925–2000) remembered the excitement the new technology generated in her small village of Arboles de Tapachula in the southern state of Chiapas. As a young girl, Montes loved the music she heard on the radio. Above all, she found Lara's voice most seductive. When Montes heard him sing her favorites "Concha nácar" (Mother of Pearl, 1933), "Talismán" (1930), and "Carita de cielo" (Tiny Face, 1934), she dreamed of going to Mexico City and someday performing on the radio.[169]

An assortment of dramatic *radionovelas* (radio dramas) sponsored by leading national and international companies (Aceite 1-2-3, Colgate Palmolive, Pepsi, etc.) complemented these musical broadcasts. Shows such as "El derecho de nacer" (The Right to Grow), "La vida de Pancha Velasco" (The Life of Pancha Velasco), "Marcelino," "Pan y vino" (Bread and Wine), "La segunda esposa" (The Second Wife), "Gigi," "El grito de la sangre" (The Bloody Scream), "Casanova," "El galante aventurero" (The Gallant Adventurer), and many others entertained audiences—particularly daytime female listeners, who avidly tuned in to catch the latest installments of their favorite programs.[170] Like the boleros themselves, radionovelas provided individuals access to a tragicomic world of love and loss. Further, promotion of a range of "modernizing goods" ranging from soap to soft drinks to refrigerators and cars enticed listeners, even if many luxuries remained out of reach.[171]

The spring of 1933 proved a busy time for Lara. Producer Ricardo Toledo invited him to join an engagement at the Teatro Politeama alongside radio personality Ricardo López Méndez, promoter José Alfonso Palacios, Pedro Vargas, and Chamaco Sandoval.[172] Around the same time, Lara also signed a contract with the Teatro Iris to take part in a revue titled "Rival" with popular baritone Moisés Rachini.[173] A short while later, he teamed up with singer/composer Pepe Guízar (1912–1980) and Joaquín Pardavé in shows at the Follies Bersère.[174] Nearly stretching himself too thin, Lara also participated in *Artistas y Modelos* at the Teatro Lírico, with Chamaco Sandoval writing the libretto.[175]

Because of his now steady employment, Agustín and Angelina were able to move again, this time to to a nicer apartment located at 47 Tokio. Unfortunately for the young couple, the composer's growing number of professional commitments caused him to spend considerable time on the road. That summer a new song titled "Languidez" (Languor) reflected a growing alienation between the two.[176]

> *Llevo en mi alma una cruz de dolor*
> *que arrastro por la vida,*
> *mi tortuoso calvario de amor*
> *fue una mentira,*
> *tengo tanta tristeza.*

> I carry in my soul a cross of pain
> that I drag through my life,
> my tortured life of love
> was a lie,
> I feel so much sadness.[177]

Lara's lyrics offer one of his standard artistic themes: that of the long-suffering romantic. From this point of view, he is the unfortunate, tortured one. But if the song is any reflection of his personal life at the time, it was clearly Agustín's many professional obligations, as well as his penchant for the occasional personal side project, that weakened his relationship with Bruschetta. Still, the composer appears to have wanted to maintain his intimate status with her, however unloving in practice at times he may have been. Reflecting this sometime later, a mid-1950s RCA Victor recording of "Languidez" opens with Lara sadly speaking the song lyrics followed by a more upbeat Foxtrot piano playing under his sorrowful testimony.[178] No doubt Agustín expresses profound loneliness in "Languidez." Exactly where that and other deeply personal feelings would take him next would remain uncertain.

## La Sensación Jarocha

Lara's rise to fame in the early 1930s came through his collaboration with a variety of talented vocalists. In August of 1933, he met a determined young singer from the Port of Veracruz named María Antonia Peregrino Álvarez (1912–1982). With an uncanny ability to interpret his songs, Peregrino (under the name Lara gave her, Toña la Negra) would record more than thirty 78 rpm and (after 1949) LP records of her own, perform on countless radio broadcasts, and tour extensively throughout Latin America while also appearing in several films.[179] Interestingly, her work with Lara provided him with an authentic connection to Veracruz jarocho culture.[180]

Toña grew up in the hardscrabble Port of Veracruz neighborhood of La Huaca.[181] She developed her singing ability as a young girl by performing alongside her guitar-playing brother Manuel. Toña later fell in love with Guillermo Cházaro, who worked as a customs agent. By mid-August 1929 they had moved in together, despite the disapproval of family members. Shortly thereafter she gave birth to a son, Ramón. She and Cházaro married soon thereafter and traveled to Mexico City. Hoping to break into the capital's music scene, Toña began performing at the El Retiro sometime in the early 1930s, where she impressed Dagoberto Campos.[182] Despite his earlier falling out with Lara, Campos suggested she get in touch with him.[183]

Legend has it that a telephone operator at radio station XEW provided Toña with the composer's address. It is more likely, however, that Campos made the introduction. She arrived at Lara's doorstep in early August 1933. Tired and seemingly indifferent, Agustín requested that the young woman come back the next day. She did, and after exchanging small talk, Toña stood next to Lara's piano and sang the bolero "Enamorada" (Smitten) while he played. When the two finished, Lara complimented the singer and then immediately asked if she would like to work with him.[184] The young woman agreed and before long the two began performing together. They traveled to Monterrey, Torreón, and other northern cities, playing to packed houses.[185] Toña made her Mexico City debut at the Teatro Iris that October (Figure 3.7).[186]

That autumn, Lara wrote several new songs for his new colleague: "Lamento jarocho" (Jarocho Lament), "Noche criolla" (Creole Night), "Palmeras" (Palms), and "La clave azul" (The Blue Clef). Then, during the early 1934 season, other melodies followed. The pair played at the Teatro Politeama and her growing repertoire included the songs "Oración caribe" (Caribbean Oration) and "La cumbancha" (The Impromptu, Rowdy Celebration).[187] Along with "Veracruz" (1936), Lara later included these in what would become known as his *Suite Tropical*. Exquisitely bringing the material to life, Agustín and Toña began performing with a small group of musicians he called his "Son de Marabú." The conjunto included Toña's husband Guillermo Cházaro on percussion, her brother Manuel Peregrino Álvarez on guitar, Chino Ibarra on trumpet, and Lauro Uranga on violin.

"Lamento jarocho" is the first in a series of musical portraits by Lara that fervently enshrine the Veracruz region, its culture, and its history. A Peerless recording of the song featuring Toña begins with a stirring fourteen measures of percussion, flute, and male chorus, after which she sings:

*Canto a la raza,*
*raza de bronce, raza jarocha*

*Figure 3.7* Toña la Negra publicity photo. Courtsey Archivo General del Estado de Veracruz.

> *que el sol quemó,*
> *a los que sufren, a los que lloran,*
> *a los que esperan, les canto yo.*
>
> I sing to the race,
> the bronze race, the jarocho,
> who the sun has bronzed,
> [I sing] to those who suffer, to those who cry,
> to those who have hope, I sing to them.

In its tribute to the people of Veracruz, the song powerfully concludes with the following stanza:

*Alma de jarocho que nació valiente*
*para sufrir toda su desventura,*
*para sufrir toda su desventura.*

Soul of the jarocho born brave
to suffer all its misfortune,
to suffer all its misfortune.[188]

"Lamento jarocho" is cast as a bittersweet anthem meant to reflect both the sadness and the strength of the Veracruz people.[189] Lara demonstrates a real talent for characterizing the feeling of a place while Toña's natural affinity for the song assured its success.

The bolero "Oración caribe" is perhaps the most dramatic of the group. Hymn-like, it honors the people of the Caribbean. The version Toña recorded for Peerless in 1943 begins with a stirring introduction with percussion and brass leading to a vocal section in which the chorus intones, "piedad, piedad para el que sufre, piedad, piedad para el que llora" (mercy, mercy for him that suffers, pity, pity for him that cries). The introduction ends as it began, with resounding percussion before giving way to the sound of a gong and Toña's commanding yet brief vocal verse sung over a clave beat with brass and flute in a mambo arrangement:

*Oración caribe,*
*que sabe implorar,*
*salmo de los negros,*
*oración del mar.*

Caribbean prayer,
that knows how to implore,
the psalm of the blacks,
declamation of the sea.

Here the chorus picks up again in halting fashion by repeating the opening before the rhythm section returns to lead Toña back into the theme:

*Piedad, piedad para el que sufre,*
*piedad, piedad para el que llora,*
*un poco de calor en nuestras vidas*
*y un poquito de luz en nuestra aurora.*

Pity for he that cries,
pity, pity for he that suffers,

*Figure 3.8* Toña la Negra performing with *son jorocho* musicians and dancers.
Courtesy of the Archivo General del Estado de Veracruz.

a bit of warmth in our lives,
and a bit of light in our dawn.[190]

The chorus concludes the arrangement with a short reprise of the opening
theme followed by the sound of chimes ringing as if from a church belfry high
above a Caribbean town.[191]

Taken together, "Lamento jarocho" and "Oración caribe" are quite similar
both musically and lyrically. Each is an impressive testament to compact arrang-
ing for a large ensemble with nearly seamless transitions between varied parts.
Toña's deep and powerful voice is effectively contrasted with a vocal chorus, percussion, brass, and flute. With arrangements inspired by Lara's new female interpreter, both begin with an overture-like introduction featuring percussion and
vocal chorus. "Lamento jarocho" is accented with flute, while "Oración caribe"
includes a brass section with which the vocals interact.

Lara's ensemble still included Pedro Vargas and Ana María Fernández, but reviewers heaped praised on the young singer from Veracruz (Figure 3.8). One critic
heard Toña at the Teatro Iris and wrote that she was "truly a jarocha—expressing
the spirit of a warm and romantic people who have a natural talent for music and
she possesses a beautiful, deep voice with a terrific range."[192] Clearly, Toña's powerful delivery and clear tone resonated with listeners. Her regular performances on
radio shows "La hora de tres flores" and Lara's "La hora íntima" quickly won her a

wide audience.[193] Riding high on their newfound success, Lara is said to have confessed to Toña that she was really the "only one" to interpret his songs. The singer reciprocated by confessing to Lara that she very much enjoyed performing his compositions.[194]

Meanwhile, Ana María Fernández indicated that she wanted to retire from professional singing and get married. Lara apparently made a halfhearted effort to retain her by gushing, "Ana María, you are the mother of [many of] my songs and now you've left them orphans."[195] Hearing of the singer's plans, critics heaped praise on Fernández. An *Excélsior* reviewer wrote that her work epitomized the "modern sound" and spoke to the "contemporary soul" of the new age. "Between Lara and Fernández," he suggested, "there is a palpable feeling of musical eroticism which can be appreciated by both the cultured and uncultured classes alike."[196] The achievements of their collaboration notwithstanding, Lara had successfully anticipated this most recent personnel change by previously cultivating a professional relationship with Toña. With Fernández soon out of the picture, she would carry on the business of interpreting the composer's music in a similarly profound, yet decidedly more soulful, tropical style.

Critics then trained their gaze on the *maestro* himself. Some detractors voiced complaints that had been aimed at the composer before: that he was insufficiently Mexican, inadequately musical, and that his lyrics were offensive. To this, a writer for *El Universal* responded:

> Yes, Lara's music is not specifically Mexican. It has its own special mark, its own particular style. It is the music of Agustín Lara that has a strange and novel appeal that has gained the enthusiasm of the public. For this reason his music has been played everywhere. Because of this popularity he is being debated—and in some cases, misunderstood— so widely. Sure, this man from Tlacotalpan draws on a mixture of rhythms including Colombian song, bambuco, tango, rumba, Foxtrot and vernacular Mexican music but the beauty of his music is that he has—like the painter Diego Rivera—created a distinctive and truly original style.[197]

While some may have preferred a more explicitly nationalist style, many enjoyed Lara's music because he provided them an opportunity to enjoy themselves and perhaps put the bitter memory of the revolutionary years behind them. After all, had not so much struggle and sacrifice been endured so that future generations would not have to worry? A female defender of Lara wrote simply, "How can people call Lara's music immoral when he has written such beautiful lyrics? . . . His music fills the heart and affects your whole nervous system—that's the way it should be!"[198] Speaking of his changing view of Lara's work, another reviewer observed:

> I had been somewhat anti-Lara before meeting him in person. Now I have had a change of heart. You see, one has to actually talk with the artist, hear him play the piano, familiarize oneself with his poetry, watch how he works before one can really judge. Certainly I do not care for his more erotic songs but at the same time I can see that he is a noble person and one should appreciate his sophisticated temperament as a poet and a musician in that light.[199]

For this relatively conservative critic, Lara's legitimacy as a Mexican artist resided in his overall integrity and sophistication. Similarly, others showed appreciation for the musician by claiming that Lara, as one put it, "was an inspired, lyrical poet [and] still in the process of maturing as an artist."[200] Another supporter could not resist taking a stab at naysayers who charged Lara with being overly cursi (kitchy or corny), and who said that his work was not appropriately national: "Ask the students in the Music Department of Bellas Artes which they prefer," he suggested, "the music of the noble Aztec or Tarahumara or Agustín Lara? . . . Undoubtedly," he surmised, "their reply will be 'Lara!'"[201] While Lara did not compose explicitly "national" music, he did produce a cosmopolitan sound that was never confused for anything other than Mexican.[202]

Considerable publicity arose once more when rumors about Lara's private life again became a matter of public discussion. As the story goes, the composer had rented a small studio in Colonia Roma at 5 Celaya Street, one block off Insurgentes, for artistic and social purposes approximately two years earlier. There, Lara later remembered dedicating himself to composing.[203] Quite naturally, he also played host to a variety of friends and acquaintances including a revolving selection of attractive young women—many of them supposedly dancers he had met performing in a variety of theater settings in the city.[204]

Things came to a head one night when, during one of Lara's parties, an allegedly drunken Chamaco Sandoval took a bath with his clothes on and then forgot to turn off the water and flooded the entire lower flat where Lara's landlady, señora Pampín, lived. Livid, she ran upstairs, tore up Agustín's lease and demanded he leave immediately. Shortly thereafter, the affair became public knowledge when the woman filed a suit against Lara for property loss and damages. In response, Agustín countered with an injunction (amparo) against Pampín and in the process managed to keep the apartment for a time. A complete sorting out of things would have to wait, for Hollywood called just after the New Year and Lara eagerly boarded a train to Los Angeles.[205]

# Los Angeles

A bevy of excited fans greeted Lara at the Southern Pacific train station in early 1934 before a motorcade escorted him to the Biltmore Hotel in downtown Los Angeles. Shortly after, Agustín performed three recitals in the city with singers María Luisa Zea (1913–2002) and Alfonso Ortiz Tirado. While in town, various Mexican clubs and associations also organized gatherings in his honor.

A column in the *Los Angeles Examiner* proclaimed Lara "the greatest poet-composer in Latin America."[206] The writer figured he would soon be offered opportunities in some of the classiest venues as well as work with motion picture production companies specializing in Spanish-language films.[207] Similarly, the *Los Angeles Times* also congratulated Lara and his musical talents. Emphasizing the excitement generated by his visit to Southern California, the newspaper introduced the Mexican artist by comparing him to the popular US composer Irving Berlin:

> The music of Old Mexico, which through the years has been changeless as the cacti on its deserts, has changed, and the man responsible for this, a slim man styled the Irving Berlin of Mexico, last night demonstrated his technique at a piano in the Biltmore. Agustín Lara is more than a composer of popular airs.

While the comparison with Berlin was perhaps apt because of his popularity, Lara clearly articulated more of a romantic style. Describing Lara's music, the writer continued:

> He writes after the manner of Mozart, Liszt, and other masters. The slight, 30-year-old composer runs the gamut of melody from jazz to sublime rhapsodies as his fingers run the keyboard. The sensational composer . . . is being aped by contemporary writers of music in the southern republic and his melodies are being played in all of Europe's gay capitals.

For the California-based reviewer, Lara's music contained a trace of "Old Mexico" while at the same time exuding a contemporary, cosmopolitan flavor:

> The young man began playing jazz compositions, which now are "best sellers" on the streets of Mexico. Then he played his better compositions of which both lyrics and music have been written by him and which reach heights attained only by dreamers of the Mozart stripe. The plaintive-haunting airs of Old Mexico make their influence felt in these

compositions. Flights into ecstasy followed and oriental effects, as the astonishing young composer demonstrated the types of songs that he has written.[208]

Having read this and many other good things about Lara, critics and the general public alike marveled at his ability.

From Los Angeles, he soon made his way to El Paso, Texas where a sympathetic public awaited. When asked by Texas critics how he composed his songs, Lara playfully said he "dreams his music while smoking, plays it by ear and then has someone write it down for him."[209] Declaring the Mexican songsmith "more popular than Irving Berlin in Latin America and along the border," one journalist described his method in the following oversimplified terms: "[He] start[s] smoking a pack of cigarettes [and] when the last is smoked he has completed a song that soon will be heard in almost every Latin American home."[210] With critics sufficiently won over, Lara seemingly defied musical categorization while impressing observers with his quick compositional skills.

Moving on to perform in Ciudad Juárez and then Chihuahua City, Lara further excited other northern critics who marveled at what they considered his somewhat "naïve" or "primitive" creative method. Many found his music refreshing with its borrowings from Cuban, Yucatecan, Colombian, and Argentine popular styles in forging a unique "tropical blend." According to one reviewer, borderlands listeners had grown weary of Tin Pan Alley songs and American vaudeville. Lara's music offered a welcome change. One reviewer even dubbed Agustín's repertoire "continental music for the masses."[211]

When Lara returned to Mexico City in the early spring of 1934, journalists expressed curiosity about his reception up north. No doubt some were suspicious not only of *gringo* motives but also of the alleged "uncultured" taste of their fellow *norteño* (northern) brethren—especially given *dichos* (popular sayings) such as "la cultura acaba donde empieza la carne asada" (culture ends where grilled meat begins).[212] Once again, some pondered the elusive question of whether Lara's music should be considered truly "Mexican."[213] For his part, Agustín seems to have largely ignored these musings.

He did, however, begin to take a greater interest in protecting the intellectual property rights to his music. To do this he enlisted the help of his sister María Teresa. Although the two siblings were not close, at this time they did engage in deliberations regarding Agustín's work. Although the details are unknown, the two hatched an agreement just before Lara sent a letter to Southern Music Publishing Company head José Briceño in New York requesting that the company no longer reproduce his material without written consent.[214] From this point, many of the composer's songs would be recopyrighted by the Mexican based Peer International Corporation—sometimes with María Teresa's name listed either as coauthor, music supervisor, or, in some cases, sole author of various songs. Ostensibly, it was a strategy devised to make an end run around claims by Southern.[215]

In addition to legal manoeuverings, Lara returned to his work on "La hora íntima" while also beginning an engagement at the Teatro Iris, where he appeared with actor and singer Jorge Negrete (1911–1953) as well as a talented female duo from Guadalajara known as the Hermanas Águila (the Águila Sisters, María Paz, 1912–2004 and María Esperanza, ?-1991).[216]

As the story goes, Lara's friend Pepe Verduzco had asked him if he would be willing to listen to his cousins Paz and Esperanza from Guadalajara. Having briefly met them before during a chance encounter, Agustín agreed to hear the young women sing.[217] Nervous in the presence of the popular composer, Paz and Esperanza apparently did not make much of a first impression.[218] Shortly there-after they returned to Guadalajara, where they made their radio debut on station XED in 1933.[219] Later that year, the sisters returned to Mexico City. One of their first activities was to make a visit to the famous XEW studios.

In awe of the many artists assembled there as well as the studio's beautiful grand piano and furnishings, they spied fellow *tapatío* (a native of Guadalajara) composer Gonzalo Curiel. Curiel greeted the Águila Sisters warmly, saying that he had been hearing good things about them. They then sang Curiel's "Deseo" (Desire) and "Mañanita fría" (Cold Little Morning) beautifully. Before the ses-sion ended, Curiel invited Paz and Esperanza to join him that night for an XEW broadcast with his orchestra El Escuadrón del Ritmo (Rhythm Squadron).[220]

The performance led to a contract with Curiel and his group. The bandleader, however, fell ill about three months later and in his absence the artistic director of XEW, Armado C. Guzmán, gave the sisters some work at the studio. In the meantime, Paz and Esperanza started performing in nightclubs, dance halls, movie houses, and theaters. They soon collaborated with many of the popular musicians of the time, including Emilio Tuero, Chucho Martínez Gil, Adelina García, and Julio Flores. Bandleaders such as Max Urbán, Elías Breeskin, Julio Cochard, and Daniel Pérez Casteñeda also featured them.[221] Initiating a cooper-ative agreement with the two, Agustín invited Paz and Esperanza to work with him at the Teatro Isis.

Before long, however, he took to the road again touring in central and northern Mexico during the summer and early fall of 1934. After he played at Guadalajara's Teatro Delgollado in July, critics praised him as one of "Mexico's new music vanguard." One journalist proclaimed, "Lara speaks to the people's taste as he gives voice to the ambience of the nation." Another reviewer added, "The jarocho composer's songs are sung by young and old alike in the salons of the wealthy as well as on the street corners of the slums." The same reviewer further asserted that the "musician-poet"—as Lara was by then being referred to—maintained his own identity as a Mexican while realizing a "harmonious blend of Latin American influences" distinct from the often "barbarous mix of styles that one often finds today in many popular songs."[222] Seeking to cash in on this growing excitement, various publications including the popular *Cancionero Picot* (Picot Songbook, established in 1931 by the Picot Laboratories) began printing lyrics to some of his works.[223]

Meanwhile, Lara continued his compositional run by producing several new songs in 1934. Boleros such as "Entrega" (Submission), "Ultimo beso" (also "El último beso," or The Last Kiss), "Viviré para tí" (I'll live for You"), the tango "Arráncame la vida" (Tear this Heart Out), and Foxtrots "Cerca" (Close), "En vano espero" (Hope in Vain), "Esclava" (Slave), and "Sola" (Alone) all began to circulate.[224] Of this group, "Arráncame la vida" has proven the most lasting.[225] First recorded by Lara in El Paso, Texas in August 1934 for Decca, the composition is a tango set in a minor key:

> *En esta noche de frío,*
> *de duro cierzo invernal,*
> *llegan hasta el cuarto mío*
> *las quejas de arrabal.*

> In this cold night
> Of the unending winter,
> I know they will come to me
> Those plaintive cries from the outskirts.

> *Arráncame la vida*
> *con el último beso de amor,*
> *arráncala, toma mi corazón.*

> Rip my life from me
> With the last kiss of love,
> Take it, take my heart.[226]

Lara's lyrics suggest a near-desperate emotional state—almost as if the protagonist is close to drowning in an unbearable loneliness. Romantic tension follows, with the possibility of redemption through love. Indeed, the last two lines suggest an inevitable kind of spiritual contact—even if the singer's hoped-for rescue is not realized. As with many of his other songs, Lara's poetic style here paints a vivid emotional portrait despite his relatively spare means. In a 1961 RCA Victor version, piano, accordion, and violin provide the main accompaniment to the vocal. To great effect, both the accordion and violin play sinuous, tango-accented lines that respond to sung vocal pleas.[227]

Following a successful visit in Guadalajara, Lara journeyed northward where he played in Culiacán, Nogales, Chihuahua City, Parral, Durango, Nuevo Laredo, and El Paso. Performing with a small ensemble that featured Chino Ibarra on trumpet, José Landeros on violin, and the vocal trio Las Tres Morenas, Lara once again gained an enthusiastic response from audiences and critics alike. This, some testified, came in contrast to what listeners disparaged as "noisy jazz" and blues heard on border radio. In overstated tones, these listeners found the "música criolla" (Creole Music) produced by the jarocho artist and his colleagues "welcome relief" from what they somewhat arrogantly considered "gringo contaminations" popular at the time.[228] Proudly praising Lara's sound, a reviewer in Durango noted that "it was not long ago that music composed in conservatories here had French titles!"[229] Indeed, times were changing as Mexicans increasingly looked to their countrymen, rather than Europe, for cultural inspiration. Far from Mexico City and close to the United States, it was in fact Spanish-speaking residents on both sides of the US–Mexico border that enthusiastically embraced Lara as an exponent of the new Mexican sound.

In the midst of all the fanfare, a brand new Chevrolet carrying Lara to a show honoring Mexican Independence at a local jail in Nuevo Laredo collided with a rented car on September 12, 1934. The musician suffered a minor head injury and was taken to the local hospital for treatment. Bruised and bandaged, he nevertheless performed the show before returning to Mexico City.[230] Back home, Lara took time to rest before performing at the newly opened Palacio de Bellas Artes a few weeks later, in a concert honoring actress Virginia Fábregas. After the show, a reporter noticed a small group calling themselves "Los defensores de la música nacional" (The Defenders of National Music) outside the auditorium. Protesting Lara's presence at the event, they declared his music unfit for national adulation. Flabbergasted, the journalist wrote the next day, "What? Lara is not a composer of Mexican music? This is preposterous!"[231] Obviously, for those who rallied against Lara, his citizenship alone did not deter them from considering him a threat. True, his songs did not explicitly render patriotic content; he occasionally did touch upon sensitive material in his lyrics, and was influenced by an assortment of foreign musical styles. Still, his growing association with the state of Veracruz should have been reassuring. Perhaps it was the fact that Lara—like other Mexican entertainment stars—had travelled to Los Angeles, western headquarters of US culture industry. Might he become corrupted by the experience and subsequently take advantage of his esteemed position back home to spread anti-Mexican ideas? For most, these and other paranoid imaginings did not add up to much of anything. In large measure, he stood as a proud example of cultural innovation and increasingly international renown.[232]

Controversy persisted. Attendees of the 1934 Congreso Feminista (Feminist Congress) in Mérida turned their attention to a number of issues, such as prostitution and various other social ills, including what they believed to be the pernicious influence of Agustín Lara.[233] They asserted that "all his songs contain an accentuated eroticism," which contributed to ongoing exploitation of women andthe age-old practice of prostitution.[234] Spokespersons Dr. Francisco Reyes and María de los Ángeles Farías y Balleza, along with other delegates, encouraged Mexicans to avoid Lara altogether—whether on stage, or radio, in films, or as featured in various entertainment magazines.[235]

These criticisms provided a field day for editorial page cartoonists, who played up the tension between the feminists and the popular composer.[236] One journalist defended Lara's music by saying that it "came as a natural product of his creativity and the tropical culture he had grown up in."[237] Drawing on contemporary currents of cultural nationalism, another reviewer saw much value in what he believed to be Lara's "miraculous" creative response to the "invasion of American jazz in recent years."[238]

Responding to the controversy, Agustín calmly defended himself by claiming that he never meant to offend anyone, "let alone the feminists."[239] He told the reporter that his songs represented only a "humble expression" of his way of thinking and feeling.[240] Echoing these sentiments, El Universal Gráfico published a column titled "Candid Sociology," which proclaimed: "While [the feminists'] mission against prostitution is a noble one, their idea to censor the songs of Lara is misguided. Surely the eroticism of Lara's songs has caused no dishonor to any woman. Moreover, women do not go into prostitution simply because of a song."[241]

Critics generally figured that feminists and fans of Lara could both have it their way. Although he did sing of prostitutes, he did so artfully. Most could appreciate the difference. Nevertheless, Mexico was a culture largely uncritical of male privilege at the time. A short while later, Illustrado magazine writer Oscar LeBlanc further responded to charges leveled at Lara. He made light of the situation and joked that that Mexicans depended on Agustín to be their "standard bearer of creole cursilería" (kitsch).[242] The composer, according to LeBlanc, could simply not help but express himself as an urbane, cosmopolitan artist fully aware of the occasional and sometimes awkward, embarrassing dilemmas every generation has had to confront. Next to a handsome drawing of the musician-poet, LeBlanc's text told a story of Lara supposedly visiting a home of an older, middle-class woman with a young daughter. After playing "one of his less controversial songs" for the señora, the girl asked if he might play a request for her. When she asked for "La Pervertida," a blushing Agustín complied.[243]

The alleged furor over Lara's music did not take shape in a vacuum. In fact, it came just as the 1934 presidential campaign heated up. Soon, the newly elected administration of Lázaro Cárdenas (1885–1970) launched a "new morals" program aimed at curtailing vice throughout the nation. These actions would eventually lead to the high-profile closings of several nightspots in Mexico City, as well as other famous entertainment sites such as the Cuernavaca casino and the Tijuana racetrack owned by former presidents Plutarco Elías Calles and Abelardo Rodríguez, respectively.[244]

Conservative voices gained ground a year later when the minister of public education temporarily prohibited the playing of Lara's music on official broadcast stations or in public educational settings because of its alleged immoral and degenerate content.[245] In line with the official government position, one critic viewed the "Lara craze" as a kind of social psychosis with fans babbling on about "drunken palms" to the beat of "some Afro-Cuban-Mexican calumnity" or the "love of a loose woman":

> Indeed, the Ministry of Education is right in not tolerating this dangerous phenomenon to continue among the impressionable younger generation. And while it may be impossible to stop it, protecting those we are responsible for from the disfavorable moral influence of the semi-original music of Mr. Lara is the least that can be done.[246]

Foreshadowing the dustup that would come with the future introduction of rock and roll music in the late 1950s, some used the Lara controversy for satirical purposes. One mock editorial by "Figaro" maligned those who took a righteous stand in "defense" of the nation's moral fiber:

> To be allowed to sing Mexican songs in the Palacio de Bellas Artes one now first needs special permission from the Fine Arts Department which will make a careful study of the throats of all those presumed to perform. . . . No singing shall be allowed on Sundays, patriotic holidays, or New Year's Eve . . . and those who violate this rule will be jailed![247]

"Figaro's" jest was soon followed by a number of cartoons and Day of the Dead *calaveras* (skull-and-bones imagery accompanied by satirical verses or décimas) that commented on the controversy. One presented humorous rewritings of some of Lara's most popular songs. Among these little ditties was "La flor de la maldad" (The Flower of Evil, to be sung to the tune of the 1930 song "Pervertida"), which featured a drawing with a succulent marijuana leaf in the background, hinting at Lara's penchant for the drug.[248] Yet while the conservative government rulings may have temporarily directed negative attention toward the musician-poet, it seemed most now had come to accept him as part of the national culture. As one writer in Tijuana put it, "he has given the public what it wants . . . and his music reflects something of our Mexican soul." The northerner added that while it was perhaps not appropriate for children to be singing along to "Aventurera," plenty of other Lara songs could be sung in schools.[249]

Interestingly, the popular composer's contribution to a developing postrevolutionary sense of *mexicanidad* came not so much through explicit patriotic refer-
encing but rather through singing of his beloved women, his adopted Veracruz,
and, ultimately, through his standing as a prolific young artist on the international
scene. With his regular work in musical revue and radio as well as near constant
touring, Lara had impressed audiences from the Southwestern United States to
Cuba and throughout Mexico. By the end of 1934, he stood as an important,
although not uncontroversial, cultural representative of modern Mexico. Lara
had established a close working relationship with the sensational Toña la Negra
and the Águila Sisters while at the same time remaining productive in turning out
new material. Powerful collaborations with Mexico's incipient film industry were
also just around the corner. Yet with all the success came certain disappointment
and loss. Perhaps most disconcerting would be his breakup with Angelina.

# Palm Trees and Pirate Nights: 1934–1941

*Yes, he is ugly but he makes up for it in personality.*
—Carmen "La Chata" Zozaya[1]

When New York dancer turned writer Verna Carleton Millan arrived in the Port of Veracruz in the mid-1930s, the first thing she heard was "the strident voice of a radio [that] throbbed forth the words of a popular danzón." For Carleton Milan this experience turned into a vivid memory for "so many, many times did I hear it: 'Palmeras borrachas de sol . . .' (Palm [trees] saturated [literally drunk] with sun).[2]

What the newly arrived *gringa*—then accompanying her Mexican husband—heard was Lara's 1933 song "Palmeras," one of Lara's tropical-themed creations that was gaining popularity at the time.[3] Her soon-to-be publicized recollection testified to the far-reaching diffusion of the composer's music as well as to his spectacular rise to the top of the Mexican entertainment industry.

As with so many of his other songs idolizing female beauty, the bolero "Palmeras" has a lively, upbeat feel with a clave beat and descending melody line that culminates in the last "borrachas del sol" stanza of the verse. The lyrics here, like so many, are economical but rich in imagery. Centered on a young woman set in a tropical paradise, Lara creates a loving portrait drawn from the natural colors of the seaside:

*Hay en tus ojos*
*el verde esmeralda*
*que brota del mar.*
*Y en tu boquita*
*la sangre marchita*
*que tiene el coral.*

There is in your eyes
The emerald green
That springs from the sea.

And on your delicate lips
Is a light blood blush
The hue of coral reefs.

After describing the woman's eyes as emerald-sea green and lips as having the color of coral, Lara goes on to consider the rhythm and rhyme of her "divine" voice before concluding with the reflection of sun-drenched palm trees just under her eyes:

Y en las cadencias
de tu voz divina
la rima de amor.
Y en tus ojeras
se ven las palmeras
borrachas del sol.

And in the rhythm
Of your divine voice
The rhyme of love.
And under your eyes
One can see palm trees
Saturated in sun.[4]

In a version of "Palmeras" sung by Alfonso Ortiz Tirado, the song's two lyric sections are sung at a relatively quick tempo with "boquita" (little mouth) rhyming with "marchita" (literally faded, here blush) in the first and "ojeras" (eyecups, or rings under one's eyes) with "palmeras" (palms) in the second.[5] The resulting combination of rhythm, melody, and romantic imagery is especially catchy, while no doubt Lara's turn of phrase "borrachas de sol" nicely complemented his womanizing, fun-loving, bohemian aesthetic that was so in vogue among Mexican men at the time. As Carleton Millan quickly discovered upon her arrival in Veracruz, "Palmeras" appealed widely to Mexican listeners, and was being heard in nearly every corner of the republic thanks to the power of radio broadcasting. To this would be added the soon to be hugely popular medium of film.

## Amor de mis amores

In 1934 Lara collaborated with expatriate Russian director Arcady Boytler (1895–1965) on a short, ten-minute film titled *Revista Musical*.[6] Agustín performed two new songs at the piano. The first, a romantic tune titled "Viviré para tí (Living for you)" featured dancer Eva Beltri, while the second, named "La cumbancha" (Drinking Spree), featured Lara and Toña la Negra performing live from the Teatro Politeama stage.[7]

On November 19, 1934, Lara and Bruschetta celebrated their sixth year together. For the occasion, Agustín dedicated a new bolero to Angelina titled "Amor de mis amores":

> *Poniendo la mano sobre el corazón*
> *quisiera decirte al compás de un son*
> *que tú eres mi vida,*
> *que no quiero a nadie,*
> *que respiro el aire,*
> *que respiro el aire*
> *que respiras tú.*

> Putting my hand on my heart
> I would like to tell you by way of a song
> That you are my life,
> And that I don't want anyone else,
> For I breathe the air,
> Breathe the air
> That joins us together in love.

Lara exalts his love, declaring he and Angelina intimately bound together in the air they breathe. After repeating the stanza above, he once again pledges his affection with the following lines:

> *Amor de mis amores*
> *vida de mi alma,*
> *regálame las flores*
> *de la esperanza;*
> *permite que ponga*
> *toda la dulce verdad*
> *que tienen mis dolores,*
> *para decirte*
> *que tú eres el amor*
> *de mis amores.*

> Love of my loves,
> Life of my soul,
> Give me the flowers
> Of hope;

> Let me put all the sweet truth
> Of my sorrows
> Into telling you
> That you are the love
> Of all my loves.[8]

The song is set in a major key, and Lara's 1953 version for RCA Victor opens with perhaps one of his most classic introductions.[9] In a romantic vein, the composition speaks of Agustín's deep and enduring commitment to Angelina.

The piano introduction leads into the first verse with Lara's vocal line accompanied by Carlos Águila's violin and light percussion (bongo).[10] When Lara arrives at the last two lines of the verse ("que respiro el aire, que respiro el aire, que respiras tú"), he only plays one quarter note at the beginning of each measure to mark time. The verse is then repeated with the same effect before Lara teasingly foreshadows the chorus by slowing the second time as he sings "que respiras tú" and then slides into the very sing-along-worthy refrain "amor de mis amores." Following a violin solo this is repeated with the same nearly warbled intonation in Lara's voice before the song ends with a light, pizzicato touch of the violin.

Lara's busy work schedule generated increased income that allowed the couple to move in late 1934 to a new residence at 50 Guadalquivir in Colonia Cuauhtémoc, a sumptuous space with two gardens along with a striking red salon and three bedrooms they had painted blue, pink, and green. The composer's frenetic work schedule precluded him from enjoying his new abode for any length of time, however. About the same time, Lara began to increasingly distance himself from Angelina—reportedly only visiting every two or three days to woo her with a bouquet of flowers and then to pick up a fresh change of clothes before heading out again. Whenever Agustín needed a place to rest he would often prefer to stay at his rented studio apartment on Celaya Street rather than return home.[11]

Despite this, Lara and Bruschetta hosted a holiday party at their new home. In attendance were Diego Rivera, Frida Kahlo, and David Alfaro Siqueiros (1896–1974), among other artistic and political notables. During the party Angelina is said to have engaged in a long conversation with Frida, who told her of her plan to divorce Diego. Bruschetta later wrote in her diary that she too had begun to think seriously about separating from Lara.[12]

In March 1935, Lara flew to El Salvador to begin a short Central American tour.[13] To promote his growing catalogue of RCA Victor recordings, he performed "Mujer," "Rosa," "Aventurera," and "Arráncame la vida," along with a new waltz titled "Farolito" during often sold-out shows.[14] Now the toast of powerful elites, Lara played for the fascist-leaning Salvadoran President Maximiliano Hernández Martínez (1882–1966) and his wife at the San Salvador Country Club.[15] He then made his way to Guatemala City.[16]

By April, Lara had returned to Mexico City before setting out for northern parts of the republic and later, San Antonio, Texas where he performed a number of benefit concerts for the Mexican Community School Association.[17] Later that year he again traveled to Central America—this time to Managua, Nicaragua for a series of radio broadcasts.[18] 1935 was one of the most prolific years in Lara's entire career, for although he had been churning out between twenty and thirty songs per year since 1929, his output in 1935 totaled nearly forty known compositions.[19]

The composer also wrote a number of new Spanish-themed songs: "Toledo," "Murcia," and "Valencia." Along with "Sevilla" (1931), as well as the hugely popular "Granada" (1932), this growing collection would be known as the "Spanish Suite." Taken together, they impressed audiences with their vivid descriptions of romantic, Iberian scenes. For this, some Mexican critics, perhaps not surprisingly, accused him of neglecting his own national culture.

Some wondered how Lara came up with this material. Neither Angelina nor any of his closest associates really knew. Not having been to Spain, Lara later claimed he had found inspiration in the 1922 book titled *El Embrujo de Sevilla* by Uruguayan writer Carlos Reyes (1878–1938).[20] Agustín's theater friend Pepe Elguero had given the composer the book while Lara recuperated at home from his bout with appendicitis in 1931.[21] Fascinated with the tale filled with exotic flamenco dancers and bullfighters, Lara imagined himself a traveler in Spanish cities contemplating local beauty. Many of the songs from his Spanish Suite suggest that the composer fancied himself a modern-day Casanova.[22] No doubt, the suite articulated a deeply felt case of Hispanophilia and fanaticized a glorious day when Lara would conquer the mother country with his charm and irresistible music. It would not be until some fifteen years later, however, that he would travel to the peninsula and visit for the first time many of the places he paid tribute to in song.

Of this group, "Granada" would eventually prove to be the most popular. Like the other Spanish-themed compositions, the song combines romanticized images of landscape and culture (sun, blood, fruit, wine, flowers, gypsies, and guitars), as well as ruminations about attractive women:

> *Granada,*
> *tu tierra está llena*
> *de lindas mujeres*
> *de sangre y de sol.*

Granada,
Your land is full
Of beautiful women
Of blood and sun.[23]

Set in a major key, "Granada" has a flowing melody most often interpreted in an operatic singing style. Pedro Vargas first recorded it for Peerless in 1932 and many others followed.[24]

In this early version, a short introduction with violin, percussion, and piano gives way to the "Granada" verse sung in Vargas's dramatic, operatic-style vocal. Here, the lyrics "Granada, tierra soñada por mi, mi cantar se vuelve gitano cuando es para ti" (Granada, land of my dreams, my song becomes gypsy-like when it is for you) unfold over a moderate tempo, march-like rhythm. This then moves into a dramatic, two-line section where the accompaniment drops off and Vargas sings "mi cantar hecho de fantasía, mi cantar flor de melancolía, que yo te vengo a dar" in an even more grandiose style (my song is fantasy, a melancholic flower that I come to give you). Following a brief passage, the song transitions into an instrumental interlude in slower habanera rhythm before giving way to a final chorus in which Lara's lyrics wax poetic about the charms of the city.[25]

Soon to be considered one of Lara's most classic songs, "Granada" would be interpreted by many other singers in years to come. Curiously, however, it does not show up on most of Lara's CD compilations—perhaps because he did not have the vocal depth to perform it. The song is different than others in his repertoire given its exceedingly sonorous, operatic approach. Aside from becoming a favorite request for countless mariachis, more recently tenors Placido Domingo, José Carreras, and Luciano Pavarotti have recorded versions. Contrasted with previous interpretations that pay closer attention to the intended character of the song, these renditions are largely showy vehicles for celebrity singers.

Back on the home front, Lara and Bruschetta's relationship became increasingly embittered. For some time the two had rarely appeared together, as Agustín preferred that Angelina stay out of the public eye.[26] He seems to have also wanted to maintain extremely tight control of Bruschetta's activities. When Emilio Azcárraga gave the couple a radio on their seventh anniversary in November 1935, it was, somewhat surprisingly, the first time that Angelina could listen to her boyfriend's broadcasts in the comfort of her own home.[27]

Lara soon rented another studio apartment. This time his private undertakings, including, many believe, visits with any number of attractive young women, were spent just off Amsterdam Street in the fashionable La Condesa neighborhood.[28] When Angelina learned of Agustín's alleged dalliances, she pleaded with him to stop but to no avail.

Deeply hurt and frustrated, Bruschetta decided to give their situation one last try. She wondered if adopting a child together might revive Agustín's love interest. Yet when the subject came up, Lara rejected the idea and instead professed a desire to travel the world and live his life without any significant family obligations. This, added to the fact that Agustín had never considered her son Jorge his own, left Angelina heartbroken. Bruschetta took solace in her family, with her mother Sofia telling her repeatedly to "forget about him" while Agustín continued to enjoy his status as a man about town (Figure 4.1).[29]

Lara carried on. In February 1936 Boris Maicon directed the composer along with Lorenzo Garza and Lucha María Bautista in Mexico's first color film: *Novillero* (apprentice bullfighter). This melodramatic, thirty-minute work was based on Lara's song about a young man about to meet his fate in the bullring. Bautista sang the title track accompanied by a parade of *manolas* (Spanish girls) and *chinas poblanas* (literally women with Asian heritage from Puebla, but more generally imagined as nineteenth-century popular feminine figures of Mexico with embroidered shawls and blouses).[30] In the drama, Agustín appeared as an orchestra director in the Mexico City El Patio nightclub. Premiering at the Cine Regis the following year (February 1937), *Novillero* may not have made for great cinema, but nonetheless represented a step forward for the Mexican film industry with cinematographer Ross Fischer's Cinecolor processing.[31] Meantime, Lara finished production work on another film project based on one of his songs, *Rival*. That same year, Agustín also traveled with

*Figure 4.1* Lara and young dancers. Agustín Lara Festival publicity card. Courtesy of Agrasanchez Film Archive.

Toña la Negra and Pedro Vargas on a northern tour with stops in Guadalajara, Tampico, Monterrey, Saltillo, San Luis Potosí, Chihuahua, Durango, Mazatlán, and Hermosillo.

It was at this time that President Abelardo Rodríguez's Minister of Public Education Eduardo Vasconcelos (1896–1953) responded to conservative critics of the musican-poet by issuing a ban of all Lara music in schools. Once again, the claim was that his lyrics contained material of an immoral and degenerate character.[32] Agustín seems to have successfully taken the situation in stride, and perhaps may have even decided to channel his frustration with the so-called guardians of public morality by continuing to write new songs. Although his output was significantly less than the previous year, among the new compositions in 1936 were the often-interpreted "Pregón" (Street Seller's Cry), "El coquero" (The Coconut Vendor, also known as "El vendedor de cocos"), and the popular bolero "Veracruz."

## Veracruz

In the late summer of 1936, Agustín visited the Port of Veracruz with his long-time friend José Luis Díaz Castilla. While staying at the Hotel Diligencias, he composed "Veracruz." As Lara would later recall, he began strumming a borrowed guitar and improvised the lines "I was born with the silvery moon" (Yo nací con la luna de plata) after enjoying a delicious dinner of red snapper and black beans along with several beers and coffee, compliments of the hotel owner Laureano Carús. Having struck up a melody, Agustín continued while his friend José Luis took note:

> Yo nací con la luna de plata,
> y nací con alma de pirata,
> yo he nacido rumbero y jarocho,
> trovador de veras
> y me fui lejos de Veracruz

> I was born under the silvery moon
> I was born with the soul of a pirate
> And I was born a rumbero and jarocho
> A real troubadour,
> And I fled, far from Veracruz.

> Veracruz, rinconcito donde hacen su nido las olas del mar.
> Veracruz, pedacito de patria que sabe sufrir y cantar,
> Veracruz son tus noches diluvio de estrellas, palmera y mujer.
> Veracruz, vibra en mi ser, algún día hasta tus playas lejanas tendré que volver.

Veracruz, little corner where the ocean waves make their nest.
Veracruz, little piece of the country that knows suffering and song,
Veracruz, with your nights filled with stars, palms and woman.
Veracruz, resonates in my being,
one day I will have to return to your distant beaches.[33]

Lara's lyrics in the first half of the song are somewhat rare in that they sketch a personal narrative, however imagined. The composer's 1951 RCA Victor recording starts with an introduction that summons the image of a storm about to break. Yet when Lara moves into the verse with the violin accompaniment of Carlos Águila playing over an upbeat rhythm, the feeling becomes lighter. In the chorus Agustín sings the praises of the beloved port city (and, by extension, the state of Veracruz) with a descending melody. Lara emphasizes the last word of each line to rhyme "mar," "cantar," "mujer," "ser," and "volver." The song includes a short, instrumental verse before repeating the "Veracruz" chorus for a final time and ending with the promising "one day I will have to return to your distant beaches." Intoning "jarocho," "rumbero," and "trovador," Agustín further identified himself as a *veracruzano* (native Veracruzan).[34]

Along with his earlier "Lamento jarocho," "Veracruz" speaks in glowing terms of the region. Many subsequently considered the two compositions as virtual state anthems as local musicians enthusiastically adapted Lara's melodies to suit their own artistic and entertainment needs.[35] These songs became an essential part of the repertoire played by marimba bands, guitar-toting troubadours, tropical groups, itinerant mariachis, players of *son* jarocho, and accordion-led *norteño* trios, as well as more classically trained bolero stylists.

By mid-September 1936 Lara was back in Mexico City, where he took part in the sixth anniversary of Mexico City radio station XEW.[36] Shortly thereafter, longtime collaborator Pedro Vargas accepted an invitation from Radio Splendid in Buenos Aires, and boarded a plane for the southern metropolis.[37] It would be some time before the once inseparable artistic friends would perform together again.

One night after one of the very few times Angelina had gone out with friends while Agustín stayed home, he composed a waltz titled "Noche de ronda." (Night Moves)[38] The song's lyrics speak of loneliness and longing:

*Noche de ronda,*
*qué triste pasas*
*qué triste cruzas,*
*por mi balcón*
*noche de ronda,*
*cómo me hieres*
*cómo lastimas,*
*mi corazón.*

Night out on the town
How sadly you pass
How sadly you cross,
By my balcony
Making the rounds,
How you hurt me
How shameful,
My heart.[39]

The 1951 RCA Victor version opens with a foreboding introduction on the piano with Lara's right hand lightly playing out what sounds like footsteps while his left hand holds down a drone-like, somber chord sequence.[40] Matching lyrics and music, "Noche de ronda" is a sad, slow waltz. It starts in a minor mode and then moves into the major. Lara sings the first verse over his melancholy piano with only a hint of movement. He sings another verse as a violin filters in to help gradually lift the tune as it enters the chorus where he then issues his final, brokenhearted plea: "[Tell her] that making the rounds is no good, it only leads to harm, and causes pain, and only ends in tears" (que las rondas, no son buenas, que hacen daño, que dan penas, que se acaba por llorar).[41] During a short instrumental break before Lara repeats the chorus for a final time, Carlos Aguila's lilting violin solo restates the bittersweet main melody over the moderate triple meter. The listener is drawn in before the final lyrics are sung ("que se acaba por llorar" repeated) and Lara's dark piano ending. "Noche de ronda" is truly romantic, even tragic, as music and lyrics combine to create a portrait of a relationship ending. It is a song that would presage events in the composer's own life.

The Christmas holiday brought a startling revelation for Angelina. While having dinner with Lara and friends, including Raulito and Adolfo Girón (with whom Agustín was allegedly in the process of organizing a small orchestra), she intercepted a telegram addressed to him signed by a young woman stating that she had arrived in the city. The message was from a Colombian dancer named Carmen "La Chata" Zozaya, whom Lara had met at the Teatro Politeama a few years earlier and with whom he had begun a relationship. Agustín had initially crossed paths with Zozaya in 1933, found her attractive, and subsequently pursued her with his characteristic wooing.[42] Acting on the belief that her boyfriend was having an affair Angelina hurriedly left with her son Jorge to live with her brother Alfonso.

Lara tried to win Bruschetta back by visiting her regularly. In typical fashion, he brought her flowers, perfume, and other gifts. Determined, Angelina held her ground during the early weeks of 1937, until word came that Agustín's father had died at the age of 79 in Tlatlauqui, Puebla. The event forced a temporary reconciliation between the two as they received an assortment of family and friends.

Shortly thereafter the composer returned to work with little apparent grief over his father's death.[43]

Meanwhile, Lara had taken part in a series of cinematic collaborations. He contributed "Noche de ronda" to the 1936 film *¡Esos hombres! (Malditos sean los hombres)* (These Men! What Bastards They Are) directed by Rolando Aguilar and starring Adriana Lamar, Arturo de Córdova (1908–1973), and Marina Tamayo.[44] Agustín would also provide songs for several other films the following year including *La gran cruz* (The Great Cross) and *Noches de gloria* (Glorious Nights). As would prove the case with quite a number of other films, Lara's compositions would serve as not only as musical material but also as the basic narrative premise. Released in 1937, *Adiós Nicanor* was titled after Agustín's rustic *ranchera* of the same name.[45]

In this picture, Lupe (played by actress Carmen Molina), the girlfriend of a young man named Nicanor (played by up-and-coming film director Emilio "El Indio" Fernández, 1904–1986), understands he is leaving her for another woman. In a pivotal scene, she sings Lara's 1930 composition:

*Adiós Nicanor,*
*sé muy bien que no vas a volver,*
*sé muy bien que tu amor es para otra mujer.*

Goodbye Nicanor,
I know well that you will not be back,
I know well that your love is meant for another woman.[46]

Curiously, Lara's art here seemed to mirror his life, as it somewhat paralleled that of the film's protagonist, Nicanor. With this and future artistic endeavors, the boundary between the composer's personal and professional worlds would become increasingly difficult to distinguish.[47] With his relationship with Angelina on the rocks, Agustín further immersed himself in his work. He also appears to have become significantly more enmeshed in the celebrity image growing up around him.

Shortly after the death of his father, Lara received a call from agent Bruno Pagliai telling him that Paramount studios in Hollywood was interested in his working on a new film. Titled *Tropic Holiday*, the project featured Dorothy Lamour (1914–1996), Ray Millard (1907–1986), popular Mexican singer Tito Guizar (1908–1999, star of the 1936 hit movie *Allá en el Rancho Grande*), as well as Guizar's wife Nanette Noriega de Guizar. Sultry singer Elvira Ríos was also slated to participate. Eager to sign on, Lara soon took up residence in Los Angeles.[48]

The story of the film follows Hollywood writer Ken Warren (Ray Milland) who goes to Mexico to develop a screenplay. Traveling with his secretary, Midge

Miller (Martha Raye), both start up romantic relations, Midge with a serenading Latin lover named Ramón (Tito Guizar) and Ken with the attractive Manuela (Dorothy Lamour). Midge's longtime boyfriend Breck Jones (Bob Burns) soon arrives and asks for his sweetheart's hand in marriage. Various adventures ensue as Midge plays off Breck and Ramón's advances. Meanwhile, Ken's romance with Manuela not only provides him with much creative material but also leaves him deeply smitten. In the end, he finds a way to remain in Mexico so the two can be together.[49]

The film featured the music of Lara for the first time in an Anglo-American context. In addition to Tito Guizar, the production included the (all-female) Ascencio del Rio Trío (Emmy del Río, Ofelia, and Sara Ascencio) and the San Cristobal Marimba Band. "Farolito," "Mujer," "Mía," "Noche tropical," and "Oractión caribe" were all included, along with Pepe Guizar's song "Guadalajara."

Various problems plagued the production from the start, however. The producers wanted control over whatever music Lara composed for the film, a situation complicated by the fact that Emilio Azcárraga, along with radio station XEW and the Sociedad de Autores y Compositores de México (Mexican Society of Composers and Authors), claimed—as they still do today—exclusive rights to Lara's music.[50] Officially, work on the film could not proceed until the go-ahead was given by Azcárraga. Represented by Bruno Pagliai, Agustín waited during the winter of 1937 in Los Angeles (initially at the Biltmore Hotel) while both sides negotiated. As expenses piled up, Lara eventually called Angelina and asked her to send money. As would be the case on more than one occasion, she went to visit Azcárraga for help, but he was unable to remedy the situation in any immediate manner. Desperate for money, Bruschetta sold their automobile and some jewelry to raise some quick cash. She then moved the couple's few remaining belongings to a modest rental home located at 26 Tuxpan in Colonia Roma.[51]

News of another death soon reached Lara. On March 18, 1937, Maruca Pérez died at the young age of thirty. According to Bruschetta, Lara became depressed upon hearing of his friend's death.[52] Yet he mentioned nothing about Maruca when he interviewed with *Todo* reporter Adolfo Fernández Bustamante for a feature story in the magazine at the end of the month. Instead, he proudly recounted his lack of formal musical training as well as a desire to write an opera that he would title *El pajaro del oro* (The Golden Bird).[53]

Lara continued to wait for Azcarraga's permission to work on *Tropic Holiday*. Finally, in late July 1937, Azcárraga and Paramount reached an agreement. Momentarily excited by the breakthrough, Agustín then called Angelina and said he wanted to get married in California. Believing that this may have been a signal that her partner was finally ready to give up his freewheeling lifestyle and settle down, Bruschetta boarded a train north for Los Angeles. When she arrived, however, Angelina found him as preoccupied and temperamental as ever. Lara told her that he had not been able to compose anything thus far during his stay. Moreover, he had apparently complained to Tito Guízar that he could not get his hands on any marijuana. Guízar is said to have been unable to score but had instead acquired some cocaine for the composer, which he then combined with his beloved cognac. The mixture may have provided some temporary emotional relief but rendered him unproductive. By the fall of 1937 production on *Tropic Holiday* finally began to gather momentum. Yet as it turned out, participation in the film proved both artistically unsatisfying and expensive, leaving Lara with a number of unpaid expenses as the difficult year came to an end.[54] At that point, any additional work on the film would have to wait. Lara returned to Mexico City for the holiday season in a funk. Feeling tired and weak, he sought medical help. Doctors soon told him he was anemic.

In the meantime, Agustín fancifully dreamed of performing in Paris with an orchestra of twenty violins and sought out Mexican government funding to pay for such a trip. This was not the first time for such a fantasy, as Lara had previously pursued a connection with former President Abelardo Rodríguez to acquire funding for European travel. Unsuccessful, he subsequently made contact with associates of President Lázaro Cárdenas, who expressed interest but told the composer that the time was not right for such an undertaking. Perhaps not surprisingly, this determination to travel to Paris also served as a pretext for Agustín's further distancing himself from Angelina, who later complained in a letter that Lara had spent Christmas Eve 1937 without her at a party in the French embassy in Mexico City.[55] Shortly thereafter, Agustín was called back to Los Angeles to complete work on *Tropic Holiday*.

In early January 1938, Bruschetta took it upon herself to again move the couple's things into a more spacious house located at 1902 Insurgentes South in Colonia Florida. Rent for the well-apportioned home amounted to only 150 pesos a month, a fact Angelina proudly told Agustín over the telephone in Los Angeles. As it turned out, there was a catch. The residence had once been home to former governor of San Luis Potosí Saturnino Cedillo (1890–1939), who had recently broken relations with President Cárdenas.[56] When Lara caught word of the fact that he was renting the former Cedillo residence, he immediately demanded that Angelina figure a way to get out of the lease before Cárdenas found out.[57]

Meanwhile, trouble was brewing in Los Angeles as members of Agustín's production team, including North American musician Ned Washington and Nanette Noriega de Guizar, were finding it difficult to mold Lara's material to fit *Tropic Holiday*.[58] As it turned out, poor translations by Noriega de Guizar ("Mujer" became "My First Love," "Oración caribe" "We Live Forever," "Farolito" "The Lamp on the Corner") deeply frustrated Lara. Nevertheless, the composer managed to keep up appearances and even waxed enthusiastic when writing to Angelina. He noted, for example, how delighted he felt with the sound of a vocal chorus singing "Farolito" (in Spanish) as well as the work of Dorothy Lamour and others on the set, including Elvira Ríos whom he believed was turning into a true "star."[59] Still, problems continued to dog the making of *Tropic Holiday*, including disputes between the director and production team that would eventually compromise the film's overall dramatic quality. Despite all this, Lara's work contributed to the realization of an admirable musical score that received a 1938 Oscar nomination.[60]

Back home, Angelina soon received news that Lara's Aunt Refugio had become quite ill. Visiting the bedside of Agustín's dying relative, Bruschetta learned that her partner had actually been married to a young woman several years earlier. The revelation distressed her greatly. She confided her desire to leave Agustín to Emilio Azcárraga, who helped her with a modest financial gift.[61]

Despite their many difficulties, the couple continued to correspond. Angelina then visited Agustín in August, finding Lara lonely and alone. Curiously, he felt little to no motivation to socialize with other Mexican artists living in Los Angeles such as Dolores del Río (1905–1983), Lupe Vélez, Ramón Navarro, and the Guizars.[62] Nevertheless, he did manage the occasional visit. For example, Agustín told Angelina about a surprise encounter with Greta Garbo (1905–1990) one afternoon while having lunch at Dorothy Lamour's house. Another happy moment occurred when Agustín received a congratulatory note from Irving Berlin. In celebration, he and Angelina dined at a restaurant named Sebastian's Club. Tension arose, however, when a casting agent approached their table and soon took an interest in Bruschetta. When he told her she looked a lot like Errol Flynn's wife at the time, French actress Lili Damita, Lara became upset and chided her.[63] With his partner attracting attention rather than he, it was becoming clear that his work on *Tropic Holiday*—and, more generally, his residency in Los Angeles—was not providing the success in the US market he had hoped for.[64]

In the spring of 1938 Angelina returned to Mexico City where, among other things, she took care of business with the staff at radio station XEW before rejoining Agustín in Los Angeles later that summer. While she was away, Lara's letters continued to address Bruschetta in endearing terms. A letter dated June 28, 1938, for example, opens with Lara referring to Angelina as the "amor de mis amores" (love of my life) before hinting at the idea that he was thinking seriously about the two getting married.[65] Once Angelina had returned to Southern California, the couple rented a small house close to Paramount Studios on Van Ness Street.

It was at this time that Agustín is said to have improvised a song one day allegedly inspired by a Dostoyevsky short story. According to Bruschetta, he titled the piece "Cuentos rusos" (Russian Stories) and recorded it along with another melody called "Vals de salón" (Salon Waltz), which he gave to Angelina as a gift shortly before her returning to Mexico City.[66] Alone again in Los Angeles, Lara continued to be frustrated with the English translations of his songs. More generally, he felt that Hollywood was ignoring him and when his contract expired at the end of the summer, he eagerly boarded a plane and flew home.

Anticipating Agustín's arrival, Angelina waited for a call from the airport—one that did not come until the next day. When Lara did telephone her, he said that he thought it better that he not come to the house because he had an appointment with President Cárdenas's secretary the following morning to see about a trip to Paris. He proposed a meeting in a downtown restaurant named La Concordia.

When they saw each other Lara once again attempted to reassure Angelina, professing his love for her and his desire to restore their relationship. But when Agustín left the table to make a phone call, she accidentally discovered a note he had left in a California magazine on the table instructing "someone" to disembark from his arriving flight well after him. Assuming that he had traveled back from Los Angeles with a female companion, Angelina decided once and for all that things were over with Lara. She got up and walked out into the street and never saw him again.[67]

## Paris, Cuba, and South America

Lara finally secured funding for a trip to Europe from Emilio Azcárraga and President Cárdenas. He left for Paris early in the fall of 1938 accompanied by his friend and sometime radio guest Fernando de la Llave.[68] Agustín had apparently also planned to make the trip with Carmen Zozaya at his side, but she fell ill at the last minute and did not travel to Europe until a short while later. Once together in the French capital, Lara and Zozaya made their residence at 23 Rue de Laos.[69] Other Mexican friends, including dancer Rosita Téllez Wood, soon joined them in the City of Lights.

Lara and Zozaya toured Paris in style as they visited a number of local attractions in a fancy Packard automobile. Agustín became acquainted with a number of resident celebrities including Charles Boyer (1899–1978), Maurice Chevalier (1888–1972), Raymond Griffith (1895–1967), Edith Piaf (1915–1963), and Josephine Baker (1906–1975). Lara also made time for several important Mexicans then living abroad, including composer Silvestre Revueltas (1899–1940), writers Narciso Bassols (1897–1959) and Carlos Denegri (?–1969), as well as painter David Alfaro Siqueiros.[70] He also made the rounds with literary friend Renato Leduc, who had arrived in the city some four years earlier. Together, they frequented some of the city's most elegant cabarets and nightspots, including the notorious Un, Deux, Deux bordello. On these and other occasions, Agustín left Carmen to fend for herself. Zozaya spoke no French and often felt lost and abandoned in Paris.[71]

Settling in the French capital, Lara set out to do what he had not achieved in Los Angeles: gain public notoriety. The situation in Europe was changing, however, as Nazi Germany had recently begun an aggressive military campaign by invading the Czechoslovakian Sudentenland. In spite of this, Agustín made the most of an artistic scene in an exciting, though increasingly anxious, pre-World War II Paris. An advertisement for one of his shows that fall announced: "Mercredi 19 Octobre, au Theatre de L'Empire, 41 Avenue de Wagram, le cèlèbre compositeur, populaire Mexicain, Agustin Lara. Gran soirèe de gala" (Wednesday, October 19 at the Empire Theater, 41 Wagram Avenue, the Celebrated Mexican Popular Composer Agustín Lara. [It Will Be] A Grand Gala Event).[72]

As word spread of the popular composer's European endeavors, Mexican journalist Carlos del Paso reported that Lara had triumphed in Paris. As he put it, Agustín's conquests included a performance for a Nicaraguan embassy reception attended by bankers, politicians, and writers. Tossing in the occasional foreign phrase, del Paso claimed that Lara had earned considerable cachet and displayed a natural savoir faire in making it on the fashionable French urban scene. Further, the journalist assumed that Lara had little interest in playing second-class theaters, but rather wished to perform only in the most expensive nightclubs. Proud of his countryman's achievements in Europe, del Paso opined that soon Lara would be "proclaimed not quite on par with virtuosos such as [Frédéric] Chopin (1810–1849), [Camille] Saint-Saëns (1835–1921), or [Claude] Debussy (1862–1918); but nevertheless would certainly be considered of equal status when compared to [Franz] Lehar (1870–1948), [Émile] Waldteufel (1837–1915), [Jacques] Offenbach (1819–1880), and other famous composers of light classical music and operetta."[73]

Other Mexican journalists soon made note of Lara's presence in Paris. Writer "Mike Gossip" later alleged that that Agustín had made a big splash in the bohemian Montmartre district, spoke decent French, and could even sing a song or two in English.[74] Fernando de la Llave also got in on the act by asserting that Agustín "now had become a continental personality . . . whose name is synonymous with Mexico [and is recognized] well beyond the borders of his country."[75]

The truth is that Lara had not taken the city by storm, despite these sympathetic claims. His fantasy of conquering the city with his personal charm and romantic melodies notwithstanding, Agustín's profile in Paris can perhaps be better understood when considering the advice he received from his musical colleague Edith Piaf, who urged him to play in smaller, more intimate settings rather than trying to win over French audiences en masse.[76]

As his time in Paris was beginning to come to an end, Lara decided he wanted to extend his European stay in order to travel to Spain. Unfortunately, civil war was raging there, and the portent of wider conflict in Northern Europe loomed. Looking for opportunities elsewhere, he accepted a British Broadcasting Company invitation to record in London.[77] There, he met a couple of rich Venezuelan businessmen who invited him to perform at a cabaret they planned to open in Caracas. When they offered to pay for Lara's ocean voyage, Agustín returned to Paris, collected his things and, it is said, took Carmen to the office of the Mexican Consulate and left her there until he could figure out a way to pay her passage home.

A 1938 bolero "Volverás/tú volverás" (You'll Return), as well as the 1939 compositions "Naufragio" (Shipwreck, also a bolero) and "Bola negra" (Dark Hoax, a java or French waltz), may have been created at the time with Carmen in mind.[78] "Bola negra" speaks of a tempting young French woman, while a section of the lyrics from "Naufragio" gives an indication of what may have been the musician's faded love:

> *De aquel sombrío misterio de tus ojos*
> *no queda ni un destello para mí;*
> *y de tu amor de ayer sólo despojos*
> *naufragan en el mar de mi vivir.*

> Of that somber mysteriousness of your eyes
> There is not even a sparkle left for me;
> And of the love you once shared, only remnants
> Shipwrecked in the sea of my existence.

The second verse gives testimony that a once vibrant relationship is all but over:

> *No te debía querer, pero te quise;*
> *no te debía olvidar y te olvidé*
> *me debes perdonar el mal que te hice*
> *que yo de corazón te perdoné.*

> I should not have wanted you, but I did;
> I should not have forgotten you, and I did
> you should forgive the pain that I caused you
> because from the bottom of my heart, I've forgiven you.[79]

Lara recorded a version of "Naufragio" in the late 1950s for Orfeón with only light percussion (bongo and timbales) accompanying him on the piano. It is set in 2/4 time, which Lara plays at a moderate tempo with a light tango feel during the verse before he moves into the final, slightly drawn out fourth line of the refrain: "Naufragan en el mar de mi vivir" (shipwrecked in the sea of my existence). Short and simple, this recording captures the mood of a lovelorn individual.[80]

It is not exactly clear where Lara went next. Earlier accounts have claimed that he boarded a ship for South America after only a brief stopover in New York. A more recent discussion of Lara's activities at the time suggests that he spent about six weeks in Cuba in late 1938 and early 1939. In this account, Agustín is described as arriving in Havana and quickly finding himself attracted to a beautiful young soprano named Xiomara Fernández. After trying to seduce her while out on the town one night, Lara is believed to have composed a song for the singer titled "Cuando mi miraste tú" (When you look at me), which she then performed in some of the island's major theaters. Inspired by this, he is alleged to have whipped up another composition, the 1939 bolero "Sueño guajiro," (Country Dream) the lyrics of which imagine a romantic union and speak in glowing terms of a beautiful queen whose memory makes the musician-poet weep.[81] Here, despite his being smitten, it is thought that Lara soon ended his stay in Cuba and returned to Mexico.[82] Once home, Lara sent for his near-forgotten companion Carmen in Paris.[83]

Somewhat surprisingly, Agustín and Carmen then sailed together to South America. They arrived in the Venezuelan port of La Guaira in early April 1939, where the musician's hosts welcomed him warmly. But when representatives of the CRESTO management agency learned that Lara had traveled with his girlfriend and not a wife, their hospitality turned cold. Determined to impose their traditional values, Venezuelan customs officials insisted that the unwed couple— pointing to Carmen in particular—could not enter the country unless they married. Forced to remedy the situation, Lara made arrangements to wed Zozaya in a civil ceremony on April 12, 1939. Reports of the event describe the impromptu bride as enthusiastic and elegant. The same could not be said of the groom, however, who must have felt more than a little uncomfortable given his longstanding bachelor tendencies.[84]

Lara and Zozaya traveled on to Caracas where he appeared on Radio Libertador. Making friends with Venezuelan musician Toñito Escobar, then touring with Mexican composer and singer Chucho Martínez Gil, with whom Agustín shared some of his music, including the newly conceived "Naufragio."[85] Lara first had Escobar transcribe it and then gave a copy to Martínez Gil, who performed it during one of his scheduled radio broadcasts. Indeed, it was thanks to the burgeoning medium of radio that Lara's music gained popularity in South America.

Lara's brief stint in Venezuela allowed him to establish important new contacts. Back in Mexico for the larger part of 1940, he picked up with his work at XEW. The previous September, the popular radio station had increased its broadcasting power to 200,000 watts. Soon, however, Agustín would return to South America for an extended tour of Brazil (Rio de Janeiro), Argentina (Buenos Aires), Uruguay (Montevideo), and Chile (Santiago, Valparaíso, and Viña del Mar).[86] As Lara effectively combined touring with presentation on an ever-expanding radio network, his music could increasingly be heard in more homes across the hemisphere than ever before. After securing a visa from the American consul in Mexico City on January 25, 1941, Agustín, Carmen, and members of their entourage traveled north and crossed into the United States at Brownsville, Texas on Jan 29 and then continued on to New York City.[87] There, they collaborated with Ramón Armengod to record several songs including a beguine of Lara's titled "Buscándote" (Looking for you), influenced by popular composer Cole Porter's "Begin the Beguine." Interestingly, Agustín would also write a bolero somewhat critical of the New York scene titled "Goodbye Broadway":[88]

> *Broadway, camino de oro,*
> *rosa en la noche de Nueva York,*
> *cuelga en tus hombros el cielo*
> *su manto de estrellas,*
> *y tus hermosas mujeres*
> *se alumbran con ellas.*
> *Broadway, muchacha rubia*
> *de ojos azules sin corazón.*

> Broadway, golden road,
> Rose in the New York night,
> On your shoulders
> The sky hangs its blanket of stars,
> And your beautiful women
> Are illuminated by them,
> Broadway, beautiful blond girl
> With blue eyes and no heart.

Acknowledging the city's allure, Lara's characterization of the Great White Way as a blond haired, blue-eyed woman without a heart largely fell on deaf ears. Yet back home in Mexico, it may have provided Lara a certain degree of social capital as his relatively unremarkable "Broadway" lyrics seemingly pandered to negative stereotypes about the US as an overdetermined, profit-obsessed, "heartless" society.[89]

Catching wind of the musician-poet's doings in New York, Mexican journalists quickly distinguished Lara not only as a cultural ambassador but an artist who—in appropriate Mexican fashion—kept his cool while in the eye of the North American entertainment industry storm (Figure 4.2). In a photo story published back in Mexico, reporter B. Fernández Aldana observed Lara in New York working with popular bandleader Guy Lombardo while also noting that the Latin music director for Decca Records (unidentified) was also maintaining close contact with the visiting Mexican composer. "Here, amidst the skyscrapers of NBC," he wrote, Lara has composed a new melody titled "Adiós Broadway." Drawing meaning from the song lyrics, Fernández Aldana wrote that he was not sure if Broadway—and by extension—New York City provided the proper creative atmosphere for the popular composer. Somewhat negatively, the journalist related that some "Latin" artists (Elvira Ríos, for example) had in fact recently become overwhelmed by the city. "What a few years ago was an example of a beautiful singer is today a vampire, a conjurer in the business of 'sex appeal' . . . in the [American] dream factory," he asserted. "In contrast," Fernández Aldana surmised, "Agustín Lara has eluded this situation, in part because he has maintained his humility. . . . Having finished his concerts at NBC," the journalist related, "he

*Figure 4.2* Lara in his prime. Courtesy of Agrasanchez Film Archive.

accepted congratulations and applause with great modesty."[90] Clearly, readers were to understand that Lara's "natural [Mexican] humility"—as Fernández Aldama put it—necessarily shone above the brash and highly commercial environment of New York's entertainment scene (Figure 4.3).

Remaining in New York until mid-March 1941, Lara then once again made his way via ocean liner to perform in Brazil, Argentina, Uruguay, and Chile for presumably more appreciative audiences. Initially, this second tour of South America was to feature singers Pedro Vargas and a young woman originally from Chihuahua named Chelo Flores. Agustín had first become acquainted with Flores the previous year while working at XEW. Yet just as final preparations were underway for the trip, Flores backed out. Taking her place was another talented young singer named Ana María González.[91]

Ana María González (1920–1983) was born María Olga del Valle Tardón in Xalapa, Veracruz on August 31, 1920. At an early age, she had demonstrated a talent for singing, often imitating her favorite performers during family gatherings.

*Figure 4.3*  Lara publicity photo. Courtesy of Agrasanchez Film Archive.

As an adolescent, she worked in a lawyer's office while listening to the radio in her spare time. While still in her teens, Ana María made her way to Mexico City.

González was drawn to Lara's music, and in 1934 sang one of his songs for a talent show broadcast on radio station XEB. Paying her dues on the capital entertainment circuit, the aspiring vocalist managed to gain employment singing in different theaters and other popular variety show venues, including the Teatro Lírico. She collaborated with musicians such as bandleader and composer Gonzalo Curiel, as well as the Cuban pianist and future mambo sensation Dámaso Pérez Prado (1916–1989), before landing a regular paying gig at the Teatro Follies in 1937 where she met a number of renowned performers including the beloved *ranchera* singer Lucha Reyes (1906–1944). When Lara first contacted Ana María, she had just returned from a variety tour to Veracruz with, among others, the comedian Mario "Cantinflas" Moreno (1911–1993). After only a short while, González would prove a powerful interpreter of Lara's music.[92]

Following passage of fourteen days and nights aboard the ocean liner "Argentina," Lara and company were greeted by the Mexican ambassador to Brazil in Rio de Janeiro on March 26, 1941.[93] As he settled in at the Casino Atlántico, the management provided Agustín with a grand piano. Ana María thrilled Brazilian audiences as she performed two new boleros, "Sólo una vez" (Only Once) and "Bendita palabra" (Blessed Word), along with other standards from the growing Lara songbook. "Sólo una vez" is a romantic fantasy that opens with the following lines:

> *Sólo una vez tu boca primorosa*
> *iluminó con besos mi querer*
> *fue un leve palpitar de mariposas*
> *fue un capricho de tu alma de mujer . . .*

> Only once your exquisite mouth
> Illuminated with kisses my desire
> It was a light palpitation of butterflies
> It was a capricious act borne out of your womanly soul.

> *Por ser tu vanidad tan exquisita*
> *con toda tu maldad y tu altivez*
> *daría toda mi sangre muñequita*
> *porque tú me besaras otra vez.*

> Since your vanity is so exquisite
> With all your wickedness and arrogance
> I would give all my blood, little doll
> For you to kiss me again.[94]

We may never know exactly in whom Lara found inspiration as he wrote these lines. It might have been Carmen. Maybe it was Ana María, who was known to have found Agustín attractive for a time, but probably not, for Lara is said to have assumed an arrogant, sometimes hurtful posture toward his newest interpreter at a relatively early point in the tour. González nevertheless held her own, and soon tension distanced the two. Perhaps harboring second thoughts about hiring González, Agustín soon enlisted the support of Paz and Esperanza Águila who were also in Rio de Janeiro at the time.[95]

The ensemble then went on to Buenos Aires in July, where listeners praised Lara for his famous tango "Arráncame la vida" during a performance on Radio Belgrano. On one occasion, just after they arrived in Argentina, singer Libertad Lamarque (1908–2000) telephoned Agustín, who later recalled:

> Libertad called that night. She said she was filming a movie called "Una vez en la vida" and needed a song to follow that theme. She needed it tomorrow and quick. I answered that I did not have time to do it right and declined the offer, doubting she would not feel insulted. I then went to visit with other Mexicans in town including Pedro Vargas, Elvira Ríos, Chucho Martínez Gil, and the Trío Los Calaveras. We first ate at the La Cabaña restaurant and then went to the house of Roberto Hinojosa who had a piano. At that point I told my friends about Libertad's offer, feeling a bit uneasy. They responded by starting right to work on a tune and quickly came up with "Solamente una vez." How great that was![96]

"Solamante una vez" would become a huge hit not only for Lara but also for various interpreters including Bing Crosby, who recorded an English-language version with Spanish bandleader Xavier Cugat (1900–1990) and his orchestra titled "You Belong to My Heart" in 1945. Agustín's original version contains the following plaintive lines:

*Solamente una vez*
*amé en la vida,*
*solamente una vez*
*y nada más.*

Only once
I loved in my life
Only once
And no more.[97]

Despite their romantic oversimplification, the lyrics to "Solamente una vez" are nonetheless appealing for their nostalgic singularity.[98]

Ana María and Agustín's professional relationship continued to deteriorate. For her part, the singer had grown weary of Lara's changing moods and occasional rude behavior toward her. Wanting to strike out on her own, González performed in Buenos Aires on Radio Belgrano only a few days after Lara had in June. Still, the two continued to work together—performing the recently crafted "Solamente una vez" on the radio and then recording it the following month for the Argentinian branch of the Odeón label.[99]

The 1956 RCA Victor version of "Solamente una vez" begins with a signature unaccompanied piano introduction, followed by an upbeat instrumental verse accompanied by light percussion (bongo and clave).[100] Lara then launches right into a vocal verse where he is followed by violin which accents his melody. The song is short and sweet: two sung verses, an instrumental verse on piano with violin and then a return to the vocal verse for a final run-through. What distinguishes this bolero in contrast to others is the descending melody line sung during the second half of the verse. The lyrics convey a bittersweet message as they suggest that the realization of "true love" only happens once in one's otherwise solitary life journey.

Meanwhile, just as they were preparing to leave Buenos Aires and travel to Uruguay and then Chile, González informed Agustín that she was leaving the tour.[101] The decision surely was not an easy one for her, since Lara had helped her achieve a considerable reputation as one of Latin America's premier vocalists. Nevertheless, Ana María's subsequent performances at the Casino Atlántico Rio de Janeiro and Teatro Politeama in Buenos Aires that year, as well as appearances on Argentine radio, proved successful. Despite this, González increasingly wished to return to Mexico to reunite with her daughter and mother. Making her way north, Ana María played for enthusiastic audiences in La Paz, Bolivia and Lima, Peru. She then went on to New York for some recording sessions with Decca.[102]

Once back in Mexico in late 1942, González appeared from time to time at the El Patio nightclub. Continuing to stay busy, she then joined a production at the Teatro Lírico in early 1943. Later that year she was featured on a new radio station called Radio Mil, and subsequently traveled briefly to Cuba for a series of performances. González again returned to performing on Emilio Azcárraga's XEW and once again at the Lírico, where she gained notoriety for her own Spanish-language version of Cole Porter's "Begin the Beguine."[103]

For their part, Lara and his ensemble had played out the remainder of 1941 entertaining receptive audiences in Montevideo, Uruguay, and in Santiago and Valparáiso, Chile. Unable to resist gambling at the casino in the resort town of Viña del Mar, Agustín reportedly lost a huge sum of money and had to perform an impromptu concert in order to collect enough to pay his way back to Mexico.[104] In doing so, he traveled a circuitous route via Brazil—leaving November 29, landing in Trinidad on December 10, New York on December 15, and Matamoros on December 21, 1941 before finally arriving home shortly thereafter.[105] Despite the long and tiring voyage, Lara's South American tour nonetheless helped secure him a loyal following.

Once back in Mexico City, Agustín wasted no time in renewing his contacts with the local entertainment world while also getting back to work at the piano. He composed several new songs including "Cada noche un amor" (Every Night a Love). "Cada noche" plays on his man-about-town bohemian reputation:

> *Cada noche un amor,*
> *distinto amanecer,*
> *diferente visión.*
> *Cada noche un amor,*
> *pero dentro de mí*
> *solo tu amor quedó.*

> Every night a love,
> A different dawn,
> A different vision.
> Every night a love,
> But inside of me
> Only your love remained.

Characteristic of the age, "Cada noche un amor" reveals Lara wholeheartedly embracing a double standard: wanting to be a playboy while at the same time professing a devotion to his one true woman at home. The last line of the second stanza, curiously, indicates that the singer's object of desire does not reciprocate his advances:

> *Oye, te digo en secreto*
> *que te amo de eras,*
> *que sigo de cerca tus pasos,*
> *aunque tú no quieras.*

> Listen, I tell you in secret
> That I love you truly,
> That I am close,
> Even though you don't want me to be.[106]

Could this woman merely be playing hard to get? Apparently, she would not stand for his declarations—most likely because she knows he makes the rounds and employs the typical male manipulative love language. This apparently does not deter the musician-poet/song narrator who declares, "within him only her love remained." From the lyrics we don't know if the two had previously enjoyed a romance or whether she is solely an imagined ideal. Either way, the tragic twist in the words to "Cada noche" is that here is a man attesting to having a new woman every night while "in secret" caring for only one true love.[107]

Adding "Cada noche un amor" to his now expansive repertoire, Lara continued with regular performances at several Mexico City theaters and nightclubs during this time. On occasion, he even reunited with Ana María González accompanied by a twenty-piece orchestra. For Lara, "Solamente una vez" and "Cada noche un amor" seemingly gave voice to a wistful feeling that had haunted him since his break-up with Angelina. Despite his being married to the younger Carmen, he revealed in these and other songs a desire for love, to the pursuit of which Agustín would dedicate himself in the coming weeks and months.

Regardless of the various changes going on in his personal life, by the end of the 1940s the music of Agustín Lara could be heard by millions. Making countless appearances in cafes, nightclubs, theaters, radio broadcast studios, on film, and out on the town, Lara had labored mightily to establish a reputation as one of Mexico's leading artistic personalities. Quintessentially cosmopolitan in a rapidly urbanizing world, the popular composer now constituted an important cultural export in great demand as the dark clouds of wartime cast a long shadow over Europe and much of the globe.

# || 5 ||

# Tales of Beauty and the Bohemian: 1942–1947

*El matrimonio con María Félix es, socialmente, una provocación magnífica.*[1]
*(The Marriage [of Lara and] María Félix is, socially, a magnificent provocation.)*

—Carlos Monsiváis

When former Minister of War Manuel Ávila Camacho (1897–1955) assumed the presidency in December 1940, the era of the Mexican Revolution came to a close. During the previous *sexenio*, Lázaro Cárdenas had overseen a number of ambitious initiatives including agrarian reform, nationalization of the oil industry, and a reorganization of the national revolutionary party. Yet in his consolidation of the Revolution, Cárdenas had also greatly centralized political power in the hands of the Executive.

Ávila Camacho led Mexico into a new, more conservative political era—one that would see economic policy increasingly turn to industrialization as Mexico entered World War II on the side of the Allies in May 1942. Upon Camacho's departure from office in 1946, national industrial development, as facilitated through a policy of import-substitution as well as the construction of important infrastructural networks such as irrigation, highways, and hotels, would become a priority under his successor Miguel Alemán Valdés (1900–1983). Investments made during the 1940s would pay high dividends, as Mexico's GDP rose handsomely. In turn, Mexican film—and the entertainment industry at large—proved to be one of the key areas for growth. In this midcentury turn of events, Agustín Lara would benefit quite handsomely.

Ávila Camacho provided Mexican cinema with a tremendous boost in the early 1940s by channeling state funding to film producers. Primarily, this support came through the establishment of the Banco Cinematográfico in 1942. Industry promotion, distribution, and demand for Mexican films then improved further when public and private investors launched Películas Mexicanas five years later.[2] Although not integrated vertically like the major Hollywood companies, which handled production and distribution under the same roof, the

Mexican film industry emulated nearly all aspects of the North American model.[3] Many of Mexico's Golden Age actors, including Dolores del Río, Andrea Palma, Pedro Armendáriz (1912–1963), Jorge Negrete, and Arturo de Córdova, had spent time in Los Angeles along with a host of producers and technicians. Similarly, Lara's two stints in Los Angeles had prepared him for regular work as an important musical collaborator in Mexican cinema during the 1940s.[4]

The popular composer became increasingly involved in Mexico's film industry, as his music provided material for imaginative screenwriters, directors, and producers. Several of Lara's boleros served not only as titles, but also provided a basic narrative structure for films.[5] Scripts often told melodramatic, film-noirish tales of love set in the shadowy Mexico City underworld populated by gangsters, dancers, musicians, prostitutes, and pimps. Indeed, the 1940s and early 1950s were the heyday of the cabaretera film in Mexico at a time when the allure of the cinema—and the celebrity star system that it supported—reached new heights.

As never before, newspaper, magazine, radio, and film media became integrated in a quest for maximum publicity and profit. By the early 1940s, celebrities had become demigods to be not only idolized, but also carefully scrutinized for clues as to the latest fashions, social attitudes, consumer choices, and cultural trends. As purveyors of taste they also provided a critical source of national pride, for they revealed the new, sophisticated, attractive, and talented modern "face" and "voice" of Mexico to the world.

## Transnational Cooperation

With the outbreak of hostilities in Europe, Mexican radio not only continued to play a critical role in helping consolidate national identity but also became a contested political terrain, with both the Axis and Allied powers competing for influence. Yet as radio historians have documented, powerful US interests ranging from executives at NBC and CBS as well as the Department of State and the then still separate Office of the Coordinator of Inter-American Affairs (CIAA) successfully convinced Mexican radio and government elites to cooperate with US war efforts.[6] To achieve this end, the CIAA had been founded in August 1940 by a presidential order and was led by Standard Oil heir Nelson Rockefeller (1908–1979), with Donald Francisco as head of the Latin American Radio Division (with offices in Washington and New York). Fluent in Spanish, Herbert Cerwin (1908–1970) very capably represented the organization in Mexico City.[7]

In the fall of 1942, Cerwin, accompanied by his wife Dag, rented an apartment on Luis Moya Street, which was just a few minutes' walk from the studios of radio stations XEW, XEQ (which Azcárraga had founded in 1938), and XEB. He set up a CIAA office for meetings and entertaining just off the corner of Juárez and Reforma, near the headquarters of Mexico City's big daily newspapers. Cerwin called his new set-up the "American Association."

Powerful US corporate interests affiliated with the CIAA and the American Association included representatives of the American Smelting and Refining Company, General Electric, General Motors, and Pan American Airlines. Further cementing his social contacts in Mexico, Cerwin sought close contact with public relations firms Grant Advertising and Sidney Ross as well as businesses that distributed heavily in Mexico such as Colgate Palmolive, Coca-Cola, and RCA Victor.[8]

It was a propitious time for radio in Mexico as broadcasting increased to approximately ninety commercial and twelve government stations. An estimated 600,000 radio receivers operated nationwide. Yet despite this, dissemination remained limited primarily to urban centers and to a relatively select audience within those areas. Nevertheless, the Mexican government promoted the development of the radio industry (as also proved true with cinema) as a way to foster its own vision of a national political culture: one directed from above by the central state and disseminated to the urban middle class in the name of modern economic and social progress. As one historian notes in the similar case of the film industry, involvement in the development of Mexican radio on the part of US agents—including Cerwin and the CIAA as well as a host of other commercial players—ironically helped make this national vision a reality during the war years.[9] To this, another observer adds, "every movement undertaken by Mexican radio operatives was carefully monitored by the North Americans."[10]

Through the supply of radio equipment (i.e., technical manuals, tubes, amplifiers, turntables, microphone equipment, and so on), as well as actual programming content, those with closest contacts to industry folk in the United States stood the best chance to succeed in Mexico. This would especially prove the case with XEW head Emilio Azcárraga, who operated his radio network with the latest broadcast technology made available in part through connections with RCA Victor, General Electric, and Westinghouse.[11]

According to a survey done in the middle of 1942 by representatives of the Sidney Ross and Colgate Palmolive Companies at the request of the CIAA, radio station XEW dominated the capital city's listening audience. Research done outside of Mexico City in several provincial cities revealed a similar command of the market by Azcárraga's operation. For this reason, a writer for the trade journal *Variety* suggested in September 1940 that XEW "clearly reached high above the city like the towers of a cathedral."[12]

Only two Mexican stations, XEW and XEB, had direct access to international press teletype service during the war: the Associated Press (which XEW had contracted with some years before) and the United Press. For a short time in 1941, XEW supported its own news bureau, headed by Adrián Lajous. Soon, however, Cerwin and the CIAA demanded that Azcárraga's outfit depend exclusively on approved US sources for nearly all their international news.[13]

Delivery of US-backed news programming was highly restricted to stations XEW, XEFO, XEB, and XEQ as well as Azcárraga's Radio Programas de México (RPM) network, which had been established in late March 1941. RPM content was transmitted to sixty affiliated stations across the country via an exchange of recorded programs and limited telephone transfer for special programming. By 1945 the network would grow to include thirty-eight stations in many parts of Latin America and the Caribbean.[14]

Provincial cities unable to tune in to either of these larger stations depended exclusively for their news on the CIAA's program *El Noticiero*, broadcast each day at 1:15 p.m. Thus, much of what Mexicans (either news or drama programs) heard came through the rebroadcast on XEW or XEQ of US-produced programs designed for Spanish-speaking Latin American audiences. A selection of these included "Contraespionaje" (Counterespionage), "La Marcha del Tiempo" (The March of Time), "Epopeya del Nuevo Mundo" (Epic of the New World), "Radioteatro de América" (Radio Theater of America) (all NBC on XEW), as well as "Las Ideas no se Matan" (Ideas Don't Kill), "La Marca del Jaguar" (Mark of the Jaguar), "Estamos en Guerra" (We're at War), "Hit Parade," and "Hacia Un Mundo Mejor" (For a Better World) (CBS broadcast on XEQ).[15]

Two industry publications, *Radio* and *Radiolandia*, supported XEW by positively reflecting Azcárraga's programming interests with (largely paid) reviews, illustrated articles, commentaries, and advertising. Praising the radio mogul and his staff, *Variety* had honored XEW with an "excellence in administration" award at the end of 1940.[16] Resulting advertising revenue produced in Mexico during the war years saw XEW well above its closest competitors. In part, this resulted from publicity afforded XEW by the Grant Advertising agency (largely a front for the CIAA), starting in June 1941.[17]

XEW also benefited from technical support and supply by the US War Production Board (WPB), which oversaw export of radio supplies to Mexico as part of a larger strategic defense campaign designed to benefit the Allied cause. The Azcárraga Group (as they had eventually become known) enjoyed a close connection with NBC executives who helped to facilitate the importation of needed materials.[18]

Given the near-monopoly power of XEW, Cerwin, Francisco, and other CIAA staffers temporarily tried supporting smaller Mexico City stations. Francisco, for example, ordered CIAA resources be used to aid in improving programming at XEQ. They also initiated a plan to support a new station called Radio Mil (call letters XEOY) beginning in March 1942. For this CIAA representatives even hired popular comic Cantinflas to perform on a live broadcast, but at the last minute the show could not be produced due to a lack of technical operators. Similar efforts by CIAA staff in conjunction with station XEOY also proved disappointing finding Radio Mil disorganized and with limited coverage, CIAA heads soon returned to full-time patronage of XEW.[19] Through it all, there remained little doubt that popular music lay at the heart of commercial radio's nationalistic programming.

More than a decade earlier staff at Mexico's Office of Cultural Radiotelephony (OCR, part of the larger Public Education Ministry or SEP) had written that "music was the primary material of radio."[20] This was true, they argued, because of music's portability, flexibility, and reproducability.[21] Moreover, Mexico boasted a variety of popular musical traditions that served as raw material in fomenting national culture and consciousness.[22]

According to a survey published in 1942, musical programming amounted to approximately 80 percent of all radio broadcasts in Mexico.[23] As the medium's leading exponent XEW promoted itself as "the station of the stars"—meaning that top-name musicians such as Miguel Lerdo de Tejada, María Grever, Juan Arvizu, Alfonso Ortiz Tirado, Gonzalo Curiel, Pedro Vargas, Toña la Negra, and, of course, Agustín Lara all could be regularly heard (Figure 5.1)

*Figure 5.1* Lara, Vargas, and. Courtesy of Agrasanchez Film Archive.

Given its prominent position as the headquarters for the national entertainment industry, Mexico City became a mecca for artists from around the country who came with the hope of gaining access to radio station XEW or, at least, one of its main competitors such as XEB or XEQ. Never mind the fact that apart from the most notable artists (who were rumored to earn close to 100,000 pesos per year for their radio work), the average salary for musicians, singers, arrangers, composers, and technicians remained substandard.[24] Still, Azcárraga and his colleagues designed what most considered an elegant, middle-class style of programming during their early years. Thousands responded to this, often crowding outside the Ayuntamiento Street studios or in the restaurant next door for a peek at their favorite celebrities.[25]

Support for Mexican cultural content came, in large part, from the state. In 1936, for example, President Lázaro Cárdenas had established the Autonomous Department of Press and Publicity (DAPP). This agency assumed regulatory control over radio, newspaper, books, magazines, film, and theater. At the same time, Cárdenas and his Secretary of Communications and Public Works Francisco Múrgica reformed communication laws under the rubric of "Regulations for Commercial, Experimental, Cultural, and Amateur Broadcasting Stations." The ruling required stations to allow for thirty minutes of government programming each day (previously set at ten). At the same time, the law enforced a previously established ban on the broadcast of political messages over the radio. It also called for a minimum of 25 percent of "typical" Mexican music to be played. Although much radio broadcasting already included significant amounts of national music, this 1936 regulation codified the percentage of music programming devoted to national artists. It also paved the way for the creation of a weekly one-hour variety program called "La hora nacional" (The National Hour), which XEW broadcast.[26]

Under President Manuel Ávila Camacho, the requirement that at least 25 percent of total music broadcast by radio stations be Mexican continued despite occasional protestation.[27] Meanwhile, La Federación Americana de Músicos (American Federation of Musicians) sought to prohibit Mexican artists from recording with the large international record companies—Columbia, Decca, and RCA Victor. For a time, smaller companies took up the slack. At the same time "Latin" music proved particularly popular during the war, as programs such as "Calling Pan America," broadcast by CBS, played songs by a number of Spanish-speaking composers and artists, including Lara. Another similar program was "Here's Mexico," distributed by the Mutual Broadcasting System across the Americas.

At a key period in the development of radio in Mexico, Emilo Azcárraga and his XEW operation benefited significantly from the technological expertise and cutting-edge professionalism of his US contacts. Although he had to engage in a constant process of negotiation between the two sides, Azcárraga astutely maintained his autonomy as a broadcaster and businessman among US agents. By the war years he commanded a more than sizeable share of the national market and therefore outsiders simply had more to deal with Azcárraga in order to gain access to Mexican listeners. This was a relationship that was even more carefully handled in early 1943 as the tide of war turned in favor of the Allies, and the CIAA sought to avoid the impression of "imposing our cultural ideas, publication, or other media of expression . . . because of our superior technical and economic resources."[28]

Emilio Azcárraga ensured his success in the face of powerful US interests by realizing early that he needed both wide broadcast coverage and a "national media image."[29] Similarly, radio historians have noted that Azcárraga shrewdly considered both state and market in crafting his product. Azcárraga managed to make effective use of government guidelines and at the same time broadcast the kind of music Mexican audiences wanted to hear.[30] Agustín Lara's urban boleros arrived on the Mexico City entertainment scene at an opportune time and readily fit this bill. Commenting on the close relationship between the two men, XEW publicist Juan Pablo O'Farril Márquez remarked that "Lara always respected Emilio for all the help he gave him and would never dream of crossing Azcárraga—he was no fool."[31]

Yet while Azcárraga's success came in part through his affiliation with ambitious US governmental and commercial heavyweights, Mexican audiences embraced modernity in a more cautious manner. Whether in the romantic strains of an urban bolero or the figure of the passionate *charro* (singing cowboy), songwriters gave voice to a nostalgic yearning many felt as they increasingly came face to face with the challenging realities of accelerating social and cultural change.[32] One singer-songwriter who deeply touched upon this sentiment was José Alfredo Jiménez.

Known for his melodramatic *ranchera-canción* style, Jiménez (1926–1973) penned hundreds of songs with the help of his close friend and arranger Rubén Fuentes. Among the many top sellers for José Alfredo were "Cuatro caminos" (Four Roads), "Sucedio en la barranca" (What Happened in the Ravine?), "El cobarde" (The Coward), "Que suerte la mía" (How Lucky I Am), "El Rey" (The King), "Hijo del pueblo" (Native Son), "Yo" (Me), and "Ella" (Her).

Jiménez adopted the persona of a poor, unfortunate country boy who, as millions of others similarly did at the time, had migrated to the big city. In 1948, José Alfredo participated in his first solo radio broadcast on station XEX.

José Alfredo's first major commercial hit came somewhat later. In 1950 he gained significant recognition with a version of "Yo" recorded by Andrés Huesca y sus Costeños. With testimonial lyrics that spoke plainly of drinking and romantic loss, Jiménez gained further popularity with a number of songs including "Llegó borracho el borracho" (The Drunk is Drunk). Rich in cultural references to Mexican rural society, history, and popular pride, José Alfredo's work was performed by a wide range of artists and embraced by the listening public.

As with Jimenez, Lara's reputation would benefit from a number of of talented singers interpreting his songs. Ramón Armengod, for example, distinguished himself not only by recording Agustín's beguine "Buscandote" in New York in February 1941, but also with nuanced versions of "Mujer" and "Mi novia."[33]

For her part, a young Lupita Alday caught the composer's attention with her version of "Bendita palabra" during a 1941 XEW-sponsored program (provocatively titled *El Colegio del Amor* or the College of Love). This Azcárraga-funded affair, in fact, was designed as a talent search dedicated to finding Lara a new female interpreter. Among the more than four hundred contestants, Alday won out and later achieved fame with "Solamente una vez" and "Puerto nuevo (New Port)," among other songs.[34]

Also from Veracruz, Chabela Durán distinguished herself as a leading interpreter of Lara's compositions starting in the 1940s. Equipped with a powerful voice and tremendous talent, Lara composed a handful of songs specifically for her, including "El mar, el cielo y tú" (The Sea, The Sky and You) and "Un beso a solas" (A Kiss for the Single Girls). She performed "Solamente una vez" on screen in the 1948 film *Señora tentación* and would soon go on to appear in two other Lara-themed films, *Mujeres en mi vida* (1949), and *La mujer que yo amé* (1950).[35]

The talented Elvira Ríos recorded renditions of "Farolito," "Janitzio," and "Santa" about the same time. Although she had begun recording Lara songs some years earlier ("Cachito de sol," Piece of Sun, and "Pensaba que tu amor," I Thought of Your Love in 1936), her version of "Noche de ronda" proved the most enduring of her deep, smoky-voiced selections from the Lara songbook.[36]

## A New Love

While his songs continued to grow in popularity, Lara's personal life remained tumultuous. As had proved the case with Angelina, Lara's demanding schedule eventually took its toll on his relationship with Carmen Zozaya. While little is known about the details, she apparently left him without explanation one day late in 1941. A small white card communicated Carmen's enduring love for Agustín with these final words: "My hope has grown weary from so much waiting and [it seems] I've been waiting for you my whole life . . . Chata."[37]

Although still legally married for the time being, Lara found himself single again. He cancelled several of his professional commitments and temporarily took refuge at a cozy seaside house in Veracruz called Villa Pepita, just south of the port.[38]

Agustín spent the next few months out of the limelight. One day in early 1942, he fell ill with tremendous pains in his stomach. Friends in Veracruz, including *decimista* poet and local historian Francisco Rivera, arranged for a plane to transport Lara to the Hospital Francés in Mexico City. Doctor Gabriel Malda's ensuing diagnosis required that Agustín be operated upon immediately to have part of his lower intestine removed. Malda performed the procedure successfully and discharged his patient shortly thereafter. He advised Lara that if he were to remain healthy he would have eat better, get more rest, and lead a life free of drinking and drugs. Lara took a dim view of his doctor's strict orders and subsequently fell into a deep depression. He gradually managed to pull himself together enough to return to work.[39] Agustín soon composed a handful of new songs including "Adiós mi Juan" (Goodbye My Dear Juan), "Sin palabras" (Without Words), "Ya me voy" (I'm Already Going), "Puedes irte de mí" (Could You Come to Me?), and a march that was adopted by the Mexican army titled "El cantar del regimiento" (Song of the Regiment). Inspired by the still ongoing global conflict, the song would be one of Lara's few compositions that dealt directly with a patriotic theme:

> *Una musa trágica hizo*
> *de una lágrima un cantar,*
> *el Cantar del Regimiento*
> *de los hombres que se van.*[40]

> A tragic muse
> Made from a tear a song,
> The Song of the Regiment
> About the men who have gone.

Here, as Lara's lyrics acknowledge, Mexican leaders had committed the nation to the Allied effort after the December 1941 Japanese attack on Pearl Harbor by lending both critical oil supplies and significant manpower.[41]

Not one to concern himself with political matters, much less linger long over patriotic melodies, Lara soon returned to performing with Toña la Negra while also restarting his collaboration with Pedro Vargas.[42] This same year saw the composer dash off a handful of new songs including "Saca los nardos morena" (Get to it, brown-skinned girl), "Te vi llorar" (I Saw You Cry), "Te quires ir" (You Want to Go), and "Silverio (a two-step written in honor of Mexican bullfighter and friend Silverio Pérez, 1915–2006).[43] In an apparent nod to wartime Holly-wood, Lara also penned "Casablanca"—no doubt inspired by the film starring Humphrey Bogart (1899–1957) and Ingrid Bergman (1915–1982), released the year before. Yearning again for the company of an attractive young woman, Agustín soon began a relationship with sixteen-year-old Raquel Díaz de León.

From an early age, Raquel had been familiar with Lara's music. She had often tuned in to "La hora íntima" with her cousin, aunt, and grandmother while living in Guadalajara. Díaz de León eventually moved to Mexico City with a boyfriend who soon forced her to begin work as a prostitute. Curiously, he installed Raquel in a bordello managed by the infamous Graciela Olmos "La Bandida" in the Condesa neighborhood. As it turned out, this same pleasure palace was one that Lara frequented—along with an assortment of politicians, artists, businessmen, and military personnel. After learning of this, Raquel one day allegedly kissed a publicity photo of Agustín owned by Olmos. La Bandida made arrangements for the popular composer to meet the curious Raquel, whereupon Lara and his young charge retired to a room with a piano. Accord-ing to Raquel, Lara then set out to seduce her. Enchanted by his new muse, Agustín subsequently met Raquel every day while the bordello madam and boyfriend kept vigilant watch.[44]

Raquel later testified that she managed to escape from her overseers one day while having her hair done at a beauty salon on the corner of Chapultepec Avenue and Frontón. After taking refuge overnight, the next day Lara somehow "rescued" Raquel and installed her in a small rental house near the Azteca Stu-dios in Coyoacán. With two beautiful pines (one taller than the other, which they figured represented their relationship) and a garden outside, they dubbed it "the farmhouse" (El cortijo) and she "the farmgirl" (La cortijera). Lara soon penned a song in honor of the place ("El cortijo") and promised his young lady friend that he would pay her expenses and also provide for a house servant, but cautioned Raquel not to spend more than 10 pesos a day.

Agustín visited his casa chica regularly at first. Soon, however, the novelty wore off. As Raquel later commented, "Agustín was very inconsistent in his emo-tions, ideas, and attitudes. . . . In reality he didn't know exactly how he felt or what he wanted. He sometimes visited more than once a day and then would not appear again for a while."[45] Perhaps this situation gave Lara the idea for a bolero-beguine he wrote in 1943 titled "Fue así" (It Was Like That). The first few lines tell of a growing distance between the two lovers:

*Tanto tiempo sin verte,*
*no me acuerdo de ti*
*si eres rubia o morena,*
*no lo podré decir.*

*Pero, en cambio, cuando hablas*
*reconozco tu voz,*
*porque son tus palabras*
*quejas del corazón.*

So much time has passed without seeing you,
I don't remember
If you are blond or brunette,
I can't exactly say.

But, on the other hand, when you speak
I recognize your voice,
Because your words
Still stir in my heart.[46]

As the song lyrics suggest, the relationship between Agustín and Raquel survived for a time. After a year or so, Lara made the acquaintance of another attractive young woman.[47] She too had also known his music and reputation as a girl listening to the radio in her Guadalajara family home. Her name was María Félix (1914–2002).

## La doña

María Félix was born María Félix de los Ángeles Félix Güereña in the town of Álamos, Sonora on May 4, 1914. Her father, Bernardo Félix, did business in the neighboring Yaqui Valley. Her mother, Josefina Güereña, came from a deeply Catholic family of Spanish descent. As a girl, María often visited her grandparents at their ranch near the town of El Quiriego. Somewhat a tomboy, she loved riding horses and preferred playing with her brothers. A rebellious student in her youth, she allegedly drew criticism from her schoolteachers.[48]

When Bernardo Félix was named by President Álvaro Obregón to a series of government posts in the early 1920s, he moved his family to Guadalajara. Blossoming into an attractive young woman, María developed an independent spirit and distinctive ways while familiarizing herself with the local *tapatío* culture. She learned how to dance and even practiced yoga.

In the spring of 1930, university students in Guadalajara chose Félix to be Carnival Queen. While at the costume ball, María met a young man named Enrique Álvarez, who worked as a representative of the popular Max Factor cosmetic company. He initiated their courtship with a home demonstration. Because María was, at least in part, eager to free herself from her parents' supervision, she accepted Enrique's marriage proposal. A priest married the two teenagers in Guadalajara during a small ceremony on January 10, 1931. Félix eventually gave birth to a baby boy named Enrique on April 6, 1934. Soon thereafter, she separated from Álvarez and briefly returned with her son to Álamos before moving to Mexico City.

After gradually establishing herself in the capital, Félix eventually made the acquaintance of engineer Fernando Palacios, who soon began to introduce her to members of the Mexican movie community.[49] At the invitation of the filmmaker Calderón Urrutia brothers (Rafael, 1882–1969 and José, 1885–1963, of Azteca Films, Inc.), María visited Los Angeles in 1940, where she adorned a float in a Mexican Independence Day parade. Félix toured Hollywood and met actors Robert Taylor (1911–1969), Ray Milland, and Walter Pidgeon (1897–1984), as well as Russian-born actor, director, and producer Gregory Ratoff (1897–1960). María also lunched with movie mogul Cecil B. de Mille (1881–1959).[50]

Despite the attention afforded the promising starlet, Félix nevertheless found only occasional work during the early 1940s in Mexico. Her big break came when she landed a part in the 1942 film *El peñón de las animas,* directed by Miguel Zacarías Nogiam (1905–2006) and costarring Jorge Negrete—now one of Mexico's leading film stars after the success of the 1941 singing *charro* film *¡Ay, Jalisco, no te rajes!*[51]

María learned quickly under her director is tutelage. She also applied some of what she had absorbed in Hollywood by assertively negotiating her salary, costumes, and an assortment of other details. Because he had hoped to costar with the better-known actress Gloria Marín (1919–1983), Negrete missed no opportunity to put the young Félix in her place. The ensuing clash of wills soon became legendary and helped make the film a popular favorite.

Félix then began work on another project that same year titled *María Eugenia.* During the filming, the actress caused quite a stir when she appeared in a white bathing suit for a beach scene and coyly sketched the word "Amor" in the sand. As photographers maneuvered for a glimpse, María provided them with the occasional "candid" shot. Not surprisingly, these photos soon appeared in publications across Mexico.[52] The entertainment press seized upon Félix and began featuring her in photos and write-ups.[53] Yet despite the fanfare, Félix would not fully distinguish herself in the movie business until the success of her next film.

One of Mexico's leading directors, Fernando de Fuentes (1894–1958), supervised Félix in the 1943 film adaptation of the 1929 novel *Doña Bárbara* by Venezuelan Rómulo Gallegos (1884–1969). The actress assumed the character of an aggressive, sometimes ruthless woman who presides over an extensive ranch stolen from the family of a handsome young doctor named Santos Luzardo, played by Julián Soler (1907–1977). At the beginning of the film we learn that

Doña Bárbara had been raped by sailors as a young girl. Embittered by this tragedy, she later abandoned her daughter Marisela (María Elena Marqués, 1926–2008). As the drama unfolds, Doña Bárbara rejects the attention of men so as to preserve her status as a powerful landowner. Assuming a tough-minded, independent attitude, she wears the local male frontier-style clothing, smokes cigarettes, and rides horses, using her beauty and cunning to dominate her rivals. Doña Bárbara falls in love with Santos Luzardo, but then finds out he is only interested in her daughter Marisela. With Félix tantalizing audiences with her femme fatale cross-dressing sex appeal, *Doña Barbara* provided viewers an exciting new female star cast in a distinctively modern role. Some observers suggest that the film also issued a warning in regard to the alleged dangers of blurring gender identity.[54]

*Doña Barbara* earned unprecedented box office receipts as well as significant praise for director Fernando de Fuentes and his young star. As audiences became enamored with María's magnetic appearance and powerful persona, her celebrity status increased significantly. Fans now referred to Félix simply as *La doña* (Lady or Madame). Building on this success, Fernando de Fuentes cast the actress in a similar role in the 1943 *La mujer sin alma*. In this film, María further added to her reputation by playing another strong, if not outright man-devouring, character.

Félix had come to embody a powerful combination of tough-mindedness and stunning beauty. As poet Octavio Paz (1914–1998) later wrote, "María Félix is a woman—such a woman—with the audacity to defy the ideas machos have constructed of what woman should be. She's free like the wind, she disperses the clouds, or illuminates them with the lightning flash of her gaze."[55] Yet while she may have appeared to defy machos with her independent on-screen persona, *Doña Barbara* and subsequent scripts nevertheless conformed to the patriarchal, so-called profamily, patriarchal standards of the day.[56] As one scholar writes, "despite titles which call attention to the female character, Félix's films are male-centered narratives, in which the spectacular pleasure lies with the woman and her masquerades of masculinity, but the narrative remains in hands of the male protagonist."[57] Careful not to go beyond the bounds of what the public would tolerate, Félix told *México Cinema* reporter Robert Browning in early 1945 that despite her bad-girl image she was indeed "a woman with a conscience," with an abiding passion for her work and life.[58]

When she became acquainted with Agustín Lara one day on the movie set, they began a courtship that provided her with gracious compliments, generous gifts, and extraordinary nights on the town. The experienced Lara also helped open entertainment industry doors for the young actress (Figure 5.2).

Agustín met Félix through mutual friend and colleague Agusto "Tito" Novaro in the spring of 1943. At the time, María had begun work on a new film

*Figure 5.2*  Félix and Lara. Courtesy of Archivo General de la Nación, Fondo Hermanos Mayo.

titled *La china poblana*. As their meetings grew more frequent, Félix and Lara attracted the attention of the press, who took pleasure in covering their every move. The two were regularly seen attending theater openings, frequenting upscale restaurants, and visiting friends. They spent Sunday afternoon at the bullfights (Figures 5.3, 5.4, and 5.5).

Photographers often hounded Agustín and his "Machángeles"—as he sometimes teasingly called her, because of her on-screen reputation as a femme fatale. Many, perhaps not surprisingly, accused María of seeking publicity. Yet the young actress stood firm in her commitment to Lara, and confessed to having had a special fondness for the still-debonair radio star ever since she was a young girl.[59] Still, society columns in magazines such as *Revista de Revistas, Jueves de Excélsior, Cinema Reporter, and Cinelandia*, speculated openly about the couple as journalists wondered how such a beautiful young woman could be attracted to an older, less attractive man such as Lara.[60] "What a shame!" one envious columnist proclaimed, "love must truly be blind."[61] Others, however, came to appreciate what they figured were the musician-poet's many appealing qualities and, presumably, his gentlemanly ways in attending to the young actress.

During the fall of 1943 and continuing through the winter of the next year, Agustín wrote a weekly column titled "Algo" in the magazine *Mañana*.[62] Published with occasional photos accompanying the text, these musings were mostly comprised of anecdotes from the musician's life In one of his first offerings, Lara positioned himself as a knowing, respectable male as he penned a short exchange with a young female fan:

*Figure 5.3* Félix and Lara spending Sunday afternoon at the bullfights. Courtesy of Archivo General de la Nación, Fondo Hermanos Mayo.

*Figure 5.4* Félix and Lara Courtesy of Archivo General de la Nación, Fondo Hermanos Mayo.

*Figure 5.5* Félix and Lara. Courtesy of Archivo General de la Nación, Fondo Hermanos Mayo.

LARA: Cigarette?

WOMAN: Sure, but it is a "Lucky"? . . . I've been told you smoke marijuana . . .

LARA: Ay!, señorita, for the love of God . . .

WOMAN, Señor Lara, is it true that you greatly enjoy (the classic Veracruz dish) crab *chilpazotle*?

LARA: Yes, indeed.[63]

This invented scene probably reflected little more than Agustín's idle fantasizing, yet it gave readers a clear sense of the composer's social standing. As rumors of the Lara and Félix romance took full flight, it was to be understood that "the man from Veracruz" had fully established himself as an artist about town. No longer struggling to make ends meet, he soon purchased a white grand piano on which he had inscribed "on this piano will only be played my most beautiful melodies for the most beautiful woman in the world."[64]

In the early 1940s, several other composers achieved notoriety. Hits such as Consuelo Velázquez's "Bésame mucho" (Oh, Kiss Me!), Federico Baena's "Que te vaya bien" (I Wish You Well), "Ven otra vez" (Come Again) and "Cuando ya no me quieras" (When You Don't Want Me), Gabriel Ruiz's "Jamás" (Never) and "La noche es nuestra" (The Night Is Ours), Gonzalo Curiel's "Amargura" (Bitterness) and "Un gran amor" (A Great Love), and Mario Ruiz Armengol's "Aunque tú no me quieras" (Although You Don't Want Me).[65] For the most part, these composers eschewed the turn-of-the-century romantic language of the modernistas in favor of a more direct bolero style that fit better with the anxious cultural climate of the wartime years. Theirs was an approach that sang of the separation, longing, and hopes for a successful reunion on the part of countless women and men at the time.[66] Increasingly associated with an aging artistic generation, Lara nevertheless continued performing at a number of Mexico City venues including the Teatros Iris and Lírico.[67] In January 1944, *El Universal* sponsored a tribute to the Mexican bolero featuring the Trío Bohemio and Trío Chachalacas. As part of the effort, organizers proclaimed Lara, along with his New York City-based counterpart composer María Grever, "truly pioneering" Mexican musicians.[68]

That May, Lara and Félix collaborated on a film for the first time. Titled *Amok*, the project was the screen adaptation of a novel by Austrian Jewish writer Stefan Zweig (1881–1942), under the direction of Spaniard Antonio Momplet (1899–1974).[69] Lara provided the main theme, a few songs, and recorded the background music. For her part. Félix famously played both blond and dark-haired characters: señoras Trevis and Belmont. As the blond "Ms. Trevis," Félix acted as a loose woman, an *aventurera*—a prostitute. In the role of the dark-haired "Ms. Belmont," she played a lady of society.

Momplet's attempt to bring to the screen one of the most cosmopolitan pictures to date in Mexican cinema came up short.[70] Apparently, the producers had a bit of additional music for the final scenes recorded at the last minute. The result proved extremely unsatisfactory to Momplet, who later told writer Paco Ignacio Taibo I (1924–2008) that "the music was flat and monotonous and did not fit the feeling the images were meant to convey . . . [it] destroyed the film."[71] Neither Momplet nor film historian Emilio García Riera (1931–2002) mention whether it was Lara or the other musical collaborator on the film, Manuel Esperón González (1911–2011), who provided the last-minute offerings. Dismal remarks from the director and critics notwithstanding, *Amok* generated several positive reviews.[72]

Lara and Félix further cultivated their romance over the next few months of 1944 and into 1945. Not surprisingly, Agustín wrote not only a number of new songs but also an occasional poem to his new love. One such offering was titled "Romance del Nuevo Amor" and contained the dedication "Para tí, María, Reina, Madre, Mujer!" (For you, María, Queen, Mother, Woman!).[73] Clearly, Lara had fallen deeply in love. Their relationship became more and more serious. By the winter of 1945, Lara and Félix had moved together to a sumptuous residence located at 211 Galileo in the fashionable Polanco district.[74]

Shortly thereafter, the adoring celebrities elegantly hosted the reporter Robert Browning with a round of highballs in their new home. Temporarily calming ongoing speculation about their private lives, Félix testified that she felt very happy with Lara.[75] A follow-up visit later that year similarly portrayed the couple as sophisticated lovers listening to freshly minted bolero recordings. When asked, the actress would repeatedly tell reporters of her contentedness.[76]

Lara added to his repertoire at this time by composing several new songs, among them the 1944 bolero-beguine "Mírame (look at me)." The first two sections read:

> Hago de mis palabras
> la más linda canción,
> súplica que es blasfemia,
> llanto del corazón.

> With my words I have made
> The most beautiful song,
> A prayer that is a blasphemy,
> The result of a weeping heart.

> Mírame,
> mírame con tus ojos
> que son dos luceros
> que Dios puso en mi corazón.

> Look at me
> Look at me with your eyes
> Eyes that are two lights
> That God put in my heart.[77]

Wooed with poetry and musical attention such as this, Félix seemed to have truly taken to Lara. When he fell ill with an undisclosed ailment in mid-April that year, paparazzi closely observed María as she visited her boyfriend at the Hospital Francés.[78] Following Agustín's release and ensuing recovery, the couple resumed their high-profile romance with appearances at film debuts and various nightspots. That fall, Félix's next film, El monje blanco, premiered and prompted several favorable reviews (Figure 5.6).

Lara continued to garner praise as "Mexico's most prolific songwriter."[79] On the international front, his reputation received a boost when Bing Crosby, accompanied by the Xavier Cugat Orchestra, recorded "You Belong to My Heart" in 1945. For the occasion, Ray Gilbert (1912–1976) had adapted the music and lyrics from Lara's 1941 hit "Solamente una vez."[80] The song had originally been used that same year for the animated Disney film The Three Caballeros with the lovely Brazilian singer Dora Luz (Aurora Miranda da Cunha, 1915–2005) performing while Donald Duck and his two cartoon colleagues fawn.[81]

*Figure 5.6* Lara and camera as friend and portrait of María look on. Courtesy of Archivo General de la Nación, Fondo Hermanos Mayo.

You belong to my heart
Now and forever
And our love had its start
Not long ago
We were gathering stars while a million guitars played our love song
When I said "I love you," every beat of my heart said it, too
'Twas a moment like this
Do you remember?
And your eyes threw a kiss
When they met mine
Now we own all the stars and a million guitars are still playing
Darling, you are the song and you'll always belong to my heart.[82]

With lyrics that included "millions of guitars" and "all the stars" rhyming with "heart," the English version of Lara's composition surely had the right stuff for a wartime romantic hit.

Crosby had come to fame during the Depression. His repertoire spanned a wide range of genres as he proved himself an important exponent of modern mass culture in the United States. He pioneered the role of the pop singer and crafted a new, more intimate approach to ballads through the use of the microphone. According to biographer Gary Giddens (1948–), "Bing was the first to render the lyrics of a modern ballad with purpose, the first to suggest an erotic undercurrent."[83] Almost single-handedly, he transformed popular music by delivering a clean, simplified melody and clearly articulated lyrics. Like other greats of his generation, Crosby's interpretive innovations derived from his natural talent and memory. He had little to no professional training. He appreciated the diversity that was American popular music as he incorporated the sound of performers such as Al Jolson, Ethel Waters, Bix Beiderbecke, and Louis Armstrong, among others.

Crosby worked with the major radio networks, Decca Records, and Paramount Studios during the difficult years of the 1930s. In 1944 he toured Europe entertaining troops. Many came to identify Bing as the voice of America as he captivated recording industry, radio, and motion picture audiences. His interpreting Lara's "Solamente una vez" brought the Mexican composer greater attention in the English-speaking world.

Meanwhile in Mexico, the entertainment press had been busy casting Félix and Lara as one of the great romantic couples of the era. Anecdotes about the two soon took on epic proportions. One story, according to Lara interpreter Alejandro Algara (1930–), occurred one late night when he, Lara, and Félix had just left the Teatro Lírico. Making their way across town, they came upon a prostitute while waiting at a stoplight. The woman approached the car and, upon recognizing Lara, asked him for a cigarette: "*Maestro*, I'm very cold, could you spare me one of yours?" Algara recounts that the famous musician offered her not only one of his Pall Malls but also María's fur coat, saying to *la doña*, "don't worry, we'll buy another one for you tomorrow."[84] At the time of the Lara-Félix romance, apocryphal tales about the two celebrities circulated wildly.

New controversy soon arose over a 1944 bolero titled "Palabras de mujer" (Words of a Woman). Musically, the short piece is set in 2/4 time and sounds relatively similar to other Lara tunes. Like the recorded work Agustín did for RCA Victor in the early 1950s, the song featured piano, violin, and percussion.[85] When initially created, it was not the music, however, but the lyrics that caused a stir. This was largely because of the insinuation of an extramarital affair:

> *Palabras de mujer*
> *que yo escuché*
> *cerca de ti, junto de ti muy quedo*
> *tan quedo como nunca,*
> *las quiero repetir*
> *para que tú, igual que ayer*
> *las digas sollozando,*
> *palabras de mujer.*

Words of a woman
That I heard
Close to you, next to you very softly
Quietly like never before
I want to repeat them
So that you, the same as yesterday
Will say them sobbing,
Words of a woman.

*Aunque no quieras tú*
*ni quiera Dios*
*lo quiero yo*
*y hasta la eternidad*
*te seguirá mi amor*
*como una sombra iré*
*perfumaré tu inspiración*
*y junto a ti estaré*
*también en el dolor.*

Although you don't want it
Nor does God, I do
And until eternity
My love will follow you
Like a shadow I will go
I will perfume your inspiration
And next to you I will be
Also in sorrow.[86]

Specifically, it was members of the Liga de la Decencia (Decency League) who worked themselves into a lather over the lines "Aunque no quieras tú/ni quiera Dios/lo quiero yo/y hasta la eternidad" (Although you don't want it/nor does God/I do).[87] They objected to what was interpreted as Lara's putting romantic desire—perhaps even extramarital sex—before God and the family. Springing into action, religious leaders hastily excommunicated the musician.[88]

Agustín found the dust-up "ridiculous" and told reporters he had meant the song to be about love and had absolutely no wish to offend anyone.[89] When a film of the same name went into production (released in early 1946), Lara changed the line in question to "Aunque no quieras tú, ni quiera yo, lo quiso Dios hasta la eternidad" (Although I didn't want it, nor you, God did until eternity).[90] This minor revision seemed to succeed in pacifying public opinion. Yet while Agustín had changed the lyric, an underlying tension would nonetheless remain in the composer's discourse about passionate, romantic love as contrasted with the more traditional loves of family and God. Spanish émigré José Díaz Morales served as director of *Palabras de mujer*. The film starred Ramón Armengod, Virginia Serret, José Luis Jiménez, and Andrés Soler. In a curious parallel to Lara's own career, Armengod plays a famous composer and bandleader named Fernando who tells the story of his early years. The narrative begins with Fernando recalling how he fell in love with an attractive young singer named Laura. Inspired by his muse, he writes a song titled "Palabras de mujer" and sings it to her.

The club owner where the two musicians work soon jealously decides that Laura can no longer perform there. Fernando begins drinking. Before long, an attractive rumbera arrives and changes into a dressing gown. Minutes later, the proprietor appears on the scene with Laura in tow to show her that Fernando is fooling around. She is crushed. The next day Fernando calls Laura to explain, but she hangs up on him. That night, he hears her perform on the radio. When Laura announces that she is on her way to South America for a tour, Fernando rushes to the club to meet her after the broadcast. Still wrongly devastated from their earlier misunderstanding, she rebuffs him.

In the meantime, Fernando's new song "Palabras de mujer" becomes a big hit. He is seen traveling to Lima, Santiago (Chile), Havana, and Madrid amid a montage of audience applause, radios, planes, trains, and boats. Once back in Mexico, he receives a phone call from a family friend named Hortencia, who informs Fernando that his mother has died. He travels to the funeral accompanied by his brother and sister. Fernando and Hortencia quickly fall in love and get married before returning to Mexico City.

One day, Fernando is called to Argentina on business. In a bar with a friend, he listens to tango music and watches drunken sailors and women dance while waiting for the evening's live entertainment to begin. Before long, his lost love Laura appears. Fernando is sad to see her in such a seedy place. Ignoring the circumstances, she sings with real conviction. Laura immediately leaves the bandstand when her song concludes and goes backstage without acknowledging Fernando. Seeing this, he makes his way to the piano and plays "Palabras de mujer" with the accompaniment of a backing band. Outside the bar, tango music can be heard as Fernando waits for Laura. When he finally sees her, he passionately professes his love. The two reunite. In one of the following scenes, Fernando is seen performing with his orchestra as Laura listens on the radio at home. A telegram arrives from Hortencia back in Mexico. Reading the message, Laura learns that the woman has just given birth. When Fernando calls to get Laura's reaction to the radio broadcast, she mentions virtually nothing. The singer hangs up the phone, packs, and leaves. She takes refuge at the house of Fernando's friend. When he comes to search for her there, she hides as Fernando shows the telegram to his friend and says that his true love is Laura. "How sad life is," the friend responds. Fernando then leaves as Laura watches. The song "Pal-abras de mujer" plays again as the credits roll.

With telephones, telegrams, radios, airplanes, and other technological trap-pings of contemporary life as background, *Palabras de mujer* presents audiences with a modern dilemma. Should romantic love be chosen above family? How-ever tragic in the end, the two lovers know they must abandon their relationship for the sake of Fernando's new baby and wife back home.

In some ways, *Palabras de mujer* foreshadowed coming difficulties for Agustín and María. By now, Lara had begun to suffer from fits of suspicion and jealousy. People sometimes even publicly teased the couple, shouting at places such as the Sunday bullfights, "there goes the beauty and the beast," "lots of salad but so little chicken," and "be tough on him, María," among other re-marks.[91] Seeking, perhaps, to stave off his insecurities, Lara marked the third anniversary of his meeting Félix with special zeal in mid-1945. Word spread suggesting that the celebrities planned to wed.[92] These rumors proved some-what true, as the two gathered in front of friends to join in civil union on Christmas Eve, 1945. Photographers captured the moment as they pictured the couple at María's recently purchased home at 127 Aristóteles surrounded by friends such as Mario "Cantinflas" Moreno, Dolores del Río, Pedro Vargas, Renato Leduc, Carlos Denegri, Libertad Lamarque, Jorge Negrete, Betty Davis, and a handful of others.[93]

Félix and Lara honeymooned in Acapulco. They stayed in the El Papaguayo Hotel with direct access to the Los Hornos beach. There, according to legend, Lara penned his famous 1946 waltz "María bonita" (Beautiful Maria) in which he proudly declares, "You've had many loves, but none so good, none so honor-able as what we've shared." Set in a major key, it is an upbeat tune that, in each verse, testifies to the wonder Lara felt:

*Acuérdate de Acapulco,*
*de aquellas noches,*
*María bonita,*
*María del alma.*

Remember in Acapulco,
Those evenings spent,
Pretty María,
Dear María.

*Acuérdate que en la playa*
*con tus manitas*
*las estrellitas*
*las enjugabas.*

Remember on the beach
With your hands
You wiped dry
The stars.

*Tu cuerpo del mar juguete,*
*nave al garete,*
*venían las olas,*
*lo columpiaban.*

Your body was the sea's toy,
A ship adrift,
The waves would come,
And sway you.

Considering María's past romances, Agustín later asserts:

*Amores habrás tenido*
*muchos amores,*
*María bonita,*
*María del alma.*

You must have had many loves
Pretty María,
Dear María.

*Pero ninguno tan bueno*
*ni tan honrado*
*como el que hiciste*
*que en mí brotara.*

But none so good
None so honorable
As the one you made bloom
in me.

As the song progresses, Lara's romantic optimism grows stronger. The final stanza of the song once again declares his love for María:

*Recíbelo emocionada*
*y júrame que no mientes*
*porque te sientes idolatrada.*

Receive it with emotion
and swear to me you will be true
because I idolize you.[94]

Perhaps the happiest of Lara's songs, it is also one of his most beloved.[95] Most famously recorded by Pedro Vargas in 1946, "María bonita" quickly made playlists nationwide and beyond. With the press framing their extensive coverage of the union as a fairytale "beauty and the bohemian" romance made in heaven, the Lara–Félix story constituted a "magnificent provocation."[96] No doubt, the celebrity couple's union had both the appearance and the impact of a successful publicity stunt. Yet it seems that there was more to their relationship than just social climbing.

Upon his return to Mexico City, Lara took part in a show that featured Toña la Negra, Pedro Vargas, and the Son de Marabú ensemble. *Revista de Revistas* profiled María in a cover story that featured her latest film, *Vértigo*.[97] Félix then teamed up with director Fernando de Fuentes to star as a strong-willed "maneater" in a new project titled *La devoradora*.[98] With a solid script and production team, the actress turned in a powerful performance. When it premiered in the spring of 1946, the film received a number of positive reviews.[99] Singer Rosalío Ramírez's interpretation of Lara's song "Aventurera" added allure.

The couple soon invited journalists into their home for another anniversary. With an assortment of friends present this time, including cinematographer Gabriel Figueroa (1907–1997), Pedro Armendariz, Rosa Castro, Andrea Palma, and Ana María González, it appeared that nearly everything was going right for the two.[100] All of Mexico—and, for that matter, much of the Spanish-speaking world—was singing along to "María bonita." If there had been any doubt before, the marriage of Félix and Lara now sealed their status as entertainment world queen and king, oddly majestic in their immediate postwar reign.

*Cinema Reporter* featured Félix as she dedicated herself to a number of projects in the fall of 1946.[101] One writer remarked that María's star appeal shone especially bright as critics christened her "the most extraordinary figure in Mexican cinema."[102] Another article covered the actress as she attended the Mexico City premiere of her film *La mujer de todos* (Everyone's Woman) with Lara that October.[103] Similarly, the publication *México Cinema* prominently featured photos of the actress in the October and November 1946 issues, while the December edition closed out the year with continued fanfare and a positive review of María's most recent cinematic release, *Enamorada*.[104]

Directed by Emilio Fernández, the picture costarred Pedro Armendáriz and adapted Shakespeare's *Taming of the Shrew* to a Revolutionary Era drama set in Cholula. Gabriel Figueroa's work set new artistic standards for the industry.

Yet with the growing list of accolades also came a new set of personal difficulties for the young actress.

Félix's next pairing with actor Arturo de Córdova in her provocatively titled film *La diosa arrodillada* (The Kneeling Goddess) spelled trouble for the increasingly insecure Lara. Filmed beginning in February 1947 in Mexico City's Churubusco Studios and released that August, the project featured Félix in the role of Raquel, a young woman wanting to find a way out of an affair with a wealthy married businessman (Antonio) played by de Córdova.[105]

Apparently, Lara was not alone in thinking the director had gone too far. A review a year later reflected mounting objections some had regarding the explicit nature of certain love scenes. Even María's father Bernardo eventually chimed in when journalists quoted him as saying that some of his daughter's recent on-screen roles had produced certain feelings of shame and embarrassment.[106] Criticism also came from members of the Catholic National Action Party, who denounced what they believed to be overly graphic material in *La diosa arrodillada*.[107]

Despite his concerns, Lara nevertheless remained busy with a string of performances including a sixteenth anniversary show for radio station XEW on September 18, 1946. A month later, he and Pedro Vargas began work on a new live radio show titled "Cómo nacieron mis canciones" (How my songs originated) on XEW.[108]

Difficulties between Félix and Lara soon became a matter of much public speculation. In the spirit of the *Día de los muertos* (Day of the Dead/All Souls Day) holiday in early November, an illustrated poem (*calavera*) made fun of María and her crumbling relationship with Lara in these lines:

> *La más bella y más desleada*
> *la que tanto amó Agustín*
> *alcanzó un hermoso fin*
> *en "La diosa arrodillada,"*
> *por ella el mundo está reza que reza*
> *pero más que ninguno Armando Valdés Peza.*[109]

> The most beautiful and the most disloyal
> She that loved Agustín so much
> Succeeded in bringing to a beautiful end
> "The kneeling goddess,"
> For her the world is praying nonstop
> But more than anyone, [costume designer] Armando Valdés Peza.[110]

With little apparent sympathy for Félix, the spoof characterized the actress as a spoiled, selfish woman—much like many of her on-screen personalities.[111]

*Figure 5.7* Jealous Lara. Collection of the author.

In late November, paparazzi captured the couple in a series of photographs at the El Patio nightclub. As it turned out, it would be one of their last public appearances together.[112] A month later, Félix graced the cover of *Revista de Revista* on December 29, 1946. The occasion was the release of *Enamorada*. In an early review published in the same issue, critic Leopoldo Pastor complimented the work of Félix, director Emilio Fernández and cinematographer Figueroa.[113]

The January 1947 issue of *México Cinema* further expressed curiosity about Félix and Lara's 's private life. One writer produced an article presumably based on *la doña's* horoscope titled "The Destiny of María Félix." This pseudo-psychological portrait cast the actress as a strong woman who could be impetuous, erratic, and even violent. Her love life, according to the stars, was subject to frequent, if not dramatic, changes (Figure 5.7).[114]

With public scrutiny abuzz, word spread that certain male admirers were showering María with expensive gifts. One rumor charged that Félix had taken part in an affair with a high-ranking military man. Other speculation had it that María might have become intimate with soon-to-be president Miguel Alemán Valdés.[115] Interestingly, Lara suspected that a wealthy businessman had come between them—most likely the flamboyant, big-spending Veracruz shipping magnate-baseball entrepreneur Jorge Pasquel (1907–1955).[116]

Marriage to "the most beautiful woman in Mexican Cinema" caused Lara's insecurity to grow more profound. Mocked by members of the press, Agustín began to act differently in public. Some worried he might explode in a jealous rage if he allowed his emotions to get the better of him. Still, Lara managed to keep his composure as he clung to his established image as a sensitive, romantic gentleman. Nevertheless, he must have feared being hurt—perhaps even betrayed. Songs composed in 1947, such as "Sombras (Shadows)" and "Cuando llegaste (When You Arrived)," reflected such concerns. Another, titled "Pecadora" (Sinner), even included the lines:

> Por qué te hizo el destino pecadora
> si no sabes vender el corazón
> por qué pretende odiarte quien te adora,
> por qué te vuelve a quererte quien te odió.
>
> Why did destiny make you a sinner
> If you don't know how to sell your heart
> Why does the one who adores you pretend to hate you,
> Why does the one who hated you go back to loving you again.[117]

The lyrics to "Pecadora" seemed to issue a bittersweet comment by Lara on the current state of his relationship with María Félix. It did not take long for the keen-eyed film industry to cash in on the tenuous Félix–Lara romance.

Directed by José Díaz Morales, *Pecadora* began production in mid-April 1947.[118] Casting featured Ramón Armengod, Emilia Guiú, and Cuban sensation Ninón Sevilla (born Emelia Pérez Castellanos in 1921).[119] The project also included Ana María González and Lara leading a new "Sinfónica" orchestra performing several songs including the title track "Pecadora," "María bonita," "Tus pupilas," and "Te quiero." The Brazilian group Los Ángeles del Infierno provided musical backing for Sevilla's nighclub dance numbers as she acted out several of her characteristic rumbera routines.

Yet another partial cross-fertilization of the musician's life and art, *Pecadora* is basically a film noir replete with mistaken identity, criminality, and tragic misunderstanding. The lead character, Antonio (played by Armengod), is condemned to a sad fate. Mixed up in a drug smuggling operation in Ciudad Juárez, he and his partner Carmen manage to escape to Mexico City and then make their way to Acapulco, where they spend a romantic few days at the beach. While there, Lara's "María bonita" plays in the background as the two protagonists enjoy what will prove to be their only happy time together. Before long, they are back in the capital.

Things get dodgy when a shady couple named Roberto and Leonor stalk Carmen and Antonio. Hatching a diabolical plan, Leonor gets Antonio drunk in a Mexico City cantina while Roberto simultaneously calls Carmen and tricks her into thinking that the aforementioned two are having an affair. Taking the bait, the young lovers split and soon Antonio lands back in Ciudad Juárez. Police arrest him on drug charges, and he is subsequently sentenced to do time at the notorious Islas Marías prison off the Nayarit coast.

Carmen, still thinking that Antonio has betrayed her, is meantime injured in an accident. With no one to care for her, she is nursed back to life by a rich man named Javier, who eventually proposes to her. By now Antonio is again free and back in Mexico City, where he defends a young woman named Ana María while drunk one night in a cabaret. She falls in love with him and subsequently invites him to meet her father Javier and his new wife Carmen. Further suspense ensues.

Roberto then reappears and Carmen discreetly pays him to protect her previous identity from Javier. Javier sees this, senses he is being deceived and confronts Roberto. Roberto tells Javier that Carmen once behaved like a loose woman (*cualquiera*) while living in Ciudad Juárez. Hearing this, Javier punches Roberto who then shoots and kills Javier. Ana María cries over the dead body of her father as the police arrive to arrest Roberto. She then accuses Carmen of killing her father.

Antonio tries to reconcile with Carmen, but she rebuffs him and turns away as "María bonita" plays. She is next seen in a dive bar and later walking the streets. A policeman finds Carmen passed out and delivers her to a seedy rooming house where she is given medicine. Someone decides to call Antonio and he arrives. Antonio tells Carmen she can come live with him and everything will be fine. On her deathbed shortly thereafter, Carmen whispers something about Ana María, who is now also present. "Why don't you two get married and be happy?" she suggests before dying. Ana María runs out while Antonio kisses Carmen for the last time. Ana María then comes back and takes Antonio's hand as the film ends.

While in many ways the film was just another second-rate cabaretera, the director's use of the songs "María bonita" and "Pecadora" helped further etch Lara's music in the collective memory. Given the title song "Pecadora," the film ensured audiences that the fate of Carmen would ultimately be a twisted and tragic one despite momentary glimpses of her "goodness."[120] Curiously, the rising popularity of "María bonita" occurred just as the relationship between

Félix and Lara went into full decline. By the time director José Díaz Morales used another of Lara's songs—this time "Solamente una vez"--for his 1947 film *Señora tentación*—one got the picture that time had run out for Mexico's most celebrated couple. Using the popular composer's 1931 creation for the film title, Diáz Morales nevertheless found inspiration in Lara's music.[121]

*Señora tentación*, as the title suggests, is an age-old story about temptation. The narrative follows composer Andrés (David Silva 1970–1976), his blind wife Blanca (Susana Guízar), and an attractive South American singer, Hortencia (Hilda Sour). Quickly, a love triangle is set up as Andrés is convinced by Hortencia to hire her to interpret his songs. Blanca consents begrudgingly. Andrés and Hortencia go on tour and temporarily live out a romantic fantasy. Meanwhile, Blanca receives an operation that restores her sight. She subsequently blossoms into a renowned concert pianist who ends up in Rio de Janeiro while performing abroad. Meanwhile, Andrés has been rejected by Hortencia, who soon dies in an accident. Andrés is detained by the police as a suspect, and it appears that all is lost for the musician. As he awaits his fate, a stroke of good fortune reunites him and his true love Blanca. Sadly, however, just as he is released, Andrés and Blanca's reconciliation is cut short when an associate of Hortencia named Ricardo shoots and kills the composer. He dies in Blanca's arms as the film ends.

*Señora tentación* is ostensibly a reinterpretation of *Santa*, with Andrés as Santa and Blanca playing the role of Hipólito. For this offering, Lara played himself and performed with his orchestra, backing singer Chabela Durán. Vocalist Kiko Mendive sparkles with Los Ángeles del Infierno, while Ninón Sevilla dances in what is a decidedly secondary and somewhat unintended humorous light. Aside from these occasional bright spots, however, the film is largely a forgettable one.[122]

In the meantime, amidst all the murmurs, speculation, and cinematic borrowings, Félix and Lara had managed to remain together through the first half of 1947. Soon, however, whatever remained of their celebrated bond came undone. That fall, Gabriel Figueroa had escorted Félix to the Cannes film festival in France. Once back in Mexico, photographers often captured her relaxing in the company of various celebrities associated with the movie industry—but not all that frequently with Lara at her side.[123] As the actress began work on a new project titled *Río Escondido*, her close relationship on and off the set with director Emilio Fernández sent a new round of rumors circulating.

Filmed in the Azteca Studios and on location in the State of Mexico, *Río Escondido* presented Félix in the role of a rural schoolteacher, Rosaura. Interestingly, the maestra sent to help rid a poor community of ignorance and disease is appointed by President Miguel Alemán, who plays himself in silhouetted shots. Stricken with a heart condition, Rosaura nevertheless manages to fend off the advances of local strongman Regino Sandoval and soon forces him to provide the support needed to repair the local schoolhouse and have the town vaccinated for smallpox. In the end, Rosaura dies after killing Sandoval in self-defense and imploring the local children to fight against "dark forces" that would keep them uneducated and poor. An artistic triumph for the Félix, Fernández, and Figueroa team, the film would go on to win the Ariel in 1949 as best Mexican film, as well as a number of international accolades.[124]

In the midst of all the fanfare over *Río Escondido*, an interview with Lara in *México Cinema* by journalist Angel Garmendia warmly praised Agustín's virtues as a creator of "sensuous melodies" that combined the "heat of the tropics with sentimental love."[125] Still, reheated compliments for the composer did little to divert attention from his failing relationship. In time, established songs such as the 1936 "Noche de ronda," 1945's "Humo en tus ojos," and "Rival" (1934), among others, took on a new, ever more personal meaning. "Rival," a waltz, tells of a relationship compromised:

Rival de mi cariño,
el viento que te besa,
rival de mi tristeza,
mi propio corazón.

Rival for my affection,
The wind that kisses you
Rival of my sadness,
My own heart.[126]

Considering "Rival" and other similar songs from Lara's repertoire, one can easily assemble a sorrowful soundtrack to accompany Agustín's growing difficulties with Félix. Struggling emotionally, Lara nevertheless kept up with the kind of chivalrous acts he had undertaken in the past. Near desperate, he sent María flowers, gifts, and romantic messages all in an effort to win his lover back. Despite Agustín's gestures, María began to tell her close friends that her relationship with Lara was over.[127]

The final straw came when Agustín confronted Félix (some say at gunpoint) about gifts sent by a fan, as well as her close relationship with Emilio Fernández. In defense, María charged Lara with having an affair with a young dancer named Clara Martínez who performed with the Conjunto Chelo La Rue.[128] Hot on the trail of these allegations, *Revista de Revistas* went public with the matter in late September: "Lara has involved himself in a new romantic complication with a young and pretty dancer from the Chelo La Rue dance group. Meanwhile, we hear that the beautiful María has also gotten involved with director Emilio Fernández."[129]

Soon making a public spectacle of the matter, Félix apparently had Lara's clothing and personal effects taken from his closet and thrown onstage just as he prepared to perform at the Teatro Arbeu.[130] When news of the confrontation hit the streets, everyone knew the romance had ended. Defending himself in the October 4, 1947 issue of *Cinema Reporter*, Lara tried to save face by once again professing his admiration for Félix and disgust for those who gossiped about their personal life.

In the meantime, Lara had begun a stint at the Teatro Follies Bergère with Toña la Negra.[131] Impressed by their performance, one writer called Lara a "lyrical Don Quixote" and compared his efforts in dignifying popular song to the work done by George Gershwin in the United States.[132] Not to be outdone, Félix attended a benefit for the Lion's Club at the El Patio nightclub with her colleagues Gabriel Figueroa and Pedro Armendaríz in mid-October.[133] Covering the actress, the magazine *Cinelandia* praised Félix who, they declared, had become the most popular star in Mexican cinema.[134]

While both personalities were seemingly unhurt professionally, official word of the Lara–Félix breakup came on October 25, 1947.[135] Not surprisingly, newspaper reports revealed little as to why Félix and Lara had separated. María indicated that she had no interest in discussing the matter publicly.[136] Instead, she announced plans to leave for Los Angeles.[137] The next day a headline in *El Universal* declared a somewhat startling revelation: "the need for divorce for María Félix is not necessary." As it turned out, the two had never been officially married—but had only been joined as common-law husband and wife.[138]

Before long Félix traveled to Spain to begin working on a film titled *Mare Nostrum*, directed by Rafael Gil and costarring Fernando Rey. Rumors later spread that Lara had wanted to follow Félix to Madrid. Unable to make the necessary arrangements, however, he did not go. Meantime, *Río Escondido* premiered in mid-February 1948, followed, however curiously, one month later with *Que díos me perdone* (*God Forgive Me*).[139]

Now back on his own, Lara signed a deal to appear in another film with Ninón Sevilla. Commenting on his upcoming work, *Revista de Revistas* remarked that the composer "once again was preparing to break hearts in the film world just has he has in real life."[140] Thus in spite of all the attention paid to his failed romance the past few months, many critics continued their unabashed promotion of the man and his music. One reviewer felt so confident of Lara that he wrote, "still nearly everything he does has been a hit."[141] Exactly how successful he would be in maintaining his popularity in the future, however, remained uncertain.

Looking back, it is clear that the mid-1940s had been a pivotal time both for Agustín Lara and Mexican society at large. As the nation increasingly turned to face a new economic and political future, entertainment industry advances provided new opportunities for both aspiring and more established artists. Enhanced publicity transformed a select few into celebrity icons who provided a welcome distraction from the brutalities of the modern world. Yet while the wartime star-maker machinery provided handsomely in many respects, the benefits of fame often came at a cost. For Lara, intimate association with María Félix had significantly revived his career despite the fact that the relationship had ended in tears.

# 6

# Postwar *Cabareteras* and Boleros: 1948–1953

All Mexicans [now will] have a Cadillac, a cigar, and a ticket to the bullfights.

—Miguel Alemán Valdés[1]

As the Lara–Félix melodrama played out during the war years, the Mexican economy had undergone a significant transformation. Import substitution policies and a resulting industrial upturn contributed to an overall average annual increase of 4.4 percent. In gross terms, Mexico enjoyed a sustained annual GDP growth of about 6 percent between 1935 and 1960—what observers of the immediate postwar decades later referred to as the "Mexican miracle." This economic dynamism provided increased opportunity for many Mexicans to join the ranks of the nation's middle class. In this pursuit, thousands made their way to the nation's capital. Combining with national population growth (3.6 percent, one of the highest in the world by the mid-1960s), Mexico City became one of the largest cities on earth, reaching approximately 4,800,000 in 1960.[2]

A flurry of new construction, international commercial exchange, and cultural cosmopolitanism contributed to what writer Salvador Novo proudly described as "New Mexican Grandeur" (Figures 6.1 and 6.2).[3] Novo, whose chronicles of the mid-twentieth century help shed light on day-to-day developments in the Mexican metropolis, here spoke of the capital's mid-twentieth-century character as articulated in modern art, architecture, automobiles, entertainments, and related technologies.[4]

Yet behind the scenes, Mexico City's infrastructure strained as thousands of newcomers crowded into already packed, low-income housing stock. Some, like the characters in Luis Buñuel's (1900–1983) 1950 film *Los Olvidados*, found the most basic accommodation in marginal settlements on the urban periphery. Others, like Jesús Sánchez and his family, as related by anthropologist Oscar

*Figure 6.1*  Arial shot of Avenida Reforma ca. 1960. Courtesy of Agrasanchez Film Archive.

Lewis, headquartered closer to the center in working-class neighborhoods.[5] Despite verifiable evidence of order and progress at the macroeconomic level, Mexico City remained a study in contrasts. Fittingly, another new official party presidential administration assumed power just as the postwar era dawned.

## Miguel Alemán

In late 1946 Manuel Avila Camacho passed the presidential sash to former Veracruz governor Miguel Alemán Valdés. Alemán had been a strong supporter of the 1938 oil expropriation. During his 1936–1939 gubernatorial term he sought to neutralize long-running social conflict by establishing a new state-sponsored peasant league, revising housing legislation, reforming prisons, and reopening churches after the Cristero conflict had raged in portions of the state just years before.[6] He then served as Manuel Ávila Camacho's campaign manager before being appointed minister of the interior in late 1940. Six years later, the deaths of Ávila Camacho's brother Máximo and Veracruz politician Manlio Fabio Altamirano (1892–1936) cleared the way for an Alemán presidency.[7]

*Figure 6.2*  Avenida Juárez ca. 1960. Courtesy of Agrasanchez Film Archive.

The ensuing 1946 campaign revealed a different kind of national leadership on the rise. Once elected, Alemán's administration confirmed what many had thought for some time: the hard-fought revolutionary ideals of the previous generation had faded. In its place emerged an elite-led business model that unabashedly pursued industrialization and a full embrace of capitalist principles. The alleged payoff, Alemán once asserted, would be that "all Mexicans [will] have a Cadillac, a cigar, and a ticket to the bullfights."[8]

The *alemanista* years saw the rise of a new national directorate comprised of businessmen and bureaucrats, all largely well-connected individuals from the postrevolutionary generation. The president and his advisors imposed import substitution policies that increased domestic production. They encouraged new building in Mexico City, including the construction of an impressive University City in the south, among other projects. At the same time, Alemán channeled massive funds into new highways, airports, and the development of Acapulco as an international tourist destination.[9] Alemán lent critical support to the film industry and enjoyed socializing with members of Mexico's entertainment elite—including Agustín Lara on certain occasions.[10]

The bolero in Mexico at this time continued to be hugely popular, yet also began to take on a nostalgic aura as original artists and audiences matured. Lara's music still attracted significant attention during this time as a number of producers and directors used his songs as raw material for a new crop of cabaretera films that would quickly gain favor, although not necessarily critical acclaim. Further enthusiasm for his songs came thanks to a new cohort of musical artists, some of whom organized into harmonizing trios who played to guitar accompaniment. One of the most popular was a group that called itself Los Panchos.

## Era of the Trios

The postwar years saw the rise of literally hundreds of bolero singing trios in Mexico and throughout the Americas. Prolific in their performances, broadcasts, recording, and appearances on film, these harmonizing groups beautifully serenaded postwar Latin America with alluring songs of love. With antecedents going back to the Trío Garnica Ascencio and the Martínez Gil brothers (Pablo and Cavlos), the Trío Los Panchos (with original members Chucho Navarro, 1913–1993, Alfredo "El güero" Gil, 1915–1999, and Puerto Rican Hernando Avilés, 1914–1986) proved most popular.[11] They not only performed widely, but also appeared in several films.[12] Their postwar collaboration proved hugely successful as it gave rise to what, in retrospect, became known as the "era of the trios."

The three original members met in New York City and began performing together in May 1944. After a successful debut at the Teatro Hispano in the Bronx, they went on to play a number of venues in Spanish Harlem and eventually, Radio City Music Hall. In 1944 and 1945 they recorded for CODA, SEECO, and Philotone, among other labels. Alfredo and Chucho soon became US citizens. Alfredo then joined the army, while Chucho was classified as unfit for military duty because of a persistent hernia. Meantime, Hernando had fallen ill while visiting Puerto Rico. Hernando and Chucho eventually recovered and began singing and playing as a duet. When the war ended, Alfredo returned to New York and the trio resumed work together.[13]

With Hernando assuming lead, Chucho sang second voice while Alfredo took on what at the time was a new lighter harmony part that complemented the other two. All three members played what was often quite stunning guitar accompaniment. Trío Los Panchos did not necessarily invent their sound, but they worked hard to distinguish themselves from the many other three-person conjuntos active at the time.[14] Together, Hernando, Chucho, and Alfredo became one of the most popular Latin acts in New York. Soon contracted with CBS for a series of recordings, the trio could be heard on the affiliated Viva América radio program. In 1946 Los Panchos began touring internationally, attracting significant attention in Venezuela, Puerto Rico, Brazil, and Cuba.[15]

In 1948 the trio decided to return to Mexico. At first, they had some difficulty getting work in the capital because Chucho and Alfredo had earlier renounced their citizenship. Nevertheless, the group's popularity as recording artists created sufficient demand, and soon the trio began performing on a Nestlé-sponsored XEW broadcast. They also entertained audiences at high-profile clubs such as La Fuente, El Patio, and Tívoli.[16]

Los Panchos soon stood atop a field that included literally hundreds of trios not only in Mexico (Los 3 Diamantes, Los 3 Ases, Los 3 Caballeros, Los Delfines, etc.) but also in much of Latin America and the Caribbean. As Carlos Monsiváis writes, they engendered the spirit of the time:

> The great period of Latin American romantic song, forged by the lived correspondences between public, composers and singers, culminates with the trios, *filin*, the composers from both brothels and conservatories, and the singers from the poor districts. Everything coincides: the maturity of the composers, the personalities of the singers, the malice and credulity of the listeners, the balance between a histrionic passion and the cynicism of a weakening machismo, the definitive images of film, the quality of the orchestras, the heyday of the trios. And in Mexico, social and political stability imposes the enjoyment of everyday life. Since we can't do politics any more, let's listen to the radio, sing a cappella, go to variety shows, love each other until we can't do it any more.[17]

Monsiváis makes a number of keen observations here about the postwar age. Just as the era of the trios dawned, celebrity culture, the popularity of mass media, changing gender roles, and politics all combined to create a particular cultural moment in the history of Latin America. Nearly everything was in a state of transition. Love songs sung by the harmonizing groups resonated with— to borrow a phrase from the cultural critic Raymond Williams—the structure of feeling of the time.

The Golden Age of Latin American popular song reached its zenith just as Mexico's Children of the Revolution feasted on the fruits of postwar modernity. Audiences and musicians craved *filin* (or "feeling"), a relatively new style first developed in Cuba and subsequently employed by the trios. As it became popularized throughout the hemisphere, artists preferred a direct, emotional approach with lyrics that were in part spoken and not sung, so as to emphasize both their private nature and poetic value.

## Charges of Cursilería

Lara was not only an important musical influence for the postwar style. He also maintained a significant presence on the entertainment scene (Figure 6.3).[18] Yet by the end of the 1940s, some critics had issued charges that his work had become tiresome and derivative. A few believed that he wantonly plagiarized. Others simply thought that he rewrote the same songs over and over. Further, detractors accused Agustín of cursilería: being imitative, kitschy, or just downright lacking

*Figure 6.3  Jueves de Excélsior.* Courtesy of Agrasanchez Film Archive.

in taste.[19] Outwardly unshaken, Lara responded by defiantly stating that he had always intended to be cursi and "enjoyed being so."[20] This was not the first time the composer had been so charged.

Commenting in *El Ilustrado* magazine some years earlier, Oscar LeBlanc had published an article in the early 1930s titled "¿Agustín Lara es un cursi?" (Is Agustín Lara a Cheezeball?). To this, the writer reassured readers by stating positively that Lara stood as "the standard-bearer of our *criollo* cursilería."[21] Presumably this meant yes—Lara's music may have been a bit cheesy, but people nevertheless embraced it. They knew and loved his lyrics and catchy melodies. Years later, writer José Alvarado revisited the issue by asserting that Lara no doubt was cursi, but qualified his remarks by identifying the composer as a proponent of a middle-class brand of cursilería rooted in the urban experience.[22] Alvarado reasserted that Lara's music was uniquely modern and represented a clear break from the rural past:

> Lara liberated us from all that . . . and gave us the idyllic modern city; its aventureras, its alienation, sadness, its street lights and deserted boulevards. His was music for the new middle class with its own nostalgia, thirst for the sentimental and inexpressible desire for the obscure and precarious. [His was an] urban music, like the tango, but with a language born of the City of Mexico [and seasoned] with an added tropical accent incorporated through Lara's connection to the Veracruz coast.[23]

Postwar critics could and did accuse Lara of being cursi, but they could not take away from his importance as a cultural pioneer. As Alvarado points out, Lara's by then well-established association with Veracruz had proven an effective way to position his art within the larger framework of revolutionary nationalism.

In the next few years, however, not everyone would take such a positive a view of Lara. For years he had been accused of being cursi, but now the allegations had begun to stick. Why? No doubt the composer's optimal time as a vanguard artist had passed, as Mexico entered a new era. No longer so taken with the novelty of Lara's bolero style, the new generation sought an artistic identity to match the changing times. Still, Agustín moved ahead. In the next few years, one of the projects he dedicated himself to was to secure the full-time backing of a full-fledged orchestra (Figure 6.4).

In 1946 Carlos Águila had convinced Agustín to expand his group. This proved a relatively easy task given that Lara had long dreamed of leading an orchestra and had on certain occasions recorded with a larger complement of contracted musicians. Listening one night to a big band led by clarinetist Everett Hoagland, Carlos and Agustín imagined that with several soloists making a larger

*Figure 6.4* Orquesta de soloists de Agustín Lara. Courtesy of Archivo General de la Nación, Fondo Hermanos Mayo.

ensemble, Lara could achieve the sound of a full-fledged orchestra. As it turned out, the two had also been influenced by bandleader Roy Carter, who, like Hoagland, played some of the top nightclubs in Mexico City with his own "orchestra of soloists."

Águila envisioned rearranging the Lara songbook so that the tunes could easily be danced to and eagerly went about selecting musicians for the group.[24] He soon added four violinists (Rafael Díaz, Manuel Medina V., Manuel Ramírez V., and Leopoldo "Polo" Dueñas). Later, xylophone, trumpet, trombone, and saxophone accompaniment would round out the mix. They called themselves the "Orquesta de Soloistas de Agustín Lara." As Carlos later explained, the new format gave Lara's music the "dignified treatment" it deserved.[25]

One of the group's first extended bookings took place at the luxurious Teocalli nightclub at the corner of Insurgentes Avenue and Nuevo León Street. The El Rosiñal proved another favorite spot where Lara and his men often broadcast the hugely popular "La hora íntima" show for XEW radio. The orchestra also performed regularly at the Teatro Lírico with Pedro Vargas and Toña la Negra as the featured singers.[26] One of the earliest recordings of the expanded line-up was the 1947 composition "Pecadora" for RCA Victor.[27]

Meanwhile, Agustín faced a series of new challenges, as he became embroiled in a conflict with the recently organized composer's union (*Sociedad de Autores, Compositores y Editores de Música* or SMACEM, Union of Authors, Composers and Editors of Music).[28] As featured on the October 23, 1948 cover of *Cinema Reporter* with the caption "I was not born to lead," details of a labor dispute within the association soon became public. The story inside, as related in an interview with Miguel Ángel Mendoza, revealed that Lara was upset with the union (which for a time he claimed to have served as Secretary General) for money supposedly owed him. Distancing himself from the group, Lara professed his undying loyalty to Emilio Azcárraga who, Agustín declared, "had put food on my table for the last eighteen years." In contrast, SMACEM leader Juan B. Leonardo accused Lara and Azcárraga of forming a publicity-hungry, monopolistic partnership that worked to the disadvantage of other composers. "Lara is trying to sell us out," Leonardo charged, "but it isn't going to happen." Bitter about disparaging remarks that Lara made criticizing Leonardo and his colleague Pablo Martínez Gil, the SMACEM leader further attacked Agustín by asserting that Chamaco Sandoval was the unrecognized and highly underpaid author of many of the musician-poet's songs. To this controversial allegation, Leonardo added, "while he [Lara] may claim to be a major creative force operating today, his work represents only a minor percentage of the total number of Mexican composers whose work is currently being performed."[29] Charging that Lara had violated the association's statutes and represented a threat to its very being, SMACEM members decided simply to kick him out. To this, Agustín seems to have paid little mind. Instead, he busied himself with a string of new film collaborations.

## B-Movie Bachelor

The late 1940s saw the apogee of the cabaretera genre. In 1948, Emilio Fernández released *Salón México*. The following year, director Albert Gout (1913–1966) premiered *Aventurera*. Taken together, the two works represent the best of postwar Mexican dance hall film both in terms of content and technical achievement. In *Salón México*, the main character, Mercedes (Marga López, 1924–2005), works as a cabaretera who turns tricks in order to support her younger sister. In contrast, *Aventurera's* main protagonist Elena (Ninón Sevilla) is deceived into becoming a nightclub dancer by a shady cast of characters in Ciudad Juárez.[30]

In each of these dramas, the leading female character struggles to survive as she navigates the depths of a dangerous, corrupt society where violence, greed, and evil men rule. Both works vividly portray women adrift in a male-dominated society as they are forced to deal in a compromised underworld despite their better intentions. Regardless of extenuating circumstances, these women are engaged in a battle of good against evil in a world gone bad.

For his part, Lara got in on the last years of the cabaretera craze by performing in a series of film projects undertaken under the direction of Alberto Gout between 1947 and 1950. Agustín's music often served as the inspiration and, on occasion, even the title song for some, as was the case with the 1948 film *Cortesana*. Previously, Lara had collaborated with director Gout by performing a handful of songs in the 1946 film *Humo en los ojos* (Smoke in The Eyes). Both

*Humo* and *Cortesana* drew inspiration from Lara's songs of the same name and featured the young actress Meche Barba (1922–2000).[31]

Continuing in this mode, the director cast Lara to play the part of a musician in a 1948 film titled after one of Agustín's recent compositions: *Revancha* (Figure 6.5). The 1947 song "En revancha" (or "Revancha," Revenge) is set in a testimonial mode where Lara recites the first section and then sings the second part twice:

Figure 6.5   *Revancha* promotion. Courtesy of the Agrasanchez Film Archive.

*Yo conocí el amor, es muy hermoso*
*Pero en mí fue fugaz y traicionero*
*Volvió canalla lo que fue glorioso,*
*Pero fue un gran amor y fue el primero*

I know love, it is beautiful
But in me it was fleeting and untrustworthy
What was glorious turned out cheap,
But it was a great love and my first


*Amor por ti bebí mi propio llanto*
*Amor fuiste mi cruz mi religión*
*Es justa la revancha y entre tanto*
*Sigamos engañando al corazón.*
*Sigamos engañando al corazón.*

My love, for you I drank my own tears
Love, you were my cross and my religion
Revenge is fair and given everything
Let's continue to be deceived in love
Let's continue to be deceived in love.[32]


"Revancha" is a bolero in the style of other Lara tunes. The 1953 RCA version features Agustín accompanied by violin and percussion (bongo), mixing Lara's melodramatic piano and vocal with a lilting string sound and light, Cuban-inspired rhythm. Midway through there is a violin and piano solo that expounds ever so slightly on the melody before returning for a final verse and ending.[33]

Featuring Lara in what would be his first major cinematic production, Gout helped the musician realize a longtime dream. Having just performed the role of blind musician Hipólito for Mexico City audiences across from talented actress Andrea Palma, Lara now had a chance to summon whatever talent he had for the silver screen.[34]

As ads appeared in various entertainment magazines beginning in July of 1948, *Revancha* received billing as "the story of Agustín Lara and some of his most famous songs."[35] The production also featured Ninón Sevilla, David Silva, Toña la Negra, and Pedro Vargas. In addition to the title track, the film featured "Oración caribe," "Rosa," "Rival," "Imposible," the 1935 song "Piensa en mi" (Think of Me), "Mia nomás" (Mine No More) from 1936, and the enchanting 1935 waltz "Farolito":

*Farolito que alumbras apenas*
*mi calle desierta,*
*cuántas noches me has visto llorando*
*llamar a su puerta.*

Streetlight that scarcely illuminates
My deserted street,
How many nights have you seen me crying
Knocking at your door.[36]

"Farolito" invoked the troubadour tradition with its chivalric lyrics and plea for love. It is perhaps one of Lara's most captivating melodies.[37] In the 1953 RCA Victor version, Agustín whistles the second verse, almost as if in the middle of an evening stroll, before guitar restates the melody and violin plays counterpoint.[38] Given the charm of "Farolito" and the quality of the other songs, it is unfortunate that their adaptation for Gout's film resulted in their largely serving as backdrop for an otherwise cheaply conceived crime caper.[39]

*Revancha* opens with a focus on Rafael (David Silva), whose mother has just died. He is sent to Veracruz by Alejandro (Lalo Malcolm), who has, unknown to Rafael, hidden contraband in his suitcase. Next, Rafael is seen in a local cabaret, where he plays one-armed bandits to pass the time before running into a dancer named Rosa, played by Ninón Sevilla. They soon develop an affection while various intrigues take shape involving drug dealers, police, and the "Veracruz musician" (Agustín Lara) himself.

We occasionally see Lara composing at the piano. In one scene, Agustín tells Rosa that she is the inspiration for a new song. Their brief, unremarkable dialogue is characteristic of late 1940s cabaretera film:

ROSA: Are you writing a song about a woman?
LARA: Yes.
ROSA: And her name?
LARA: Rosa.
ROSA: Like me?
LARA: Yes.

On cue, Rosa gives Lara a kiss and then stands back to admire him from a distance. As with the blind piano-playing Hipólito of *Santa* fame, Agustín plays the role of an older, sensitive man who cares deeply for his female friend. He often urges Rosa to be careful and to wait for him to accompany her. On more than one occasion, Agustín's last-minute intervention causes menacing Veracruz thugs to leave Rosa alone.

Various nightclub performances reflect upon the pianist's love for young Rosa. Yet while Agustín's affection is appreciated, it cannot compete with that of the male protagonist Rafael. At one point, Lara is pictured alone playing "Imposible" in a nightclub with his trademark cigarette and glass of cognac. As the song suggests, his love, however profound, will nevertheless remain unrequited.

Still, Agustín continues to care for Rosa. Somewhat hesitatingly, he confers with Rafael:

AGUSTÍN: Can you make Rosa happy?

RAFAEL: Yes, I love her, I love her completely.

AGUSTÍN: You haven't known her for very long.

RAFAEL: Why do you ask—do you love her too?

AGUSTÍN: Yes, I love her more than my own life.

Deferring to her suitor, the musician offers Rafael and Rosa the use of a small house in Mexico City. Confrontation ensues as Rafael and Alejandro fight over Rosa. Guns are drawn. Alejandro shoots at Rafael and misses. Other shots are fired before Rosa and Rafael escape to begin a new life together. The police take Alejandro away. Now seen alone back in the club, Agustín feels in his coat and finds blood. He stumbles to the piano, the lights go out, and he dramatically plays one last song before falling dead. In the end, the piano player's sacrifice enables Rosa and Rafael to leave the Veracruz underworld behind and embark upon a new life as a "legitimate" couple.[40]

In addition to work on *Revancha*, Lara soon contributed several songs for Fernando A. Rivero's 1949 film *Coqueta* (Flirt), including "Noche criolla" (Creole Night) "Siempre te vas" (You Always Go), "La marimba," the two-steps "Madrid" and "Escarcha" (Frost), as well as "Noche de ronda" and "Amor de mis amores." For the production Agustín again drew upon the Hipólito archetype—this time literally assuming the role of a blind musician, Rubén (Figures 6.6 and 6.7).[41]

With Ninón Sevilla and Victor Junco (1917–1988) starring, the narrative centers on an innocent young girl named Marta (Sevilla) who, after being separated from her brother Mario, finds herself embroiled in a number of conflicts. As was the case with *Revancha*, the Port of Veracruz is the site where the action takes place.

Meeting a character named Luciano, Marta is taken to a cabaret, where she gets drunk. She is next on stage filling in for one of the club dancers, surprisingly with great success. Subsequently envious of Marta, the two women fight. Catching wind of this, Rubén comes to Marta's rescue and welcomes her into his home. After she has had a chance to heal her wounds, she takes a job as a dancer and moves in with a man named Rivera, who is the owner of the club. Marta and Rivera eventually disagree and she becomes very sick after he attempts to poison her. With this, Marta again relies on the charity of the blind man who idolizes her (Figure 6.8).

*Figure 6.6 Coqueta* publicity poster. Courtesy of the Agrasanchez Film Archive.

Once recovered, Marta then meets an attractive young man named Rodolfo. They fall in love. We soon learn, however, that Rodolfo is the son of Rubén, and so it becomes clear that Marta's love for the young man will most likely lead to the undoing of his father. And so it goes: as Marta and Rodolfo get ready to leave Veracruz we see Rubén appear. He approaches the couple and shoots Marta in a jealous rage before collapsing in the street. Tragically, she dies in the arms of Rodolfo and the film ends.

Like the archetypical *Santa, Coqueta* offers up a sympathetic relationship between the characters of the blind musician and the fallen woman.[42] They seek

*Figure 6.7* Lara as blind musician Rubén. Courtesy of Agrasanchez Film Archive.

*Figure 6.8* Rubén and Marta. Courtesy of the Agrasanchez Film Archive.

each other in a familiar way—their intimacy providing a shelter from the threat-ening social circumstances they face. In a classic film noir turn of events, Marta's fall and subsequent plight is a dramatic (however exaggerated) device conceived to draw in the viewers, who then empathize with the "good" characters as they negotiate confusion, deception, and moral conundrum.

Yet as the narrative progresses and Marta is rescued and somewhat restored, complications ensue. Just as she is set to embark on what appears to be a happily ever-after scenario with the innocent and admiring Rodolfo, an incestuous plot twist which pits the blind man against his former charge robs the young couple of their much anticipated future. In contrast with *Revancha*, *Coqueta* produces a tragic confrontation between father and son that dooms the young couple. Such was often the dramatic formula for these films as they advanced narrative ele-ments crossing family values with the tantalizing yet corrupt influence of the urban underworld. However poignant the best of the genre might have been, by the end of the decade interest in the cabaretera had diminished. Further, Mexi-can cinema had slipped into a period of crisis from which it would not emerge until the early 1960s.[43]

## Biopics

Despite a general decline in the industry, Agustín's work in film continued as producers and directors persevered in exploiting the composer's music and life story. Following *Coqueta*, Lara's next cinematic endeavor came when Fernando A. Rivero directed a picture titled *Mujeres en mi vida* (Women in My Life). Pro-duced in mid-August 1949 at the Churubusco Studios and released the fol-lowing year, the movie starred Agustín as Armando, Emilia Guiú as Magdelena (a rendering of Chata Zozaya), and Chilean actress Hilda Sour as María (similarly, María Félix). Trío Los Panchos, Toña la Negra, and Pedro Vargas performed various musical numbers including "Mujer," "Noche tropical," and "María bonita" (Figures 6.9 and 6.10).[44]

Advance promotion for the film advertised it as ostensibly a biography of Lara in which the composer played a gallant, mustachioed, and pure-hearted version of himself. Once it premiered, the production's obvious glorification of Agustín irritated many, including a critic for the magazine *El Duende Filmo* who commented harshly on the production, saying that "Lara has unleashed all his resentment for María Félix in this movie." Indeed, Hilda Sour's portrayal of the character "María" made her appear very much like La doña with a strikingly similar on-screen voice and costuming. Despite early criticism, ads in several Mexico City newspapers spoke highly of the new production. One such promo-tion tempted potential viewers with the promise that the film offered a look back

*Figure 6.9* Lara in *Mujeres en mi vida*. Courtesy of Agrasanchez Film Archive.

*Figure 6.10* Lara in *Mujeres en mi vida*. Courtesy of Agrasanchez Film Archive.

at "the sentimental love life of the most brilliant lyrical genius in the last twenty years."[45] Some made fun of this claim, including one cartoonist who offered a caricature of Lara asking his mirror, "Who is the most dashing and handsome?" In the background an image of María Félix replied, "You, Agustín, at least according to the crazy (*chiflado*) who wrote the screenplay for *Mujeres en mi vida*."[46] Later, film historian Emilio García Riera commented that the production generally portrayed "Lara's women" as "idiots possessed with a near-suicidal passion for a man who looked like he had just crawled out of an Egyptian tomb looking like a cross between a mummy and Frankenstein."[47] Clearly for most, *Mujeres en mi vida* had failed to render an attractive portrait of the musician-poet.

Yet the biographic movie mill kept rolling. In Lara's next project Agustín played himself, sharing the bill with Elsa Aguirre (1930–) who played Rosita, an unlucky, handicapped daughter of a bordello madame. The collaboration Saw Chilean Tito Davidson (1912–1985) directing the 1950 release titled *La mujer que yo amé* (*The Woman I Loved*). This production included a number of Lara tunes including "Oración caribe," "Por qué negarlo" (Why Deny It?), "Te vendes" (You Sell?), "A solas tú y yo" (You and I alone), "Si fueras una cualquiera" (You Used to Go With Anyone), "Mujer," and "El cielo, el mar y tú" (The Sky, The Ocean, and You). Drawn somewhat from the composer's own life events, the film presented a bordello scene dramatization of Lara being attacked and stabbed in the face.[48]

Fernando A. Rivero next cast Agustín as a neurotic musician in *Perdida*.[49] The director paired the soon-to-be fifty-three-year-old Lara with Ninón Sevilla in the hope that she could carry the picture.[50] Trío Los Panchos performed Lara's song "Perdida." A host of other musicians made cameo appearances including Amalia Cristerna, Linda Rey, Pedro Vargas, Matilde Sánchez, the group Los Ángeles del Infierno, and Mariachi Vargas de Tecalitlán, as well as the up-and-coming Cuban mambo sensation Dámaso Pérez Prado (1916–1989).[51]

The film is a cross between cabaretera and Pygmalion drama.[52] It opens as Sevilla's young dancer character Rosario recounts to a matador friend Antonio Velázquez that she had been violated by her stepfather and then fled to Mexico City. In a series of flashbacks we see how she is picked up along the road and taken to a bordello in the capital. From there a wealthy man named don Pasquel buys her and takes her home. As she becomes fed up with his drunken abuses, Rosario abandons Pasquel and takes to the streets. Desperate, she steals some bread and is arrested.

In the women's jail a famous composer, Agustín (again playing himself) discovers Rosario and pays for her release. He takes her to his luxurious home and begins to care for her. Relaxing before bed one night, she tries on some women's clothing and jewelry found in a closet in the room where she is staying. Before long, the two visit a nightclub where Pedro Vargas sings "Miseria" by Miguel Ángel Valladares (1919–1969). Agustín compliments Rosario on her extraordinary transformation.

After hearing the older composer mysteriously talking one night, Rosario asks her host to level with her. He takes her to a room upstairs and shows her a painting of a woman who turns out to be his dead wife. Agustín tells Rosario that she reminds him of her. "When I am with you it is like I am with her again," he says. He confesses that his wife had been his inspiration and that he has kept all her things. Since her passing his heart has been so broken that he has had no further desire to compose music. He is a lost soul, strangely talking to her portrait every night. Standing by a piano that has not been touched in years, Agustín gives Rosario a key that he says "can open his heart." Moved, Rosario calls him "uncle" after he plays her a beautiful melody.

Rosario meets a young man named Armando, and the two soon plan to marry despite the strong misgivings of Agustín. Armando takes Rosario to meet his father who—to her absolute horror—turns out to be don Pasquel. She breaks with Armando and takes up work as a cabaret dancer. One night Agustín shows up. He cries and tells her how lonely he is. Rosario tells him she is going to see Antonio the bullfighter the next day. "If that is what you wish," Agustín says, "then go ahead—even as you turn my happiness to sadness."

We then see Rosario in a house with Antonio. She worries about him and prays to the Virgin for protection. Rosario listens to his next bullfight on the radio and then goes to meet him afterward. She finds out that she has been deceived, for as it turns out Antonio is married with a small boy. Dejected, Rosario is back on the street again. She sits in a cantina and drinks while the song "Miseria" plays. Rosario goes to another bar and by now is quite intoxicated. As another song plays, lamenting the life of a spurned lover, Agustín enters and finds Rosario in a stupor. Having had some kind of poison put in her drink, she falls over. Agustín picks her up and sadly says, "She is my wife . . . and as she dies I, too, die again." With this, the musician's attempt to use Rosario to fill the void left by his dead wife is foiled and the film ends.[53]

By this time, Lara's participation in various film projects on top of his regular schedule of personal appearances had exhausted him. In November 1949 he checked into the Hospital Francés in Mexico City. Plagued for years by what he described as a dull yet constant pain in his groin (he had been diagnosed with a hernia years earlier while in Cuba during the summer of 1932), on November 14 Agustín underwent a two-and-a-half hour operation to have a testicle removed.[54]

After his release a few days later, doctors performed a follow-up operation, this time at his home on December 7. Medical attention left the composer in a particularly nervous and fearful state, as his agenda from late 1949 attests. Brief entries for the above-mentioned dates express trepidation ("*Qué horror, qué fea es la Eternidad*"; "What a horror, how ugly is Eternity") and finally, relief ("*Qué bueno que se acabó este pinche año*," "Thank goodness that this damn year is over") as he made his way to Veracruz and back at the end of 1949.[55] Incurring surgery on his manhood temporarily challenged yet nevertheless did not seem to negatively impact his musical career. As he recovered, the composer enjoyed a newfound popularity in the music world as he returned to performing with his Soloists.

The temporary trauma did not seem to slow his seemingly never-ending search for young women, either. Agustín had now begun appearing at some of the finest restaurants and nightclubs in Mexico City with Clara Martínez. As it turns out, the composer had for some time been acquainted with Martínez before he ended his relationship with María Félix. Once Félix and Lara split, Agustín, as was his custom, showered the young woman with flowers, perfume, and jewelry.

Before long, they began appearing on Sunday afternoons at the bullfights. Agustín and Clara then moved in together. First, they took up residence in Coyoacán in the same small house where Lara had kept Raquel Díaz de León some years back. They next moved to #119 Avenida del Castillo in the northern Tlalnepantla district. It is said that one day María Félix, having returned from her film work in Spain, made a visit to this address and angrily fired several shots into the house. If the rumors had any truth to them, fortunately, no one was hurt.[56]

By the end of 1948, Lara and Martínez had relocated again to a residence located on Pirineos Avenue in the Las Lomas neighborhood on the city's west side. There they would spend the next four years together. Attended to by a live-in cook and personal assistant named David "Verduguillo" Rodríguez, whom Lara had essentially rescued from the Mexico City streets, the two lived comfortably.[57]

Over the past two years, Lara had composed a few new songs. In 1948, his new work included "Anoche" (Last Night) (also known as "Anoche te sentí"), "Caña brava" (Strong Cane), "Mensaje" (Message), "Tirana" (Tyranny), "Tu retrato" (Your Portrait), and the eponymous "Corrido de Agustín Lara." This ballad opens with the lines "I give songs to the people because I always carry the thought of them in my soul . . . I know that I am very ugly."[58]

Lara had also teamed up with Chamaco Sandoval to write a *chotís* called "Madrid" that same year. Different than his existing two-step "Madrid," this new song drew upon the nineteenth-century Spanish country dance (somewhat of a slow polka) associated with the zarzuela theater and long performed at traditional festivals.[59] "Madrid" soon would become immensely popular once singers Esmerelda and Ana María González, among others, recorded it.

With "Madrid," Lara again hoped to travel to Spain. Soon, however, Francisco Franco disappointed the Mexican composer by turning down his request for a visa. Franco justified the decision by claiming that Lara had made certain antiregime comments. In response, Agustín is said to have penned a song titled

"Mexicano" that Spanish born Sara Montiel (1928–) would record. The lyrics to "Mexicano" offered an imagined word of thanks for "Madrid," despite the fact that Lara's desire to visit his beloved motherland would have to wait.[60]

The musician-poet again soon settled in for a series of dates in his hometown. Lara played a number of Mexico City venues, including a stint at the Teatro Lírico in April 1950 with his Soloists and singers Pedro Vargas, Chabela Durán, actor Fernando Soto "Mantequilla" (1911–1980), and the comedian Adalberto Martínez Chávez "Resortes" (1916–2003). For her part, Durán had achieved success with Agustín's 1949 songs "Un beso a solas" and "El mar, el cielo y tú."[61] Lara subsequently performed a demanding eighteen months of daily shows at the Follies Bergère. Following this, he returned the Lírico accompanied by singer Juan Arvizu and later by singer Ramón Armengod.[62]

Lara and his orchestra then traveled to Cuba for a two-week stint in July 1950 with young singer Jorge Fernández and another talented vocalist named Consuelo "Chelo" Vidal.[63] Once installed on the island, Lara and his group successfully played a number of dates at Havana's Montmartre nightclub.[64] One young woman who had begged her father to take her to see the elegant el flaco later testified that Lara's presence thrilled her immensely. When he sang his erotic lyrics "tu párvula boca que siendo tan niña me enseñó a pecar" (your mouth is that of a girl but it taught me to sin), she admitted to feeling an unforgettable rush of excitement. As the story goes, later that same night her boyfriend wooed her with a bolero of his own and the two were subsequently married.[65]

Inspired by his Cuban visit, Lara would later compose a song in 1964 titled "Havana" that Jorge Fernández debuted:

*Princesa del caribe*
*yo te ofrezco mi cantar*
*Habana, cuando mi mano escribe,*
*quieren mis ojos llorar.*

Caribbean princess
I sing for you
Havana, when my hand writes,
My eyes want to weep.

*Déjame que ponga en tu regazo*
*mi ferviente gratitud*
*Habana, Veracruz es La Habana*
*cielo y mar la misma vibración*
*tu estrellita solitaria la llevo en mi*

Let me express my fervent gratitude
Havana, Veracruz is like Havana
Sky and sea vibrating together
I carry your solitary star in me.[66]

Altogether, the ensemble's stay in Cuba proved a memorable one.[67] Travel in 1951 included performances in Central and South America, including several spots in Brazil (Rio de Janeiro, São Paulo, Santos, Belo Horizonte, Natal, Campinha Grande, Bahia, and Minas Gerais), where audiences warmly received the Mexican musicians.

Lara's interpreters for this visit again included Jorge Fernández and Chelo Vidal. On one occasion, Pedro Vargas arranged for Lara and Carlos Águila to dine with Brazilian President Getúlio Vargas (1882–1954). Following the dinner, the two serenaded Vargas and his wife along with a small number of other guests.[68] True to form, Lara dashed off a few new compositions while on tour. One piece called "Brasil" pays tribute to the country and—not surprisingly—the beautiful women who live there.[69]

Brasil, donde el Río Amazonas,
Templo de sirenas,
Es llanto del mar.
Brasil, como tu grandeza,
En el mundo no hay.

Brazil, where the Amazon River,
Temple of sirens,
Overflows from the sea.
Brazil, you have a greatness
Which is unmatched anywhere else in the world.[70]

Clearly impressed by what they saw of Brazil, Lara and his ensemble then played a handful of dates in Colombia on their return home. After taking a bit of time off, Lara and his group of soloists then traveled again to Cuba in June 1951. Arriving at the Havana airport, a number of fans, along with a welcoming delegation sent by President Carlos Prio Socarrás (1903–1977), enthusiastically received the ensemble. On this trip Clara Martínez accompanied Lara. After extending their stay in Havana, Lara and his ensemble eventually made it home just two days in advance of a new tour to Central America. There they appeared in several cities including Managua and Guatemala City.[71]

Exhausted, Lara returned to the Mexican capital just as the *sexenio* of President Alemán was coming to an end. When news arrived in January 1953 that

Clara's mother had died, Agustín apparently showed little sympathy. After seven years together he had grown weary of his female companion and did little to hide his apathy. A short while later, Martínez moved out of the house on Pirineos Avenue.[72]

The postwar years had witnessed the continued popularity of Agustín Lara as a composer and performing musician. Sustained interest came in part thanks to the efforts of talented young artists who interpreted his compositions as well as an assortment of film directors who made creative use of his songs and life story. Now in his fifties, Lara showed little sign of slowing down as he maintained his a busy work schedule both at home and abroad.

# 7

# To Spain and Veracruz: 1954–1970

*To live with Agustín was like a fairytale.*

—*Yolanda Santacruz Gasca*[1]

*How beautiful is my Veracruz?*[2]
—Lara at a civic gathering on his seventy-first birthday in Tlacotalpan,
Veracruz, 1967

In December 1952, Miguel Alemán Valdés ceded the presidential sash to his Institutional Party successor Adolfo Ruiz Cortines (1890–1973), who charted a more conservative path for the nation over the next six years. Early in his administration the dance hall film began to be interpreted not so much as tantalizing entertainment for men provided by often scantily clad rumberas, but as a sign of a larger social and moral crisis affecting the nation.[3] A host of editorial writers weighed in by denouncing cabareteras. Ensuing government oversight would significantly impact Mexican media and the entertainment industry at large.[4]

For their part, Mexico City mayor Ernesto P. Uruchurtu (1906–1997) and Oficina de Espectáculos (Major Events Office) head Adolfo Fernández Bustamante (1898–1957) began an antivice campaign that targeted unhygienic conditions and the spread of what they viewed as immoral material in the capital's entertainment centers. A host of reform groups allied under various "committees for moral, civic and material improvement" supported the offensive.[5] In mid-February 1953, high-ranking Catholic leaders strategized in Guadalajara.[6] The Association of Radio Broadcasters then joined the campaign by imposing stricter controls over media content. The process left some cabarets, theaters, and nightclubs, as well as several movie houses, either temporarily or permanently closed.[7] In the meantime, incipient television programming sought to bridge the entertainment gap, first under the Azcárraga family-owned Grupo Televisa (initially termed Telesistema Mexicano).[8]

# Yiyi

As a new conservative era took shape, Agustín Lara continued to receive accolades from adoring fans. The composer also remained productive, penning "De riguroso chotis" (A Strong Schottische) and "Por qué ya no me quieres" (Why Don't You Want Me?), both in 1951, and "Sultana" the following year. In 1952 the International Olympic Committee asked him if he would be willing to write a song for the upcoming Helsinki games. Honored, Agustín agreed and recorded "Himno al deporte" (Hymn to Sport) in Los Angeles that year.[9] Then, in 1953, Agustín spotted a woman he quickly took an interest in while working with the Chelo la Rue group at the Teatro Lírico. Her name was Yolanda Santacruz Gasca.

Lara courting Yolanda by sending a red rose each day with a card that simply had the letter "L" written on it. When she quit Chelo La Rue and joined another dance group called the Continental, Gasca soon found herself performing along with Lara at the Teatro Margo.[10] One night, Yolanda and a friend visited the Capri nightclub inside the luxurious Hotel Regis where Lara was performing.[11] Following him after his performance, the two young women tried to get the composer's attention before he boarded a taxi. Apparently he saw them, but only as the vehicle sped away. The next night at the Lírico, Yolanda approached Agustín directly, making up a story suggesting that the reason she and her friend had followed him the previous evening was because she did not have a car. Hearing this, Lara saw his chance and quickly made arrangements to have a brand new Cadillac delivered to Yolanda the following day. From this point Agustín seriously set his chivalric sights on her, continually regaling her with roses and expensive gifts.[12]

As the two began to be seen around town, many again wondered how a man so unattractive (not to mention being forty years her senior) could win over a beautiful eighteen-year-old. By this time, the composer's courtship ritual revealed a well-crafted romantic discourse: one that progressed—as French scholar Roland Barthes has noted—from archetypal station to station. Here, key aspects of this contemplative practice include reflections on "the meeting," "declaration," leading to "coupling," "commitment," "marriage," and so on.[13] Interestingly, one finds evidence of this "lover's discourse" reflected in both Yolanda and Agustín's letters and mementos from the time (Figure 7.1).[14]

Lara began calling Yolanda by a number of endearing nicknames, the most regular of these being "Yiyi." Numerous messages from Lara spoke of the two embarking on a romantic journey together. Further, Agustín's correspondence recorded his close attention to Yolanda's emotional state. Letters would often begin with "when you laugh" (*cuando ries*), "when you pray" (*cuando rezas*), or "when you cry" (*cuando lloras*). Still others commented on her various activities: "when you sleep" (*cuando duermes*), "when you gaze" (*cuando miras*), "when you kiss" (*cuando besas*), "when you are far away" (*cuando estás lejos*), or "when you

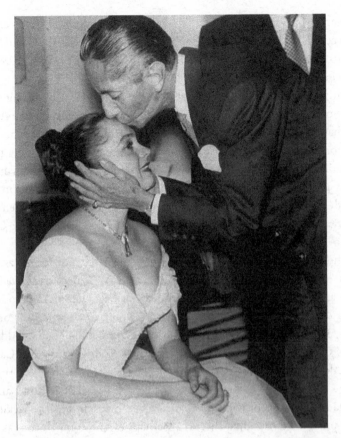

*Figure 7.1* Agustín and Yolanda. Courtesy of Agrasanchez Film Archive.

dance" (*cuando bailas*). Some referred specifically to parts of her body: "your hands," "your eyes," "your mouth," and so on. Lara's love letters were usually set in a dramatic context with imagery such as "the sky", "the sea", "the moon", "flashing of lights," and "veils of mist." Obviously, Lara's romantic confessions (what he termed his "divine madness of love") to his sweetheart drew heavily upon his long experience as a bolero songsmith.

As with his previous lovers, el maestro Lara trained Yolanda in the art of fine living. He encouraged her social development and stressed the importance of female beauty. For her part, Yolanda appears to have cooperated willingly in this effort. As she once testified, "He taught me how to act and feel like a real woman and being at his side proved satisfying and tranquil because I admired and loved him."[15] Yolanda later testified that "being with Agustín was like a dream."[16]

Writing songs for his new love, Agustín produced "Aquel amor" in 1953 and an instrumental titled "Yiyi" around the same time. Before long, the two went looking for a house together and eventually found a beautiful home at 308 Homero in the Polanco district of Mexico City, where they lived along with a pair of fancy automobiles, a chauffeur, two house servants (Marcos and Germán), a cook (Huang Hai Chung), and Lara's steadfast assistant David "Verduguillo" Rodríguez.[17] The couple would wed in a civil ceremony in 1953 at the Xala hacienda in the State of Mexico.[18]

Following the postwedding afterglow, Lara fell ill one day during the late summer of 1953 with another severe pain in his side. Medical tests revealed a tumor that needed to be removed immediately.[19] Following a successful surgery by Doctor Gabriel Malda, Agustín remained in the hospital. Wanting to show appreciation for the ailing musician, *Excélsior* journalist Félix Anguiano organized a tribute to Lara in the Palace of Fine Arts on the eve of the composer's fifty-sixth birthday. With a wide array of government officials and members of the Mexican entertainment elite, more than 250 stations broadcast the October 12 event.

For the occasion, invitations had gone out to many of Lara's former associates and past interpreters including Raulito, Alfonso Ortiz Tirado, Ana María Fernández, Paz and Esperanza Águila, Sofía Álvarez, Chabela Durán, Amparo Montes, Amanda del Llano, María Conesa, Mario "Cantinflas" Moreno, Néstor Mesta Chayres, Libertad Lamarque, Elvira Ríos, Avenda Landín, Lupita Alday, and Las Tres Conchitas. Former presidents Abelardo Rodríguez, Lázaro Cárdenas, Miguel Alemán, and Emilio Portes Gil sent congratulatory notes honoring Lara, while the orchestras of Daniel Pérez Casteñeda, Rafael de Paz, and Lara's own Orquesta de Soloistas provided the vocalists with a rich musical backing. The evening proved a resounding success—perhaps even too much so—as a huge crowd gathered outside the Palacio unable to enter because the event had sold out. There appeared so many people that the Águila Sisters were unable to gain entrance.[20]

Yet while the nation's aging entertainment stars performed in the Fine Arts Palace, Mexican youth were discovering something new. From Cuba came exciting new groups performing mambo, such as the one fronted by Damaso Pérez Prado (1916-1989) and singer Beny Moré (1919–1963), who were playing to packed houses and recording for RCA Victor.[21] At the same time musicians in the United States had begun to fashion an up-tempo blend of rhythm and blues that would soon be dubbed rock and roll. Artists such as Jackie Wilson (1934–1984), Elvis Presley (1935–1977), The Platters, James Brown (1933–2006), and The Four Tops all began their careers in the mid-1950s and would help change the sound of popular music forever.

Lara acknowledged these changes by settling into semiretirement in his adopted homeland of Veracruz in December 1953 (Figure 7.2). There, he received a hero's welcome from a cheering crowd and the keys to the city from municipal officials in the Plaza de Armas.[22] Soon after his arrival, the fashionable oceanfront Hotel Mocambo hosted a party in the composer's name. Master of

*Figure 7.2* Lara reviewing press coverage. Courtesy of Archivo General de la Nación, Fondo Hermanos Mayo.

ceremonies Francisco Rivera honored his friend with a *salutación* in verse that began with an invitation for Lara to return to his beloved *patria chica*: "Agustín: please accept this tribute from here—the heart of your stomping grounds."[23]

In the meantime, Veracruz governor Marco Antonio Muñoz Trumbull (1914–2001) paid his own tribute to Lara by having a house built for him at 8 Calzada Costa Verde, just south of the historic port. With a direct view of the beach and the Isla de Sacrificios at a distance, the composer's Veracruz residence featured a terrace on the second level and a garden in back. From his oceanfront "little white house" (*La casita blanca*), as it would soon become known, Lara could relax. Excited, he would later compose a short song in 1963 about the waterfront site—one to which he not so surprisingly added his own mythic touch:

> *En la playa solitaria*
> *en la costa en que nací*
> *hay una casita blanca*
> *que parece de marfil.*
>
> *Casita blanca de mi niñez,*
> *donde las horas,*
> *donde las noches feliz pasé.*

*Tiesto fragrante lleno de luz,*
*cómo me acuerdo*
*de aquellas noches de Veracruz.*

On the solitary beach
Along the coast where I was born
There is a little white house
That looks like it is made of ivory.

Little white house of my childhood,
Where the hours,
Where the happy nights pass.

Fragrant flowerpot filled with light,
That is how I remember
Those Veracruz nights.[24]

Clearly Lara felt a great deal of affection for his seaside residence, and whenever he spent time in his Veracruz home he often enjoyed the company of a wide array of friends and admirers.[25] The composer regularly hosted artists such as poet Dr. Horacio Díaz Cházaro, singers Amparo Montes, José Luis Caballero, and Rebeca Silva ("Rebeca"), as well as local musical groups such as the Trío Veracruz, Trío Azul, and Los Tigres de la Costa.[26] Further, Agustín often had his "soul mates" Dr. Mauro Loyo, José Pérez de León ("Popocha"), "El Pirata" Fuentes, Beto Ávila, Carlitos López, and his cousin Enrique Lara nearby.[27] With the help of his friend Francisco Rivera, Lara soon began broadcasting radio programs from a small performance space located on the second floor of his house. Still intact today, it was designed as an art deco replica of the XEW studio in Mexico City.[28]

The musician frequented the famous Portales de Lerdo city center (on the periphery of the Plaza de Armas), where he patronized one of the popular businesses such as the Café Parroquia, the lobby bar of the Hotel Diligencias, or one of the other many Veracruz watering holes. He often attended the colorful annual Carnival celebration during the 1950s. Seen regularly at the festival with the orchestra of Gabriel ("Gaby") Moreno, Pedro Vargas, Toña la Negra, Lola Beltrán (1932–1996), and Alejandro Algara, Lara and his associates contributed to the fun as they performed at various venues in the port including the Carrillo Puerto, Reforma, Variedades, and Clavijero theaters.[29]

In 1954, US officials invited Lara to participate in a government-sponsored program called "Himno Panamericano" in Chicago. Lara obliged and soon traveled to the Windy City for the occasion, along with Alejandro Algara.[30] Aside from his participation in the Chicago program, Agustín penned a few new songs that year including "Luna, luna, luna" (moon, moon, moon) and "Tesoro mío." (My Treasure) David Lama and Linda Arce recorded "Luna, luna luna" with much success, while Carmela Rey's renditions of "Tesoro mío" and the following year's "Por qué te vas" (why are you leaving?) also proved popular.[31] At the same time, however, Lara grew increasingly conscious of the fact that he still had not yet achieved his long-imagined conquest of Spain.[32]

## Spain

Despite the fact that Mexico continued to have no official diplomatic relation with the Spanish government since dictator Francisco Franco had come to power in the late 1930s, Lara again began making plans to travel to Spain. This time, he selected singers Olga Darson, Carmela Rey, and Alejandro Algara to head up his entourage. Soon, however, it became painfully clear that the project lacked sufficient financial backing.[33] Then, in what would prove a fortunate turn, Emilio Azcárraga introduced Lara to a member of the Mexico City Casino Español association named Santiago Ontañón, who agreed to help pay for a visit to Spain—but only if the composer traveled alone. With this, Agustín made the necessary rearrangements, packed his bags, and flew to the Spanish capital of Madrid in early June 1954. Upon his arrival Lara knelt and kissed the ground, saying, "Hello mother, how have you been?" as an assemblage of photographers and television cameras documented the moment.[34] After a few days, Yolanda joined him.[35]

Mayor José Finat Escriva soon organized a party to honor the Mexican composer.[36] The city official gave Lara a "Batuta de Oro y Plata" with an inscription paying tribute on behalf of the nation. Agustín's hands trembled with emotion as he received the gift. Following the ceremony, Lara's hosts then escorted him to an evening festival where he led the city band in a spirited rendition of "Madrid." By now, the song had gained tremendous popularity in Spain and had even been recorded in Japanese.[37] Curiously, when Agustín asked the mayor which of his songs Spaniards generally preferred, he answered that most favored his compositions "Rosa," "Solamente una vez," "Farolito," and "Veracruz."[38]

Lawyer José María "Chema" Lozano regularly hosted the Mexican couple. He took Agustín and Yolanda on a tour of the city and then introduced them to Gran Vía bar owner Perico Chicote.[39] Both devoted drinkers of cognac, Chicote and Lara saw each other regularly and became good friends. As one observer noted at the time, "Agustín is drinking more cognac than all of Spain can produce."[40] Pursuing his love of the bullfight, the musician also frequented Madrid's famous Plaza de Toros (Figure 7.3).[41] Overall, time spent in Madrid proved quite memorable for Lara and he later remarked how city residents had welcomed him so warmly:

*Figure* 7.3  Lara at the bullfights. Collection of the author.

The hospitality of the *madrileños* is undeniable and classic. From his Excellency the mayor to the anonymous baker, everyone has a warm embrace, a kind word, a sympathetic and amiable gesture to share with me. Look, that is how it is—incredible—when I think that I really did nothing all that extraordinary when I wrote that song "Madrid."[42]

Indeed, Lara's 1948 song had served as a kind of musical calling card for the Mexican composer as he and his young girlfriend were treated like royalty during their first-ever visit to Madrid. Following this, Agustín and Yolanda traveled south to Toledo and then the spectacular Andalusian cities of Seville, Jerez, and

Granada. Subsequently feted in Valencia, local journalists organized a performance by an eighty-piece orchestra and a rendering of Lara's 1935 song "Valencia," which deeply impressed the Mexican composer.[43]

Once back in Mexico after spending a total of six months abroad, Agustín thanked his sponsors for their generosity during a banquet held in his honor at the Casino Español.[44] Not surprisingly, some criticized Lara for his deep affection for the "mother" country by calling him a "bad Mexican" or even "malinchista" (a sell-out).[45] To this the musician would later comment, "I care for Mexico as I would my own mother while my relationship with Spain is something I consider an eternal; I've always been in love with her."[46]

Not one to linger, Lara and Yolanda soon took off on a Caribbean tour. Among the highlights of the trip was a visit to the Dominican Republic, where the couple dined with General Leónidas Trujillo (1891–1961) and his entourage.[47] The encounter may have inspired Lara to begin recording his recollections of various famous people he had come to know. In what reads as a kind of Who's Who for early- to mid-twentieth-century Mexican art and culture, Lara drafted a series of remembrances starting in late 1955 and continuing into 1956 for inclusion in his regular radio broadcasts.

He titled these reflections "Como los conocí" (How I Know Them). As a group, they constituted a nostalgic collection of anecdotal commentaries on figures such as composers María Grever and Miguel Lerdo de Tejada; singers María Conesa, Lola Flores, Elsa Aguirre, Ana María Fernández, Toña la Negra, Elvira Ríos, Juan Arvizu, the Águila Sisters, and Libertad Lamarque; actors Gloria Marin, Lupe Vélez, Maurice Chevalier, Arturo de Córdova, Jorge Negrete, and Andrea Palma; film director Emilio Fernández; entertainers Josephine Baker, Esperanza Iris, and Roberto Soto; painters Diego Rivera and David Alfaro Siquieror; newspaperman (*Excélsior*) Rodrigro de Llano; and Veracruz governor Marco Antonio Muñoz Trumbull. These remembrances offer mainly superficial commentary and thin description and do not bear up to much in the way of analysis.[48]

Lara appeared in the 1956 film *Los tres bohemios* along with costars Luis Aguilar (1917/18–1997), Pedro Vargas, and Miguel Morayta (1907–). He also took part in *El teatro del crimen*, directed by Fernando Cortés and featuring Cuban rumbera María Antonieta Pons (1922–2004). The film *Mujer en Condominio* from the same year saw Agustín perform as a pianist along with actor Carlos López Moctezuma (1909–1980) and actress-rumbera María Esquivel (?–2007). His many other contributions included the 1935 composition "Arroyito (Little Greek)," the 1950 piece "Compás de espera" (Awaiting), and a new song, conceived in 1956, called "Si supieras" (If you knew). Lara also took part in Juan José Ortega's production of *Tropicana*; Tito Davidson's *Música de siempre*, where he sang "Granada"; another project titled *Un mundo nuevo*, directed by René Cardona; and a work dubbed *Locos por televisión*.[49]

Soon, however, Mexican society witnessed another social and cultural shift as urban middle-class youth began to shape their own generational culture in conjunction with the apparent invasion of new, African American-inspired rhythms. An indication of this generational change in regard to Lara's career came when the musician-poet costarred with his longtime collaborator Pedro Vargas and singer Luis Aguilar in the 1956 spoof *Los chiflados de rock 'n' roll* ("Crazed for Rock and Roll").

This comedy featured Agustín and his collaborators performing a number of sanitized tunes as they attempted to show that they could sing the new, still largely imported music. The film's release strangely coincided with a controversy surrounding Elvis Presley that broke in early 1957 after rumor spread that the popular singer had allegedly said "[he would] rather kiss three black girls than a Mexican."[50] The charge turned out to be false, but not before promoters of *Los chiflados* redesigned their advertising for the film to capitalize on the Presley attacks by pitting "the King" against the rapidly maturing Golden Age Mexican stars. The new ad attempted to emasculate Presley while conversely asserting that Lara, Aguilar, and Vargas stood as the more authentic avatars of rock and roll. Advertisements even went as far as to proclaim "¡Muera Elvis Presley!" (Die, Elvis Presley!). Ensuing public debate included sensationalist rhetoric from naysayers such as journalist Federico de León who believed Presley represented a real threat to all things Mexican. More open-minded pundits accepted the quite reasonable fact that the younger generation wanted their own music, while figuring that Mexican youth could at the same time remain patriotic and respectful of social traditions.[51]

Tremendous excitement along with biting criticism of the new music extended throughout the Americas and much of Europe in the late 1950s. Many dismissed not only Presley but a whole cohort of musicians thought to be upsetting the relative social peace.[52] At the same time, the postwar period had seen the rise of a new generation of youthful consumers who, although increasingly identified with their peers rather than their parents, nevertheless helped entertainment industry executives realize unprecedented profits. For his part, Lara stuck with the old guard, believing that the new music ostensibly amounted to a new kind of cultural colonialism. Condescending in his musical appraisal of the American popular music, he viewed rock and roll not as artistry but as a gymnastic exercise. Of course, many of his generation agreed.[53]

Still, Lara kept busy. In 1957 he traveled to Colombia with Alejandro Algara. Upon his return, a song he had completed the previous year titled "Regalo de viaje" (A Travel Gift) was recorded by Donna Mason—a regular performer at the Capri nightclub.[54] Meantime, Agustín followed up his efforts in *Los chiflados del rock 'n' roll* with a 1957 performance of the song "Amor de mis amores" in the film *Mis padres se divorcian*. This cinematic consideration of what otherwise remained a taboo subject in Mexican society was curiously followed the next year with the composer playing "Enamorada" in *Mi mujer necesita marido* (My Wife Needs a Huband).

Obviously still enjoying considerable cachet among film producers and directors, Lara's music appeared in several other films that year.[55]

## La Vida de Agustín Lara

Soon, a new project directed by Alejandro Galindo (1906–1999) titled *La vida de Agustín Lara* (*The Life of Agustín Lara*) set out to cash in on what remained of the composer's star power by characterizing his life in wholly hagiographic terms. For the title role in this 1958 production, Galindo chose not to have Lara play himself but instead cast a younger, more attractive actor named German Robles (1929–). It was a move that angered Lara and immediately put him at odds with the director.[56] Nevertheless, the aging composer did not fail to co-operate with the production and in the years to come would reap the financial benefits afforded him by Tropical Films, Inc.[57]

The picture opens with a well-dressed woman and her younger female companion browsing in a Mexico City music store filled with brand new pianos. In walks a dapper young musician apparently just in from Veracruz, who sits down and begins playing a tune. The older woman approaches him in a friendly manner and asks if he might be willing to teach her attractive associate. When the pianist agrees, she provides him with her address and a small advance payment.

In the next scene we see our man Lara (Robles) arrive outside a fashionable home where a moving truck is delivering a new piano. There are several nicely dressed young women inside who express a girlish excitement when Agustín begins to play. The woman who had propositioned Lara in the music store soon appears at the top of the stairs and orders the young women to "hurry up and get ready." Slightly confused, the young musician continues playing for a while before realizing that he has been hired to work in an upscale bordello.

It is not long before the film recounts one of the formative scenes from Lara's life. Playing night after night, Agustín takes a fancy to one of the resident sex workers and writes a song for her. Performing it for her one night, he sings "Rosa" but is then deeply saddened to see his new love swept up by one of the johns and taken away. With everyone applauding his music, a heartbroken Lara angrily takes a beer bottle and smashes it against a mirror as the scene ends.

A day or so later, he is once again at the piano. This time, however, Rosa is listening intently. When Agustín shows caution in dealing with her, she begins to grow anxious. Lara is then called into another room by a phone call. Following him, Rosa grows extremely agitated, breaks a liquor bottle, and slashes Agustín's left cheek. The attack—as we all know—leaves the piano player scarred for life, a tragic event that would require the artist to rise above personal adversity to create beautiful music.

*Figure 7.4 Los chiflados publicity poster. Courtesy of Agrasanchez Film Archive.*

The composer's emotional depth is dramatized in a subsequent scene when, after performing a radio date, he encounters an attractive young woman who insists they talk. Sitting down in a cabaret, Agustín is very conscious of his still-healing wound and tells her that he has lived a no-good life in dance halls and bordellos. The young woman tells him it doesn't matter; "she knows everything." Lara then sings "Noche de ronda." Yet when she realizes he is remembering a long-lost love he still cares for deeply, she abruptly clutches her purse and leaves.

Agustín soon appears in a police station where he encounters yet another bordello madam. She introduces the musician to a call girl named Mariposa (Butterfly). Gazing at her, Agustín is transfixed. The two are then seen together happily cavorting on a date in the southeastern canal district of Xochimilco. Soon, however, a client of Mariposa's jealously tracks her down. When he finds her and Lara together kissing in her apartment, the man pulls out a gun, pushes Lara aside, and then forces the young woman to dance to a recording of "Aventurera" before shooting her. In a melodramatic last act, she and Agustín kiss one last time before she dies.

Subsequent scenes show Lara with a famous film star named María. They honeymoon in Acapulco and live a seemingly blissful life together on the set of one of her productions. Soon, however, they each go their own ways. Agustín is seen next in a cemetery where his former love Mariposa is buried. She, as it turns out, is his one true muse and her memory is immortalized when he sees her in a vision while visiting her gravesite. Celestial music plays in the background as the camera pans toward the heavens and the film ends. With this, audiences are led to the conclusion that Lara, despite access to the rich and famous, is ultimately a man of the people whose loyalty is to the hard-luck, working girl Mariposa.

Another tribute to the popular composer soon came during a stint at the El Señorial club in Colonia Juárez.[58] One night after completing a series of recording sessions in Mexico, Nat King Cole (1919–1965) appeared at the venue.[59] With Lara and his group backing the celebrated visiting musician, Cole sang "Noche de ronda" and "Solamente una vez."[60] In a dramatic gesture, he then kissed Agustín's ring on stage just as photographers caught the image on film. Seeing the encounter as a validation of Mexican music internationally, publicists widely disseminated the photograph of the two stars.[61] Cole subsequently recorded Lara's "Nunca" along with a number of Spanish language tunes before his death from lung cancer in 1965.

Lara soon appeared on some of the first television broadcasts in Mexico with a variety of other singers, dancers, and performers (Figure 7.5). Some shows featured him playing across from accomplished artists such as Consuelo Velázquez (1916–2005) or Vicente Garrido (1924–2003) in what was called a "Duelo de pianos." Lara's performances on the new medium provided much pleasure for viewers.[62] Diehard fans enjoyed seeing their favorite songs performed as the maestro made several appearances with some of his most beloved interpreters including Ana María González, Toña la Negra, and Pedro Vargas (Figure 7.6).[63]

Meantime, Lara continued to live happily with Yolanda Gasca.[64] During their time together Yiyi and Agustín adopted a boy, whom they named Gerardo Agustín Lara Santacruz. At various points during their relationship, however, Agustín would give in to fits of jealousy. Other times, he apparently felt the need to reaffirm his self-image as a Don Juan. According to some sources, he had a short affair with singer Chabela Durán—an event that may have led to his

*Figure* 7.5 Lara in the studio. Courtesy of Archivo General del Estado de Veracruz.

eventual breakup with Yiyi.[65] Whatever the circumstances, Yolanda and Agustín ended their nine-year relationship in 1961.[66]

The composer set out to find yet another girlfriend. Before long, he won the attention of a nineteen-year-old model and dancer named Vianey Lárraga. Taken into his home, Lárraga was politely informed about the older musician's preferences and public reputation. When interviewed by US journalist June Kay, Lara had proudly recounted his previous "work" in similarly "preparing" María Félix, Clara Martínez, and Yolanda Gasca "to meet the world."[67] Privately, Vianey eventually revealed that she had a young son whom the musician-poet soon adopted and gave the name Agustín Lara Lárraga.[68] The two are said to have married in 1962 as they went on to enjoy many fun-filled nights in Mexico City and Veracruz.[69] The fact that Lara often

*Figure 7.6* Lara at work. Courtesy of Archivo General del Estado de Veracruz.

found himself at odds with Vianey's young son, however, did little enhance their bond and the two soon drifted apart.[70] Before long, Agustín was seen in the company of an attractive dancer named Irma Palencia. He then took up with a young woman named Rocío Durán, whom he had first met more than ten years earlier when he first began working with her mother Chabela.

## My Fair Lady

When Chabela Durán would occasionally visit Lara at his home in Polanco she would often do so with young Rocío in tow. Agustín took a liking to the girl, calling her "mi hijita" (my little daughter) and she referring to him as "papi." When Rocío's grandmother died he supported her for a time and then paid for her to attend a private college in 1952. Eight years later, the two became reacquainted. Lara then took up with the eighteen-year-old as a lover in 1963. In an odd coincidence, Alan Jay Lerner (1918–1986) and Frederick Loewe's (1901–1988) smash hit *My Fair Lady*, based on George Bernard Shaw's (1856–1950) *Pygmalion*, had recently enjoyed a long run on Broadway and was being made into a film to be released in 1964.[71] In his own curious way, Lara would play Henry Higgins to Rocío's Eliza over the next few years.

The musician-poet, as with all the others, initially dedicated himself to his new muse. Durán moved into Agustín's house in Polanco. She often traveled with Lara to the Casita Blanca in Veracruz where he added tile, fountains, and plants to a second floor outside area and dubbed it "El Patio de la Rocío."[72] Agustín and Rocío soon welcomed friends and family over for parties.[73] Interviewed by journalist José Natividad Rosales, Lara professed that he felt young for a man in his sixties. Yet at the same time he noted that he had become weary of certain bothersome aspects of fame.[74] Here, Lara explained that he retreated to his house in Veracruz to escape from publicity hounds. He often traveled south to Tlacotalpan, where he was always received with tremendous warmth, either at the bar of Tobías Carvajal or the homes of any number of friends.

Before long, Agustín and Rocío traveled to Los Angeles, where one night he joined Frank Sinatra (1915–1998), Dean Martin (1917–1995), and Sammy Davis Jr. (1925–1990) in making an appearance at the Coconut Grove nightclub in Beverley Hills. Eddie Fisher (1928–) happened to be scheduled that night, and when Sinatra and company walked in, he invited the singer on stage. Sinatra then took the microphone and announced: "Here with us, is, directly from Mexico the famous author of 'Granada' and 'You Belong to My Heart,' Mr. Agustín Lara." The musician-poet then accompanied Sinatra as he sang "You Belong to My Heart." Later that evening the actress Bette Davis (1908–1989) is said to have paid additional tribute to the composer by singing versions of "Imposible," "Palmeras," and "Noche de ronda" in Spanish.[75]

Lara soon felt the need to tour again. In early 1964, he and his Soloists, with singers Alajandro Algara and Rebeca in tow, boarded a plane for Bogotá. From there they traveled to Lima, where the group performed at the Teatro Municipal Lara made a television appearance on the *Super Show de Radio La Cronica*.[76] During this trip the musician hinted to a friend that he had contracted cancer and wanted to marry again. When then asked about his young girlfriend, Lara quipped, "Can you imagine a sixty-four-year-old man actually looking for a sixty-four-year-old woman to marry?"[77]

Once back in Mexico, Lara received word that the mayor of Granada had invited him to Spain.[78] Without having to give the matter much thought, the composer accepted and began making plans. He needed to raise some money, however, and soon sold his automobile—much to the chagrin of Rocío. Hearing of the pending trip, newspaper satirists anticipated the event with verses and cartoons once again accusing the musician-poet of Hispanophilia (Figure 7.7).[79]

Agustín and Rocío flew to Madrid in June 1964, where a throng of well-wishers welcomed the two with "flowers, *olés* and cheers for the elegant Lara."[80] For his part, Agustín had packed several bottles of mescal and fresh chipotle peppers to give as gifts. Officials arranged a concert with the municipal band with Lara

...de Granada

*Figure 7.7*   Lara in Granada. Collection of the author.

directing.[81] Shortly thereafter, the association of Spanish composers gathered to honor Agustín.[82] Then, flying the musician from Madrid to Granada in a plane provided by Francisco Franco, several friends (Perico Chicote, among others) warmly greeted Agustín and Rocío. The mayor of Granada praised Lara for his composition honoring his city, and declared him an "adopted son" in a ceremony with hundreds present at the base of the Alhambra castle. Warmly welcoming their Mexican guests, the musician's hosts prepared a house in the center of the city for Agustín and Rocío.[83] Taken together, all the fanfare sparked a series of news stories and photos in the Spanish press, and later in Mexico as well.[84]

In the conservative climate of post war Spain, however, Agustín and Rocío's unwed status gave rise to a series of critical comments. Hearing this, Lara decided that it was time to propose. When Rocío agreed, Agustín made arrangements for a church ceremony that took place on June 24, 1964.[85] A few days later, dictator Franco met briefly with the Mexican composer and the local press. Supposedly, Lara greeted the fascist leader with a familiar "How are you doing, don Paco?"[86] When later asked what he thought of Franco, he replied "although many stand against him, the generalissimo is a gentleman who has dedicated himself to nothing other than the betterment of Spain . . . he honored me not for my political views but because I am an artist."[87]

Duly welcomed, the couple then returned to Madrid, where the mayor provided a limousine and driver. Madrileños welcomed el flaco and his new bride at a number of banquets, theater performances, and other special events including one where Agustín received a Medal of Honor.[88] Two days later, Lara and Franco met again, this time to attend a bullfight. On this and other occasions, various matadors including the famous "El Cordobés" (Manuel Benítez Pérez, 1936–) saluted Agustín and Rocío from the ring.[89] Sufficiently inspired by the experience, Lara composed a two-step dedicated to the popular idol the following year. It was rumored, however, that "El Cordobés" did not care much for the song.[90] Nevertheless, it was added to Lara's relatively minor repertoire of bullfight-themed songs created over the years, which he had entitled "Suite Taurina."[91]

In contrast, the more noteworthy Suite Española had now been expanded to include songs about several cities in Spain: "Madrid," "Granada," "Valencia," "Toledo," "Sevilla," and "Murcia," as well as the region "Navarra." Among the other compositions associated with the ongoing collection were "Clavel sevillano," "Cuerdas de mi guitarra," "De riguroso chotís," "Rosa castellana," "Triana," "Los cuatro gatos," and "Españolerías."[92]

While in Madrid, Lara appeared on Spanish television with Alejandro Algara to perform a selection of these Spanish-themed compositions. At the same time, Agustín is also said to have also appeared in a film about matador El Cordobés with talented Spanish singer and actress Sara Montiel.[93] In between commitments, Agustín and Rocío made time to visit Valencia and Bilbao. Yet according to Francisco Rivera, Lara constantly worried about money and on several occasions telegrammed Mexican President Adolfo López Mateos (1909–1969) asking for financial support.[94] Lara and his new bride then made their way in early August to Sopot, Poland, where Agustín performed at an international music festival.[95] The couple then went on to Paris where the composer cashed a much-needed royalty check.[96] Back in Mexico in early October 1964, Lara told reporters of his warm reception in Spain and his desire to possibly even die there.[97] Hearing of his enthusiasm for the country some poked fun at him, declaring "Old Lady Spain" his "newest muse."[98] Others once again criticized him sharply, calling him a "Malinchista." Undaunted, Agustín kept on (Figure 7.8).

...y su nueva musa

*Figure 7.8* Lara and "Spain." Collection of the author.

In early December 1964, US promoters paid Lara handsomely for performances in San Francisco and Los Angeles.[99] While visiting in Hollywood, the Mexican musician strongly expressed his disapproval of an alleged film project based on his life that supposedly had none other than Frank Sinatra playing the lead. Shortly thereafter Agustín made a trip to Tijuana, where he played two nights and received the keys to the city from city officials.[100] At this point, Lara claimed he had sworn off writing songs in favor of more monumental works. Apparently, he was working on a symphonic arrangement for "Veracruz." The composer also suggested that he was writing a light opera titled "El Pájaro de Oro" (The Golden Bird).[101]

The dubious veracity of these assertions notwithstanding, Agustín soon returned home. Continuing to divide his time between Mexico City and Veracruz, he settled into semiretirement (Figure 7.9).[102] He soon began drinking and smoking heavily despite polite words of caution from his assistant, Verduguillo. Still, Lara's friends welcomed him unconditionally. Often Francisco Rivera's wife, Imenia ("doña Pico"), would help Agustín shop in the city markets and then cook up wonderful soups and other traditional Veracruz dishes. Sometimes a group would venture out to enjoy the fresh seafood available at one of the many restaurants in central Veracruz or in the neighboring town of Boca del Río.

The musician-poet would fondly recall these days by saying, "The jarochos are my most beloved friends and, perhaps, those who love me the most."[103] Apart from his closest friends, however, Lara kept his distance from the Veracruz public. When he frequented the Café Parroquia, for example, he would sit erect at his table, smoke his cigarettes, and only occasionally acknowledge passersby. Everyone, it was said, knew to leave el maestro alone.[104]

In late August 1965 Agustín and Rocío celebrated their anniversary in Mexico City. The couple invited many friends to their house in Polanco including Antonio "Chacho" Ibáñez, Alberto Solórzano, Pedro Vargas, José Luis Caballero, Toña la Negra, Chango Cabral, and even María Félix, whose antipathy for Lara had subsided over the years.[105] Ever loyal, Francisco Rivera and his friend Mauro Gómez traveled from Veracruz especially for the event. With members of his Soloists orchestra present, Lara invited Toña la Negra to sing a new song titled "A poco no" (Almost Not). The party continued long into the night with much drinking and dancing (Figures 7.10 and 7.11).

On a growing number of occasions, Agustín shunned the company of even his closest friends. When, for example, former President Miguel Alemán paid for Lara's Spanish friend Perico Chicote to visit Mexico City, Lara refused at first to answer the door. After much persistence Perico managed to roust Agustín, who then greeted him with much affection. Aside from the occasional visitor, however, Agustín preferred to remain secluded.

On May 1, 1966 at the age of sixty-eight, Lara separated from Rocío.[106] In the coming months, Agustín soldiered on with the help of Verduguillo, along with a

*Figure 7.9*  Lara at the piano. Courtesy of the Archivo General de la Nación, Fondo Hermanos Mayo.

rotating roster of house staff including maids and cooks. During this time the aging composer grew increasingly lonely, ornery, and tired. A sampling of household payment receipts made to his employees includes occasional marginal comments about certain individuals. Some of these seem to indicate Agustín taking pity. Others explicitly curse those in his employ and condemn them as incompetent. Amusingly, one of these pay book pages describes a woman named Magdalena Reyes, who Lara hired as a cook for three days in July 1966. He explains her short stay by noting that "she did not even know how to cook up a batch of refried beans and had to be kicked out swearing and screaming." Another annotation from the same month mentions a maid named María Hernández, who, besides being tall and ugly, according to Agustín, seemed to spend an

*Figure 7.10* Toña la Negra and Cuban sensation Celia Cruz. Courtesy of Archivo General de la Nación, Fondo Hermanos Mayo.

*Figure 7.11* Lara in his radio glory. Courtesy of Archivo General de la Nación, Fondo Hermanos Mayo.

inordinate amount of time hiding away in the top floor bathroom. Looking with a degree of compassion upon another poverty-stricken cook named Alicia Cruz Sánchez, Lara considered her yet "another one of [anthropologist Oscar Lewis's] children of Sánchez."[107] At this juncture nearly no one, it seemed, could satisfy him.

Weary of keeping tabs on employees while continuing to live alone in such a large residence, Lara eventually wrote a short letter to Chacho Ibáñez asking for help in mid-December 1967. Ibáñez responded by having a small house built in Tetelpa in the Federal District as a refuge for Lara. Dubbed "La malcontenta," the modest property provided the melancholy musician a backyard garden to stroll in as well as a view of downtown Mexico City.[108]

Back in Veracruz for the holidays, Lara met with reporters from *Life Magazine en Español* (Figure 7.12). Remembering his life and career with pride, he disclosed his last wishes in a melancholy tone:

> I want my ashes—if there are any—to be scattered in the sea. Putting them out to sea is the best. Please, no serenades, no guitars. Please, don't make a fuss. Just leave me in peace and give whatever I have or give my songs to the Mexican Cancer Institute. I can't go on much longer. I am poor and want to die poor, like I was born.[109]

On his seventy-first birthday that year Lara made another visit to Tlacotalpan, Veracruz. Nearly everyone turned out for the occasion as the mayor presided over an extraordinary banquet in honor of the reputed prodigal son.[110] Contemporaries of the composer offered warm remembrances of a "mischievous, frolicking, intelligent young boy who had gone off in search of fame and fortune." As the story goes from the celebrated afternoon in 1967, a wheelchair-bound blind schoolteacher fondly remembered "his old student" as Lara and his admirers walked to have dessert in the local church. Carta Blanca Beer funded a television shoot of the composer in the river city, a program that would subsequently air regularly on Mexican television. Indeed, it was a glorious day for Agustín as he savored thoughts of earlier times amidst the lavish praise heaped upon him by his adopted townsfolk. Lara sat at a banquet table not far from the famed Río de Mariposas and exuberantly exclaimed to the gathered multitude: *Que linda es mi Veracruz* ("How Beautiful is My Veracruz").[111] The internationally known musician had returned in triumph one last time to his imagined Veracruz home.

Now largely out of the spotlight, Lara surfaced about a year later for the occasion of XEW's thirty-eighth anniversary on September 18, 1968. Accompanied by members of his Soloists orchestra, the composer took part in a program that featured the Águila Sisters, Alejandro Algara, actress Silvia Pinal (1931–), and Venezuelan actor and singer Enrique Guzmán (1943–).[112] The following year,

*Figure 7.12  Life en español.* Collection of the author.

Mexican television organized a tribute concert for Lara that was broadcast from the Alameda in central Mexico City. A number of performers participated, including the composer himself. This was the last time he would be seen in public.[113]

In the meantime, Agustín reconciled with Rocío. The reunion did not last long, however, as this time she was the one who soon decided to leave. Alone again, Lara suffered from stomach pains, rheumatoid arthritis, and allergies. Nearly incapacitated, he could no longer shave or bathe himself. Attending to the reclusive musician, Dr. Joaquín Fernández de Castro later testified that Lara would lie in his bed for days on end. The once dapper musician grew a long beard and, at times near delirium, constantly asked for Rocío.[114]

Observing Lara's declining health some time earlier, Emilio Azcárraga, along with his secretary Amalia Gómez Cepeda, had offered the musician whatever help he needed for medical care. The Mexican Society of Authors and Composers had done the same.[115] Waving off their generous offers, Lara persisted in his reclusive state and refused medical care.[116]

## The Black Cadillac

In mid-October 1970 Lara mustered the necessary energy to host a visit from Carlos Águila and a friend. After preparing a round of drinks, Agustín accidentally fell to the ground and broke his hip. On the advice of his doctor, the staff at the Hospital Inglés admitted Lara (under the name Carlos Flores) on October 16, 1970. His caretakers then scheduled hip replacement surgery.[117]

While undergoing treatment, Agustín suffered a respiratory failure; he survived, but his condition remained critical.[118] Once word got out, hundreds of well-wishers including government officials, industry chiefs, and several foreign dignitaries jammed the hospital telephone lines, crowded the lobby, and gathered outside. Hospital staff permitted only Lara's family and close friends to visit him, including sister María Teresa Lara and her husband Nicanor Guzmán, Verduguillo, Emilio Azcarraga's secretary Amalia Gómez Zepeda, Rocío Durán, and her nephew. Hearing the news, many other friends, such as Francisco Rivera, rushed to Mexico City to pay their last respects.[119] For the next eighteen days Lara lay in a virtual coma before dying of a heart attack on November 6, 1970. He was seventy-three years old.

Saddened, government and civic leaders quickly responded by organizing a massive tribute for the artist on November 7. Federal District chief Alfonso Corona del Rosal oversaw the event, while thousands mourned the loss of Mexico's most influential twentieth-century composer of popular song. The governor of Veracruz, Rafael Murillo Vidal (1904–1986), convened a memorial at the state university stadium while also transmitting a televised message. "We have lost one of our distinguished sons," he declared.[120]

Lara's remains first rested at the offices of the Mexican Society of Authors and Composers where for twelve hours "countless men, women, children and the aged from all walks of life paid their last respects to the man who brought tremendous joy to the Mexican people with his music."[121] At 10:30 on the morning of November 7, a black Cadillac accompanied by a squadron of motorcycle police slowly transported the casket to the Fine Arts Palace by way of the Monument of the Revolution (Figure 7.13). Along the route journalists noted that

*Figure 7.13*  The funeral procession. Courtesy of Archivo General de la Nación, Fondo Hermanos Mayo.

"an infinite number of admirers appeared at windows while street vendors and pedestrians quietly said a prayer as the black hearse passed."[122]

Just before 11:00 a.m., Federal District Chief Alfonso Corona del Rosal and a host of dignitaries including Department of Education Secretary for Cultural Affairs Mauricio Magdaleno, film industry head director del Banco Cinematográfico Rodolfo Echeverría Alvarez, National Institute of Fine Arts chairman José Luis Martínez, Labor Congress leader and Secretary General of the Theater Federation Fernando Benítez, Mexico City chronicler Salvador Novo, and representatives of the National Association of Actors received the funeral procession on the steps of Belles Artes. Pedro Vargas, Verducuillo, and others served as pallbearers (Figure 7.14).

Director of Social Action for the Federal District Jesús Salazar Toledano proclaimed the following in honor of Lara:

> Agustín Lara has shared with his people and his land the triumphs of his artistic success. His career, songs and unique musical style are all testimony to the persistence of inspiration and lyrical imagination that has served as a treasury for romantic song in recent decades. Everything that he experienced was transformed into songs of love . . . and his work will forever live in the sensibility and spirit of our people.[123]

With this, the gathering left the Fine Arts Palace as the funeral procession made its way toward Dolores Cemetery. As it traveled east on Juárez Avenue, heading

*Figure 7.14* Outside of the Palacio de Belles Artes. Courtesy of Archivo General de la Nación, Fondo Hermanos Mayo.

southeast along Reforma Boulevard toward Chapultepec Avenue, Constituyentes, and then on to the gravesite, countless mourners hung memorials from balconies. Onlookers waved white handkerchiefs and some tossed red roses as the Cadillac slowly passed, while others joined the entourage as it solemnly carried the musician-poet to his final resting place in the *Rotunda de los Hombres Ilustres* (Rotunda of Distinguished Men). A huge crowd greeted the funeral procession as it arrived at the Dolores Cemetery. After those gathered had taken their seats, Paco Pildora read one of his famous décimas in honor of his friend Agustín. Later, at a tribute inside Mexico City's Teatro Blanquita, a minute of silence was observed before Toña la Negra sang a chilling rendition of "Noche de ronda."

Obituaries filled the Mexico City papers and periodicals across the Spanish-speaking world as journalists wasted no time in crafting a number of effusive tributes to the recently deceased national hero.[124] Former president Gustavo Díaz Ordaz (1911–1979) and his successor Luis Echeverría Álvarez publicly expressed their regrets.[125]

In November and December 1970, a series of articles published in the magazine *Cine Mundial* and titled "Vida, pasión y muerte de Agustín Lara" chronicled the composer's life. Around the same time, Francisco Rivera wrote a number of columns for the Veracruz newspaper *Notiver* that described Lara's later life in the port during the 1960s. Don Paco also remembered Lara with the following description:

Happy, accommodating, affectionate, sometimes irritable, on occasion vul-
gar, caring and other times stingy, he suffered mood swings as do others like
him, always careless about everything but nevertheless a man of the utmost
professionalism and good pay in regard to his artistic commitments. Occasionally he would seem gloomy, blaming his most intimate feelings, but he
kept things alive. He never became a father—something that sometimes
bothered him and he would occasionally talk bitterly and with frustration
about his relationships; he would sigh and say "so many women and none
really loved me, no one loved me!!" That was truly how it was, and he knew
it. He had felt it and suffered it, that all of his women had left him.[126]

Upon hearing of Lara's death, fans in Spain also expressed their grief. "Madrid
cries . . . the whole world cries for Agustín Lara," declared one journalist.[127]
Remembering Lara's last visit, Madrid residents hung memorials from their balconies in honor of the composer. One article declared, "Agustín Lara was a
Mexican nobleman; an untiring songwriter of all the beauty he saw around him;
a true romantic gentleman . . . Lara always felt at home in Spain—as if Spain was
his country."[128] Numerous celebrities including singers Lola Flores and Carmen
Sevilla mourned the loss of the great musician.

People in Granada felt a special bond with the musician-poet.[129] On the day
of his funeral a plane flew overhead with a trailing banner announcing the news
of Lara's death. Below, fans waved farewell. In an official response, Mayor José
Luis Pérez Serrabona proclaimed that his city would dedicate a monument in
honor of the composer.

In Caracas, Venezuela, several newspapers printed word of Lara's death on their
front pages. Radio stations played lengthy tributes. Long exposés detailing his life
and career supplemented details regarding his demise. Newspaper, radio, and television reports in Brazil, Colombia, and Uruguay also spread the news that one of
Latin America's most beloved musicians had died.[130] Nicaraguans fondly remembered el flaco and his last visit to their country in 1952, while to the north Spanish-
speaking residents of New York received the news either through the paper El
Diaro-La Prensa or while listening to radio station WHOM. "Lara has left the
world a rich musical inheritance that will live on despite his death," one reporter
commented.[131] Admirers made plans to interrupt regular broadcast programming
in order to air a special tribute in honor of the Mexican composer. Elsewhere in
cities such as Bogotá, Lima, Santiago, Montevideo, Buenos Aires, Havana, and
many other places throughout the hemisphere, fans of Lara mourned his death.

On the first anniversary of Lara's passing, many dignitaries and friends gathered at the Rotunda de Personas Ilustres in Mexico City to pay tribute (Figure
7.15). María Teresa Lara, Consuelo Velázquez, Salvador Novo, Román Garzón,
Francisco Rivera, Tobías Carvajal (who brought a bit of soil from Tlacotalpan to

*Figure 7.15* Rotunda de Personas Ilustres in Mexico City. Courtesy of Archivo General de la Nación, Fondo Hermanos Mayo.

lay next to Lara's grave), Pedro Domínguez Moscovita, José Pérez de León, and María Luisa C. Covarrubias all attended. The Mexican Society of Authors and Composers hosted a reception afterward.[132]

On May 13, 1975 madrileños erected a statue of Lara in the Spanish capital's Lavapies district. Some of the musician-poet's collaborators attended the unveiling ceremony, including Pedro Vargas, Alejandro Algara, Lola Beltrán, Ana María González, Rocío Durcal (1944–2006), and actress, singer, and master of ceremonies Nati Mistral (1923–). With the flags of Spain and Mexico draped from the image of Lara, a band played a resounding version of "Madrid" while those in attendance sang along. Later, Pedro Vargas performed "Mujer" and "María bonita."[133] Alejandro Algara then added "Valencia" and "Granada" from Lara's Suite Española.[134] Nearly two years later, on October 8, 1977, Lara's love for Spain would facilitate an official meeting (*reencuentro oficial*) between Mexico and Spain in honor of the seventh anniversary of the composer's death.[135]

Four years after his death, the governor of Veracruz, municipal officials in the cities of Veracruz, Boca del Río, Tierra Blanca, Xalapa, Córdoba, and Orizaba, and an array of distinguished artists, labor, military, and commercial elites presided over a massive tribute to Lara in the Port of Veracruz. Nearly seventy musical groups honored the musician-poet as they performed a number of his beloved melodies. Virginia Cordero de Murillo Vidal, wife of Governor Marco Antonio Muñoz, headed up a committee of local retailers from the Hidalgo Market and other outlets who had collected money to pay for the crafting of a bronze statue of

Lara to be erected along the seaside Ávila Camacho Boulevard, approximately halfway between Veracruz and its southern neighbor Boca del Río. The festival attracted tremendous attention as radio, television, and print journalists covered the event. Scores of local residents gathered to catch a glimpse of visiting celebrities. Nearly seven hundred tourists traveling aboard the cruse liner Atlas came ashore to join in the fun. Caught up in the excitement, some even spoke of establishing an international Agustín Lara day to be celebrated annually.[136]

On the eve of the 1984 Summer Olympics in Los Angeles, Mayor Tom Bradley named Lara's song "Granada" as the official song of the games.[138] A statue of Lara was erected in the Los Angeles neighborhood of Lincoln Heights (*Parque México*), with the composer's interpreter Alejandro Algara present for the ceremony. Residents in Bell Gardens paid tribute to the musician-poet with a concert of the maestro's music in Anson Ford Park. Similarly, the Wyndham Garden Hotel in Commerce also hosted a concert.[139]

Since then, the Lara legend has only continued to grow. Celebrating Lara's ninetieth birthday, *porteños* organized a tribute for October 29–31, 1987. Over the three days, admirers of Lara attended a variety of events including a screening of *Santa*, a presentation by Francisco Rivera and Ignacio Taibo I titled "El Agustín que yo conocí," and several musical performances. In 1995 the Mexican Postal Service issued a special series of stamps titled "Idolos Populares de la Radio." Among those featured was Lara along with some of his most notable interpreters: Toña la Negra, Pedro Vargas, and the Águila Sisters.

In 1997, a national celebration of Lara's one-hundredth birthday took place. At that time a number of concerts, radio programs, and television specials paid tribute to Mexico's esteemed musician-poet. The first of several performances was held that summer in the Palace of Fine Arts where Amparo Montes, Eugenia León, and Alejandro Algara shared a bill entirely dedicated to the music of Lara. Later that fall in Los Angeles, Alejandro Algara represented the Mexican people during a ceremony there next to a statue of the composer. In Mexico City, a mass was held in the Dolores Cemetery near Lara's gravesite. Following the service, a concert with ten trios and Las Hermanas Huerta honored Lara. Several radio and television programs featured Lara's music while *Radiópolis* dug up some old material from his La hora azul broadcasts during the 1930s. Radio ABC hosted singers Amparo Montes and Carmela Rey, while the station Grupo Radio Centro entertained audiences with a series of programs highlighting the work of Lara as interpreted by several popular singers. Montes also performed at the Archbishop's Palace to mark the one-hundredth birthday of el flaco. The Mexican Society of Authors and Composers also held a series of commemorative events including an honor guard and mass at the Dolores Cemetery.[137]

Tributes to Lara continue in Mexico to this day (Figure 7.16).[140] Each November the Veracruz Cultural Institute sponsors a Lara festival that features a competition

*Figure 7.16* Poster for Lara Festival in Tlacotalpan, Veracruz in 1998. Collection of the author.

*Figure 7.17* Poster for Lara Festival in 2001. Collection of the author.

for interpreters of his songs. In 2003 the festival extended to the cities of Madrid, Buenos Aires, and Havana (Figure 7.17).

Agustín Lara wrote hundreds of songs that have been recorded by a vast array of performers. He traveled widely, performing in countless auditoriums, theaters, and radio studios. His songs served as the soundtrack for many Mexican

*Figure 7.18* Lara, women, and flowers. Courtesy of Archivo General de la Nación, Fondo Hermanos Mayo.

films. As his love life proved the stuff of legend and regularly mixed with the content of his music, he came to epitomize for many the luxurious lifestyle of a mid-twentieth-century male celebrity. Some, of course, never cared for the man, but nevertheless appreciated his work. Upon his death, one Mexico City journalist put the musician-poet's life in perhaps the most accurate and concise terms when he wrote, "In a world so filled with practicalities and egoism, Agustín Lara was a bohemian, a romantic who lived more in the world of illusions, affectations and dreams than in reality" (Figure 7.18).[141] Lara had remained true to his self-styled romantic vision both in life and death (Figure 7.19). One of the most important composers of the modern bolero, he will always be fondly remembered not just as an iconic figure from Mexico's Golden Age, but as a true giant in the twentieth-century history of popular song.

*Figure 7.19*  *Revista de Revistas* tribute to Lara, October 1997. Collection of the author.

# NOTES

## Epigraph

1. Eduardo Galeano, *Memory of Fire: Century of the Wind,* trans. Cedric Belfrage (London: Quartet Books, 1989), p. 110.

## Prelude

1. Daniel Barenboim, *Music Quickens Time* (London: Verso Press, 2009), p. 10.
2. Lyrics from Mario Arturo Ramos (ed.), *Agustín Lara: Cien años, cien canciones* (Mexico City: Océano, 2000), p. 28. All translations are mine unless otherwise noted. My punctuation and verse lines generally follow Ramos.
3. Ramos, *Agustín Lara: Cien años, cien canciones,* p. 28.
4. Television performance from DVD *Las Número Uno: Agustín Lara,* Sony/BMG 2005, #828767585222. Originally composed in 1930, "Aventurera" was first recorded by actress Adria Delhort. Pável Granados, liner notes to the compact disc *Rarezas discográficas Agustín Lara,* included in Pável Granados, *Agustín Lara, Canciones* (Mexico City/Veracruz: Océano/Gobierno de Veracruz, 2008). Lara then recorded it for Victor Records with singer Juan Arvizu in 1931.
5. John Mraz, "Today, Tomorrow and Always: The Golden Age of Illustrated Magazines in Mexico, 1937–1960," in Gilbert M. Joseph, Anne Rubenstein, and Eric Zolov (eds.), *Fragments of a Golden Age: The Politics of Culture in Mexico since 1940* (Durham, NC: Duke University Press, 2001), p. 151.
6. Among a handful of primarily Spanish-language publications that touch upon aspects of Lara's career and music, two full-length biographies of Lara lay at the foundation of my study: Javier Ruiz Rueda's *Agustín Lara: Vida y pasiones* (Mexico City: Editorial Novaro, 1976) and Gabriel Abaroa Martínez's *El flaco de oro* (Mexico City: Editorial Planeta, 1993). Also extremely helpful has been the more recent chronicle of Lara by Guadalupe Loaeza and Pável Granados *Mi novia, la tristeza* (Mexico City: Océano, 2008).
7. Leo Charney and Vanessa R. Schwartz, "Introduction," in Leo Charney and Vanessa R. Schwartz (eds.), *Cinema and the Invention of Modern Life,* Berkeley: University of California Press, 1995, pp. 3–4; Laura Doyle and Laura Winkiel, "Introduction: The Global Horizons of Modernism," in Laura Doyle and Laura Winkiel (eds.), *Geomodernisms: Race, Modernism, Modernity* (Bloomington: Indiana University Press, 2005), p. 1 and passim.
8. For a concise treatment of this emerging culture in Mexican history see, for example, Robert M. Buffington and William E. French, "The Culture of Modernity," in Michael C. Meyer and William H. Beezley (eds.), *The Oxford History of Mexico* (New York: Oxford University Press, 2000), pp. 397–432. One of the best recent treatments of Mexican cultural nationalism can

be found in John Mraz, *Looking for Mexico: Modern Visual Culture and National Identity* (Durham, NC: Duke University Press, 2009).

9. On nineteenth-century innovations in sound technology see Jonathan Sterne, *The Audible Past: Cultural Origins of Sound Reproduction* (Durham, NC: Duke University Press, 2003). Rubén Gallo champions the 1920s as the dawning of Mexican modernity and focuses on photography, typewriters, radio, cement, and stadiums as key mediums that helped forge the new sensibility. Rubén Gallo, *Mexican Modernity: The Avant-Garde and the Technological Revolution* (Cambridge, MA: MIT Press, 2005).

10. Jeffrey Herf, *Reactionary Modernism: Technology, Culture, and Politics in Weimar and the Third Reich* (Cambridge: Cambridge University Press, 1984). Herf appropriately opens with the statement, "There is no such thing as modernity in general. There are only national societies, each of which becomes modern in its own fashion." Herf, p. 1.

11. Since the mid-nineteenth century, various Latin American nations have proudly played host to a variety of modernist writers, visual artists, musicians, architects, engineers, scientists, businessmen, and other creative types. Evaluating this tradition in relation to more present-day problems of persistent social and economic inequality, some, including Mexican anthropologist Néstor García Canclini, have suggested that individuals who stand as examples of modernity in Latin America did not necessarily contribute in any real way to the social development of their native lands. For García Canclini, modernity in Latin America has proven merely a cultural façade "conjured up by the elites and the state apparatuses [to] cultivate vanguard poetry and art while most of the population is illiterate." Néstor García Canclini, *Hybrid Cultures: Strategies for Entering and Leaving Modernity*, trans. Christopher L. Chiaparri and Silvia L. López (Minneapolis: University of Minneapolis Press, 1995), p. 7.

12. Despite the fact that literary modernism and its main proponents in Mexico were identified with the regime of President Porfirio Díaz and therefore largely on the wane by Lara's time, one can nevertheless assert that his aesthetic was clearly in the modernist tradition.

13. On this complex mass communication process see, for example, Stuart Hall's classic essay excerpt "Encoding, Decoding," in Simon During (ed.), *The Cultural Studies Reader* (New York: Routledge, 1993), pp. 90–103.

14. Carlos Monsiváis, "Bolero: A History," in Carlos Monsiváis, *Mexican Postcards*, trans. John Kraniauskas (London: Verso Press, 1997), p. 179. "Carlos Monsiváis: Mexican who wrote of the great and the humble, dies at 72," *New York Times*, June 22, 2010.

15. An example of more avant-garde artistic work in Mexico during the 1920s can be seen in the loosely affiliated group known as the *Estridentistas* (Stridentists). One of their more provocative as well as quite amusing antiestablishment slogans at the time was "Chopin . . . to the electric chair!" Elissa Rashkin, *The Stridentist Movement in Mexico: The Avant-Garde and Cultural Change in the 1920s* (Lanham, MD: Lexington Books, 2009).

16. On this discursive process in Mexican music during the critical decade of the 1920s see Alejandro Madrid, *Sounds of the Modern Nation: Music, Culture, and Ideas in Post-Revolutionary Mexico* (Philadelphia: Temple University Press, 2009).

17. See Mraz, *Looking for Mexico*, chapter 3.

18. Salvador Novo quoted in José Salvador Orozco Farías, "El flaco de oro: Agustín Lara," *Revista de Revistas*, November 19, 1990, p. 52.

19. Daniel Castañeda, *Balance de Agustín Lara* (Mexico City: Ediciones Libres, 1941), p. 79 and passim.

20. Pável Granados, *Apague la luz . . . y escuche* (Mexico City: Biblioteca de ISSSTE, 1999), p. 82.

21. De la Peza Casares, *El bolero y la educación sentimental en México*, p. 406.

22. While legend has it that Lara penned over five hundred compositions in his lifetime, Moreno Rivas lists 194 of Lara's most renowned songs by year. Yolanda Moreno Rivas, *Historia de la música popular Mexicana* (Mexico City: Alianza Editorial Mexicana, 1979, 1989), pp. 156–58. Abaroa Martínez organizes 422 of Lara's songs alphabetically. Abaroa Martínez, *El flaco de oro*, pp. 345–50. The Archivo General de la Nación (AGN), Ramo Propiedad Artística y Literaria, offers documentation on Mexican popular music, theater, and film beginning in 1890. The earliest mention of Lara is his song "Volviste," which

appears in box 491, folder 11641 (1928). Significant listings ensue covering years 1929 and 1930 before extending to 1961.

23. Here, I am drawing on ideas expressed by John Bush Jones in *Our Musicals, Ourselves: A Social History of the American Musical Theater* (Lebanon, NH: Brandeis University Press, 2003), pp. 1–2.

24. For example, some of Lara's early sheet music can be found in the AGN in Mexico City while many copyright records for Lara's music can be reviewed at the Library of Congress (www.copyright/gov/records) and some recordings can be found at the Biblioteca Nacional de España (National Library of Spain, Madrid). A registry of Lara compositions and listing of major interpreters is available via the Sociedad de Autores y Compositores de México (Mexican Society of Authors and Composers, SACM) website (www.sacm.org.mx) and a few selections of Lara's music published by the Southern Music Publishing Company can be found at the San Francisco Public Library as well as the University of New Mexico General Library Center for Southwest Research where a fair number of Golden Age musical scores including a number by Lara have been collected. I had less luck coming up with much other than title listings when surveying more commercial outlets such as Decca, Peer, RCA Victor, and Orfeón records. Searches conducted in person by the author in Madrid, Granada and Havana, despite Lara's residing in each of these cities, did not turn up much.

25. Many of the newspaper articles referenced in the text have come from scrapbook and assorted clip files that, unfortunately, do not always include a full citation. For this reason, I have not been able to include specifics—including, at times, the author's name, date, and page numbers. Nevertheless, material include in these references is often worth noting and I have indicated the location and collection.

## Chapter 1

1. Carlos Monsiváis, *Mexican Postcards*, trans. John Kraniauskas (London: Verso Press, 1997), p. 179.

2. Juan José Arreola, "Lara imaginario," in Eugenio Méndez (ed.), *Agustín, rencuentro con lo sentimental* (Mexico City: Editorial Domés, 1980), pp. 44–45; Javier Ramos Malzárraga, "El último día feliz de Agustín Lara," in Guillermo Mendizábal and Eduardo Mejía (eds.) *Todo lo que quería saber sobre Agustín Lara* (Mexico City: Grijalbo, 1993), pp. 22–23.

3. Renato Leduc, in *Agustín, rencuentro con lo sentimental*, pp. 268–70. Leduc, like many of his contemporaries, makes comparisons to Buenos Aires and the rise of the tango as an urban-based, "national" music.

4. Juan José Arreola and Lilian Scheffler, *México: ¿quires tomarte una foto conmigo? Cien años de consumo* (Mexico City: Procuraduría Federal del Consumidor/Editorial Gustavo Casasola, 1996), pp. 26–37. On department stores in Mexico see Steven B. Bunker, "Consumers of Good Taste:' Marketing Modernity in Northern Mexico, 1890–1910," *Mexican Studies / Estudios Mexicanos*, Vol. 13, No. 2 (Summer, 1997), pp. 227–69, as well as Steven B. Bunker, *Creating Mexican Consumer Culture in the Age of Porfirio Díaz* (Albuquerque: University of New Mexico Press, 2012). On the history of the department store see Michael B. Miller, *The Bon Marché: Bourgeois Culture and the Department Store, 1869–1920* (Princeton, NJ: Princeton University Press, 1981) as well as Susan Porter Benson, *Counter Cultures: Saleswomen, Managers, and Customers in American Department Stores, 1890–1940* (Champaign: University of Illinois Press, 1986).

5. T. Philip Terry, *Terry's Guide to Mexico* (Boston: Houghton Mifflin Company, 1935). Other informative insights to life in the capital include Frances Toor's *New Guide to Mexico* (New York: McBride, 1936) and *A Treasury of Mexican Folkways* (New York: Bonanza Books, 1933, reprint edition 1985), as well as her *Mexican Folkways* journal. Emphasis in the original.

6. Arreola and Scheffler, *México: ¿quieres tomarte una foto conmigo?*, pp. 81–113.

7. Arreola and Scheffler, *México: ¿quieres tomarte una foto conmigo?*, pp. 57–72 and passim.

8. On modernizing Mexico City see William Beezley, *Judas at the Jockey Club and Other Episodes of Porfirian Mexico* (Lincoln: University of Nebraska Press, 1987); Michael Johns, *The*

*City of Mexico in the Age of Díaz* (Austin: University of Texas Press, 1997); Peter Ward, *Mexico City* (New York: Wiley, 1990, 1998), pp. 41–86; Pablo Piccato, *City of Suspects: Crime in Mexico City, 1900–1931* (Durham, NC: Duke University Press, 2001), pp. 17–33; Patrice Elizabeth Olsen, *Artifacts of Revolution: Architecture, Society and Politics in Mexico City, 1920–1940* (Lanham, MD: Rowman and Littlefield, 2008); John Lear, *Workers, Neighbors and Citizens: The Revolution in Mexico City* (Lincoln: University of Nebraska Press, 2001), pp. 30–35; William Schell Jr., *Integral Outsiders: The American Colony in Mexico City: 1876–1911* (Wilmington, DE: SR Books, 2001), pp. xviii–xix, 31–41, 51–59; Diane E. Davis, *Urban Leviathan: Mexico City in the Twentieth Century* (Philadelphia: Temple University Press, 1994), pp. 26–32.

9.  Alberto Dallal, *El "dancing" mexicano* (Mexico City: Secretaria de Educación Pública 1986), p. 97.

10. Here, Mexico City is the jurisdiction defined only as the subdivisions of Miguel Hidalgo, Cuauhtémoc, Benito Juárez, and Venustiano Carranza. Growth in the larger Federal District jurisdiction rose from 541,516 in 1900, to 729,153 in 1910, and to 903,063 in 1921. Census material cited in El Colegio de México, *Dinamica de la poblacíon de México* (Mexico City: Colegio de México, 1970), p. 137. Rodríguez Kuri discusses discrepancies in the various late nineteenth-century census reports. Ariel Rodríguez Kuri, *La experiencia olvidada: El Ayuntamiento de México: pólitica y gobierno, 1876–1912* (Mexico City: Colegio de México/UAM Azcapotzalco, 1996), pp. 82–85.

11. On worker housing in the Port of Veracruz, Mexico City and elsewhere in the republic see Andrew Grant Wood, *Revolution in the Street: Women, Workers and Urban Protest in Veracruz, 1870–1927* (Lanham, MD: Rowman and Littlefield/SR Books, 2001).

12. Andreas Huyssen, *After the Great Divide: Modernism, Mass Culture and Postmodernism* (Bloomington: Indiana University Press, 1986), pp. 18–19.

13. On the context of Mexican national development see Alan Knight, "Popular Culture and the Revolutionary State in Mexico, 1910–1940," *Hispanic American Historical Review*, Vol. 74, No. 3 (August 1994), pp. 393–444.

14. On nineteenth-century development and ideology see, for example, Fridrich Katz, "The Liberal Republic and the Porfiriato, 1867–1910," in Leslie Bethell (ed.), *Mexico since Independence* (Cambridge: Cambridge University Press, 1985, 1991), pp. 49–124 and Stephen Haber, *Industry and Underdevelopment: The Industrialization of Mexico, 1890–1940* (Palo Alto: Stanford University Press, 1989). Mexicans presented elaborate examples of national progress at international expositions including a dazzling "Aztec Palace" display at the 1889 Universal Exposition in Paris. Mauricio Tenorio Trillo, *Mexico at the World's Fairs: Crafting a Modern Nation* (Berkeley: University of California Press, 1996). On imports see Arnold Bauer and Benjamin Orlove (eds.), *The Allure of the Foreign: Imported Goods in Postcolonial Latin America* (Ann Arbor: University of Michigan Press, 1997).

15. See, for example, Friedrich A. Kittler, *Discourse Networks 1800/1900* (Palo Alto: Stanford University Press, 1990) and Friedrich A. Kittler, *Gramophone, Film, Typewriter* (Palo Alto: Stanford University Press, 1999).

16. Lina Opena Gûemes H. (ed.), *Guía general del archivo histórico del Distrito Federal* (Mexico City: Gobierno del Distrito Federal, 2000), pp. 192–95. See also Beezley, *Judas at the Jockey Club*.

17. Pierre Bourdieu, *Distinction: A Social Critique of the Judgement of Taste*, trans. Richard Nice (Cambridge, MA: Harvard University Press, 1984).

18. Newspaper observations and commentary on the advent of film are collected in Felipe Garrido, *Luz y sombra: Los inicios del cine in la prensa de la ciudad de México* (Mexico City: Consejo Nacional para la Cultura y las Artes, 1997). On the larger transformation in work and leisure time see William H. Beezley, "The Porfirian Smart Set Anticipates Thorstein Veblen in Guadalajara," in William H. Beezley, Cheryl E. Martin, and William E. French (eds.), *Rituals of Rule, Rituals of Resistance: Public Celebrations and Popular Culture in Mexico* (Wilmington, DE: SR Books, 1994), pp. 173–90 and Bunker, "'Consumers of Good Taste:' Marketing Modernity in Northern Mexico, 1890–1910."

19. See for example, Carlos Monsiváis, *Celia Montalván (te brindas, voluptuosa e imprudente)* (Mexico City: Cultura/Secretaría de Educatión Pública (SEP), 1984) as well as Ángel

Miguel (ed.), *Placeres en imagen: fotografía y cine eróticos, 1900–1960* (Morelia: Universidad Autonómica del Estado de Morelos, 2009).

20. Thomas Edison had undertaken a trial run of his kinetoscope (or nickelodeon) in 1895 with mixed results. On the early history of film in Mexico see Juan Felipe Lara et al., *Anales del cine en México, 1895–1911* (Mexico City: Ediciones y Gráficos Eón, 10 volumes, 2003).

21. See Luis G. Urbina, "El Cinematógrafo," *El Universal*, August 23, 1896 as well as other columns published in Mexico City papers (*El Tiempo, El Globo, El Mundo, El Nacional, El Siglo XIX, El Monitor Republicano*, and others after the Lumiere brothers film debut that month in Mexico City. Garrido, *Luz y sombra*, pp. 43–76 and passim.

22. Carl Mora, *Mexican Cinema: Reflections of a Society, 1896–1988* (Berkeley: University of California Press, 1982), pp. 6–27.

23. Archivo Histórico del Distrito Federal (hereafter AHDF), "Diversiones," tomo 28, exp., 317–61, 853–54. By 1921 inspectors had visited a majority of the city's movie houses and theaters, often commenting on the overall condition of the building, ventilation, fire prevention, bathrooms, number of seats, and the like. Officials occasionally commented on the "public morality" of various shows—especially if they had received complaints. On the proliferation of movie houses see Aurelio de los Reyes, *Cine y sociedad en México*, vol 1 (Mexico City: Universidad Nacional Autónoma de México (hereafter UNAM), 1996), pp. 25–32, 61–66.

24. Jesús Flores y Escalante, *Salón México: Historia documental y gráfica del danzón en México* (Mexico City: Asociación Mexicana de Estudios Fonográficos, 1993), pp. 83–94, 117–20; Jeffrey Pilcher, *Cantinflas and the Chaos of Mexican Modernity* (Lanham, MD: Rowman and Littlefield, 2001), pp. 23–26; de los Reyes, *Cine y sociedad en México*, 1996, p. 30; Katherine Bliss, *Compromised Positions: Prostitution, Public Health and Gender Politics in Revolutionary Mexico City* (University Park: Pennsylvania State University Press, 2001), pp. 84–85; Alberto Dallal, *La danza en México: La danza escénica popular, 1877–1930* (Mexico City: UNAM, 1995), pp. 153–62; Armando Jiménez, *Sitios de rompe y rasga en la Ciudad de México* (Mexico City: Océano, 1998), p. 141. On one of the earliest hotels in the area see Sergio H. Peralta Sandoval, *Hotel Regis: Historia de una época* (Mexico City: Editorial Diana, 1996).

25. AHDF, "Diversiones." See also Enrique Olavarría y Ferrari, *Reseña histórica del teatro en México, 1538–1911* 3rd ed., 5 vols. (Mexico City: Porrua, 1961) and Pablo Dueñas, *Las divas en el teatro de revista mexicano* (Mexico City: Asociación Mexicana de Estudios Fonográficos/Dirección General de Culturas Populares, 1994), pp. 34–49 for a listing of the city's theaters. On the Teatro Esperanza Iris see Sergio López Sánchez and Julieta Rivas Guerrero, *Esperanza Iris, la tiple de hierro: Escritos 1* (Mexico City: Instituto Nacional de Belles Artes Centro Nacional de Investigacíon Documentación e Información Teatral Rodolfo Usigli/ Gobierno del Estado de Tabasco, Secretaria de Cultura, Recreación y Deporte, 2002).

26. On the history of *carpa* theater see Socorro Merlín, *Vida y milagros de las carpas: La carpa en México, 1930–1950* (Mexico City: Institucion Nacional de Belles Artes [hereafter INBA], 1995).

27. Early twentieth century travelers to Mexico are discussed in Helen Delpar, *The Enormous Vogue of Things Mexican: Cultural Relations between the United States and Mexico, 1920–1935* (Tuscaloosa: University of Alabama Press, 1992).

28. For description and portraits of turn-of-the-century street vendors, see Juan José Arreola and Lilian Scheffler, *México: ¿quires tomarte una foto conmigo?*, pp. 38–46.

29. The habanera can be traced to the turn of the nineteenth century when Afro-Caribbean musicians "creolized" French contradance brought to Cuba by émigrés from Haiti and the Dominican Republic. During the next few decades, this mixture would become known successively in Cuba as the *contradanza, danza, danza habanera*, and, finally, habanera. John Santos, "The Cuban Danzón and its Antecedents and Descendents," liner notes to *The Cuban Danzón*, Folkways FE 4066, 1982, http://media.smithsonianglobalsound.org/liner_notes/folkways/FW04066.pdf. On the influence of this music in Mexico see, for example, Helmut Brenner, *Juventino Rosas: His Life, His Work, His Time* (Warren, MI: Harmonie Park Press, 2000), pp. xvii–xviii.

30. On nightclubs and other leisure spaces in Mexico City see Armando Jiménez, *Cabarets de antes y de ahora en la Ciudad de México* (Mexico City: Plaza y Janes, 1992); Armando

Jiménez, *Lugares de gozo, retozo, ahogo y desahogo en la Ciudad de México* (Mexico City: Océano, 2000); and Jiménez, *Sitios de rompe y rasga en la Ciudad de México*.

31. Simón Jara Gámez, Aurelio Rodríguez Yeyo and Antonio Zedillo Castillo, *De Cuba con amor . . . el danzón en México* (Mexico City: Grupo Azabache/CONACULTA, 1994), pp. 39–113; Flores y Escalante, *Salón México Historia Documental y Graáfica del Danzón en México* (Mexico City: Asociación Mexicana de Estudios Fonográficos, 1993), pp. 99–111, 120–24. Salón México was the site for the 1948 *cabaretera* film of the same name directed by Emilio "El Indio" Fernández and starring Mercedes López. See Flores y Escalante, *Imagenes del danzón: Iconografia del danzón en México* (Mexico City: Asociación Mexicana de Estudios Fonográficos, 1994), pp. 76–77, 80–83 for descriptions of Salón México in its heyday. Aaron Copland's orchestral work "El Salón México" pays homage to this important Mexico City site.

32. Jonathan Sterne, *The Audible Past: Cultural Origins of Sound Reproduction* (Durham, NC: Duke University Press, 2003), pp. 70–85.

33. William Howland Kenney, *Recorded Music in American Life: The Phonograph and Popular Memory, 1890–1945* (New York: Oxford University Press, 1999), p. 24.

34. Kenney, *Recorded Music in American Life*, pp. 24–28.

35. Kenney, *Recorded Music in American Life*, pp. 46–56, American Memory Project; Library of Congress, http://memory.loc.gov/ammem/berlhtml/berlgramo.html. For more on Berliner see *Emile Berliner and the Birth of the Recording Industry and the American Memory Project*, Library of Congress, http://memory.loc.gov/ammem/berlhtml/berlhome.html. For a listing of Berliner recordings see Paul Charosh, *Berliner Gramophone Records, American Issues, 1892–1900* (Westport, CT: Greenwood Press, 1995).

36. During the second half of the nineteenth century, a variety of US publishing companies (W. A. Pond, G. Schirmer, etc.) took interest in the work of Mexican composers. John Koegel, "Crossing Borders; Mexicana, Tejana, and Chicana Musicians in the United States and Mexico," in Walter Aaron Clark (ed.), *From Tejano to Tango: Latin American Popular Music* (New York: Routledge, 2002), p. 99. For a more complete discography see Richard K. Spottswood, *Ethnic Music on Records: A Discography of Ethnic Recordings Produced in the United States, 1893–1942, volume 4: Spanish, Portuguese, Philippine, Basque* (Champaign: University of Illinois Press, 1990). Odeon did not have a significant presence in Mexico but a presence nonetheless. See www.mustrad.org.uk/articles/odeon.htm.

37. Quoted in Katz, "The Liberal Republic and the Porfiriato," in Bethell (ed.), *Mexico since Independence*, p. 15.

38. On Adams see Mark Clague (ed.), *The Memoirs of Alton Augustus Adams, Sr.: The First Black Bandmaster of the United States Navy* (Berkeley: University of California Press, 2008).

39. On Curti see Jean Dickson, "¿Quién fue Carlos Curti?," *Heterofonía*, Vol. 140, January–June 2009, pp. 61–75.

40. John Koegel, "Crossing Borders; Mexicana, Tejana, and Chicana Musicians in the United States and Mexico," p. 99; John Koegel, "Canciones del país: Mexican musical life in California after the Gold Rush," *California History*, Vol. 78, No. 3, pp. 160–87, 215–19; John Koegel, "Compositores mexicanos y cubanos en Nueva York, c.1880–1920." *Historia Mexicana*, Vol. 56, No. 2 (October–December 2006), pp. 533–612.

41. Archivo Histórico del Distrito Federal/Universidad Autnónoma Metropolitana-Iztapalapa, *Gran baile de pulgas en traje de charácter: Las diversiones públicas en la Ciudad de México del Siglo XIX* (Mexico City: Archivo Histórico del Distrito Federal/Universidad Autnónoma Metropolitana-Iztapalapa, 1999), p. 97.

42. Quoted in Katz, "The Liberal Republic and the Porfiriato," in Bethell (ed.), *Mexico since Independence*, p. 29.

43. *Danza*, in contrast to the earlier *contradanza*, refers to a more independent form of figure (couples) dancing that developed in the nineteenth century as well as the music that accompanied it. Peter Manuel, "Cuba: From Contradanza to Danzón," in Peter Manuel (ed.), *Creolizing Contradance in the Caribbean* (Philadelphia: Temple University Press, 2009), p. 67. The contradanza consisted of a rhythmic cell then called the tango (and later changed to habanera) that Afro-Cuban musicians had developed on the island in the nineteenth

century as they performed and added their own improvisational touches to the French *contradanse* as they transformed it into a "creolized" musical form during the late eighteenth and early nineteenth century. Alejo Carpentier, *Music in Cuba*, Timothy Brennan (ed.), trans. Alan West-Durán (Minneapolis: University of Minnesota Press, 2001), pp. 158–59; Ned Sublette, *Cuba and its Music: From the First Drums to the Mambo* (Chicago: Chicago Review Press, 2004), pp. 133–34. Peter Manuel provides extensive consideration of the contradance in Cuba as well as more recent debates regarding its origins on the island. Peter Manuel, "Cuba: From Contradanza to Danzón,"pp. 51–112.

44. Alejo Carpentier, *Music in Cuba*, pp. 222–32; Peter Manuel, "Cuba: From Contradanza to Danzón," p. 92.

45. Robin Moore, *Music in the Hispanic Caribbean: Experiencing Music, Expressing Culture* (Oxford: Oxford University Press 2010), p. 212.

46. Cristobal Díaz-Ayala, "El Danzón," in *Encyclopedic Discography of Cuban Music*, Díaz-Ayala Cuban and Latin American Popular Music Collection, Florida International University, http://gislab.fiu.edu/smc/discography.htm.

47. Flores y Escalante, *Imagenes del danzón*, pp. 1–4. For a sampling of early Cuban danzón see "Cuban Danzón: Its Ancestors and Descendents," Washington, D.C., Smithsonian Folkways #4086, 2010, "The Cuban Danzón: Various Artists," Arhoolie Records #7032, and "Orquesta Cuba: Charangas y Danzón," Nimbus records #7058.

48. Peter Manuel, "Cuba: From Contradanza to Danzón," p. 93.

49. Flores y Escalante, *Salón México*, p. 1; John Charles Chasteen, *National Rhythms, African Roots: The Deep History of Latin American Popular Dance* (Albuquerque: University of New Mexico Press, 2004), pp. 73–74; Simón Jara Gámez, Aurelio Rodríguez Yeyo and Antonio Zedillo Castillo, *De Cuba con amor . . . el danzón en México*, pp. 205–53.

50. Francisco Rivera, "Breve semblanza de Emilio Cantarell Vela," *Notiver*, no date, Fondo Francisco Rivera, file 1V, Archivo Municipal del Puerto de Veracruz (hereafter AMV).

51. Maria del Rosario Ochoa Rivera, personal communication with the author, May 2005. See also Mark Pedelty, *Musical Ritual in Mexico City: From the Aztec to NAFTA* (Austin: University of Texas Press, 2004), p. 147.

52. On danzón in Mexico City see Robert Buffington, "La 'Dancing' Mexicana: Danzón and the Transformation of Intimacy in Post-Revolutionary Mexico City," *Journal of Latin American Cultural Studies*, Vol. 14, No. 1 (March 2005), pp. 87–108. For information on the history of social dance see Julie Malnig, *Dancing till Dawn: A Century of Exhibition Ballroom Dance* (New York, New York University Press, 1995); *America Dances! 1897–1948: A Collector's Edition of Social Dance in Film*, DVD, Dancetime Publications, 2003; and *An American Ballroom Companion*, American Memory Project, United Status Library of Congress, http://memory.loc.gov/ammem/dihtml/dihome.html.

53. Simón Jara Gámez, Aurelio Rodríguez Yeyo, and Antonio Zedillo Castillo, *De Cuba con amor*, p. 46. On the history of danzón see Flores y Escalante, *Imagenes del danzón*; John Storm Roberts, *The Latin Tinge: The Impact of Latin American Music on the United States* (New York: Oxford University Press, 1979), pp. 5–6; Alejo Carpentier, *Music in Cuba*; pp. 148–50 as well as Ned Sublette, *Cuba and its Music: From the First Drums to the Mambo*, pp. 133–34 and Peter Manuel, *Creolizing Contradance in the Caribbean*.

54. Antonio García de León, "Los patios danzoneros," *La Jornada Seminal*, #223, September 19, 1993, p. 34; Flores y Escalante, *Imagenes del danzón*, pp. 73–76. Personal communication with Veracruz historian Miguel Angel Montoya Cortés, February 11, 1995, Port of Veracruz, Veracruz. At the AGN in Mexico City, sheet music publications beginning in 1897 (when the first collecting began) become more frequent during the first decade of the new century. One catchy title is the 1913 danzón for piano titled "El triunfo del feminismo" by Cándido Saínz in Havana, Cuba. The cover shows a uniformed woman with in a police uniform lording over a multitude of men on the march. AGN, Ramo Propiedad Artistica y Literaria, box 242, file 1002.

55. Jaime Rico Salazar, *Cien años de boleros* (Bogotá: Centro Editorial de Estudios Musicales, 1987), p. 65. On the history of bolero see, for example, Pablo Dueñas, *Bolero: historia*

*documental del bolero mexicano,* (Mexico City: Asociación de Estudios Fonograficos, 1993); Rodrigo Barzán Bonfil, *Y si vivo cien años... Antología del bolero en México* (Mexico City: Fondo de Cultura Económica, 2001); María del Carmen de la Peza Casares, *El bolero y la educación sentimental en México* (Mexico City: Universidad Autónoma Metropolitana-Xochimilco, 2001); Elena Tamargo et al., *Clave del corazón, bolero* (Mexico City: Alejo Peralta Fundación, 2004); Helio, Orovio, *El bolero latino* (Havana: Editorial Letras Cubanas, 1995).

56. Although quite different than what would later take shape in Cuba and elsewhere in the Americas, the first documented mention of "bolero" is associated with the Mediterranean Balearic Islands where a Mallorcan dancer named Sebastián Lorenzo Cerezo is said to have introduced a new music to accompany a couples dance in the Spanish court during the 1780s. Bazán Bonfil, *Y si vivo cien años,* p. 17; Dueñas, *Bolero,* p. 14.

57. Dueñas, *Bolero,* p. 13; Helio Orovio, *El bolero latino,* p. 7; Adela Pineda Franco, "The Cuban Bolero and Its Transculturation to Mexico: The Case of Agustín Lara," *Studies in Latin American Popular Culture,* vol. 15 (1996), pp. 119–30. See also Francisco González Clavijo, "Los colores interiors de la música Afrocubana," in Jesús Galindo Cáceres (ed.), *Entorno de miradas* (Veracruz: Instituto Veracruzano de Cultura, 2003), pp. 15–42.

58. Juan S. Garrido, *Historia de la música popular en México. Mexico City, 1876–1973* (Editorial Extemporáneos S.A., 1974), p. 49.

59. Tamargo et al., *Bolero: Clave del corazón,* pp. 25–49.

60. "Tristezas me dan tus quejas, mujer, No hay prueba de, amor que deje entrever, Cuánto sufro y padezco por ti. La suerte es adversa conmigo, No deja ensanchar mi pasión. Un beso me diste un día, Lo guardo en mi corazón." Dulcilia Cañizares, *La trova tradicional cubana,* Havana: Editorial Letras cubanas, 1992. Quoted in Tamargo et al., *Bolero: clave del corazón,* p. 29. See also Dueñas, *Bolero,* p. 14.

61. Orovio, *El bolero latino,* p. 8.

62. Dueñas, *Bolero,* pp. 16–17.

63. Interview with Agustín Lara Museum director and composer Guillermo Salamanca Herraga, June 24, 2006, Port of Veracruz, Veracruz. Adela Pineda Franco, "The Cuban Bolero and Its Transculturation to Mexico: The Case of Agustín Lara," and Radamés Giro, "Los pasos perdidos del bolero cubano," *El Nacional* (Mexico City), Janurary 17, 1994.

64. Elena Tamargo et al., *Bolero: clave del corazón,* p. 72; Dueñas, *Bolero,* pp. 18–19.

65. Interview with Guillermo Salamanca Herraga, June 24, 2006, Port of Veracruz, Veracruz. Salamanca Herraga describes early boleros by Cárdenas as "more ballad-like in style" rather than what would later appear in Lara's music. Liner notes to CD "La voz y guitarra de Guty Cárdenas: El ruiseñor yucateco," Mexico City: Discos Corasón, 1993, CO 004.

66. Garrido calls it "Concurso de canciones mexicanas." Garrido, *Historia de la musica popular en México,* p. 60. Moreno Rivas (p. 116) and Armando Pous (liner notes to "Guty Cárdenas: Grabaciones 1928–1930 restoradas") both list the event as taking place on August 19, 1927. For his part, Dueñas suggests sometime in July, Bolero (p. 19).

67. Liner notes to CD "Guty Cárdenas: Grabaciones 1928–1930," Mexico City: ICREM-003, 1999. Guty's boyhood friend Chalín Cámara says that Tata Nacho had invited Cárdenas to Mexico City for a song contest that he had organized. Liner notes to CD "La voz y guitarra de Guty Cárdenas: El ruiseñor yucateco," Mexico City: Discos Corasón, 1993.

68. "Alma criolla," "Nunca," "Presentimiento," "Qusiera," "Aléjate," "Si yo pudiera," "Para olvidarte," "a que negar," "Dios te bendiga," "Caminante del Mayab," "Yucalpetén," and "Xtabay" rank among his most famous recordings. Pablo Dueñas, *Historia documental del bolero mexicano,* p. 190; Jaime Rico Salazar, *Cien años de boleros,* p. 115.

69. Loaeza and Granados, *Mi novia, la tristeza* (Mexico City: Océano, 2008), p. 172. There exists an anecdote that that the same Vigil y Robles similarly turned down the chance to record some of Lara's early material when presented with the opportunity a few years later. This charge, however, remains unsubstantiated.

70. Cárdenas recorded some of Lara's earliest songs. Sergio Nuño, liner notes to "Guty Cárdenas: Grabaciones 1928–1930," Mexico City: ICREM-003, 1999; Zac Salem, liner notes for "La voz y guitarra de Guty Cárdenas: El ruiseñor yucateco," Mexico City: Discos Corasón, 1993, CD CO004.

71. www.depeliculasgratis.com/pelicula/la-dama-atrevida.

72. De la Peza Casares, *El bolero y la educación sentimental en México*, pp. 135–39.

73. De la Peza Casares, *El bolero y la educación sentimental en México*, pp. 24–29. Carlos Monsiváis briefly discusses how the romantic poetry of Amado Nervo and others was carefully memorized and recited so as to cultivate one's identity as a learned and spiritual person. Carlos Monsiváis, "Agustín Lara: El harem ilusorio (Notas a partir de la memorización de la letra de 'Farolito')," in *Amor perdido*, (Mexico City: Ediciones Era, 1977), pp. 63–64. For an attempt at a more universal cataloguing of romantic language, gesture, and interaction see Roland Barthes, *A Lover's Discourse, Fragments*, trans. Richard Howard (New York: Hill and Wang, 1978).

74. Mark Couture, "The Importance of Being Agustín Lara: Cursilería, Machismo and Modernity," *Studies in Latin American Popular Culture*, vol. 20 (2000), p. 79.

75. Mario Martín-Flores, "Nineteenth-Century Prose Fiction," trans. David William Foster, in David William Foster (ed.), *Mexican Literature: A History* (Austin: University of Texas Press, 1994), p. 126; Antonio Plaza, *Album de Corazón: Poesías Completas de Antonio Plaza* (Mexico City: Casas Editoriales, 1899), pp. 84–88; Carlos Monsiváis, "Profetas de Un Nuevo Mundo: Vida Urbana, Modernidad y Alternidad en América Latina (1880–1920)," in Carlos Monsiváis, *Aires de Familia: Cultura y sociedad en América Latina* (Barcelona: Editorial Anagrama, 2000), pp. 181–210.

76. Biographical information on Nervo was drawn from a newspaper clip file at the Instituto Nacional de Bellas Artes [INBA] Centro Nacional de Información y Promoción de la Literatura, Mexico City.

77. Amberson Imbert quoted in Gerald Martin, "Literature, music and the visual arts, 1870–1930," in Leslie Bethell (ed.), *A Cultural History of Latin America: Literature, Music and the Visual Arts in the 19th and 20th Centuries* (Cambridge: Cambridge University Press, 1998), p. 66.

78. Imbert, "Literature, music and the visual arts," p. 66

79. Ibid., p. 69.

80. "El prismo roto," *Crónica*, October 15, 2000.

81. Recent reconsiderations of Nervo include Carlos Monsiváis, "Yo te bendigo vida," *Contenido*, November 1, 2003, pp. 118–44.

82. Alaíde Foppa, "Mujer Divina," in *Agustín, rencuentro con lo sentimental*, p. 117. Allegedly, Lara's song "Mujer divina" was written for his friend Celia Montalván just before she and her sister Issa Marcué returned to Mexico from a stay in Paris in the mid-1930s. Unidentified clipping, Salvador Lara Scrapbooks, Casita Blanca de Agustín Lara, Boca del Río, Veracruz (hereafter SLS), vol. 15.

83. Martín-Flores, "Nineteenth-Century Prose Fiction," pp. 127–29; Casteñeda, *Balance de Agustín Lara*, pp. 100–01; Carlos Monsiváis, "Agustín Lara: El harem ilusorio," in *Amor perdido*, pp. 70–71; Carlos Monsiváis, *Mexican Postcards*, trans. John Kraniauskas (London: Verso Press, 1997), p. 182.

84. Monsiváis, *Mexican Postcards*, p. 170.

85. See testimony as to the centrality of bolero in Juan Carlos H. Vera and Mauricio Sarabia Garrido (eds.), *El bolero en mi vida* (Mexico City: Dirección General de Culturas Populares, 1991).

86. María del Carmen de la Peza Casares, *El bolero y la educación sentimental en México*, p. 406. The term "lovers' discourse" is borrowed from Roland Barthes.

87. Others, more recently, worked to adapt the tradition to more contemporary situations—as one hears today in the popular *narcocorrido* (drug trafficking related) subgenre. Still, the early twentieth century saw the emergence of a Mexican bolero that differed both musically and lyrically in that it dealt with contemporary urban world. Mark Pedelty, *Musical Ritual in Mexico City*, pp. 139–79, and Mark Couture, "The Importance of Being Agustín Lara: Cursilería, Machismo and Modernity, pp. 69–80.

88. John Lear, "Space and Class in the Porfirian Capital, 1884–1910," *Journal of Urban History* 22:4 (May 1996), p. 455.

89. Patrice Elizabeth Olsen, "Artifacts of Revolution: Architecture, Society and Politics in Mexico City, 1920–1940," PhD thesis, Pennsylvania State University History Department, 1998. Of course, urban renewal during the 1920s led to a number of complications while also exacerbating the already stark contrasts in standards of living.

90. Anita Brenner, *The Wind that Swept Mexico* (Austin: University of Texas Press, 1942), p. 80.

## Chapter 2

1. Epazote (aka wormseed or Jesuit's tea) is a Mexican herb used for cooking. Besides its savory flavor, it is used to reduce flatulence caused by ingesting legumes.

2. Quoted in Jesús Flores y Escalante, *Salón México: Historia documental y gráfica del danzón en México* (Mexico City: Asociación Mexicana de Estudios Fonográficos, 1993), p. 47.

3. Copies of Lara's birth certificate are on file in the Colección Juan Antonio Pérez Simón (hereafter JAPS), Archivo Agustín Lara, Carpeta #1, "Documentos Personales." The JAPS collection also contains a handful of family photographs, including a picture from his parents' wedding as well as photos of Agustín in 1898 and 1900 (the latter with the inscription "three years old"). Carpeta "Fotografias familiares." Lara's Mexico City birth certificate and baptismal records are also reproduced in Gabriel Abaroa Martínez, *El flaco de oro* (Mexico City: Editorial Planeta, 1993), pp. 12–13. Despite the existence of these documents, many still fervently assert that the musician was born in Tlacotalpan. Mónica Barrón Echauri, personal communication, November 22, 2008. Lara and Tlacotalpan.

4. Abaroa Martínez, *El flaco de oro*, pp. 12–25; Javier Ruiz Rueda, *Agustín Lara: Vida y pasiones* (Mexico City: Editorial Novaro, 1976), pp. 21–24; Paco Ignacio Taibo I, *La música de Agustín Lara en el cine* (Mexico City: UNAM, 1984), p. 27; Guadalupe Loaeza and Pável Granados, *Mi novia, la tristeza* (Mexico City: Océano, 2008), pp. 245, 330. See also María Teresa Lara in Eugenio Méndez (ed.), *Agustín, rencuentro con lo sentimental* (Mexico City: Editorial Domés, 1980), pp. 197–98.

5. Libretto by Alberto Michel. On Castro see Ricardo Miranda, "Los valses de Ricardo Castro: música de raro encantamiento," *Revista de Investigación Musical Heterofonía* (Mexico City: Órgano del Centro Nacional de Investigación, Documentación e Información Musical, Instituto Nacional de Bellas Artes [INBA], July–December 2007), pp. 9–26.

6. Ruiz Rueda, *Agustín Lara: Vida y pasiones*, pp. 24–27; Abaroa Martínez, *El flaco de oro*, 20–22; "Agustín por Agustín," in *Agustín: Rencuentro con lo sentimental*, p. 176; *La Vida de Agustín Lara*, nos. 1, 2. Published initially in 1965, *Vida de Agustín Lara*, issue #1, gives production credit to Antonio Gutiérrez, Jorge P. Valdés, Gustavo Vidal, Gabriel Madrid, and Guillermo Yépez, whereas issue #135 lists Ruben González, Jorge Avina, Gustavo Vidal, A. Acosta, and Gabriel Madrid.

7. Lara quoted in Abaroa Martínez, *El flaco de oro*, p. 22.

8. *Vida de Agustín Lara*, no. 3; "Agustín por Agustín," *Agustín: rencuentro con lo sentimental*, pp. 178–79; Ruiz Rueda, *Agustín Lara: Vida y pasiones*, pp. 29–33; June Kay, *Las siete vidas de Agustín Lara*, trans. F. de Riba Millon (Mexico City: El Universal Gráfico, 1964), pp. 31–45.

9. Ruiz Rueda, *Agustín Lara: Vida y pasiones*, pp. 39–41; Abaroa Martínez, *El flaco de oro*, p. 25; *Vida de Agustín Lara*, nos. 4, 5, 6; Lara, "La vida íntima de un gran músico," p. 53.

10. Abaroa Martínez, *El flaco de oro*, pp. 27–30; Ruiz Rueda, *Agustín Lara: Vida y pasiones*, pp. 42–46. Loaeza and Granados do not stipulate what bordello Lara first took up work in as a teenager but instead rely on the composer's own testimony in affirming that by 1922 he was performing at a high-end bordello called "Córdoba," owned by the infamous Francisca "la Paca" Betancourt. *Mi novia, la tristeza*, p. 339. On the association between prostitution and musical entertainers see, for example, Alan Lomax, *Mr. Jelly Roll: The Fortunes of Jelly*

*Roll Morton, New Orleans Creole and "Inventor of Jazz"* (Berkeley: University of California Press, 1973), pp. 41–109.

11. Carlos Monsiváis, "Agustín Lara: El harem ilusorio," in *Amor Perdido* (Mexico City: Biblioteca Era, 1977), p. 66. Loaeza and Granados, *Mi novia, la tristeza*, pp. 339–41. For details regarding prostitution in Mexico City and various official efforts to regulate the trade see Katherine Elaine Bliss, *Compromised Positions: Prostitution, Public Health and Gender Politics in Revolutionary Mexico City* (University Park: Pennsylvania State University Press, 2001). Patronizing a bordello—at least a higher-class bordello—was not just about sex. For men, it also constituted a way of socializing with friends and associates. A middle-class or elite man's visit to a brothel served as an important rite of passage. Bliss, *Compromised Positions*, p. 47.

12. Bliss, *Compromised Positions*, pp. 66–70.

13. Among the more recent commentaries on the Mexico City erotic entertainment and sex trade is a series of short essays by travel writer David Lida. See his *First Stop in the New World: Mexico City, the Capital of the Twenty-First Century* (New York: Riverhead Books, 2008); chapters "Sex Capital" and "The Last Cabaret."

14. Alejandro Aura, *La hora íntima de Agustín Lara* (Mexico City: Cal y Arena, 1990), pp. 21–23.

15. Abaroa Martínez, *El flaco de oro*, pp., 26–30; Ruiz Rueda, *Agustín Lara: Vida y pasiones*, pp. 39–47; *Vida de Agustín Lara*, no. 8.

16. Ruiz Rueda, *Agustín Lara: Vida y pasiones*, pp. 44–45; Abaroa Martínez, *El flaco de oro*, pp. 31–32; *Vida de Agustín Lara*, no. 9. On the Decena Trágica see Alan Knight, *The Mexican Revolution* (Lincoln: University of Nebraska Press, 1986), vol. 1, pp. 482–90; John Womack, "The Mexican Revolution," in Leslie Bethell (ed.), *Mexico Since Independence* (Cambridge: Cambridge University Press, 1985, 1991), pp. 138–40; and Michael J. Gonzáles, *The Mexican Revolution: 1910–1940* (Albuquerque: University of New Mexico Press, 2002), pp. 92–99.

17. Agustín Lara, "La vida íntima de un gran músico 'con alma de pirata,'" *Life en español*, January 15, 1968, p. 55.

18. Remembering these days in 1968, Lara wrote that he took a train to Veracruz and then went south to Tlacotalpan where he enjoyed a short vacation before returning to Mexico City. Agustín Lara, "La vida íntima de un gran músico," pp. 55–56. Not surprisingly, Lara's 1968 recollections gloss over the details of his leaving the academy. Instead, he tells the story of losing one of the school's horses after going on a date with a young woman named Amalia.

19. Ramos, "Notas para una rapsodia," in *Agustín, rencuentro con lo sentimental*, p. 21; "Agustín por Agustín," in *Agustín: rencuentro con lo sentimental*, p. 180; Abaroa Martínez, *El flaco de oro*, p. 37–38; Ruiz Rueda, *Agustín Lara: Vida y pasiones*, pp. 46–49; *Vida de Agustín Lara*, nos. 11, 12, 13.

20. Alan Knight, "Popular Culture and the Revolutionary State in Mexico, 1910–1940," *Hispanic American Historical Review*, Vol. 74, No. 3 (August, 1994) pp. 393–444.

21. Roger D. Hanson, *The Politics of Mexican Development* (Baltimore: The Johns Hopkins University Press, 1971), pp. 39–40.

22. James Wilkie's 1967 study attempting to assess the degree to which the revolution promoted a reduction in Mexico's "poverty index" concluded that despite increases in the GDP during the 1920s and the 1930s, significant reductions in poverty levels began only after 1940. James Wilkie, *The Mexican Revolution: Federal Expenditure and Social Change since 1910* (Berkeley: University of California Press, 1967). From national reports, evidence suggesting positive economic growth comes from the fact that GDP per capita increased gradually during the 1920s and then nearly doubled during the 1930s. Clark W. Reynolds, "The Structure and Growth of the Mexican Economy, 1900–1960," cited in Wilkie, p. 261. For a discursive analysis of middle-class Latin Americans see David S. Parker, *The Idea of the Middle Class: White Collar Workers and Peruvian Society, 1900–1950* (University Park: Pennsylvania State University Press, 1998) and Brian P. Owensby, *Intimate Ironies: Modernity and the Making of Middle Class Lives in Brazil* (Palo Alto: Stanford University Press, 2001).

23. Katherine Elaine Bliss and Ann S. Blum, "Adolescence, Sex, and the Gendered Experience of Public Space in Mexico City," in William E. French and Katherine Elaine Bliss (eds.), *Gender, Sexuality and Power in Latin America since Independence* (Lanham, MD: Rowman and Littlefield, 2007), p. 165.

24. One of the better recent studies of this process is Rick A. López, *Crafting Mexico: Intellectuals, Artisans and the State after the Revolution* (Durham, NC: Duke University Press, 2010). Related discussion in English can be found in Dina Berger and Andrew Grant Wood, *Holiday in Mexico: Critical Reflections on Tourism and Tourist Encounters* (Durham, NC: Duke University Press, 2010) as well as Gilbert Joseph, Anne Rubenstein, and Eric Zolov (eds.), *Fragments of a Golden Age: The Politics of Culture in Mexico since 1940* (Durham, NC: Duke University Press, 2001) and John Mraz, *Looking for Mexico: Modern Visual Culture and National Identity* (Durham, NC: Duke University Press, 2009).

25. Yolanda Moreno Rivas, *Historia de la música popular mexicana* (Mexico City: Alianza Editorial Mexicana, 1979) p. 17. See also Richard Miranda, *Manuel M. Ponce: Ensayo sobre su vida y obra* (Mexico City: Consejo nacional para la cultura y las artes, 1998) as well as Jorge Velasco and Ricardo Miranda on Ponce in Emilio Casares Rodicio (ed.), *Diccionario de la música española e hispanoamericana*, vol. 8 (Madrid: Sociedad General de Autores y Editores, 1999), p. 57.

26. For a discussion of Ponce in the larger debate over national music see Alejandro Madrid, *Sounds of the Modern Nation: Music, Culture and Ideas in Post-Revolutionary Mexico* (Philadelphia: Temple University Press, 2009) as well as Richard Miranda, *Manuel M. Ponce: Ensayo sobre su vida y obra.*

27. In the mid-1920s, avant-garde composers who identified themselves as "serious" considered this work done by mere "arregladores" (arrangers) and generally turned against this particular tendency. In September 1926, several met at the First National Congress of Music in Mexico City to discuss the question of a national music. See Madrid, *Sounds of the Modern Nation*, pp. 111–37.

28. Carlos Monsiváis, *Mexican Postcards*, trans. John Kraniauskas (London: Verso Press, 1997), p. 173 and passim.

29. Colección JAPS, Archivo Agustín Lara, Carpeta #6 "Textos de Agustín Lara," unidentified writing.

30. He is buried in the Francés de la Piedad Cemetary near Cuauhtémoc Avenue in Mexico City. Loaeza and Granados, *Mi novia, la tristeza*, p. 339.

31. Abaroa Martínez, *El flaco de oro*, pp. 41–42. In November 1970 Esther found herself in the same hospital as Lara lay dying. Reporters soon took relish in the coincidence by interviewing Esther about her former husband. Rivas Elorriaga enthusiastically denounced the idea that Lara came from Veracruz. She also told television reporter Jacobo Zabludowsky that she and Lara had produced a child, which they named Agustín, but that the boy had died shortly after birth. Irma Fuentes, "La primer mujer que se casó con Agustín revela la otra imagen de él," *Novedades*, November 9, 1970.

32. Ruiz Rueda, *Agustín Lara: Vida y pasiones*, pp. 54–60; Abaroa Martínez, *El flaco de oro*; pp. 43–46. Flores y Escalante locates this establishment at 74 Cuauhtemoctzín and notes that it was overseen by a woman named Margarita Pérez. Flores y Escalante, *Imagenes del Danzón, Iconografia del danzón en México* (Mexico City: Asociación Mexicana de Estudios Fonográficos, 1994), p. 78. The same name and address is presented in Armando de María y Campos, "Agustín Lara, se presenta como actor, cara, cruz y canto del principe de la canción Mexicana," *Novedades*, August 5, 1948.

33. Ruiz Rueda, *Agustín Lara: Vida y pasiones*, pp. 54–60; Abaroa Martínez, *El flaco de oro*, pp. 43–46.

34. Abaroa Martínez, *El flaco de oro*, pp. 46–48; Ruiz Rueda, *Agustín Lara: Vida y pasiones*, pp. 65–66; Flores y Escalante, *Salón México: Historia documental y gráfica del danzón en México* (Mexico City: Associación Mexicana de Estudios Fonograficos, 1993), p. 152, note 44 mentions June Kay, *Las siete vidas*, but her mention of the attack is slight and does not offer a specific date. June Kay, *Las siete vidas de Agustín Lara*, p. 133; Loaeza and Granados, *Mi novia, la tristeza*, p. 346. The brothel at 61 Libertad was allegedly owned by a woman named Rosario. Flores y Escalante, following June Kay as well as a radio

Notes to Pages 26–29

interview with Lara realized in 1958, suggests that Lara fell victim to the sex worker's attack at a place title "El Jacalito" located at 90 Santa María la Redonda. Flores y Escalante, *Salón México*, p. 152, note 44. A 1997 article on Lara identifies the bordello as located on or near "Meave" Street. Rubén García Cruz, "Agustín Lara, el día que nació un a leyenda," *El Nacional*, October 30, 1997. Loaeza and Granados assert that Lara suffered the attack in 1923. They speculate that he may have been knifed at La Marquesa although they do not say for sure. *Mi novia, la tristeza*, p. 339.

35. Archivo Histórico del Distrito Federal (hereafter AHDF), "Sanidad" public health records—which run until October 1920—suggest that 61 Libertad and another bordello in the Santa María la Redonda area were owned by a woman named María Martínez. Abaroa Martínez, *El flaco de oro*, pp. 45–46 and José Galindo in *Agustín, rencuentro con lo sentimental*, p. 199 refer to the owner as "Rosario."

36. On Ortiz Tirado see Enriqueta de Parodi (Enriqueta Montaño Peralta), *Alfonso Ortiz Tirado: su vida en la ciencia y en el arte* (Mexico City: s.n., 1964). This work is largely an anecdotal history of Ortiz Tirado and, somewhat strangely, makes little mention of Lara. María Grever is discussed briefly, pp. 76–87.

37. Agustín Lara, "Como los conocí," Colección JAPS, Archivo Agustín Lara. Ortíz Tirado's interpretations of works by composers such as María Grever, Gonzalo Curiel, and José Sabre Marroquín helped elevate them to esteemed status. Ortiz Tirado dedicated a portion of his earnings to establishing and maintaining an orthopedic clinic in Mexico City where, word was, he attended to painter Frida Kahlo by providing her with a reinforced corset for her many back and leg problems. Loaeza and Granados, *Mi novia, la tristeza*, pp. 206–07.

38. Loaeza and Granados, *Mi novia, la tristeza*, p. 346.

39. Abaroa Martínez, *El flaco de oro*, pp. 46–48; Ruiz Rueda, *Agustín Lara: Vida y pasiones*, pp. 65–67; Angelina Bruschetta, in *Agustín, rencuentro con lo sentimental*, p. 206; June Kay, *Las siete vidas de Agustín Lara*, p. 150; Lara, "La vida íntima de un gran músico," p. 56. Taibo I suggests that Lara was attacked in 1927 and fled to Puebla that year. Taibo I, *La música de Agustín Lara en el cine*, pp. 30–31. *Vida de Agustín Lara*, no. 45 recounts that "Marichú" attacked him with a nail file after hearing from Lara that a former boyfriend named Hugo was engaged.

40. Flores y Escalante, *Salón México*, p. 152, note 4.

41. Abaroa Martínez, *El flaco de oro*, p. 47. Pável Granados, *Canciones*, p. 379 notes the song not being recorded.

42. Abaroa Martínez, *El flaco de oro*, pp. 48–49; Ruiz Rueda, *Agustín Lara: Vida y pasiones*, pp. 67–70; June Kay, *Las siete vidas de Agustín Lara*, p. 151; Loaeza and Granados, *Mi novia, la tristeza*, p. 330. Doña María and Lara's father Joaquín had moved in 1920 to Tlatlauquite-pec, Puebla.

43. Flores y Escalante, *Salón México*, p. 96. Ruiz Rueda mentions Garbanzo, but does not offer a specific date when he and Lara collaborated. *Agustín Lara: Vida y pasiones*, p. 54. Loaeza and Granados write—following Lara's friend José Galindo in *Agustín, rencuentro con lo sentimental*, p. 201—that Agustín and Garbanzo met in 1921 and cocomposed a piece titled "Si alguna vez comprendes." Curiously, Galindo offers no date. *Mi novia, la tristeza*, pp. 341–42.

44. Abaroa Martínez, *El flaco de oro*, pp. 42–44; Flores y Escalante, *Salón México*, p. 96; Paco Pildora, "Revolviendo papeles," *Notiver*, no date, Fondo Paco Pildora, file 4E, AMV.

45. Abaroa Martínez, *El flaco de oro*, pp. 43–44; Loaeza and Granados, *Mi novia, la tristeza*, p. 341.

46. Flores y Escalante, *Salón México*, pp. 95–98.

47. See Flores y Escalante, *Salón México*, pp. 101–11 for details on various "decency" campaigns beginning in the late teens, as well as Katherine Bliss, *Compromised Positions*, pp. 1–5.

48. Jorge Loyo, "La vida íntima de Agustin Lara," *El Ilustrado*, April 26, 1934, p. 37.

49. "Agustín por Agustín," in *Agustín, rencuentro con lo sentimental*, p. 176.

50. See, for example, Toña la Negra, in *Agustín, rencuentro con lo sentimental*, p. 249.

51. On Montalbán see Carlos Monsiváis, *Celia Montalbán (te brindas, voluptuosa e impudente)* (Mexico City: SEP, 1982); Armando de María y Campos, *Las tandas del Principal* (Mexico

City: Editorial Diana, 1989); Museo Nacional de Culturas Populares, *El país de las tandas: Teatro de revista, 1910–1940* (Coyoacán, Mexico: Dirección General de Culturas Populares/SEP, 1984); and Enrique Alonso, *María Conesa* (Mexico City: Océano, 1987).

52. Two different recordings of this song can be found at the UCLA Strachwitz Frontera Collection of Mexican and Mexican American Recordings, http://frontera.library.ucla.edu.

53. Alberto Dallal, *La danza en México, La danza escénica popular, 1877–1930* (Mexico City: UNAM, 1995), pp. 157–59. For a time Montalván was allegedly the lover of President Obregón's Secretary of War Enrique Estrada. Pablo Dueñas, *Las divas en el teatro de revista mexicano* (Mexico City: Asociación Mexicana de Estudios Fonográficos, 1994), p. 80. See also Museo Nacional de Culturas Populares, *El país de las tandas: Teatro de revista, 1910–1940*.

54. June Kay, *Las siete vidas de Agustín Lara* p. 81.

55. "Para siempre," 2001 Festival de Agustín Lara, www.agustin-lara.com/txtembrador.htm; Robert McKee Irwin, *Mexican Masculinities* (Minneapolis: University of Minnesota Press, 2003), pp. xvii-xix, 27 and passim. On the more complex realities behind the stereotypical "Mexican macho" see Matthew C. Gutmann, *The Meanings of Macho: Being a Man in Mexico City* (Berkeley: University of California Press, 1996) as well as the essays collected in Matthew Gutmann (ed.), *Changing Men and Masculinities in Latin America* (Durham, NC: Duke University Press, 2003). It is said that other men did not view Lara as a rival but as a brother who, above all, sang to his muses and wholly dedicated himself to his art. "Para siempre," 2001 Festival de Agustín Lara, www.agustin-lara.com/txtembrador.htm.

56. Oscar LeBlanc (pseudonym of Demetrio Bolaños Espinosa), "Agustín Lara: sus amores y sus canciones," *El Universal*, November 9, 1970. The early seventeenth-century Spanish courtier Don Miguel de Mañara—a libertine who chased after cloistered nuns—may have served as the original inspiration for the legendary character of Don Juan. Philip IV provided the foundation, for it was he who gained notoriety for presiding over a court known for its sexual adventures, illegitimate children, and all-too-frequent inbreeding. Over the course of his career, the king sired some thirty bastard children but only recognized one male child, whom he had with actress María Calderón. They named him "Don Juan." Don Juan traveled widely throughout Europe and, like his father, had many lovers while his hapless half-brother Charles II ("the bewitched") became heir to the throne and the final Hapsburg monarch in Spain. Carlos Fuentes, *The Buried Mirror: Reflections on Spain and the New World* (Boston: Houghton Mifflin, 1992), pp. 182–88. The legendary character of Don Juan first appeared in Tirso de Molina's 1634 play *El burlador de Sevilla*. This was followed by Molière's 1665 *Dom Juan ou le festin de pierre*, Mozart's 1787 *Don Giovanni*, Byron's 1821 *Don Juan*, Pushkin's 1830 *Kamenniy Gost,*' José Zorilla's 1844 *Don Juan Tenorio,* and Baudelaire's 1861 *Don Juan aux enfers*. Richard Strauss wrote a tone poem titled *Don Juan* in 1889. Articulated in these and other works, the idea of Don Juan was that of the Iberian *hidalgo*, meaning literally "son of something" or inheritor, man of honor, nobleman. Don Juan's image was basically that of consummate seducer who has one affair after another. He was portrayed as a man virtually obsessed with women—or at least the idea of being in love.

57. Ruiz Rueda, *Agustín Lara: Vida y pasiones*, p. 70; Abaroa Martínez, *El flaco de oro*, p. 53; Ramos, "Notas para una rapsodia," in *Agustín, rencuentro con lo sentimental*, pp. 26–27. On the rise of dancings see Aurelio de los Reyes, 1993, *Cine y sociedad en México*, Vol. 1, (Mexico City: UNAM, 1996), p. 290 and Alberto Dallal, *El "dancing" mexicano* (Mexico City: Secretaria de Educación Pública, 1987), pp. 93–113. The term "active environments" is adapted from sociologist Erving Goffman's "action environment," used by Erenberg to describe cabarets in New York City. See Erenberg, *Steppin' Out: New York Nightlife and the Transformation of American Culture* (Westport, CT: Greenwood Press, 1981), pp. 113–45.

58. Lara quoted in *Agustín, rencuentro con lo sentimental*, p. 182. See also Santiago X. Sierra, "Viñetas frívolas: Nuestra música," unidentified newspaper clipping, SLC vol. 6. On the history of jazz in Mexico see Alain Derbez, *El jazz en México: Datos para una historia* (Mexico City: Fondo de Cultura Económica, 2001), especially pp. 35–44. New York City's

dance craze had flowered some ten years earlier (roughly between 1912–1916), as couples looking for something more exciting than the waltz moved to the turkey trot, Texas Tommy, Foxtrot, tango, bunny hug, and lame duck, among others. Many of the new dances, like the Charleston that would soon follow, had their origins in African American culture. Erenberg, *Steppin' Out*, pp. 150–58. Combined with the proliferation of cheap theaters, movie houses, and other urban attractions such as the amusement park, these leisure pursuits contributed significantly to the demise of Victorian culture in US cities. See Lary May, *Screening Out the Past: The Birth of Mass Culture and the Motion Picture Industry* (New York: Oxford University Press, 1980), pp. 34–42 and Kathy Peiss, *Cheap Amusements: Working Women and Leisure in Turn-of-the-Century New York*. Philadelphia: Temple University Press, 1986), pp. 88–163.

59. "The First Jazz Records," www.redhotjazz.com/jazz1917.html. By the late 1920s, Mexico City played host to the sweet-sounding dance music ensemble led by Paul "the King of Jazz" Whiteman. Yet while Whiteman may have considered himself a jazz bandleader and created important opportunities for fledgling musicians such as Bix Beiderbecke, Eddy Lang, Red Nichols, and many others, his work is generally considered overly commercial. Ted Gioia, *The History of Jazz* (New York: Oxford University Press, 1997), p. 88 and passim. Regular advertisements for the Paul Whiteman Band in Mexico City appear in *El Universal* during the late 1920s.

60. "Agustín por Agustín," in *Agustín, rencuentro con lo sentimental*, p. 182.

61. For various reactions to the music in Mexico City see Derbez, *El jazz en México*, pp. 36–42. Considering the dissemination of early American "jazz" in France, Michael Dregni describes how gypsy guitarist Django Reinhardt, although powerfully drawn to the liberating sounds and improvisational elements of the music, nevertheless kept his distance from the clamorous approach of early white ensembles such as Nick La Rocca's Original Dixieland Jazz Band with its "furious tempos fired by [drummers'] heat and instrumental histrionics, from barnyard mews to howling gimcrackery." Michael Dregni, *Django: The Life and Music of a Gypsy Legend* (New York: Oxford University Press, 2004), p. 41.

62. Lerdo de Tejada interview in *El Universal*, November 20, 1921, quoted in Derbez, *El jazz en México*, p. 41.

63. "Agustín por Agustín," in *Agustín, rencuentro con lo sentimental*, p. 182; Jorge Loyo, "La vida íntima de Agustin Lara," *El Ilustrado*, April 26, 1934, p. 37.

64. Luis de Valle, "Juan de Arvizu o el secreto del micrófono," *Jueves de Excélsior*, December 18, 1930. On the early history of blues see Peter C. Muir, *Long Lost Blues: Popular Blues in America, 1850–1920* (Champaign: University of Illinois Press, 2009).

65. Loyo, "La vida intima de Agustin Lara," *El Ilustrado*, April 26, 1934, p. 37.

66. Loyo, "La vida intima de Agustin Lara," p. 37. See also Luis Sandi, "Agustín Lara y la canción mexicana," *Música: Revista Mexicana*, December 1930–January 1931, pp. 46–49. Basically, Sandi considers the influence of Cuban and Colombian music agreeable but, like Lara, casts a more critical eye on the character and tone of US jazz and Argentine tango.

67. Luis de Valle, "Juan de Arvizu o el secreto del micrófono," *Jueves de Excélsior*, December 18, 1930.

68. Chavela Vargas, *Y si quieres saber de mi pasado*. (Madrid: Aguilar/Santillana Ed., 2001, p. 130.)

69. The establishment's name invokes the 1862 historical novel *Salammbô* by French writer Gustave Flaubert, set in third century B.C.E. Carthage. Thanks to Guadalupe Loeza and Pável Granados for alerting me to this reference.

70. Angelina died in 1985. Mónica Barrón Echauri, *Álbum fotográfico de Agustín Lara* (Mexico City: Océano, 2008), p. 8.

71. Angelina Bruschetta, *Agustín Lara y yo: 1928–1938* (Xalapa, Veracruz: Author's edition, 1979), pp. 8–9. Angelina's father had died when she was three years old.

72. Mario Arturo Ramos (ed.), *Agustín Lara: Cien años, cien canciones* (Mexico City: Océano, 2000), p. 60.

73. "Imposible" was first recorded by the Trío Garnica Ascencio in New York on October 2, 1928 for Victor Records (Victor 81786). Agustín himself would not record the composition until 1948. Granados lists the song with Anfión 10-122 (Granados, *Canciones*, p. 25) while

Dueñas and Flores y Escalante list RCA Victor 092076 catalogue 70-8339 as well as Anfión AB-192 (catalogue no.) 10-122. Pablo Dueñas and Jesús Flores y Escalante, *Discografía de Agustín Lara*, November 2008, unpublished discography, collection of the author. Lara also mentioned to Angelina that he had seven other compositions to his name including "Copla," "Adiós Nicanor," "Ojos negros," "Boca chiquita," Reliquia," "De noche," and "Marucha." Angelina Bruschetta, in *Agustín, rencuentro con lo sentimental*, pp. 204–06; Bruschetta, *Agustín Lara y yo*, pp. 12–14. Carlos Monsiváis believes that Lara originally composed the song in 1926. Elizabeth Velasco Contreras, "Carlos Monsiváis habla de Agustín Lara," *Revista de Revistas*, November 19, 1999, p. 32.

74. Bruschetta, *Agustín Lara y yo*, pp 16–17. Curiously, Sofía claimed to have had Lara's own mother María Aguirre del Pino as one of her elementary school teachers.

75. Ramos, *Agustín Lara: Cien años, cien canciones*, p. 81.

76. "Orgullo" would be recorded in 1932 by Tito Guízar and the Orquesta Internacional de Eduardo Virgil y Robles for Victor Records (30309-A). Granados, *Canciones*, p. 27.

77. Bruschetta, *Agustín Lara y yo*, pp. 34–40.

78. Abaroa Martínez, *El flaco de oro*, pp. 55–56, 66, 72; Bruschetta, *Agustín Lara y yo*, pp. 42–60; *Vida de Agustín Lara*, nos. 52–56.

79. Other leading Mexican tenors who studied with Pierson included José Mojica, Pedro Vargas, and Alfonso Ortiz Tirado. Mojica later became a Franciscan friar after a storied operatic and screen career. His bestselling autobiography *Yo pecador* was translated into English as *I, a Sinner* (Chicago: Franciscan Herald Press, 1963). He appeared briefly at the end of the 1959 film version of *Yo pecador*. On Mojica see John Koegel, "Mexican Musicians in California and the United States, 1910–50," *Californa History*, vol 84, no. 1, (Fall 2006), pp. 14–20.

80. Luis de Valle, "Juan de Arvizu o el secreto del micrófono," *Jueves de Excélsior*, December 18, 1930; Elena Tamargo et al., *Bolero: Clave del corazón*, p. 92;(Mexico City: Alejo Peralta Fundación, 2004) José Octavio Sosa and Mónica Escobedo, *Dos siglos de ópera en México* (Mexico City: Secretaria de Educación Pública, 1988), 2 vols. No. 1, p. 260. I am indebted to John Koegel for this reference. On opera in Mexico, see also Edgar Ceballos, *La historia de México a través del teatro: Un siglo de contraste. La ópera, 1901–1925* (Mexico City: CONACULTA/Escenología, 2002).

81. Noemi Atamoros, "Yo descubrí a Agustín Lara en el Café Salambó dice Juan Arvizu." Unidentified newspaper article, October 4, 1972, clipping file collection, "Agustín Lara," Biblioteca Miguel Lerdo de Tejada (hereafter BLT), "Archivos Economicos." After working for four years with Lara, Arvizu would spend nearly twenty years living in Argentina where some say he compared favorably with the great Carlos Gardel.

82. Pável Granados, *XEW: 70 años en el aire* (Mexico City: Editorial Clío, 2000), p. 24; Loaeza and Granados, *Mi novia, la tristeza*, pp. 192–93.

83. Juan Arvizu, in *Agustín, rencuentro con lo sentimental*, p. 220; Noemi Atamoros, "Yo Descubrí a Agustín Lara en el Café Salambó dice Juan Arvizu," October 4, 1972, clip file collection; "Agustín Lara," BLT, "Archivos Economicos"; Ruiz Rueda, *Agustín Lara: Vida y pasiones*, pp. 73–74.

84. Juan Arvizu, in *Agustín, rencuentro con lo sentimental*, p. 220. Arvizu mentions "Beso" and "Sintiendo una pena." Arvizu's recollection of "Beso" might actually be the 1931 bolero "Besa," which he recorded in 1932 for Victor (30704). "Sintiendo una pena" was written in 1929 and recorded by Arvizu for Victor in 1929. Granados, *Canciones*, p. 55.

85. Agustín Lara, "Como los conocí," Colección JAPS.

86. "Chamaco" is slang for "boy." Jaime Rico Salazar, *Cien años de boleros* (Bogotá: Centro Editorial de Estudios Musicales, 1987), p. 111. Loaeza and Granados state that Sandoval was born in 1919. Loaeza and Granados, *Mi novia, la tristeza*, p. 219.

87. Some charged that Sandoval actually wrote the lyrics for Lara and that tragically, Agustín paid him with alcohol. Sandoval, of course, always denied this. Salazar, *Cien años de boleros*, p. 111. On Sandoval and his undocumented relationship with Lara see Loaeza and Granados, *Mi novia, la tristeza*, pp. 219–21.

88. Loaeza and Granados, *Mi novia, la tristeza*, p. 187.

89. Ruiz Rueda, *Vida y pasiones*, pp. 77–81; Abaroa Martínez, *El flaco de oro*, pp. 60–61; *Vida de Agustín Lara*, nos. 55, 64. Ramos claims the recording took place in 1927

(*Agustín Lara: Cien canciones, cien años*, p. 28). According to Abaroa Martínez, Azcárraga paid 45 pesos for the song. It is unclear whether Azcárraga purchased the publication and/ or recording rights as well. Loaeza and Granados write that Lara remained painfully poor and resorted to selling copies of the Trío Garnica Ascencio Victor disc in the street. *Mi novia, la tristeza*, p. 190. Abaroa Martínez as well as Loaeza and Granados write that a singer named José Rubio backed by the Adelaido Casteñeda orchestra had earlier recorded "Imposible" in Mexico City for the Artex label. Abaroa Martínez, *El flaco de oro*, p. 60–61; Loaeza and Granados, *Mi novia, la tristeza*, p. 184. Further, Loaeza and Granados assert that a Cuban singer named Pilar Arcos had realized another recording of the song with a singing group backing her called The Castillians. Allegedly, this took place without Lara's knowledge. Loaeza and Granados, *Mi novia, la tristeza*, p. 190. Angelina Bruschetta comments that Lara sold the rights to "Imposible" for 40 pesos and that the ensuing transcription of the song was written in a quite different *tiempo de danza* style. *Agustín Lara y yo*, p. 13.

90. Claudia Fernández and Andrew Paxman, *El Tigre: Emilio Azcárraga y su imperio Televisa* (Mexico City: Grijalbo, 2000, 2001), p. 42.
91. Granados, *XEW: 70 años en el aire*, p. 28; Fernández and Paxman, *El Tigre*, p. 43. See also Alex M. Zaragoza, *The Monterrey Elite and the Mexican State, 1880–1940* (Austin: University of Texas Press, 1988), pp. 140–43, who mentions in passing Azcárraga's participation in the Monterrey Rotary Club.
92. Granados, *XEW: 70 años en el aire*, p. 28. Fernández and Paxman say that Azcárraga first began selling automobiles in Monterrey before extending his dealerships to other cities. Fernández and Paxman, *El Tigre*, p. 43.
93. Pérez's parents nicknamed her "mocosita" (literally snot-nose, or, more kindly, rugrat) when she was young and the phrase seemed to have lived on among her bohemian friends. Loaeza and Granados write that Pérez suffered from a spinal deformity for which her pharmacy-owning father (and family) tried for some time to find suitable orthopedic and medical remedies. *Mi novia, la tristeza*, p. 178.
94. Loaeza and Granados, *Mi novia, la tristeza*, p. 177.
95. "Clavelito" was first recorded by Tito Guízar with guitar accompanient for Victor in 1930 (46683-A). Granados, *Canciones*, p. 35. Granados lists an undated, later recording of the song by Lara for Orfeón (LP-12-06) while Dueñas and Flores y Escalante indicate Lara having recorded "Clavelito" between 1957–59 for an album released in 1970 under the title "Agustín Lara" (Orfeón LP 12-653). They say the recordings were culled from the radio program "Momentos íntimos de Agustín Lara." Dueñas and Flores y Escalante, *Discografía*.
96. Ramos, *Agustín Lara: Cien años, cien canciones*, p. 40. Although he references the Renaissance/early Baroque musical-poetic form of the madrigal, it is unclear what Lara knew of this European singing tradition. Still, as a young man growing up in Mexico, the influence of European music and culture—despite the nationalist posturing of revolutionary elites—was never much in doubt. Madrigals, and their various New World derivations, were in the air.
97. Agustín Lara, "Como los conocí," Colección JAPS.
98. "Poco a poco" was never recorded. Granados, *Canciones*, p. 379.
99. Bruschetta, *Agustín Lara y yo*, pp. 31–33; Abaroa Martínez, *El flaco de oro*, p. 61; Ramos, "Notas para una rapsodia," in *Agustín, rencuentro con lo sentimental*, p. 27; *Vida de Agustín Lara*, nos. 60–62.
100. Álvarez later wrote the popular "Angelitos negros" (Little Black Angels) recorded by Alfonso Ortiz Tirado and Toña la Negra.
101. Bruschetta, *Agustín Lara y yo*, p. 61.
102. Granados, *Canciones*, p. 363.
103. Bruschetta, *Agustín Lara y yo*, pp. 61–63; Loaeza and Granados, *Mi novia, la tristeza*, pp. 190–92.
104. Publicity letter signed by W. Glass with Mexican Music Co. stationery announcing a tour on September 30, 1929. Salvador Lara Scrapbooks: Casita Blanca de Agustín Lara (hereafter SLS), vol. 12. Loaeza and Granados, *Mi novia, la tristeza*, p. 246.
105. Loaeza and Granados, *Mi novia, la tristeza*, p. 198. "Panzón" means potbelly. Soto was a high-profile actor on the Mexico City scene who often poked fun at politicians, labor leaders, and other revolutionary elites.

106. Politeama artists associated with Fernández at the time included Margarita Carbajal, Maruja Grifell, and dancer Eva Beltri under the name "Gran Companía de Revistas Modernas." Biographical information on Ana María's early years is particularly scant. Ads for a show at the Teatro Variedades in the Port of Veracruz for the Gran Companía de Revistas Modernas indicate that their tour appeared in the city in late December 1928. *El Dictamen* (Veracruz), December 9, 10, 1928.

107. Ana María Fernández, in *Agustín, rencuentro con lo sentimental*, p. 227. "Cuate" is buddy. "Cuatezón" can be translated to big drinking buddy. Beristáin skewered politicians of the day with the slurred speech of his "drunken Indian from Xochimilco" character. Jeffrey M. Pilcher, *Cantinflas and the Chaos of Mexican Modernity*, p. 13.

108. Ana María Fernández, in *Agustín, rencuentro con lo sentimental*, pp. 227–28; Granados, *XEW: 70 años en el aire*, p. 56. Fernández writes that after debuting with Beristáin in October 1929, she later, along with members of the audience after a performance by Lara and Arvizu, sang a version of the brand new song "Rosa." The composer observed the performance and subsequently asked her to be his interpreter. Granados writes of this as happening "one night in 1929," which I figure occurred very late in the year and just after "Rosa" had become popular. Monsiváis mentions that Minister of Education José Vasconcelos had commissioned Joaquín Beristáin (not to be confused with the early nineteenth-century composer, Joaquín Beristáin, 1817–1839) to develop a collection of songs that revealed the Mexican "popular soul." This work had begun under Manuel M. Ponce. Monsiváis, *Mexican Postcards*, p. 173.

109. Angelina mentions 50 pesos and then 10 pesos for each melody when delivered to the record company. Bruschetta, *Agustín Lara y yo*, pp. 64, 69. Many at the time also felt exploited by the incipient radio industry, which played records but did not necessarily pay royalties. Others lamented the fact that Mexican officials did little to enforce civil codes aimed at protecting artistic material. A.F.B., "Los fenicios del arte." Unidentified clipping, SLS, vol. 12.

110. Also known as *The Broadway Melody of 1929*, this was recorded on 16-inch phonographic disc process that played as the film projected. *El Dictamen*, November 9, 1929. The movie was the first sound film to win an Academy Award for Best Picture. It contained a Technicolor sequence that would inspire other musical theater films during the early 1930s. www.imdb.com/title/tt0019729.

111. *El Dictamen*, November 9, 1929.

112. *El Dictamen*, November 9, 1929.

113. Loaeza and Granados speculate that Lara had traveled previously to the port with his family—perhaps sometime in 1915—but this is uncertain. Loaeza and Granados, *Mi novia, la tristeza*, p. 339. That year Veracruz was still occupied by the Constitutionalist faction of the Revolution headed by Venustiano Carranza. The previous year the city had been bombarded and invaded by US forces. See Berta Ulloa, *Veracruz, capital de la nación, 1914–15* (Mexico City: Colegio de México/Estado de Veracruz, 1986) as well as Andrew Grant Wood, *Revolution in the Street, Women, Workers, and Urban Protest in Veracruz, 1870–1927* (Lanham, MD: Rowman and Littlefield/SR Books, 2001), pp. 21–45.

114. Bruschetta, *Agustín Lara y yo*, pp. 64–68.

115. Abaroa Martínez, *El flaco de oro*, pp. 73–74; *Vida de Agustín Lara*, no. 67. See also "Agustín Lara: Una revelación del arte musical mexicano" by Pinelo, unidentified clipping, SLS, vol.1. Colleagues in Xalapa once told me that "Lara allegedly was from several places in Mexico but the least surely must have been Tlacotalpan." Conversation with Olivia Domínguez Pérez and friends, Xalapa, Veracruz, June 26, 2002.

116. Lara's career would parallel other popular early twentieth-century artists such as tango singer Carlos Gardel, American Broadway great George Gershwin, Delta bluesmen Robert Johnson and Muddy Waters, and jazz pioneers Jelly Roll Morton and Louis Armstrong, whose uncertain beginnings (i.e., Armstrong saying he had been born on the fourth of July), would be manipulated in the service of myth. On Gardel see Simon Collier, *The Life, Times and Music of Carlos Gardel* (Pittsburgh: University of Pittsburgh Press, 1986). Robert Johnson's saga is chronicled in Robert Palmer, *Deep Blues* (New York: Penguin Books, 1981). Palmer also writes extensively on Muddy Waters. For a full biographical treatment

of Waters see Robert Gordon, *Can't Be Satisfied: The Life and Times of Muddy Waters* (Boston: Little, Brown and Company, 2002). Other inportant biographies of artists who might be compared to Lara include Alan Lomax, *Mister Jelly Roll: The Fortunes of Jelly Roll Morton, New Orleans Creole and "Inventor of Jazz"* (Berkeley: University of California Press, 1950), Gary Giddens, *Satchmo: The Genius of Louis Armstrong* (New York: DaCapo Press, 1988), and Edward Jablonski, *Gershwin: A Biography* (New York: DaCapo Press, 1998). For information on many of Brazil's late nineteenth/early twentieth-century musicians see Hermano Vianna, *The Mystery of Samba: Popular Music and National Identity in Brazil*, trans. John Charles Chasteen (Chapel Hill: University of North Carolina Press, 1999) and Bryan McCann, *Hello, Hello, Brazil: Popular Music in the Making of Modern Brazil* (Durham, NC: Duke University Press, 2004).

117. Bruschetta, *Agustín Lara y yo*, p. 55.

118. See the exposé on Lara and his "native" Tlacotalpan in "La tierra de Agustín Lara," *Jueves de Excélsior*, January 14, 1932 as well as his testimony in a series of interviews with North American journalist June Kay in the early 1960s. June Kay, *Las siete vidas de Agustín Lara*, trans. F. de Riba Millon (Mexico City: El Universal Gráfico, 1964), pp. 17–20. Her cover story on Lara in *Life* magazine also began with the claim of Tlacotalpan as the place of his birth. Agustín Lara, "La vida íntima de un gran músico 'con alma de pirata,'" *Life en español*, January 15, 1968, pp. 50–60. As recently as the fall of 2008, the myth of Lara as a veracruzano/jarocho lives on. During the proceedings leading up to the presentation of Guadalupe Loaeza and Pável Granados's three-volume luxury edition of *Mi novia, la tristeza*, representatives of the Veracruz governor's office insisted upon Lara being a native son. Record of his actual birth certificate was cast aside and in its place was inserted an "honorary" certificate produced in 1937 claiming Tlacotalpan as his birthplace. Personal communication, Monica Barrón (designer and iconographer for *Mi novia, la tristeza*), Mexico City, November 23, 2008. The actual fake birth certificate is located in Colección JAPS, Archivo Agustín Lara, Carpeta #1 "Documentos Personales." Dated September 19, 1937, the document states that Lara was born "30 de October, 1900" and since "no record of his birth apparently exists elsewhere," a new birth certificate needed to be drawn up. Witnesses Señores Carlos Calvo, Juan E. Lara B. (77 years old), and Profesor Luis Alavés Román were present. All claimed to be residents of Tlacotalpan and to have known Agustín, his parents, family, and so on. The professor said he knew Lara from the Escuela Municipal and was familiar with the boy's parents, whom he described as "humble local folk" (*gente humilde del pueblo*). Not surprisingly, Lara maintained that he was born in Tlacotalpan for much of his life and a passport issued in January 1941 lists his place of birth as such. Colección JAPS, Archivo Agustín Lara, Carpeta #1, "Documentos Personales." On the history of Tlacotalpan see Armando Pous (ed.), *Tlacotalpan: Veracruz, Patrimonio de la humanidad imágenes fotográficas, 1880–1950* (Mexico City: Author's edition, 1998) and Gema Lozano y Nathal (ed.), *Con el sello de agua: Ensayos históricos sobre Tlacotalpan* (Veracruz: Instituto Veracruzano de Cultura, 1991). Lara's good friend Francisco Rivera also notes that he and Lara once attended a party in Tlacotalpan. Walking along the town's well-preserved nineteenth-century streets the composer casually pointed to a house where he said he had been born. When Rivera returned some years later and asked the longtime owners of the house about Lara, they told him they had never known the Lara family. Today the house sports a historic marker claiming it was Lara's original home. Francisco Rivera, in *Agustín, rencuentro con lo sentimental*, p. 217.

119. Interview with Guillermo Salamanca Herraga, June 24, 2006. Tlacotalpan is renowned for its extraordinary Virgin of Candelaria/Encuentro de jaraneros y decimistas festival at the end of January each year.

120. On the lure of Tlacotalpan and other mythic origins associated with Lara see Alejandro Aura, *La hora íntima de Agustín Lara*, pp. 9–11.

121. On the shaping of jarocho identity see: Ricardo Pérez Montfort, *Estampas de nacionalismo popular mexicano: Ensayos sobre cultura popular y nacionalismo* (Mexico City: Centro de investigaciones y estudios superiores en anthropología social, 1994) and Bernardo García Díaz and Ricardo Pérez Montfort, *Veracruz y sus viajeros* (Xalapa, Veracruz: Estado de Veracruz/Grupo Sansco, 2001).

122. Not only foreigners but local people contributed significantly to this imagining process. In the case of the Port of Veracruz, residents revived the celebration of Carnival in 1925 as a means to encourage citizens to identify with the new postrevolutionary order both at home and at the national level. On Carnival see Andrew Grant Wood, "Introducing *La Reina del Carnaval*: Public Celebration and Postrevolutionary Discourse in Veracruz, Mexico" in *The Americas: A Quarterly Review of Inte-American Cultural History,* Vol. 60, No. 1 (July 2003), pp. 87–107.

123. On the history of Veracruz see Anselmo Mancisidor Ortiz, *Jarochilandia* (Veracruz: Author's edition, 1971); Roberto Williams, *Yo nací con la luna de plata: antropología e historia de un puerto* (Mexico: Costa-Amic, 1980); Bernardo García Díaz, *Puerto de Veracruz imágenes de su historia* (Xalapa: Veracruz: Archivo General del Estado de Veracruz, 1992); Andrew Grant Wood, "Modernity and Mobilization: Politics and Culture in the Port of Veracruz, Mexico, 1880–1930," in Johanna Von Grafenstein (ed.), *El Golfo-Caribe y sus puertos, siglos XVIII–XIX* (Mexico City: Instituto Mora/CONACYT, 2006), 2 vols., pp. 441–82; and Andrew Grant Wood, *Revolution in the Street: Women, Workers and Urban Protest in Veracruz, 1870–1927* (Lanham, MD: Rowman and Littlefield/SR Books, 2001).

124. On the history of tourism in Veracruz and Mexico more generally, see Dina Berger and Andrew Grant Wood (eds.), *Holiday in Mexico: Reflections on Tourism and Tourist Encounters.*

125. Ramos, *Agustín Lara: Cien años, cien canciones,* p. 116.

126. "Veracruz," RCA Victor 094232 (catalogue no. 70-9163). Dueñas and Flores y Escalante, *Discografía.* Lara first recorded the song for Victor in 1936 according to Granados and 1937 according to Dueñas and Flores y Escalante. The actual CD "Agustin Lara" (Serie de 20 Exitos, RCA Victor 1991) actually lists the recording as 1953.

127. Ramos, *Agustín Lara: Cien años, cien canciones,* p. 116.

128. Unidentified Mexico City paper, January 14, 1931. SLS, vol. 3.

129. S. R. Gallardo, "El creador de la canción actual está en San Luis." Unidentified newspaper clipping from San Luis Potosí, March 1931, SLS, vol. 3.

130. One pictured the artist standing next to a horse with the caption "[before becoming a famous entertainer] Lara was a friendly revolutionary whose actual life was more down to earth than his songs suggest." *El Ilustrado,* February 2, 1934, p. 21. The first issue of *El Ilustrado* premiered on November 1, 1928.

131. *El Illustrado,* April 5, 1934.

132. *El Illustrado,* April 5, 1934.

133. *El Ilustrado,* April 12, 19, 26, 1934.

134. Lara's story would be syndicated on stations such as XEB, XEW, XEFO, XEYZ, XEN, XEWZ and XEYZ (*El Illustrado,* December 13, 1934). The magazine notes in its December 24, 1936 issue that radio station XEBZ was broadcasting a satirical program called "El doble de Agustín Lara" with a personality known as Tatatín Taralara.

135. "Paco" is a nickname commonly assigned to men named Francisco. "Píldora," translated literally, means pill. One can surmise from this alliterative combination that Francisco Rivera was a character, witty and animated. Indeed, from what I know of his larger than life reputation/legend in the port, this all makes good sense.

136. Quoted in Flores y Escalante, *Salón México,* p. 47.

137. Loaeza and Granados, *Mi novia, la tristeza,* p. 241.

138. *Vida de Agustín Lara,* no. 1.

139. *Vida de Agustín Lara,* no. 1.

140. *Vida de Agustín Lara,* no. 1.

141. "Acta de nacimiento expedida en Tlacotalpan, Veracruz el 5 de abril de 1941. Donde ante juez y con testigos hacen constar que Agustín Lara, nació en 1900." Colección JAPS, Archivo Agustín Lara, "Documentos Personales."

142. As Carlos Monsiváis observed, Lara overcame this apparent moral conflict by "magnificently positioning himself right at the edge of what people would tolerate." Monsiváis, "Agustín Lara: El harem ilusorio," in *Amor Perdido* pp. 76–78.

143. "Rosa," Peerless (7079). Granados, *Canciones,* p. 52. Again, the story of Ana María Fernández singing this song earlier in the fall raises the question as to exactly when Lara composed it.

144. From the CD *Mejor de lo major: Agustín Lara 40 temas originales.* RCA Victor/BMG 2000, # 74321-72825-2.
145. Ramos, *Agustín Lara: Cien años, cien canciones,* p. 96.
146. Angelina Bruschetta, in *Agustín, rencuentro con lo sentimental,* pp. 207–08. Angelina indicates clearly that "Rosa" was composed in Guadalajara in late November 1929 and then delivered as a kind of Christmas gift shortly thereafter.
147. Granados suggests "Rosa" was recorded in 1929 (*Canciones,* p. 52) while Dueñas and Flores y Escalante list 1930 (Peerless #7079). Guty Cárdenas recorded it in April 1930 for Columbia. Spottswood, *Ethnic Music on Records,* Vol. 4, p. 1743. Lara later recorded it in 1953 for RCA Victor.
148. Aside from a few figures scribbled in notebooks and other marginalia, I have unfortunately not been able to find any comprehensive material indicating Lara's income.
149. Juan Arvizu, "Monísima" (also known as "Monísima mujer"), RCA Victor 1930. Granados, *Canciones,* p. 42.
150. Lara to Bruschetta, undated letter, ca. late 1929, quoted in Loaeza and Granados, *Mi novia, la tristeza,* pp. 207–08.
151. Abaroa Martínez, *El flaco de oro,* p. 81; Ruiz Rueda, *Agustín Lara: Vida y pasiones,* pp. 83–84; Bruschetta, in *Agustín, rencuentro con lo sentimental,* pp. 208–09; Bruschetta, *Agustín Lara y yo,* pp. 82–83.
152. Jaime Rico Salazar, *Cien años de boleros,* p. 74.
153. Interview with Juan Pablo O'Farrill, June 29, 2006. Mexico City.
154. Loaeza and Granados, *Mi novia, la tristeza,* p. 210. "Mujer," Peerless 1930 #7079.
155. Singer Ramón Armengod was the first to perform "Mujer" live with Lara accompanying on piano. Loaeza and Granados, *Mi novia, la tristeza,* p. 210.
156. "La música mexicana antes de Lara era perfectamente campesina, ranchera." Renato Leduc, in *Agustín: rencuentro con lo sentimental,* p. 269.

## Chapter 3

1. "Sin Emilio Azcárraga no hubieran existido ni la radio ni la televisión Mexicana." Quoted in Jorge Mejía Prieto, *Historia de la radio y televisión en México* (Mexico City: Ángel Urraza, 1972), p. 291.
2. In an effort to stabilize the nation's still tumultuous social and political environment, revolutionary elites under Calles's leadership established *Partido Revolucionario Nacional* (National Revolutionary Party or PNR) in 1929.
3. Arnaldo Córdova, *En una época de crisis (1928–1934)* (Mexico City: Siglo XXI/UNAM, 1980), p. 37.
4. Michael Kantor and Laurence Maslow, *Broadway: The American Musical* (New York: Bulfinch Press, 2004), pp. 18–27; John Bush Jones, *Our Musicals, Ourselves: A Social History of the American Musical Theatre* (Lebanon, NH: Brandeis University Press, 2003), pp. 52–78. See also Andrew Lamb, *150 Years of Popular Musical Theater* (New Haven, CT: Yale University Press, 2001); Kurt Gänzl, *The Musical: A Concise History* (Freeport, MA: Northeastern Press, 1997); and also Gerald Bordman, *Days to be Happy, Years to be Sad: The Life and Music of Vincent Youmans* (New York: Oxford University Press, 1982).
5. Kantor and Maslon, *Broadway,* p. 52.
6. Museo Nacional de Culturas Populares, *El país de las tandas: Teatro de revista, 1910–1940* (Coyoacán, Mexico: Dirección General de Culturas Populares/Secretaría de Educación Pública (SEP), 1984), p. 127. The book provides a listing of productions and the dates they premiered from late 1899 to the summer of 1940. See a similar listing in Moreno Rivas, *Historia de la música popular en México,* (Mexico City: Alianza Editorial Mexicana, 1979), pp. 75–79.
7. Museo Nacional de Culturas Populares, *El país de las tandas: Teatro de revista,* p. 18. See also Nicolás Kanellos and Claudio Esteva Fabregat, (eds.) *Handbook of Hispanic Cultures in the United States,* Volumes 1–2 (Houston: Arte Publico Press, 1994), pp. 252–54.
8. Museo Nacional de Culturas Populares, *El país de las tandas,* pp. 9–21, 35–47, 61–66, 81–83, 89–96, 111–14. The Fábregas was owned by actress Virginia Fábregas while actress

Esperanza Iris presided over the Iris. See pp. 127–31 for information on theater openings, closings, and other details.

9. John Koegel, "Mexican Musicians in California and the United States, 1910–50," *California History*, vol. 85, no. 1 (Fall 2006), pp. 23–24. See also Carlos Monsiváis, "Instituciones: María Conesa," in *Escenas de pudor y liviandad* (Mexico City: Grijalbo 1992, 2002), pp. 333–45. See also actor Enrique "Cachirulo" Alonso's (1892–1978) account. Enrique Alonso, *María Conesa* (Mexico City, Océano, 1987). Alonso lived with Conesa for many years.

10. Jeff Pilcher, *Cantinflas and the Chaos of Mexican Modernity* (Lanham, MD: Rowman and Littlefield, 2001), p. 20.

11. See Pablo Dueñas, *Las divas en el teatro de revista Mexicano* (Mexico City: Asociación Mexicana de Estudios Fonográficos/Dirección General de Culturas Populares, 1994) for individual profiles, revues, and photos.

12. Pilcher, *Cantinflas and the Chaos of Mexican Modernity*, pp. 20–21; Monsiváis, *Escenas de pudor y liviandad*, pp. 24–26. On portrayals of the "modern girl" in comic books see Ann Rubenstein, *Bad Language, Naked Ladies and Other Threats to the Nation* (Durham, NC: Duke University Press, 1998) and Joanne Hershfield, *Imagining la Chica Moderna: Women, Nation and Visual Culture in Mexico, 1917–1936* (Durham, NC: Duke University Press, 2007).

13. Moreno Rivas, *Historia de la música popular en México*, pp. 80–81. Ziegfeld's influence in the burgeoning Hollywood film industry also represents a powerful link between revue-style theater and cinema. Kantor and Maslon, *Broadway*, p. 24.

14. Gabriel Abaroa Martínez, *El flaco de oro* (Mexico City: Editorial Planeta, 1993), pp. 78–81. For a sampling of music from the era see the LP "El pais de las Tandas / Cachitos de Mexico," MEX LP VG + MNCP-0012. Release date unknown.

15. Manuel López de la Parra, "México y la época de Agustín Lara," *Revista de Revistas*, November 19, 1990, p. 28. Granados indicates the "Rosa Castellana" was never recorded. Granados, *Canciones*, p. 379.

16. Unidentifed clippings, Salvador Lara Scrapbooks (SLS), vol. 16, Loaeza and Granados, *Mi novia, la tristeza*, (Mexico City: Océano, 2008) p. 215.

17. Lara quoted in Loaeza, Guadalupe and Pável Granados, *Mi novia, la tristeza*, p. 217.

18. Ads and short note by "Fradique" in SLS, vol. 12, Dueñas, *Las divas en el teatro mexicano*, 1994, p. 172.

19. Dueñas, *Las divas en el teatro mexicano*, pp. 185–88. See clippings of ads and reviews in SLS, vols. 13 and 14. The "Casita Blanca" (Little White House) former residence and now Lara Museum located between the Port of Veracruz and its southern neighbor Boca del Río contains a handful of photos of Lara, as well as promotional posters and programs for a few of these shows. Fragments of a 1932 musical revue script as well as a few radio program themes are part of the Colección Juan Antonio Pérez Simón (JAPS), Archivo Agustín Lara, Carpeta "Giones para radio y teatro." When "Mujeres y canciones" closed, Roberto Soto and company embarked on a tour to Spain. He asked permission to use Lara's music but did not extend a travel invitation to the composer. In fact, a tension developed between the two as Soto began to criticize Lara for "seducing the public with simple melodies and banal lyrics." Soto quoted in Loaeza and Granados, *Mi novia, la tristeza*, pp. 217–18.

20. Walter Winchell, excerpted from *New York Daily Mirror*, March 31, 1928. Quoted in Kantor and Mason, *Broadway: The American Musical*, p. 127.

21. For illustrations associated with *revista* theater, see Museo Nacional de Culturas Populares, *El país de las tandas: Teatro de revista, 1910–1940* as well as Pablo Dueñas, *Las divas en el teatro de revista mexicano*. On advertising and the rise of consumer culture in the United States see Roland Marchand, *Advertising and the American Dream: Making Way for Modernity, 1920–1940* (Berkeley: University of California Press, 1985).

22. Bruschetta, Angelina, *Agustín Lara y yo: 1928-1938* (Xalapa, Veracruz: Author's edition, 1979), pp. 84–86.

23. Radio broadcasts from the United States initially arrived in Mexico during the early 1920s as a growing number of commercial stations in cities such as New York, Los Angeles, San

Francisco, Chicago, and Fort Worth came on the air. José Luis Garza Ortiz, *La guerra de las ondas: Un libro que desmiente la historia "oficial" de la radio Mexicana* (Mexico City: Planeta, 1992), p. 18. Meanwhile, a handful of gringo impresarios established powerful stations along the US–Mexico border. Gene Fowler and Bill Crawford, *Border Radio: Quacks, Yodelers, Pitchmen, Psychics and Other Amazing Broadcasters of the American Airwaves* (Austin: University of Texas Press, revised ed., 2002). The most notorious of these radio men was the eccentric "goat gland doctor" John Brinkley. See Pope Brock, *Charlatan: America's Most Dangerous Huckster, The Man Who Pursued Him and the Age of Flimflam* (New York: Crown Books, 2008).

24. Claudia Fernández and Andrew Paxman, *El Tigre: Emilio Azcárraga y su imperio Televisa* (Mexico City: Grijalbo, 2000), p. 44.

25. Manuel Maples Arce, 1923. First published in *El Universal Ilustrado*, radio issue, April 5, 1923. Maples Arce was part of a literary art group called the Estridentistas (Stridentists) who promoted new ideas about art and society. On the Estridentistas see Luis Mario Schneider, *El estridentismo o una literatura de la estrategia* (Mexico City: Consejo nacional para la cultura y las artes, 1997) and Elissa Rashkin, *The Stridentist Movement in Mexico: The Avant-Garde and Cultural Change in the 1920s* (Lanham, MD: Lexington Books, 2009).

26. Jorge Mejía Prieto, *Historia de la radio y televisión en México* (Mexico City: Angel Urraza, 1972), pp. 26–26; Pável Granados, *XEW: 70 años en el aire*, p. 15; *Agustín Lara*: Ruiz Rueda, *Agustín Lara: Vida y pasiones*, (Mexico City: Editorial Nouno, 1976), p. 88.

27. See Rubén Gallo, "Mexican Radio goes to the North Pole." *Cabinet*, Issue 22, Summer 2006. www.cabinetmagazine.org/issues/22/gallo.php.

28. Joy Elizabeth Hayes, *Radio Nation: Communication, Popular Culture and Nationalism in Mexico, 1920–1950* (Tucson: University of Arizona Press, 2000), p. 36; Mejía Prieto, *Historia de la radio y televisión en México*, p. 28, 29.

29. Hayes, *Radio Nation*, pp. 28–29.

30. Mejía Prieto, *Historia de la radio y televisión en México*, pp. 31–37. See also Jesús Flores Escalante and Pablo Dueñas, "XEB : Una estación de radio con historia," www.imer.com.mx/EstacionesIMER/XEB/xeb_historia.pdf.

31. Ruiz Rueda, Javier, *Agustín Lara: Vida y pasiones*, p. 88.

32. Hayes, *Radio Nation*, p. 33.

33. "Imagined Community" is drawn from Benedict Anderson, *Imagined Communities: Reflections on the Origin and Spread of Nationalism* (London: Verso Press, 1983), 2006.

34. Mejía Prieto, *Historia de la radio y televisión en México*, p. 38.

35. Granados, Pável, *XEW: 70 años en el aire*, p. 29.

36. Ruiz Rueda, *Agustín Lara: Vida y pasiones*, pp. 89–92; Granados, *XEW: 70 años en el aire*, pp. 26–31.

37. María del Carmen de la Peza Casares, *El bolero y la educación sentimental en México* (Mexico City: Universidad Autónomia Metropolitana-Xochimilco, 2001), pp. 192–97. Curiously, Lara at this time preferred not having a radio in his own home. Loaeza and Granados, *Mi novia, la tristeza*, p. 229.

38. *El Universal*, September 18, 1930.

39. Apparently President Abelardo Rodríguez had been invited but was sick and sent Sáenz in his place. Loaeza and Granados, *Mi novia, la tristeza*, p. 227.

40. Barcelata and his Trovadores Tamaulipecos did not attend. Loaeza and Granados, *Mi novia, la tristeza*, p. 227.

41. Angelina Bruschetta, *Agustín Lara y yo: 1928–1938*. Xazapa, Veracruz (1979, author's edition), p. 95. Although Lara is pictured along with a number of other performers in the *El Universal* advertisement for XEW's opening program, Loaeza and Granados claim that he was not present at the inaugural broadcast. *Mi novia, la tristeza*, pp. 227, 242.

42. "Campanitas de mi tierra" was classified as a "Mexican song" and first recorded in late 1932 by Jorge M. Dada for Brunswick in New York City. Alfonso Ortiz Tirado recorded it in 1936 for Victor (30115). Granados, *Canciones*, p. 33. "Campanitas" is often attributed to Guty Cárdenas who also recorded and performed it.

43. "Aventurera" was composed in 1930 and first recorded by Adria Delhort for Peerless in 1930 (7115). Pável Granados, *Agustín Lara: Canciones* (Mexico City: Gobierno de

Veracruz/Océano 2008), p. 61; Elena Tamargo et al., *Bolero: Clave del corazón, bolero* (Mexico City: Alejo Peralta Fundación, 2004), pp. 106–07; Granados, *XEW: 70 años en el aire*, p. 21; Bruschetta, *Agustín Lara y yo*, p. 95; Ruiz Rueda, *Agustín Lara: Vida y pasiones*, pp. 91–93. Historian Armando Pous suspects that many of the early XEW program recordings have unfortunately been lost. Personal communication with the author, Mexico City, August 13, 2002. Long-time XEW employee Juan Pablo O'Farrill confirmed this during an interview with the author in Mexico City on June 29, 2006.

44. *El Ilustrado*, April 19, 1934; p. 24; Ortiz Garza, *La guerra de las ondas*, p. 184; Granados, *XEW: 70 años en el aire*, p. 124; Hayes, *Radio Nation*, pp. 32–33.

45. Granados, *XEW: 70 años en el aire*, pp. 122–24.

46. Interview with retired XEW employee Juan Pablo O'Farrill, June 29, 2006, Mexico City.

47. Julio Moreno, *Yankee Don't Go Home!: Mexican Nationalism, American Business Culture, and the Shaping of Modern Mexico, 1920–1950* (Chapel Hill: University of North Carolina Press, 2003), p. 80.

48. Pedro Vargas remembered the title of the film being the 1928 production "Corazones sin rumbo" but Harding does not appear on the cast list. Quite likely the film was either "Holiday" or "Girl from the Golden West"—both produced in 1930. José Ramón Garmabella, *Pedro Vargas Una vez nada más* (Mexico City: Ediciones de Comunicación, 1984), p. 84, IMDB Ann Harding filmography, www.imdb.com/name/nm0362267/. Competitions like this were a regular part of the Mexico City music scene as people like Guty Cárdenas, Tata Nacho, and Luis Martínez Serrano had previously won prizes for their songs. Typically, Lara steered away from these contests. Ruiz Rueda, *Agustín Lara: Vida y pasiones*, p. 99.

49. Teresa Campos Juaregui de Vargas, in Eugenio Méndez (ed.), *Agustín, rencuentro con lo sentimental* (Mexico City: Editorial Domés, 1980), p. 242. Then girlfriend and future wife of Pedro Vargas, María Teresa worked as a secretary for Jorge Pezet for the Pathé Films office on Uruguay Street and urged Pedro (as well as Lara) to participate in the competition. Allegedly, Pedro proposed marriage during the contest and she accepted despite the alleged misgivings of her family.

50. "Con broche de oro se cerró el concurso del vals 'Ann Harding.'" Unidentified clipping, SLS vol. 15.

51. Ruiz Rueda calls him Juan José Espinosa de los Monteros. Rumor has it that he persuaded a number of his fellow railroad workers to attend in support of his bid. Ruiz Rueda, *Agustín Lara: Vida y pasiones*, pp. 100–01; Granados, *XEW: 70 años en el aire*, p. 35. A recording of Espinosa de Monteros's composition on Brunswick by the "Orquesta de Carter" can be found at the UCLA Frontera Collection, Los Angeles, http://frontera.library.ucla.edu/viewItem.do?ark=21198/zz00002vs6.

52. Del Moral had had recent success with "Pierrot," "Tú, tú, tú" and other songs recorded by Juan Arvizu. Ruiz Rueda, *Agustín Lara: Vida y pasiones*, p. 101.

53. Roberto Ayala (ed.), *Canciones y poemas de Agustín Lara: Colección completa*. (Mexico City: Selecciónes Orfeón, 1969), p. 86. "Cortesana" was first recorded by Adolfo Utreta and Perla Violeta Amado with the orchestra of Enrique Madriguera in New York in October 1930 for Columbia. Eduardo Vigil y Robles and his International Orchestra also recorded it for Victor that same year. Granados, *Canciones*, p. 65. Alfonso Ortiz Tirado recorded it for RCA Victor at some point but it appears as if Lara never did.

54. Granados, *XEW: 70 años en el aire*, p. 35; Ruiz Rueda, *Agustín Lara: Vida y pasiones*, pp. 100–01; Bruschetta, *Agustín Lara y yo*, pp. 93–94; Ramos, "Notas para una rapsodia," in *Agustín, rencuentro con lo sentimental*, pp. 31–32; Loaeza and Granados, *Mi novia, la tristeza*, p. 239. Alfonso Esparza Oteo's "Íntimo secreto" sung by Juan Arvizu took fourth place. Lara's "Diploma de Honor" is on display at the Casita Blanca Museo de Lara in Boca del Río.

55. Unidentified clipping, SLS, vol. 15.

56. See Mario Talavera, *Miguel Lerdo de Tejada: Su pintoresca y anecdotica* (Mexico City: Editorial Compas, no date). Lara remembers that he first met Lerdo de Tejada years earlier when "I was playing in an ice cream shop [*nevería*] below a photographic store one afternoon when maestro Lerdo arrived for his daily pecan-flavored dessert. I was playing some of his compositions including 'México Bello,' 'El Faisán,' and 'Perjura' among others, and Miguel took an interest. He asked me my name and I told the maestro that I worked evenings in a cabaret on Héroes Street." Agustín Lara, "Como los conoci," Colección JAPS.

57. Garmabella, *Pedro Vargas*, pp. 75–86; Manuel Robles, "Samurai de la canción," interview conducted in 1973. Reprinted in David Martin del Campo, *100 Entrevistas Personajes* (Mexico City: Grupo Azabache, 1991), pp. 262–63.

58. José Ramon Garmabella, *Pedro Vargas*, pp. 35–36.

59. Garmabella, *Pedro Vargas*, pp. 45–49.

60. Garmabella, *Pedro Vargas*, p. 49.

61. Richard K. Spottswood, *Ethnic Music on Records*. Vol 4: *Spanish, Portuguese, Philippine, Basque* (Champaign: University of Illinois Press, 1990). p. 2008.

62. Loaeza and Granados, *Mi novia, la tristeza*, pp. 170–71, 239.

63. Pedro Vargas interview, "Mi compadre es la canción," *Excelsior*, November 7, 1970.

64. Pedro Vargas, in *Agustín, rencuentro con lo sentimental*, p. 237; Garmabella, *Pedro Vargas*, pp. 89–91. Vargas and Lara continued to associate both professionally and personally for the rest of their lives. Lara also served as godparent for Pedro's son Alejandro.

65. José Luis Velasco, "Un cancionero romantico," *Excélsior*, January 5, 1930.

66. Juan Arvizu, in *Agustín: rencuentro con lo sentimental*, p. 221.

67. Juan de Ega, "Mi mejor canción? No la he escrito todavía; entrevista con Agustín Lara." Unidentified clipping, SLS, vol. 12.

68. Ernesto Belloc, in *Agustín, rencuentro con lo sentimental*, pp. 223–25. Interestingly, this process paralleled the work of Irving Berlin in New York, who also contracted associates to transcribe his compositions and suggest harmonizations that the composer would then accept, modify, or reject. On Berlin see Charles Hamm, *Irving Berlin: Songs from the Melting Pot, the Formative Years, 1907–1914* (New York: Oxford University Press, 1997). See also Charles Hamm, *Irving Berlin: Early Songs, 1907–1914*, 3 vols., Music of the United States of America series (Madison, WI: A-R Editions, 1994).

69. Pedro Centellas, "Microfonos candillejas y celluloide." Unidentified clipping. SLS, vol 14.

70. Two undated pages in Lara's handwriting produced between circa 1930 and 1933 reveal his growing repertoire of original works—many presumably to be recorded for Victor Records. The first list includes only tangos: "Mujercita," "Poco a poco," "Más tarde," "De noche," "Canella," "Mentira," "Perdida," "Adios," "Lo de siempre," "Sentiendo una peña," and "Adios nicanor." The second is a mix of twenty-four songs including boleros, Foxtrots, bambucos, waltzes, and canciones jaranas. "Selecciónes Victor," Colección JAPS, Archivo Agustín Lara, Carpeta #2. Moreno Rivas suggests 38 new songs created by the end of 1929 and then a total of 150 by 1935. Moreno Rivas, *Historia de la música popular mexicana*, p. 141.

71. Ayala, *Canciones y poemas de Agustín Lara*, p. 160.

72. "Mi novia" was recorded by Ramón Armengod for Peerless in 1930 (801), Juan Arvizu on Seeco and Jorge Fernández on Orfeón (s/n) around the same time. Lara later waxed his own version for RCA Victor in 1953 while also realizing versions on Camden, Trébol, and Orfeón. Granados, *Canciones*, p. 74. See, for example, Orfeón *Agustín Lara* LP 12-653, 1970 (compilation of recordings from the late 1950s). Dueñas and Flores y Escalante, *Discography*.

73. From the CD "Agustín Lara: 40 temas originales," RCA Victor/BMG 2000.

74. Mario Arturo Ramos (ed.), *Agustín Lara: Cien años, cien canciones*, (Mexico City: Océano, 2000), p. 41.

75. First recordings of "Como dos puñales" were made by Ramón Armengod in 1931 (Peerless 801) and Guty Cárdenas (Columbia 4518-x in April 1931) in New York City. Spottswood, *Ethnic Records*, vol. 4, p. 1744; Granados, *Canciones*, p. 63.

76. Mario Arturo Ramos, *Agustín Lara: Cien años, cien canciones*, p. 41.

77. Ayala, *Canciones y poemas de Agustín Lara*, p. 76. The 1948 version of "Como dos puñales" is from Granados, *Canciones*, disc one, track 7.

78. Armengod (1931 Peerless 802); Cárdenas (Columbia s/n May 1931 in New York); Arvizu (1931 Victor 30339); Granados, *Canciones*, p. 64.

79. Ramos, *Agustín Lara: Cien años, cien canciones*, p. 42.

80. 1953 RCA Victor Mkl-1333. From the CD "Mejor de lo majoR: Agustín Lara 40 temas originales," RCA Victor/BMG 2000 #74321-72825-2. Previously released as "Palabras de mujer . . . Agustín Lara, su piano y su conjunto," 1961 (compilation of recordings from 1950–1955). Dueñas and Flores y Escalante, *Discography*; Granados, *Canciones*, p. 64.

81. "La tortuada inspiración de un músico poeta." Unidentified author, *Revista de Revistas*, November 23, 1930.
82. "Una pelicula sensacional y Agustín Lara en el Olimpia." Unidentified clipping, SLS, vol. 12. The film discussed in the review was *The Spoilers* starring Gary Cooper.
83. "La canción mexicana y Agustín Lara." Unidentified newspaper clipping, SLS, vol. 3.
84. Rafael de la Cerda, "Arenitas y cantos rodados." Unidentified clipping, SLS, vol. 9.
85. de la Cerda, "Arenitas y cantos rodados."
86. Ayala, *Canciones y poemas de Agustín Lara*: p. 68. "Cautiva" was recorded by Rafael Trova in 1931 (Peerless 806) and Ana María Fernández in 1932 (RCA Victor pel-125). Lara recorded it for Peerless at an unidentified time and then for RCA Victor in 1953 (MKL-1333) on the album *Palabras de mujer ... Agustín Lara, su piano y su conjunto*. RCA Victor 1961. Granados, *Canciones*, p. 91; Dueñas y Flores y Escalante, *Discography*.
87. From the CD *Mejor de lo major: Agustín Lara 40 temas originales*. RCA Victor/BMG 2000.
88. Jacobo Delevuelta, "Cosas del día: Agustín Lara; Músico y poeta," "Agustín Lara: El músico de moda." Unidentified clippings, SLS, vol. 9.
89. A.F.B. "El mundo y la canción mexicana." Unidentified clipping, SLS, vol. 11.
90. A small assortment of photographs documenting Lara's burgeoning career in film is located in the Colección JAPS, Archivo Agustín Lara, Carpeta "Fotografias del cine."
91. Debra A. Castillo, *Easy Women: Sex and Gender in Modern Mexican Fiction* (Minneapolis, University of Minnesota Press, 1998), pp. 37–62. Gamboa served in Victoriano Huerta's cabinet as foreign minister and then ran as a Catholic candidate against Huerta in the ill-fated election of late 1913. The presidential result—which favored Huerta—was declared void by Congress. Nevertheless, they approved an extension of Huerta's provisional term to July 1914. *The New International Year Book: A Compendium of the World's Progress* (New York: Dodd, Mead and Company, 1914), pp. 438–39.
92. Bruschetta, *Agustín Lara y yo*, pp. 120–21.
93. Ramos, *Agustín Lara: Cien años, cien canciones*, p. 97.
94. Lara recorded "Santa" in 1953 and released it on the 1956 album *Rosa: Agustín Lara*. RCA Victor MKL 1131. This version was accessed via *Agustín Lara 20 exitos*, RCA Victor/BMG 1991 CDM-3352. Lara also recorded a live version in the late 1950s for Orfeón. Orfeón JCD-1908, n/d.
95. The 1953 version includes Carlos Águila on violin along with percussion provided by Lara's otherwise unidentified ensemble.
96. *Radiolandia*, unidentified clipping, SLS, vol. 2.
97. Carlos Monsiváis, *Mexican Postcards*, trans. John Kraniauskas (London: Verso Press, 1997), p. 182.
98. Oscar LeBlanc, "Lara, el larismo y las mujeres," *El Illustrado*, unidentified clipping, SLS, vol. 12.
99. Melodrama has many connotations including: a specific dramatic genre, spoken dialogue over orchestral music in a play or opera, as well as its use as an adjective. In the context of postrevolutionary Mexico, literary historian Nina Gerassi-Navarro's comments on the beginnings of modern melodrama some years earlier in Europe are worth noting. She writes: "in its origin, melodrama provided popular classes a way to dramatize the intensity of the violent events of the French Revolution while reestablishing at the same time order and stability as justice triumphed in the end. In spite of the cultural and political differences in Europe, the popularity of this dramatic form enabled it to reflect the intense social and economic changes stemming from the large-scale industrial production of the nineteenth century and the breakdown of two important institutions: the monarchy and the Church. Traditional values society had held until then as imperatives were violently questioned. As a response to the void formed by the crude dismantling of precepts and traditional lifestyles, melodrama presented itself as a unifying and structuring expression. . . . Through its extremism, melodrama sought to configure a specific order and alleviate the sense of rupture." Nina Gerassi-Navarro, *Pirate Novels: Fictions of Nation Building in Spanish America* (Durham, NC: Duke University Press, 1999), pp. 148–49.
100. Alaíde Foppa, "Mujer Divina," in *Agustín, rencuentro con lo sentimental*, p. 124.
101. Carl Mora, *Mexican Cinema*, pp. 34–35; Hugo Lara Chávez, *Una ciudad inventada por el cine* (Mexico City: Reflections of a Society, 1896–1988 (Berkeley: University of California Press, 1982) CONACULTA/Cineteca Nacional/Nueva Era, 2006). Quoted in Loaeza and

Granados, *Mi novia, la tristeza*, p. 263. The film was realized between November 3, 1931 and January 5, 1932 and released later that year. Because of this, I list it as a 1932 film. Emilio García Riera, *Historia documental del cine mexicano*, vol. 1 (Guadalajara: Universidad de Guadalajara, 1992), pp. 47–51, however, lists it as a 1931 product. There would be a total of three Mexican-produced versions of *Santa*: Moreno's 1932 debut, a 1943 remake directed by Norman Foster, and another in 1968 directed by Emilio Gómez Muriel.

102. Emilio García Riera, *Historia documental del cine mexicano* vol 1., pp. 47–51.

103. Unidentified clipping, SLS, vol. 11. Lara performed the role of Hipólito in a 1947 Mexico City stage production at the Fábregas Theater in 1947. Andrea Palma played the role of Santa. Loaeza and Granados, *Mi novia, la tristeza*, pp. 263–64.

104. Carl Mora, *Mexican Cinema*, p. 35. For an illustrated presentation of Mexican movie houses see Francisco H. Alfaro and Alejandro Ochoa, *La república de los cines* (Mexico City: Clío Editions, 1998). Likewise, a bevy of actors and actresses are pictured in Carlos Monsiváis, *Rostros del cine mexicano* (Mexico City: Américo Arte Editors S.A., 1993).

105. A fascinating take on the Mexican film industry and in particular the role of American William O. Jenkins can be found in Miguel Contreras Torres, *El libro negro del cine mexicano* (Mexico City: Editora Hispano-Continental Films, 1960) as well as Andrew Paxman, "William Jenkins, Business Elites, and the Evolution of the Mexican State: 1910–1960," PhD diss., University of Texas, Austin, 2008.

106. Carlos Monsiváis, "Mexican Cinema: Of Myths and Dymystifications," in John King, Ana M. López, and Manuel Alvarado (eds.), *Mediating Two Worlds: Cinematic Encounters in the Americas* (London: British Film Institute, 1993), p. 143.

107. As Ana M. López put it, the Mexican "country[side] seemed ungovernable and the city [constituted] an unruly Mecca [as the] revolution [had] changed the nature of public life." Ana M. López, "Tears and Desire: Women and Melodrama in the 'Old' Mexican Cinema," in John King, Ana M. López, and Manuel Alvarado (eds.), *Mediating Two Worlds: Cinematic Encounters in the Americas*, p. 152.

108. Andrew Grant Wood, "Blind Men and Fallen Women: Notes on Modernity and Golden Age Mexican Cinema," in *Post Identities*, vol. 3, no 1 (Summer 2001), pp. 11–24; Carlos Monsiváis, "Santa: El cine naturalista," *Anuario*, Departamento de Actividades Cinematográficas (Mexico: UNAM, 1966).

109. García Riera later said that *Santa* was "mysteriously lacking in the poetry that time tends to attach to even the worst of films." Quoted in Carl Mora, *Mexican Cinema: Reflections of a Society, 1896–1988*, p. 35.

110. Carl Mora, *Mexican Cinema*, pp. 34–35.

111. "El cine como industria nacional." Unidentified clipping, SLS, vol. 12. The advent of sound in Hollywood is discussed in Scott Eyman, *The Speed of Sound: Hollywood and the Talkie Revolution, 1926–1930* (Baltimore: Johns Hopkins University Press, 1997).

112. "Agustín Lara se halla fuera de peligro y ha recuperado su sonrisa." Unidentified clipping, SLS, vol. 9. Bruschetta wrote that Refugio, while working at the Hospico de Niños in Coyoacán, remembered Angelina and her mother as well as an incident where Angelina and Agustín had collided and both broken their arms. Bruschetta, *Agustín Lara y yo*, pp. 99–105.

113. Jorge Rachini-Chino Herrera and Luis G. Roldán both recorded "A tus pies" in 1931 for Peerless (809 and 821 respectively). "Sevilla" was first recorded by Ortiz Tirado for Victor in 1935 (75244). Granados, *Canciones*, p. 87. See also the University of California, Santa Barbara Victor Discography Project, www.victor.library.ucsb.edu.

114. Unidentified newspaper advertisement, SLS, vol. 6. See notices and reviews for "Mujer" in *Excélsior* and *El Universal*, January 1931.

115. Contestants included Yolanda Millán, María Alcalá, Esperanza López, Aida E. Peralta, Lilia Morlet, Rosita Estévez, Amparo Ortiz, and Carmen Garrido. Unidentified newspaper clippings, SLS, vol. 3., vol. 8.

116. Bruschetta, *Agustín Lara y yo*, pp. 108–19.

117. Loaeza and Granados, *Mi novia, la tristeza*, p. 246.

118. Abaroa Martínez, *El flaco de oro*, pp. 103–04, 110–11. Garmabella, *Pedro Vargas*, pp. 19–64.

119. Unidentified San Luis Potosí newspaper clipping, March 1931. SLS, vol. 3.

120. *El Sol* (Querétaro) July 8, 1931. "Comida Rotaria en honor de Agustín Lara" and assorted advertisements for show at the Coliseo del Victoria-Durango. SLS, vol. 5.

121. "Ojo de pajaro: Agustín Lara." Unidentified newspaper clipping, SLS, vol. 6; unidentified newspaper clipping, July 1931, SLS, vol. 2; *La Prensa* (San Antonio, TX), August 9, 1931.

122. Unidentified newspaper clippings, July 1931, SLS, vol. 5.

123. "Lara, su canción y su espectaculo," *El Siglo* (Torreón, Coahuila), July 27, 1931.

124. "Lara, su canción y su espectaculo."

125. On Rudy Vallée, Bing Crosby, and the new crooning style in the United States and its appeal to female audiences, see Allison McCracken, "Real Men Don't Sing Ballads: The Radio Crooner in Hollywood, 1929–33," in Pamela Robertson Wojcik and Arthur Knight (eds.), *Soundtrack Available: Essays on Film and Popular Music* (Durham, NC: Duke University Press, 2001), pp. 105–33 and Allison McCracken, "God's Gift to Us Girls': Crooning, Gender and the Re-Creation of American Popular Song, 1928–33," *American Music* 17.4 (1999), pp. 365–95. For a biography of Crosby see Gary Giddens, *Bing Crosby: A Pocketful of Dreams: The Early Years, 1903–1940* (New York: Little, Brown, 2001). For a taste of the times see punk rock guitarist Lenny Kaye's historical novel based on the lives of beloved crooners such as Russ Columbo, Vallée, and Crosby. Lenny Kaye, *You Call it Madness: The Sensuous Song of the Croon* (New York: Villard Books, 2004).

126. Pável Granados notes that Vicente Bergmann was the first crooner in Mexico. Liner notes to "Rarezas discográficas Agustín Lara." Included in Granados, *Canciones*.

127. McCracken, "Real Men Don't Sing Ballads," p. 107.

128. Greg Grandin mentions live broadcasts by Vallée from Green Bay, Wisconsin listened to by employees of Henry Ford's rubber plantation town (Fordlandia) deep in the Amazon jungle. Greg Grandin, *Fordlandia: The Rise and Fall of Henry Ford's Forgotten Jungle City* (New York: Picador, 2009), p. 196.

129. Pablo Dueñas, *Las divas en el teatro revisista mexicano*, pp. 185–88 lists a number of songs from various revistas that were recorded. From this I surmise the 1932 production described was probably "Su amado."

130. "Su amado" was not recorded. Granados, *Canciones*, p. 379.

131. For these Laurelio L. Campos (violin) and Jesús Camacho Vega (cello) joined Lara. Unidentified newspaper clippings, SLS, vol. 3. These songs appear to have never been recorded. Granados, *Canciones*, p. 379.

132. Ayala, *Canciones y poemas de Agustín Lara*, p. 285.

133. Rodrigo Barzán Bonfil, *Y si vivo cien años . . . antología del bolero en México* (Mexico City: Fondo de Cultura Económica, 2001), pp. 40–41.

134. "Sal de uvas Picot" was a Mexican product similar to Alka-Seltzer. The company sponsored the *Cancionero Picot*—an illustrated annual compendium of popular songs and ephemera.

135. Noemi Atamoros, "Yo descubrí a Agustín Lara en el 'Café Salambo,' dice Juan Arvizu." Unidentified clipping, October 4, 1972, BLT, "Archivos Economicos."

136. Shortly after Guty's death, Lara received a letter addressed to him at radio station XEW from Jorge M. Dada, head of Dada-Dada & Co., Brunswick and Columbia record distributors in San Salvador, El Salvador, lamenting the death of Cárdenas while also praising Lara's "suggestive and sentimental" hits. Dada mentions that the music and name of "Agustín Lara" is well known both in New York and Central America. Jorge M. Dada to Agustín Lara, April 7, 1932. Colección JAPS, Archivo Agustín Lara, Carpeta #2. On Cárdenas see Álvaro Vega and Enrique Martin (eds.), *Guty Cárdenas: Cancionero*, Serie Cancioneros 2 (Merida, Yucatán: Instituto de Cultura de Yucatán, Centro Regional de Investigacíon, Documentacion y Difusión Musicales "Geronimo Baqueiro Foster," 2006).

137. "De charla con Agustín Lara," *La Nación* (Mérida, Yucatán) June (no date indicated) 1932. SLS, vol. 11. Bruschetta, *Agustín Lara y yo*, p. 122.

138. Lara, Fernández, and Vargas are pictured arriving in Havana in *El Mundo* (Havana, Cuba), June 24, 1932. Assorted clippings from SLS, vol. 8. The volume also includes occasional documentation of the Cuban tour, photos of Lara, and various notes about his performances.

139. "Hoy despedida de Lara," *El Mundo* (Havana), June 11, 1932; "Agustín Lara en El Encanto," "De teatros, cines y música: nuestro galeria." Unidentified clippings, SLS, vol. 8. Ruiz Rueda, *Agustín Lara: Vida y pasiones*, p. 165. Allegedly Lara subsequently received many letters from Cuban fans. References to civil conflict do not exactly coincide with the August 1933 revolution that ousted Machado. Instead, the Mexican entourage must have witnessed sporadic violence the previous summer. For recent recordings of Lara songs by contemporary Cuban artists see the CD *Agustín Lara a la cubana* (Havana: EGREM 2001), CD #0520.

140. Clippings from the 1932 visit contain a photo of Lara in the offices of Havana's *El Mundo* newspaper. SLS, vol. 8. One titled "Arreglando el mundo: Triguñita y Lara" described a complaint by a Cuban named Billiken claiming that Lara had plagiarized one his songs in crafting "Trigueñita." The Mexican composer denied the charge.

141. Abaroa Martínez, *El flaco de oro*, p. 100; Loaeza and Granados, *Mi novia, la tristeza*, p. 279.

142. Maria M. Garrett, "Agustín Lara en El Encanto." Unidentified clipping, SLS, vol. 8.

143. Bruschetta, *Agustín Lara y yo*, pp. 124–25.

144. Bruschetta, *Agustín Lara y yo*, pp. 124–25.

145. Bruschetta recalls that the phone call took place on July 31. Other accounts suggest events occurred about a month earlier. Other references are somewhat conflicting: Bruschetta writes that the tour happened in 1932. *Agustín Lara y yo*, pp. 123–33. She also relates that civil strife had required that all flights into Havana be diverted. *Agustín Lara y yo*, pp. 126–27. Similarly, Abaroa Martínez describes the visit as happening in 1932. Abaroa Martínez, *El flaco de oro*, pp. 98–102. Vargas later claimed, however, that they arrived on July 10, 1933. Garmabella, *Pedro Vargas*, p. 95. Granados suggests that the stay in Cuba lasted through the remainder of the summer and fall of 1932 and into early 1933 as a photo of Pedro Vargas and Ana María Fernández in his book on XEW includes the caption, "in Havana, 1932," while a few pages later his text describes Lara and company back in Mexico in mid-1933 after a "disastrous tour." Granados, *XEW: 70 años en el aire*, pp. 58, 77.

146. "El compositor Agustín Lara: Gravemente enfermo en Cuba." Unidentified clipping, SLS, vol. 9. "Murió ayer en la Habana el musico-poeta Agustín Lara." Unidentified clipping, SLS, vol. 11.

147. Loaeza and Granados, *Mi novia, la tristeza*, p. 281.

148. Ruiz Rueda, *Agustín Lara: Vida y pasiones*, pp. 166–67; Bruschetta, *Agustín Lara y yo*, pp. 126–27. Loaeza and Granados suggest Agustín manipulated his malady so as to have Angelina join him. *Mi novia, la tristeza*, pp. 279–81.

149. Pedro Vargas, in *Agustín, rencuentro con lo sentimental*, p. 238. In Garmabella's biography of Vargas he simply calls the ship "Reca." Garmabella, *Pedro Vargas*, pp. 93–100. Having sampled a bitter taste of Cuba's tumultuous political climate, Lara and his colleagues would watch from a safe distance as a coalition of labor, students, middle-class groups, and marginalized politicians took part in the ill-fated Revolution of August 1933 that deposed Machado.

150. Named after Veracruz poet Salvador Díaz Mirón (1853–1928).

151. One reporter alleged that Lara had written a waltz titled "Sierra ventana"—inspired by his outbound journey to the island republic. No reference to this can be found, however, in either Granados's or Dueñas and Flores y Escalante's discographies.

152. Pepe Bulnes S., "Nuestras entrevistas con el músico y poeta," "Teatro y cines: Un bello espectáculo," "De teatros, cines y música: Cronica [de] Agustín Lara: Compositor y pianista," "Agustín Lara y el público de Habana," "Encanto: Agustín Lara y su espectaculo." Unidentified clippings, SLS, vol. 8. Apparently upon hearing rumors that Lara had died in Cuba, porteños had erected a memorial in the doorway of the Veracruz Hotel Diligencias.

153. Unidentified clipping, SLS, vol. 7, Another United Press article from Havana stated "Agustín Lara goza de una gran salud." Unidentified clipping, SLS vol. 11.

154. Sigriedo Ariel, "La cumbancha cubana de Agustín Lara," in Bernardo García Díaz and Sergio Guerra Vilaboy (eds.), *La Habana/Veracruz, Veracruz/La Habana: Las dos orillas* (Veracruz and Havana: Universidad de Veracruz, Universidad de Havana, 2002), pp. 497–98. Rita Montaner arrived in Mexico with composer and pianist Ernesto Lecuona in early March 1933. Having met Lara in Cuba shortly before, she is said to have included his song "Palmera" in her repertoire for a show at the Teatro Iris on March 10 for which she received much praise. A review in the magazine *Diversiones* that April complimented Montaner on her interpretation of the song but then went on to mention that she and Lara had gotten into some kind of tiff after

another publication had suggested that Montaner possessed more all-around talent than Lara's newfound interpreter Toña la Negra. Word was that Lara had subsequently prohibited the Cuban from singing his songs. The disagreement eventually set off a rivalry the following year that played out mostly in the Mexican and Cuban press. At one point, Montaner along with Bola de Nieve accompanying her on piano appeared together with Lara and Toña la Negra at the Teatro Politeama. Lara's recollection of this show claims that Toña sang a rendition of "Noche criolla" that provoked such a favorable response from the audience that "applause could be heard from as far away as the North Pole." Agustín Lara, "Como los conocí," Colección JAPS, Archivo Agustín Lara. Subsequent gossip pitted the Cuban and Mexican musicians against each other. Ruiz Rueda, _Agustín Lara: Vida y pasiones,_ pp. 127–29. Sigriedo Ariel, "La cumbancha cubana de Agustín Lara," in Diaz and Vilaboy, p. 497; Ramón Fajardo Estrada, _Rita Montaner: Testimonio de una época_ (Havana: Casa de las Americas, 1997), pp. 110–17; Loaeza and Granados, _Mi novia, la tristeza,_ pp. 288–89.

155. "Agustín Lara seguro de su triumfo," "El doble de Agustín Lara permanece insepulto," "Agustín Lara que dara una serie de recitales en el Teatro Regis." Unidentified clippings, SLS, vol. 8. An unidentified clipping from SLS, vol. 17, pictures Lara responding to mail from fans across the country as well as in Los Angeles, Dallas, and Cuba. Granados, _XEW en el aire,_ p. 80; personal communication with Pável Granados, Mexico City, August 19, 2002. Granados writes elsewhere that Lara and Bruschetta would survey stacks of fan letters and open the most interesting-looking envelopes and then amuse themselves by reading various passionate love proposals. Pável Granados, _Apague la luz ... y escuche_ (Mexico City: Biblioteca de ISSSTE, 1999), p. 87. See also Loaeza and Granados, _Mi novia, la tristeza,_ pp. 39–43, 120–21.

156. Letters were often printed with Lara's "responses" in newspapers such as _Excélsior_ and in a special section of _El Illustrado_ magazine.

157. José Alvarez, "La "purificación de Agustín Lara," _El Universal,_ September 5, 1932. "Agustín Lara listo para su prentación," "Agustín viene a iniciar una nueva época en la canción mexicana." Unidentified clippings, SLS, vol. 8. "Grandes exitos ha tenido Agustín Lara." Unidentifed clipping, SLS, vol. 8.

158. Ruiz Rueda, _Agustín Lara: Vida y pasiones,_ p. 168. Ad for "Xochimilco" show at the Teocalli, SLS, vol. 11.

159. "Teatralerias: Agustín Lara triumfó." Unidentified clipping, SLS, vol. 8. "La presentación de Agustín Lara y sus intérpretes en El Gran Teatro Azteca anoche." Unidentified clipping, August 25, 1932, SLS, vol. 7.

160. "Tuvo un nuevo triumfo ayer en el Regis," _El Universal Gráfico,_ September 1, 1932. "Agustín Lara en el Regis," "Agustín Lara hoy vuelve a la escena en el Regis con una canción purificada," "Agustín Lara que hoy reaparece" (ad for show at Regis). Unidentified clippings, September 1, 1932, SLS, vol. 8. A note from the same time mentioned that Lara's recording contract with the Southern Music Company had expired. His lawyer is listed as Adolfo Fernández Bustamante with an office on Tacuba Street, Mexico City.

161. "Canciones de Lara en escuelas de Ciudad Juárez." _El Universal,_ September 29, 1932. "Comentarios radios." Unidentified clipping dated September 29, 1932, SLS vol. 8.

162. A sampling of the program is available on You Tube, www.youtube.com/watch?v=QOgi_hAcDck

163. Bayer Aspirin of Mexico later became the main sponsor.

164. El Vate translates to poet or, perhaps more precisely, bard.

165. Juan José Zavala, "El radio cominador: Figuras nuevas de la época; el compositor Agustín Lara y los que lo siguen." Unidentified clipping, SLS, vol. 7. The article states that much has been written about "the melancholy, the women, the flowers—all part of the growing legend of Lara whose new radio show starting tomorrow will enter hundreds of homes and reach many listeners."

166. Jorge Laso de la Vega, "Las historias de una leyenda," _Revista de Revistas,_ November 19, 1990, p. 48.

167. The show was broadcast from 1932 to 1944. Loaeza and Granados, *Mi novia, la tristeza*, p. 285.

168. Interview by the author with Pablo Dueñas and Jesús Flores y Escalante, Mexico City, August 13, 2008; Ruiz Rueda, *Agustín Lara: Vida y pasiones*, pp. 106–10; Ramos, "Notas para una rapsodia," in *Agustín, rencuentro con lo sentimental*, pp. 32–33; Loaeza and Granados, *Mi novia, la tristeza*, p. 39. See photos and description of the new studio in Granados, *XEW: 70 años del aire*, pp. 99–105. About the same time, Pedro de Lille presided over another popular show titled "La hora azul," which featured many of the same artists including Lara. Unfortunately, there appear to be few, if any, surviving recordings of these programs.

169. *Siempre*, July 1991, p. 65. Her first encounter with Lara's music as a young girl is also quoted in Javier Galindo Ulloa, "Hoy, centenario del natalico de Agustín Lara," *El Financiero*, October 30, 1997.

170. Pável Granados, *XEW: 70 años en el aire*, pp. 249–56. For testimony from various actor-participants see Bertha Zacatecas, *Vidas en al aire: Pioneros de la radio en México* (Mexico City: Editorial Diana, 1996).

171. The term "modernizing goods" is borrowed from Arnold J. Bauer, *Goods, Power and History: Latin America's Material Culture* (Cambridge: Cambridge University Press, 2001).

172. For a brief overview of Toña la Negra and Lara's history see "Toña la Negra, sí, la de la voz tropical," www.agustin-lara.com/txtfrente.thm.

173. Ruiz Rueda, *Agustín Lara: Vida y pasiones*, p. 168 says that Joaquín Pardavé and Roberto "El Panzón" Soto—whom he knew from ten years earlier working in some of the first *revista* shows at the teatro Lírico—invited him to play at the Teatro Fábregas on Donceles Street (formerly Espalda de San Andrés).

174. Ruiz Rueda, *Agustín Lara: Vida y pasiones*, pp. 171–77.

175. Unidentified clipping, SLS vol. 8; Loaeza and Granados, *Mi novia, la tristeza*, p. 221.

176. Bruschetta, *Agustín Lara y yo*, pp. 134–38, 142–46.

177. "Languidez" sheet music published by Editorial Promotora Hispano Americana de Música, S.A., 1954. "Languidez" was first recorded by Lara for Peerless in 1933 (s/n). The 1933 original version by Lara was accessed from Granados, *Canciones*, disc one, track 15.

178. Accessed via RCA Victor disc titled "Agustín Lara y su orquesta."

179. Although not explained, presumably Lara nicknamed Peregrino "Toña" as short for "Antonia" and "la Negra" because of her darker skin and other Afro-Mexican physical attributes.

180. Abaroa Martínez, *El flaco de oro*, p. 113; "Beatriz Reyes Nevares, Sensualidad jarocha," interview conducted in February 1962; reprinted in David Martin del Campo (ed.), *100 Entrevistas Personajes*, pp. 265–57.

181. A statue of Lara and Peregrino Álvarez is located just across from La Iglesia del Cristo del Buen Viaje at the entrance of the La Huaca neighborhood in the Port of Veracruz. On Toña's legacy see Paco Pildora, "Homenaje de Paco Píldora a la gran Toña la Negra," *Excélsior*, no date, Fondo Francisco Rivera, file 1V, AMV. In the working-class La Huaca neighborhood Hornos alley was subsequently renamed "Toña la Negra" in the 1980s. Traveling to Veracruz for the occasion, Carlos Monsiváis was quoted as saying "here there remains a lifestyle (and culture) that has long been lost in Mexico City." "Homenaje a Toña la Negra," unidentified clipping, Fondo Francisco Rivera, file 1V, AMV. Testifying to the richness of the port's popular culture, the same rustic alleyway was home to another beloved local musician named Pedro "Moscovita" Domínguez Castillo. A singer of boleros and other songs in the "tropical" style (including works by Lara and Gonzalo Curiel), Moscovita was especially known for his song "Se estaba poniendo Viejo"—often performed with the University of Veracruz orchestra. Athletic in his youth, Moscovita was friends with Veracruz baseball stars Chacho Hernández and Pepe Moll as well as Cuban film star Ninón Sevilla. As his friend Santás Ximenez fondly remembered, "to speak of Moscovita is to evoke the bohemian and romantic age in Veracruz." He died of a heart attack in 1989. The atmosphere of this neighborhood with its many musicians and personalities is also recounted in Paco Pildora, "Un barrio, una mujer y una voz incomparable!" Unidentified clipping, Fondo Francisco Rivera, file 1V, AMV.

182. Toña states that she first performed with Lara at the El Retiro on December 16, 1932 and there again at the end of the month. Toña la Negra, in *Agustín, rencuentro con lo sentimental*,

p. 247. These may have been preliminary, informal meetings of the two before they began working together regularly the following year because Bruschetta and Abaroa Martínez both date her meeting with Lara and subsequent collaboration approximately a year later. In her 1980 interview with journalist Cristina Pacheco, Toña remembers having met Lara in August 1932. Cristina Pacheco, *Los dueños de la noche* (Mexico City: Plaza y Janés, 2001), p. 105.

183. Agustín later claimed that he had met Peregrino in the Port of Veracruz in 1928 and then at the El Retiro in 1930. Agustín Lara, "Como los conoci," Colección JAPS, Archivo Agustín Lara.

184. Alejandro Campos Bravo, "Toña la Negra: Anédotas de su vida privada." Unidentified clipping, SLS, vol. 9; Bruschetta, *Agustín Lara y yo*, pp. 138–41.

185. "Apoteósico triunfo sin precedente de Agustín Lara y Toña la Negra," *El Siglo de Torreón* (Torreón, Coahuila), August 28, 1933, SLS, vol. 16; *El Viajante* (Monterrey, Nuevo León), September 1933; and other unidentified clippings, SLS, vol. 10.

186. A favorable review of the show "Bambalinas" appeared in an unidentified illustrated magazine dated October 21, 1933. The theater is not identified. SLS, vol. 10.

187. Alejandro Campos Bravo, "Toña la Negra: Anecdotas de su vida privada," "Teatros: Los estrenos del Sabado," "Politeama Maravilla!" along with an advertisement for the show dated April 17, 1934 and a review "Teatro en Mexico" from *Mexico al Día* (Mexico City), May 15, 1934, among other short reviews. Unidentified clippings, SLS, vol. 9. The show "Carnival" is mentioned in SLS, vol. 10. Other reviews of the "Toledo" and "Carnival" shows at the Princesa and Politeama theaters appear in SLS, vol. 17. *Diversiones* magazine, April 28, 1934 mentions Lara returning to the Politeama. See also Dueñas, *Las divas*, pp. 173–76 and Garmabella, *Pedro Vargas*, pp. 102–03.

188. Ramos, *Agustín Lara: Cien años, cien canciones*, p. 62.

189. Undated version of "Lamento jarocho" accessed via *Toña la Negra: La sensación jarocha*, Peerless 1990, CD # PCD-098-9.

190. Ramos, *Agustín Lara: Cien años, cien canciones*, p. 79.

191. "Oración caribe" accessed via *Toña la Negra: La sensación jarocha*, Peerless 1990.

192. H. Camino Díaz, "La Negra Toña" el hit del año." Unidentified clipping, SLS, vol. 15.

193. Another show titled *Talismán* featured Ana María Fernández. Filling in for Fernández one night, singer Sofía Álvarez impressed Lara with her rendition of "Cabellera negra." The composition became her signature song. Later, she also claimed to be the inspiration for his song "Muñeca" despite earlier claims to the contrary. Sonia Álvarez, in *Agustín, rencuentro con lo sentimental*, p. 243–45. She would continue to collaborate with Lara on future occasions including various *La Hora Íntima* radio broadcasts on XEW, certain films where producers made use of his compositions (i.e., *Lágrimas de sangre*, 1946), and in theaters.

194. Toña la Negra, in *Agustín, rencuentro con lo sentimental*, p. 249.

195. Ana María Fernández, in *Agustín, rencuentro con lo sentimental*, p. 229.

196. Querido Moheno, "Paréntesis lírico," *Excélsior*, July 16, 1935.

197. "Agustín Lara," *El Universal*, May 26, 1933. SLS, vol. 17.

198. Indiana (pseudonym), "Opiniones femininas: Otra vez Agustín Lara." Unidentified clipping, SLS, vol. 17.

199. Antonio de Cárdenas,"Origin de las viejas canciones mexicanas," *El Illustrado* (Mexico City), no date, SLS, vol. 17.

200. Salvador Landázuri D., "Agustín Lara según lo ve S. Landázuri." Unidentified clipping, SLS, vol. 17.

201. Querido Moheno, "Paréntesis lírico," *Excélsior*, July 16, 1935.

202. For a fascinating discussion of music and nationalism see Andrew F. Jones, *Yellow Music: Media and Colonial Modernity in the Chinese Jazz Age* (Durham, NC: Duke University Press, 2001) as well as Jeffrey H. Jackson, *Making Jazz French: Music and Modern Life in Interwar France* (Durham, NC: Duke University Press, 2003).

203. "Como los conoci," Colección JAPS, Archivo Agustín Lara.

204. Loaeza and Granados, *Mi novia, la tristeza*, pp. 274–75.

205. Lara later acknowledged that the incident "cost him a lot of money." "Como los conoci," Colección JAPS, Archivo Agustín Lara. Abaroa Martínez, *El flaco de oro*, p. 96; Loaeza and

Granados, *Mi novia, la tristeza*, pp. 277, 307. Bruschetta also mentions Pampín and the incident. *Agustín Lara y yo*, pp. 147–48.

206. Quoted in *El Universal*, January 11, 1934,

207. *El Universal*, January 11, 1934; see also *El Ilustrado*, January 18, 1934, p. 4. A while later, a picture of Lara and some friends in Los Angeles appeared in the May 3, 1934 issue. For a history of Mexican musicians working in Hollywood see John Koegel, "Mexican Musicians in California and the United States, 1910–50," pp. 6–29.

208. "New Mexican Music Heard: Agustin Lara, Irving Berlin of Southern Republic, Demonstrates Technique at Biltmore." *Los Angeles Times*, January 9, 1934.

209. "Famous song writer can't read music, he confesses." *El Paso Herald Post*, January 20, 1934; "Agustín Lara obtuvo un señalado triumfo en El Paso, TX," *El Universal*, January 30, 1934. SLS, vol. 11.

210. "Famous song writer can't read music, he confesses."

211. Jorge Labra, "Lara, el arte y la música." Unidentified clipping, SLS, vol. 11. Ads for Lara performing in El Paso, Juárez, and Chihuahua City (*El Heraldo*) where he played the Alcázar Theater can be seen in SLS, vol. 11.

212. I thank my colleague Alejandro Madrid for alerting me to this saying.

213. On the practice of US State Department "cultural diplomacy" between 1950 and 1970 see, for example, Penny M. Von Eschen, *Satchmo Blows up the World: Jazz Ambassadors Play the Cold War* (Cambridge, MA: Harvard University Press, 2004).

214. Unsigned copy of letter from María Teresa Lara and Agustín Lara to José Briceño at Southern Music Publishing Company in New York City, March 22, 1934. Colección JAPS, Archivo Agustín Lara, Carpeta #1 "Documentos Personales."

215. Personal communication with Pablo Dueñas, September 20, 2008, Loaeza and Granados, *Mi novia, la tristeza*, pp. 244–45. See also various sheet music publications of Lara's music copyrighted both by Southern (late 1920s/early 1930s) and then Peer International (early 1940s). The Mexican Society of Authors and Composers in Mexico City (SACM) presently owns the copyrights.

216. Bruschetta, *Agustín Lara y yo*, pp. 150–54. Given the obvious nationalist imagery of the sisters' names "Peace" and "Hope" along with their surname "Eagle" one might suspect that these were stage names. I have found no evidence to support this notion, however.

217. Allegedly, Lara had met Paz and Esperanza as he was fleeing from someone who purportedly to want to kill him for whatever reason. "Como los conoci," Colección JAPS, Archivo Agustín Lara. See also Loaeza and Granados, *Mi novia, la tristeza*, pp. 274–75.

218. Las Hermanas Águila, in *Agustín, rencuentro con lo sentimental*, p. 251; Abaroa Martínez, *El flaco de oro*, p. 110.

219. Bertha Zacatecas, *Vidas en al aire: Pioneros de la radio en México*, p. 33. Zacatecas writes that the sisters first performed professionally in 1934. They actually did so a year earlier. See Tamargo, *Bolero: Clave del corazón*, p. 154.

220. Zacatecas, *Vidas en al aire*, p. 34; Granados, *XEW: 70 años en el aire*, pp. 66–67.

221. Las Hermanas Águila, in *Agustín, rencuentro con lo sentimental*, p. 253.

222. "El arte musical y nuestro pueblo; Agustín Lara: Esponente de la raza y de la época." Unidentified clipping, Guadalajara newspaper, July 1934, SLS, vol. 13.

223. On the product and associated radio advertising see Mexico Bob's blog, June 5, 2008, "Sal de Uvas," http://mexicobob.blogspot.com/2008_06_01_archive.html; Daniel Castañeda, *Balance de Agustín Lara* (Mexico City: Ediciones Libres, 1941), pp. 15–16.

224. Granados, *Canciones*, pp. 389–90; Juan S. Garrido, *Historia de la música popular en México, 1896–1973* (Mexico City: Editorial Extemporáneos S.A., 1974), p. 73; Moreno Rivas, *Historia de la música popular mexicana*, p. 157.

225. A 2008 film of the same name based on the 1985 book by novelist Ángeles Mastratta won several awards.

226. Ramos, *Agustín Lara: Cien años, cien canciones*, p. 24.

227. Lyrics from Granados, *Canciones*, p. 152. Music accessed via *Las Número Uno: Agustín Lara*, Sony/BMG 2005, BMG 205 CD # 828767585222.

228. "Vida Parralense: Alcanzó un gran triumfo el compositor Lara," *Correo de Parral* (Parral, Chihuahua), September 5, 1934.
229. Alberto M. Alvarado, "Agustin Lara," *Diario de Durango* (Durango). Unidentified clipping, SLS, vol. 13.
230. "Agustín Lara a punto de morir," *El Heraldo del Norte* (Nuevo Laredo, Tamaulipas), September 13, 1934; "Resulto herido Agustín Lara en Nuevo Laredo, Tamps.," *La Prensa* (San Antonio, TX), September 14, 1934. SLS, vol. 13.
231. "Desde la Ciudad de México: Que os ha hecho Agustín Lara!," *El Dictamen* (Port of Veracruz, Veracruz) October 28, 1934. SLS, vol. 13. Unidentified clipping, SLS, vol. 14.
232. "Desde la Ciudad de México."
233. Monsiváis refers to this gathering as the "Congreso de Mujeres Intelectuales contra la Prostitucíon" (Congress of Female Intellectuals against Prostitution). Carlos Monsiváis, Agustín Lara: El harem ilusorio (Notas a partir de la memorización de la letra de "Farolito"), in *Amor Perdido* (Mexico City: Biblioteca Era, 1977), p. 79.
234. Quoted in Ángeles Magdelano, "Introduccíon," Archivo de Agustín Lara de la Colección JAPS, p. 4.
235. "El exótico Agustín Lara será bicoteado," *La Prensa* (San Antonio, TX), June 24, 1934. Monsiváis mentions a Señora Monterrubio who, perhaps in an effort to be diplomatic, had invited Lara to attend the conference.
236. A cartoon in *El Universal* portrayed a classroom of school kids being given a choice between orchestra music and the recordings of Lara by their teacher. Enthusiastically, they choose Lara. *El Universal*, no date, SLS, vol. 7.
237. "Nuestro Agustín." Unidentified clipping, SLS, vol. 7.
238. "Galería bohemia: México de noche." Unidentified clipping, SLS, vol. 10.
239. Quoted in "Nuestro Agustín." Unidentified clipping, SLS, vol. 7.
240. Quoted in "Nuestro Agustín." Unidentified clipping, SLS, vol. 7.
241. "Sociología candorosa," *El Universal Gráfico*, June 25, 1934.
242. On cursilería in Spain see Noël Valis, *The Culture of Cursilería: Bad Taste, Kitsch and Class in Modern Spain* (Durham, NC: Duke University Press, 2002).
243. Oscar LeBlanc, "Lara, el larismo y las mujeres," *El Illustrado*, no date. SLS, vol. 7.
244. Chavela Vargas, *Y si quieres saber de mi pasado* (Madrid: Aguilar/Santillana Ediciones Generales, 2002), pp. 47–48. On the reform in northern Mexico, see Eric Michael Schantz, "From Mexicali Rose to the Tijuana Brass: Vice Tours of the United States Mexico Border, 1910–1965." PhD dissertation, History Department, University of California, Los Angeles, 2001.
245. Untitled *Universal* clipping dated January 11, 1936. Archivo Silvino González, Biblioteca Nacional de México, Fondo Reservado. Even Guadalupe Marín (ex-wife of Diego Rivera) got in on the action a few years later when in 1941 she condemned Lara for his opulent tastes and objectification of young, scantily clad women. Carlos Monsiváis, "Agustín Lara: El harem ilusorio, in *Amor Perdido* p. 79.
246. "Lara en el indice." Unidentified clipping, SLS, vol. 14.
247. "La reglamento del canto." Unidentified clipping, SLS, vol. 17.
248. Carlos Leon G., "Nuestros concursantes: Interpretando a Lara." Unidentified clipping, SLS, vol. 15. As the illustration suggests, rumors that Lara was a longtime pot smoker circulated freely.
249. Rafael Sánchez Escobar, "El alma del pueblo mexicano," *El Hispano Americano* (Tijuana, BC), February 5, 1936. SLS, vol. 10.

## Chapter 4

1. Quoted in Antonio Salazar Paez, "El flaco de oro, un hombre atormentado y de contrastes que cantó siempre al amor," *Novedades* (Mexico City), November 9, 1970.
2. Verna Carleton Millan, *Mexico Reborn* (Boston: Houghton Mifflin, 1939), p. 1. The article was originally published in the US magazine *Musical Courier* a few years earlier. Carleton Millan had married a Mexican doctor and the two made their home in Mexico City. She

makes virtually no further mention of popular music in her book. Instead, she comments on the high art, classical Mexican composers: Silvestre Revueltas, Carlos Chavez, and their followers, who sought to incorporate indigenist and other folkloric elements into their music. At one point, Millan writes disparagingly of the cultural climate of the capital: "The musicians in Mexico were faced with a situation even more difficult than that which confronted the writers. In spite of Mexico City's pretense of being a cultural center and the capital of the nation, there was no musical life whatsoever beyond a few stray concerts by visiting celebrities or enterprising students. The flamboyant theater of the Fine Arts Palace was only occupied on rare occasions by the Symphonic Orchestra, the local opera company, which we shall charitably pass over without a comment, and a stray pianist or two. . . . During the years that I have been correspondent here for the *Musical Courier* I have spent a great portion of my time trying to explain to the more than patient editors why I do not send regular material. There is really nothing to send." Carleton Millan, *Mexico Reborn*, p. 183.

3. Gringa/gringo is a Mexican term for people from the United States, Canada, Britain, and most of Northern Europe. More generally, it includes all whites, although it is not to be confused with *güera*, which refers to someone with a light complexion. "Palmeras" was first recorded by Pedro Vargas in 1933 on Peerless (875).

4. Mario Arturo Ramos (ed.), *Agustín Lara: Cien años, cien canciones* (Mexico City: Océano, 2000), p. 83.

5. Undated version with Alfonso Ortiz Tirado singing. Accessed via *Tenores inolvidables de México*, RCA Victor/BMG 2004, CD # 82876654652-1.

6. Boytler had studied with Stanislavsky in Russia before the Revolution and became acquainted with Eisenstein once in Mexico. He had just directed the groundbreaking *Mujer del Puerto* in 1933. Carl Mora, *Mexican Cinema: Reflections of a Society, 1896–1988*, p. 37. On Boytler, see Eduardo de la Vega Alfaro, *Arcady Boytler: Pioneros del cine sonoro II* (Guadalara, Mexico: Universidad de Guadalajara (Centro de Investigación y Enseñanza Cinematográficas [CIEC]), 1992.

7. Paco Ignacio Taibo I lists this film as being produced in 1930. Paco Ignacio Taibo I, *La música de Agustín Lara en el cine* (Mexico City: UNAM, 1984), p. 71.

8. Ramos, *Agustín Lara: Cien años, cien canciones*, p. 22.

9. "Amor de mis amores," from the album *Rosa: Agustín Lara*, RCA Victor MKL-1131, (compilation of recordings between 1950–1953), released in 1956. Dueñas and Flores Escalante, *Discography*. Ana María Fernández first recorded the song for RCA Victor in 1936. Pável Granados, *Agustín Lara: Canciones* (Mexico City: Gobierno de Veracruz/Océano, 2008), p. 151. Version accessed via *Agustín Lara: 20 exitos*. RCA Victor/BMG 1991, CD #CDM-3352.

10. I had the opportunity to meet Carlos Águila (brother of Paz and Esperanza) at the Hostería Santo Domingo on 72 Belisario Dominguez. After I introduced myself, Carlos agreed to meet and talk with me about Lara, about whom he said, "he'd tell me many things that have not ever been written about by his former wives [and many girlfriends]." Unfortunately, I had to leave Mexico City the next day but planned to return the following spring to interview Águila. When I did, the other musicians at the restaurant told me he had died a few months before.

11. Gabriel Abaroa Martínez, *El flaco de oro* (Mexico City: Editorial Planeta, 1993), p. 115; Angelina Bruschetta, *Agustín Lara y yo: 1928–1938* (Xalapa, Veracruz: Author's ed., 1979), p. 156; Guadalupe Loaeza and Pável Granados, *Mi novia, la tristeza* (Mexico City: Océano, 2008), pp. 304–05.

12. Bruschetta quoted in Loaeza and Granados, *Mi novia, la tristeza*, pp. 308–09.

13. *La Prensa* (San Salvador), March 17, 1935.

14. Victor had merged with RCA in 1929 when RCA bought the Victor Talking Machine Company, then the largest producer of photographs (including the famous "Victrola").

15. La Prensa, March 17, 1935. Hernández Martínez presided over one of the most tragic peasant revolts (led by the legendary Agustín Farabundo Martí Rodríguez) and subsequent massacre in 1932.

16. *El Liberal Progresista* (Guatemala City), March 27, 1935. An article by Gustavo Ávila Arevalo, "Panegírico de Agustín Lara," in *Imparcial* (Guatemala City, Guatemala) the previous

year (March 23, 1934) extolled the virtues of Lara and claimed that in his music there was "nearly something for everyone."

17. "Leading Mexican Composer Flying to San Antonio," *San Antonio Evening News* (San Antonio); "Enthusiasmo por la presentación del compositor mexicano Agustín Lara," *La Prensa* (San Antonio). Unidentified clippings, Salvador Lara Scrapbooks (SLS), vol. 10.

18. *La Noticia* (Managua, Nicaragua), December 14, 1935.

19. Granados, *Canciones*, pp. 386–91.

20. June Kay, *Las siete vidas de Agustín Lara*, trans. F. de Riba Millon (Mexico City: El Universal Gráfico, 1964), p. 273.

21. Loaeza and Granados, *Mi novia, la tristeza*, pp. 247–48.

22. On this legendary figure see Ian Kelly, *Casanova: Actor, Love, Priest, Spy* (New York: Penguin, 2011).

23. Ramos, *Agustín Lara: Cien años, cien canciones*, p. 57.

24. Pedro Vargas, "Granada," Peerless (830) accessed via *Pedro Vargas: Época de oro de la radio, grabaciones de 1932–1935*. Instituto de conservación y recuperación musical S.C. 1996, CD #ICREM-01.

25. Many ensuing versions would employ a similar style and structure: 1) instrumental introduction foreshadowing the melody, 2) descending, cadenza-like transitional section with a solo instrument (often trumpet), 3) march-like verse, 4) instrumental interlude in slower, habanera time, 5) chorus. Personal communication with John Koegel, Summer 2010.

26. Loaeza and Granados write that Lara had dinner with film producer Santiago Reachi at the El Retiro one night. When Reachi asked Agustín if he thought Angelina might be interested in a screen test, Lara apparently reacted defensively, telling Reachi "my wife is simply my wife." *Mi novia, la tristeza*, p. 312.

27. Bruschetta, *Agustín Lara y yo*, pp. 174–75.

28. Pável Granados, personal communication, Mexico City, August 19, 2002.

29. Bruschetta, *Agustín Lara y yo*, pp. 158–61; Loaeza and Granados, *Mi novia, la tristeza*, p. 305.

30. Stereotypical Mexican "types"—especially the *china poblana*, conceived as an independent rural woman dressed in a white cotton blouse, skirt, and rebozo (shawl). See Ricardo Pérez Montfort, *Expresiones populares y estereotipos culturales en Mexico: Ensayos sobre cultura popular y nacionalism* (Mexico City: Centro de investigaciones y studios superiores en anthropología social, 1994), pp. 119–46.

31. Emilio García Rivera, *Historia documental del cine mexicano*, Vol. 1, 2nd edition (Guadalajara: Universidad de Guadalajara, 1992), pp. 249–50; Taibo I, *La música de Agustín Lara en el cine*, p. 26. A *novillero* is a bullfighter aspiring to full mastery as a matador working in a "minor league" context (*novilladas*) where bulls are between two and four years old. In full *corridas* matadors typically fight five-year-old bulls. Adrian Shubert, *Death and Money in the Afternoon: A History of the Spanish Bullfight* (Oxford: Oxford University Press, 1999), p. 58.

32. Pável Granados, *Apague la luz... y escuche* (Mexico City: Biblioteca de Instituto de Seguridad y Servicios Sociales de los Trabajadores del Estado [ISSSTE], 1999), p. 79. Fellow composer Manuel M. Ponce is said to have commented that all [Lara] was missing in his repertoire were two songs appropriately named "Whore" (*Ramera*) and "Laid" (*Horizontal*). No doubt Lara enjoyed much of this presumed rebellious play with public morality. Quoted in Ángeles Magdelano, "Introducción," Colección de Agustín Lara JAPS, p. 4.

33. Ramos, *Agustín Lara: Cien años, cien canciones*, p. 116; Abaroa Marínez, *El flaco de oro*, pp. 121–22; "Himno a la tierra jarocha," www.agustin-lara.com/txtsisupieras.htm. Loaeza and Granados note that the original contained the lyrics "sangre de pirata" (blood of a pirate), which Lara later changed. Nevertheless, Emilio Tuero, Valente Garza, and Antonio Badú made recordings of this earlier version of "Veracruz." *Mi novia, la tristeza*, p. 313.

34. Lara first recorded "Veracruz" for RCA Victor in 1936. Granados, *Canciones*, p. 232. 1951 version accessed via *Agustín Lara: 20 exitos*. RCA Victor/BMG 1991, track 6.

35. "Un canción de Lara: Adoptada como himno en Veracruz." Unidentified clipping, SLS, vol. 8. Bruschetta, *Agustín Lara y yo*, pp. 132–34.

36. *El Universal*, September 17, 1936. SLS, vol. 11.

37. Garmabella, *Pedro Vargas: "Una vez nada más"* (Mexico City: Ediciones de communicación, 1984) p. 105.

38. Bruschetta, *Agustín Lara y yo*, pp. 221–22, and Loaeza and Granados, *Mi novia, la tristeza*, p. 312, mention that she attended the opening of the Teocali nightclub with friends José Galindo and Raulito.

39. Ramos, *Agustín Lara: Cien años, cien canciones*, p. 77.

40. Version accessed via *Agustín Lara: 20 exitos*. RCA Victor/BMG 1991.

41. Ramos, *Agustín Lara: Cien años, cien canciones*, p. 77.

42. Lara met her in 1933 and was never clear whether she was Colombian or Venezuelan. He would later write, "Some say she was Venezuelan, others Colombian—all I know is that she was a beautiful woman." Agustín Lara, "La vida íntima de un gran músico 'con alma de pirata,'" *Life en español*, January 15, 1968, p. 57; Antonio Salazar Paez, "El flaco de oro, un hombre atormentado y de contrastes que cantó siempre al amor," *Novedades*, November 9, 1970. Loaeza and Granados claim her father was a Revolutionary General. *Mi novia, la tristeza*, p. 81.

43. Bruschetta, *Agustín Lara y yo*, pp. 183–90.

44. Taibo I, *La música de Agustín Lara en el cine*, p. 71. García Riera, *Historia documental del cine mexicano*, vol. 1, pp. 245–46.

45. January 1937 Mexico City newspaper ad for *Novillero*, SLS, vol. 11; Taibo I, *La música de Agustín Lara en el cine*, p. 71; Mora, *Mexican Cinema*, p. 149.

46. Ramos, *Agustín Lara: Cien años, cien canciones*, p. 21.

47. "Adios Nicanor" was first recorded by Juan Arvizu in 1930. Granados, *Canciones*, p. 59. No company information is given. Ana María González and Lara recorded it for Anfión in 1948. Dueñas and Flores y Escalante, *Discography*. The film also featured the Trío Calaveras known for backing singer and actor Jorge Negrete and for participating in the 1945 Disney film *The Three Caballeros*, along with the Trío Ascencio del Rio.

48. Abaroa Martínez, *El flaco de oro*, p. 126–28.

49. Summary from UCLA Film and Television Archive catalogue, http://cinema.library. ucla.edu.

50. A visit by the author to the SACM Mexico City headquarters in July 2003 and subsequently in August 2008 unearthed no available records on Lara. I suspect that they have material on Lara but guard it closely. Their website offers a basic list of the songwriter's work but not much else (www.sacm.org.mx).

51. Bruschetta, *Agustín Lara y yo*, pp. 232–34; Loaeza and Granados, *Mi novia, la tristeza*, p. 316.

52. Bruschetta, *Agustín Lara y yo*, pp. 223–25.

53. Adolfo Fernández Bustamante, "Habla Agustín Lara, el compositor intuitivo," *Todo*, March 30, 1937. Some say that he secretly paid for the upkeep of Maruca's gravesite at the Panteón Español until his death. Pável Granados, *XEW: 70 años del aire* (Mexico City: Editorial Clío, 2000), pp. 85–86.

54. Loaeza and Granados, *Mi novia, la tristeza*, pp. 316–20. Details on Lara's contract with Paramount are unknown.

55. Angelina Bruschetta to Agustín Lara, January 4, 1938. Loaeza and Granados *Mi novia, la tristeza*, pp. 52–53.

56. On Cedillo see Dudley Ankerson, *Agrarian Warlord: Saturnino Cedillo and the Mexican Revolution in San Luis Potosí, 1890–1940* (DeKalb: Northern Illinois University Press, 1985).

57. Bruschetta, *Agustín Lara y yo*, pp. 232–33.

58. About this same time, a number of popular English-language composers (Irving Berlin, George Gershwin, Cole Porter, and Hoagie Carmichael, among others) took to adapting Afro-Cuban rhythms (often loosely termed "rhumba") to their repertoire. See Gustavo Pérez Firmat, "Latunes: An Introduction." *Latin American Research Review*, Vol. 43, No. 2, (Spring 2008), pp. 180–203.

59. Agustín Lara to Angelina Bruschetta, February 9, 1938. Quoted in Loaeza and Granados, *Mi novia, la tristeza*, p. 56.

60. A prolific musical director and double agent (he spied for the Soviets), Boris Morros actually received the nomination for the *Tropic Holiday* music. www.imdb.com/title/tt0030897.

61. Loaeza and Granados, *Mi novia, la tristeza*, pp. 60–65.

62. Undated composite letter/remembrance from Angelina Bruschetta to Agustín Lara. Quoted in Loaeza and Granados, *Mi novia, la tristeza*, p. 28.

63. Loaeza and Granados, *Mi novia, la tristeza*, p. 320.

64. Loaeza and Granados, *Mi novia, la tristeza*, pp. 30–32, 55–59; Abaroa Martínez, *El flaco de oro*, pp. 123–26; Bruschetta, *Agustín Lara y yo*, pp. 193–219. For his part, Javier Ruiz Rueda, *Augstín Lara: Vida y pasiones* (Mexico City: Editorial Novaro, 1976), pp. 138–39, 143–47, incorrectly says this all happened in 1934. In her memoir, Bruschetta occasionally mentions "los ninos" (the children) or, while in Los Angeles, "el bebé" (the baby) during this time. Aside from her son Jorge, the younger child is later identified as her brother Alfonso's six-year-old son, whom she and Lara often talked of adopting. Early in 1938, however, Alfonso was seriously injured in a car accident while his son (then six) was also hit by a truck and injured about the same time. *Agustin Lara y yo*, p. 252.

65. Lara to Bruschetta, June 28, 1938. Reproduced in Mónica Barrón Echauri, *Álbum Fotográfico de Agustín Lara* (Veracruz/Mexico City: Gobierno de Veracruz/Océano, 2008). The two-page letter was written on Ravenswood Hotel stationary—570 North Rossmore, Los Angeles.

66. Bruschetta, *Agustín Lara y yo*, pp. 226–28. Angelina claims Lara never played these two songs again.

67. Bruschetta, *Agustín Lara y yo*, pp. 277–81; Abaroa Martínez, *El flaco de oro*, pp. 132–36; Loaeza and Granados, *Mi novia, La tristeza*, pp. 66–72. Ruiz Rueda does not include many details but nevertheless says Lara had been paying attention to other women. *Agustín Lara: Vida y pasiones*, pp. 160–61.

68. Support for the trip from Cárdenas was commented on during a personal communication with Pável Granados, Mexico City, August 19, 2002.

69. Carte d'Identité 1938–39. Colección JAPS, Archivo Agustín Lara, Carpeta #1, "Documentos personales."

70. Siqueiros and Revueltas both traveled to Spain to support the Republicans in the Civil War. On Revueltas during this period see Carol A. Hess, "Silvestre Revueltas in Republican Spain: Music as a Political Utterance," *Latin American Music Review/Revista de Música Latinoamericana*, Vol. 18, No. 2 (Autumn-Winter, 1997), pp. 278–96.

71. Loaeza and Granados, *Mi novia, la tristeza*, pp. 73–83.

72. Colección JAPS, Archivo Agustín Lara.

73. Carlos del Paso, "Agustin Lara, Genio Musical Mexicano, Conquista a Paris." n/d, unidentified Mexican newspaper, Colección JAPS, Archivo Agustín Lara.

74. Mike Gossip, "Ojo mágico," *Cine*, October 21, 1939. p. 46.

75. Fernando de la Llave, "Mole de olla en Francia," unidentified Mexican newspaper, ca. April 1939, Colección JAPS, Archivo Agustín Lara. See also "El Arribo de Lara," unidentified newspaper photo (n/d) showing Lara, back from Europe after an allegedly long and successful stay. JAPS, Archivo Agustín Lara.

76. Renato Leduc, in Eugenio Méndez (ed.), *Agustín, rencuentro con lo sentimental* (Mexico City: Editorial Domés, 1980), p. 271; Loaeza and Granados, *Mi novia, la tristeza*, p. 88.

77. Ruiz Rueda, *Agustín Lara: Vida y pasiones*, pp. 182–83.

78. Renato Leduc, in *Agustín, rencuentro con lo sentimental*, pp. 272–73; Bruschetta, in *Agustín, rencuentro con lo sentimental*, p. 211; Ruiz Rueda, *Agustín Lara: Vida y pasiones*, pp. 183–84.

79. Ramos, *Agustín Lara: Cien años, cien canciones*, p. 76.

80. Accessed via the CD *Agustín Lara: Su voz, su piano y sus canciones*. Orfeón JCD-1908 (n/d). "Naufragio" was first recorded by Johnny Rodríguez y Su Conjunto in New York on August 8, 1939 for Decca (21026). Lara first recorded it for RCA Victor in 1953. Granados, *Canciones*, p. 247. In a 1956 version of the song, a brass section provides an upbeat introduction before Lara launches into the first verse. This more commercial, show-biz interpretation runs somewhat contrary to the song's character given the relatively somber material presented in the lyrics.

81. "Guajiro" refers to someone from the Cuban countryside.
82. For a brief comment on meeting Lara by Fernández see "Xiomara Fernández, una joya de las ondas radiales y la pantalla televisiva," www.radiocubana.cu/historia/la_memoria_radial/xiomara_fernandez.asp.
83. Abaroa Martínez, *El flaco de oro*, p. 139, writes that Lara went to New York briefly on his way to Venezuela from France as does Ruiz Rueda, *Agustín Lara: vida y pasiones*, pp. 184–85. Loaeza and Granados believe that he visited Cuba starting in late November 1938 and then returned to Mexico before leaving for Venezuela via New York. *Mi novia, la tristeza*, pp. 96–115. The above testimony by Xiomara Fernández gives credence to Loaeza and Granados's version.
84. Apparently no religious record exists of the marriage, although Lara would remain wedded to Zozaya and she would claim to be one of his widows. She later received rights to one quarter of his work, which she donated to the Actors Guild. Loaeza and Granados, *Mi novia, la tristeza*, pp. 96–98; Abaroa Martínez, *El flaco de oro*, pp. 139–40; Ruiz Rueda, *Agustín Lara: vida y pasiones*, pp. 184–85. On the question of his previous marriages, Lara's "deathbed marriage" to Angelina was never made official despite their ten years together. His first marriage to Esther Rivas Elorriaga still remained on the books. Later, Lara writes untruthfully that his union with Carmen "was his first marriage." Lara, "La vida íntima de un gran músico," p. 57.
85. Escobar married Paz Águila.
86. Somewhat confusingly, Ruiz Rueda, *Agustín Lara: Vida y pasiones*, pp. 184–99, and Abaroa Martínez, *El flaco de oro*, pp. 139–43, describe the trip as originating in Venezuela and then following a series of extensions to Brazil, the Río de la Plata region, and Chile rather than two separate trips with the second including a visit in New York.
87. Colección JAPS, Archivo Agustín Lara, Carpeta #1, Passport (and visa stamps), issued January 1941, "Documentos Personales." The description of Lara did not fail to mention the pronounced scar on his left cheek among other physical characteristics, including his height (165 centimeters), hair color (black), eye color (brown), and skin color (white).
88. Loaeza and Granados, *Mi novia, la tristeza*, pp. 101, 292.
89. Rueda, *Agustín Lara: Vida y pasiones*, p. 185. Ruiz Rueda also gives the title "Goodbye Broadway." "Broadway Adiós" was first recorded by Lara on March 17, 1942 in New York City for Decca (10530). Granados, *Canciones*, p. 267. While Granados lists the recording as taking place in 1942, newspaper accounts of Lara and company in the city are from the previous year. See, for example, "Agustín Lara, presentado ante críticos de Nueva York," *Excélsior*, clipping dated February 5, 1941, Archivo Silvino González. At that time, Lara took part in a series of programs broadcast by the National Broadcasting Company.
90. B. Fernández Aldana, "Agustín Lara en Nueva York." Unidentified Mexican Newspaper (n/d), Colección JAPS, Archivo Agustín Lara.
91. Loaeza and Granados, *Mi novia, la tristeza*, pp. 103–04.
92. Ana María González, *Mi voz y yo: memorias* (Madrid: Biblioteca Nueva, 1955), pp. 85–89; Antonio Subirana, liner notes for *Ana María González: Todas sus grabaciones vols. 1 & 2 (1948–1953)*, Madrid: Rama Lama, 2004, CD # RQ-52442. Subirana also writes that Ana María toured Brazil and Argentina with Lara in 1941. Ruiz Rueda and Abaroa Martínez seem to conflate this tour with the earlier one that took place in late 1939.
93. Lara's passport is stamped with a visa by the Brazilian embassy dated March 12, 1941 and then again upon his arrival in Rio de Janeiro on March 26, 1941. Colección JAPS, "Documentos personales."
94. Ramos, *Agustín Lara, Cien años, cien canciones*, p. 104.
95. Loaeza and Granados, *Mi novia, la tristeza*, pp. 106–07. "Solamente una vez" was first recorded by Manolita Arriola in 1941 for Peerless (1779). Granados, *Canciones*, p. 264. Ana María González recorded it for Decca the following year in New York.
96. Agustín Lara, "Como los conocí," Colección JAPS.
97. Ramos, *Agustín Lara: Cien años, cien canciones*, p. 103.

98. Mexican tenor José Mojica (1896–1974), famous for his opera, recital, and film appearances as well as his version of María Grever's "Júrame," also occasionally joined Lara when he was in Buenos Aires. In 1942, Mojica began training in the Franciscan order. Pedro Vargas claims that Mojica impressed Lara and allegedly served as an inspiration for "Solamente una vez." Pedro Vargas, in *Agustín, rencuentro con lo sentimental*, p. 239. In 1956 Mojica published his autobiography *Yo pecador* (Mexico City: Editorial Jus, 1956). On Mojica, see John Koegel, "Mexican Musicians in California and the United States, 1910–50," *California History*, Vol. 84, No. 1 (Fall 2006), pp. 14–20.

99. Loaeza and Granados, *Mi novia, la tristeza*, p. 111. Coming just five years after the tragic death of 44-year-old Carlos Gardel (1887/90?–1935) in a plane accident in Medellín, Colombia in 1935, Lara's presence in the South American capital may have reminded Argentine music fans of their fallen hero. After all, the careers of Gardel and Lara run somewhat parallel up until the tango singer's death. Both began their careers under very modest circumstances. Each articulated a modern melancholia with songs telling heartfelt tales of desire, love, and loss set in an urban context. As Gardel and Lara rose to fame, each transformed his respective popular song genres (tango, bolero) into uniquely modern "American" music. Thanks in part to them, tango and bolero had evolved from a turn-of-the-century music performed by singers to the sound of a guitar into new arrangements that featured singers as part of a larger ensemble. On Gardel see Simon Collier, *The Life, The Music and Times of Carlos Gardel* (Pittsburgh: University of Pittsburgh Press, 1986). On tango see Simon Collier, Artemis Cooper, María Susana Azzi, and Richard Martin, *Tango!: The Dance, The Song, The Story* (London: Thames and Hudson, 1995), pp. 122–26.

100. "Solamente una vez" accessed via *Agustín Lara: Las numero uno*. SONY/BMG, 2005.

101. Subsequently, González achieved success as she again played Rio de Janeiro's Casino Atlántico before returning to Buenos Aires for stints at the Avenida and Politeama Theaters in 1942. She also appeared on Argentine radio.

102. González, *Mi voz y yo*, pp. 103–24.

103. González, *Mi voz y yo*, pp. 125–40.

104. Loaeza and Granados, *Mi novia, la tristeza*, p. 115; Abaroa Martínez, *El flaco de oro*, pp. 139–43; Ruiz Rueda, *Agustín Lara: Vida y pasiones*, pp. 196–99. Lara's passport is stamped with a two-month Chilean visa dated September 15, 1941. Abaroa Martínez and Ruiz Rueda state that the Chilean performances occurred in 1939.

105. Coleccíon JAPS, Archivo Agustín Lara, "Documentos personales."

106. Roberto Ayala (ed.), *Canciones y poemas de Agustín Lara: Colección completa* (Mexico City: Selecciónes Orfeón, 1969), p. 53.

107. "Cada noche un amor" was first recorded by Manolita Arriola in 1942 for Peerless (1855). Granados, *Canciones*, p. 268.

## Chapter 5

1. "The marriage [of Lara] with María Félix is, socially, a magnificent provocation." Carlos Monsiváis, *Amor Perdido* (Mexico City: Ediciones Era, 1977), p. 82.

2. Carl J. Mora, *Mexican Cinema: Reflections of a Society, 1896–1988* (Berkeley: University of California Press, 1982), pp. 52–53; Paulo Antonio Paranaguá, "María Félix: imagen, mito y enigma," *Archivos de la Filmoteca*, no. 31, February 1999, pp. 77–87; Eduardo de la Vega Alfaro, "The Decline of the Golden Age and the Making of a Crisis," in Joanne Hershfield and David R. Maciel (eds.), *Mexico's Cinema: A Century of Film and Filmmakers* (Wilmington, DE: SR Books, 1999), p. 175.

3. Seth Fein, "From Collaboration to Containment: Hollywood and the International Political Economy of Mexican Cinema after the Second World War," in Hershfield and Maciel, *Mexico's Cinema*, pp. 123–63.

4. For an overview of Lara's work in film during the 1940s see Paco Ignacio Taibo I., *La música de Agustín Lara en el cine* (Mexico City: UNAM, 1984), pp. 72–76 and Vicente Leñero, "En casa de la doña," interview conducted in September 1966, reprinted in David Martin del Campo, *100 Entrevistas personajes* (Mexico City: Grupo Azabache, 1991), pp. 75–77.

5. Lara sang "Rosa" in a 1939 film starring Sofía Álvarez, Miguel Arenas, and Tony Díaz titled "Carne de cabaret." He also provided background music for a second-rate ranchero movie titled *Mujeres y toros*, released that same year. María del Carmen de la Peza Casares figures that more than 30 percent of Mexican films produced between 1943 and 1953 were based on boleros. María del Carmen de la Peza Casares, *El bolero y la educación sentimental en México* (Mexico City: Universidad Autónoma Metropolitana-Xochimilco, 2001), p. 200.

6. An executive order on August 31, 1945 transferred the Office of Inter-American Affairs to the Department of State. A year later another executive order abolished the Office and transferred its duties to the Department of State.

7. The CIAA's somewhat interventionist practices during the early years of the war stood in contrast to the US ambassador George Messersmith's belief that such programming would inevitably be insulting to Mexicans and therefore do much harm to binational relations. For discussion on Francisco and others who previously worked for the J. Walter Thompson advertising agency, see Julio E. Moreno, "J. Walter Thompson, The Good Neighbor Policy, and Lessons in Mexican Business Culture, 1920–1950," *Enterprise & Society*, Vol. 5, No. 2 (June 2004), pp. 254–80 as well as Julio Moreno, *Yankee Don't Go Home: Mexican Nationalism, American Business Culture and the Shaping of Modern Mexico, 1920–1950* (Chapel Hill: University of North Carolina Press, 2003).

8. Cerwin had a solid command of Spanish after living in Guatemala for several years. José Luis Ortiz Garza, *La guerra de las ondas: Un libro que desmiente la historia "oficial" de la radio Mexicana* (Mexico City: Planeta, 1992), pp. 27–29.

9. Seth Fein, "From Collaboration to Containment: Hollywood and the International Political Economy of Mexican Cinema after the Second World War," in Maciel and Hershfield, *Mexican Cinema*, pp. 123–63.

10. Ortiz Garza, *La guerra de las ondas*, p. 43.

11. Joy Elizabeth Hayes, *Radio Nation: Communication, Popular Culture, and Nationalism in Mexico, 1920-1950* (Tucson: University of Arizona Press, 2000), p. 34.

12. Quoted in Garza, *La guerra de las ondas*, pp. 48–49.

13. Garza, *La guerra de las ondas*, pp. 94–100.

14. See Miriam D. Baer, "Television and Political Control in Mexico." PhD Dissertation, Department of Communication, University of Michigan, 1991.

15. Garza, *La guerra de las ondas*, p. 122. In 1947, President Miguel Aleman's visit to Washington facilitated XEW's obtainment of "una grabadora de cable magnetizado," with which Álvaro Gálvez y Fuentes conducted interviews and gave reports from Washington, D.C. These were then edited and broadcast on XEW days later. Garza, *La guerra de las ondas*, p. 90.

16. Garza, *La guerra de las ondas*, pp. 36–45.

17. Garza, *La guerra de las ondas*, pp. 149–51.

18. When station XEB sought to expand its broadcasting power in early 1942 they ran into technical trouble because of a shortage of high power tubes, cautiously guarded by the staff at the WPB.

19. After difficulties with XEW, the Coca Cola Company temporarily switched their sponsorship to XEOY for a brief time toward the end of 1943. Unsatisfied, the company soon restarted advertising on XEW. Meanwhile, in December 1942, ten Mexico City stations had banded together to create what was called the Cadena Radio Continental. Both British and American propaganda providers made effective use of Radio Continental during the war until disorganization and bureaucratic problems caused the effort to be reformed under the title Radio Centro. Garza, *La guerra de las ondas*, pp. 48–52.

20. Quoted in Hayes, *Radio Nation*, p. 46.

21. Cited in Hayes, *Radio Nation*, p. 21.

22. Hayes effectively uses Raymond William's term "selective tradition" to discuss how popular music was extracted from its social context and idealized as part of an imagined national community. Hayes, *Radio Nation*, pp. 50–52.

23. Garza, *La guerra de las ondas*, p. 68.

24. Garza, *La guerra de las ondas*, p. 152.

25. Author interview with Juan Pablo O'Farrill Márquez, June 29, 2006. Mexico City.

26. See Cole Norris Renfro, "A History of *La Hora Nacional*: Government Broadcasting via Privately Owned Radio Stations in Mexico." Ph D diss., Department of Speech and Theater, University of Michigan, 1963.

27. In 1942, ASCAP composer's union in the United States called for a boycott of music exports to Mexico. See Yolanda Rivas Moreno, *La historia de la música popular en México* (Mexico City, Alianza Mexicana, 1989), p. 240.

28. Quoted in Hayes, *Radio Nation*, p. 105.

29. Baer, "Television and Political Control in Mexico," p. 58, quoted in Hayes, *Radio Nation*, p. 70.

30. Ortiz Garza considers how, with the help of US propagandists and commercial sponsor such as Sydney Ross (Sterling Drug), Bristol Meyers, Coca-Cola, Colgate Palmolive, and others, Mexican radio began once again to play American music on the airwaves during the early 1940s. According to surveys, however, the featured broadcast of a show called "The Hit Parade" did very poorly. Garza, *La guerra de las ondas*, pp. 71–73.

31. Author interview with Juan Pablo O'Farrill Márquez, Mexico City, June 29, 2006.

32. On Jiménez see, for example, Carlos Monsiváis, *Y sique siendo el rey: homenaje a José Alfredo Jiménez* (Mexico City: Museo Nacional de Culturas Populares, 1998).

33. Guadalupe Loaeza and Pável Granados, *Mi novia, la tristeza* (Mexico City: Océano, 2008), p. 292. Spottswood only lists "Buscandote" on Decca 21189, when Armengod allegedly sang with Lara's group. Richard K. Spottswood, *Ethnic Music on Records: A Discography of Ethnic Recordings Produced in the United States, 1893–1942*, vol. 4 (Champaign: University of Illinois Press, 1990), p. 2003.

34. Loaeza and Granados, *Mi novia, la tristeza*, pp. 293–94.

35. Loaeza and Granados, *Mi novia, la tristeza*, pp. 292–99; Taibo I, *La música de Agustín Lara en el cine*, pp. 75–76. Taibo I lists José Díaz Morales's *Señora tentación* as released in 1947.

36. Loaeza and Granados, *Mi novia, la tristeza*, pp. 292–99; Carlos Monsiváis, *Amor Perdido*, pp. 80–82. On Ríos see Christine Erich, "Radio Transvestism and the Gendered Soundscape in Buenos Aires and Montevideo, 1930s-1940s," in Alejandra Bronfman and Andrew Grant Wood (eds.), *Media, Sound and Culture in Latin America and the Caribbean* (Pittsburgh: University of Pittsburgh Press, 2012).

37. In 1947 Zozaya charged Lara with bigamy, saying that he had married María Félix without first obtaining a divorce from her. Lara pleaded ignorance, saying that he was uncertain whether paperwork existed that certified his union with Carmen Zozaya in Venezuela and that he had subsequently obtained a divorce from her on November 6, 1945 in Yautepec, Morelos before becoming involved with Félix. *Excélsior* reported that judge Próspero Olivares Sosa had declared the charges false after reviewing divorce papers presented by both Lara and Félix. "Un lío jurídico el doble casamiento de Agustín Lara" and "Confianza en Agustín Lara," *Excélsior*, March 20, 21, 1947; "Llueve en la milpa de Agustín: estando solo lo acusan de bígamio," *Novedades*, October 25, 1947; "Agustín Lara sigue casado con Zozaya," *Excélsior*, October 25, 1947. Others would simply marvel, however enviously, at Lara's ability to attract the attention of some of Mexico's most beautiful women. See, for example, J. L. de Guevara, "Guía de turista," *La Prensa*, March 31, 1947.

38. Gabriel Abaroa Martínez, *El flaco de oro* (Mexico City: Editorial Planeta, 1993) p. 148; Javier Ruiz Rueda, *Agustín Lara: Vida y pasiones* (Mexico City: Editorial Novaro, 1976), pp. 215–16.

39. Abaroa Martínez, *El flaco de oro*, p. 149; Ruiz Rueda, *Agustín Lara: Vida y pasiones*, pp. 216–17.

40. Mario Arturo Ramos (ed.), *Agustín Lara: Cien años, cien canciones* (Mexico City: Océano, 2000), p. 36.

41. Alan Knight, "The Rise and Fall of Cardenismo, ca. 1930–ca. 1946," in Leslie Bethell (ed.), *Mexico since Independence* (Cambridge: Cambridge University Press, 1991), pp. 302–07.

42. *Jueves de Excélsior*, February 11, 1943.

43. On Pérez see Heriberto Murrieta, *Silverio Pérez* (Mexico City: Editorial Clío, 1999).

44. Raquel Díaz de León, "De como con Agustín Lara cualquier mujer estaba de paso," in Eugenio Méndez (ed.) *Agustín, rencuentro con lo sentimental*, p. 149; Loaeza and Granados, *Mi novia, la tristeza*, pp. 129–38.

45. Díaz de Leon, p. 151.

46. Roberto Ayala (ed.), *Canciones y poemas y de Agustín Lara: Colección completa* (Mexico City: Selecciónes Orfeón, 1969), p. 124. "Fue así" was first recorded by Miguel Aceves Mejía in 1943 for Peerless. Pável Granados, *Agustín Lara: Canciones* (Mexico City: Gobierno de Veracruz/Océano, 2008),p. 276.

47. Some say he had an abortion without telling Lara and when he found out he was furious. See Abaroa Martínez, *El flaco de oro*, p. 158. Loaeza and Granados add that Rosa Fernández Téllez Wood encouraged Raquel to avoid upsetting Lara by telling him she was pregnant and to have an abortion with a doctor she knew. Loaeza and Granados, *Mi novia, la tristeza*, pp. 144–45. Loaeza and Granados write that Lara maintained a casual interest in Raquel for some time until she attended a performance of his at the Regis Hotel in 1953. Still apparently filled with anger at his former lover, Lara lashed out at her in front of the assembled public, cursing at her and staring angrily from behind his piano. *Mi novia, la tristeza*, pp. 147–48.

48. An earlier version of this section was published as "The Public Romance of María Félix and Agustín Lara," in Jeffrey Pilcher (ed.), *The Human Tradition in Mexico* (Latham, MD: Rowman and Littlefield/SR Books, 2003), pp. 185–97.

49. Details on Félix's early years in Mexico City are covered in her autobiography in relatively short order. María Félix, *Todos mis guerras* (Mexico City: Editorial Clío, 1993), pp 53–59.

50. Félix, *Todos mis guerras*, p. 60.

51. In 1952, the actress would marry Negrete, who died two years later. On Negrete see Enrique Serna, *Jorge el bueno: La vida de Jorge Negrete* (3 vols.) (Mexico City: Editorial Clío, 1993).

52. *Jueves de Excélsior*, April 1, 1943; "La actriz más bella del cine mexicana," *Jueves de Excélsior*, June 24, 1943.

53. María again traveled with Arturo de Córdova and others to Los Angeles where she met with Cecil B. DeMille and did a screen test for Max Factor cosmetics. "María Félix en Hollywood," *Jueves de Excélsior*, June 10, 1943.

54. Ana M. López, "Tears and Desire: Women and Melodrama in the 'Old' Mexican Cinema," in John King, Ana M. López, and Manuel Alvarado (ed.), *Mediating Two Worlds: Cinematic Encounters in the Americas* (London: British Film Institute, 1993), pp. 155–56; Joanne Hershfield, *Mexican Cinema/Mexican Woman, 1940-1950* (Tucson: University of Arizona Press, 1996), pp. 109–16.

55. Quoted in Sam Dillon, "María Félix, 87, Feisty Heroine Who Reigned Supreme in Mexican Cinema, Dies," *New York Times*, April 9, 2002. See also Chris Kraul, "Mexican Film Star Dies on 88th birthday," *Los Angeles Times*, April 16, 2002.

56. *Doña Barbara* premiered on September 16, 1943 at the Cine Palacio and ran for six weeks. At the same time Dolores del Río was starring in *Flor Silvestre* directed by Emilio Fernández.

57. López, "Tears and Desire: Women and Melodrama in the 'Old' Mexican Cinema," p. 156.

58. "Yo soy una mujer con alma," *México Cinema*, March 1945, pp. 22–24.

59. Even as late as her 1993 memoir, she still maintained that "Agustín was *muy sexy* [and had] the most exciting voice in the world." Félix, *Todas mis guerras*, p. 78.

60. A *Revista de Revistas* column named "Mientras México duerme" (While Mexico Sleeps) often featured pictures of the celebrity couple and related gossip. See for example, *Revista de Revistas*, October 1, 1943, May 7, 1944, September 11, 1944, February 4, 1945, June 3, 1945, September 2, 1945, and September 30, 1945.

61. *Nuestro Cinema*, February 13, 1944.

62. No doubt, portions of the column could have been ghostwritten.

63. Agustín Lara, "Algo: Una entrevista original," *Revista Mañana*, October 21, 1943. Colección Agustín Lara, Fundación Pérez Simón, Scrapbook #9.

64. Carlos Monsiváis, "Agustín Lara: El harem ilusorio in *Amor Perdido*, p. 83. *Jueves de Excélsior*, February 11, 1943 featured a picture of Félix and commented on her as a "new star." "Agustín Lara murió en paz con el gran amor de su vida." Unidentified clipping, November 8, 1970, BLT.

65. Jaime Rico Salazar, *Cien años de bolero* (Bogotá: Centro Editorial de Estudios Musicales, 1987), pp. 84–98; Loaeza and Granados, *Mi novia, la tristeza*, pp. 349–50. "Cuando ya no me quieras" is listed as being popular in 1932. Among those popular on the bolero hit parade during the early 1940s was also composer Javier Ruiz Rueda, who would later write a book on Lara. On Ruiz Armengol see Carlos Díaz Barriga, *La calle de los sueños: Vida y obra de Mario Ruiz Armengol* (Veracruz: Instituto Veracruzano de la cultura, 2002).

66. Loaeza and Granados, *Mi novia, la tristeza*, p. 152.

67. *El Universal*, October 22, 31, November 5, 1943.

68. *El Universal Gráfica*, January 19, 1944.

69. Zweig committed suicide two years earlier while living in Brazil.

70. Working with screenwriters Erwin Wallfisch and Max Aub, the director's desire to deploy "realistic" dialogue represented one of the most significant problems.

71. Paco Ignacio Taibo I, *La doña* (Mexico City: Planeta, 1985), pp. 79–80.

72. Among those who praised the film was poet Efraín Huerta in the daily *Esto*. Meantime, Mexican star Lupe Veléz committed suicide in mid-December 13, 1944 in Los Angeles. A February 18, 1945 *Revista de Revistas* two-part article paid tribute to the actress.

73. August 21, 1944. Colección JAPS, Archivo Agustín Lara, Carpeta #11, "Lara escritos." Translation assistance thanks to Bruce Dean Willis.

74. Abaroa Martínez, *El flaco de oro*, p. 161. Ruiz Rueda says the address is 308 Edgar Allan Poe corner of Homero Street. Ruiz Rueda, *Agustín Lara: Vida y pasiones*, p 227.

75. "Yo soy una mujer con alma," *México Cinema*, March 1945, pp. 22–24; see also *Cinema Reporter*, May 12, 1945.

76. Angel Mora, "Grandes amores del cine mexicano," *México Cinema*, April 1946.

77. Ramos, *Agustín Lara: Cien años, cien canciones*, p. 72. "Mírame" was first recorded by Aurora Muñoz for Peerless (2106) in 1944. Pedro Vargas and Bobby Capó soon followed with versions for RCA Victor and Seeco, respectively. Granados, *Canciones*, p. 281.

78. *Revista de Revistas*, April 29, May 13, 1945. María Félix writes in her memoir that Lara, Félix, and her son Enrique were involved in a car crash (a flat tire at relatively high speed) on the México-Puebla highway when returning from a visit to the municipality of Tehuacán. No specific date is given in regard to the incident although it is presumed to have happened before their "marriage" in late 1945. Félix, *Todas mis guerras*, p. 82. The accident was kept out of the press for fear that Enrique's father would use the incident to claim full custody of Enrique.

79. Review of *El monje blanco* and article by Salvador Pineda "Canciones de México," in *Revista de Revistas*, October 21, 1945.

80. The song would later be interpreted by many others including Pérez Prado, Marty Robbins, The Flamingos, Frank Sinatra, Elvis Presley, Slim Whitman, Tommy Garrett, and Juan Esquivel.

81. *Cinema Reporter*, February 17, 1945. Taibo I, *La música de Agustín Lara en el cine*, p. 73.

82. Decca Records 23413, 1945. Singer-songwriter Phil Brito initially recorded and released the song in 1944. Later, Roy Rogers performed the song in the 1948 film *The Gay Ranchero*. In 1951 Ezio Pinza sang it in a film titled *Mr. Imperium*.

83. Gary Giddens, *Bing Crosby: A Pocketful of Dreams: The Early Years, 1903–1940* (New York: Little, Brown, 2001), p. 7. Material for this section is drawn from pp. 3–12.

84. Algara quoted in Benito Vázquez González, "María Félix: La mujer que más amo Agustín Lara," *Revista de Revistas*, November 19, 1990, p. 39.

85. "Palabras de mujer" accessed via *Agustín Lara: 20 exitos*. RCA Victor/BMG 1991. The song was first recorded by Fernando Rosas in 1944 for the Azteca label and Fernando Fernández the same year for RCA Victor. Toña la Negra recorded it in 1945 for Peerless (2153). Granados, *Canciones*, p. 282.

86. Abaroa Martínez, *El flaco de oro*, pp. 165–66.

87. Ramos, *Agustín Lara: Cien años, cien canciones*, p. 82.

88. "Solo faltaba que me acusaran de ateo, dice Agustín Lara," *Excélsior*, June 6, 1945.

89. "Solo faltaba que me acusaran de ateo, dice Agustín Lara."

90. Abaroa Martínez, *El flaco de oro,* pp. 165–66; Elizabeth Velasco Contreras, "Carlos Monsiváis habla de Agustín Lara," *Revista de Revistas,* November 19, 1999, p. 32.

91. Quoted in Loaeza and Granados, *Mi novia, la tristeza,* p. 157.

92. *Cinema Reporter,* August 31, 1945 covered this party which Sara Mateos, Gabriel Figueroa, Pedro Armendariz, Rosa Castro, Efrain Huerta, Andrea Palma, and Ana María González attended while members of Lara's soon to be formed "Sinfonica" played. "El Duende Filmo" (sic) reported in the Sunday, October 17, 1943 magazine section of *El Universal* that a young journalist unleashed "a torrent" of gossip when he wrote that Lara and Félix had secretly wed. This rumor was subsequently denied by Roberto Soto and other friends. *El Universal,* October 22, 1943. Still, commentary would continue as seen in a cartoon printed in the paper two days later with a caption suggesting that "since Lara's songs had been used in film, what better than to marry the beautiful Félix." *El Universal,* October 24, 1943.

93. Ruiz Rueda lists nearly the entire gourmet menu served. *Agustin Lara: Vida y pasiones,* p. 228. June Kay also provides an impressionistic account of the civil ceremony and subsequent party. June Kay, *Las siete vidas de Agustín Lara,* trans. F. de Riba Millon (Mexico City: El Universal Gráfico, 1964), pp. 238–44. Somewhat mysteriously, María had inherited a sum of money from a millionaire in Guadalajara. Loaeza and Granados, *Mi novia, la tristeza,* p. 163. She nevertheless lived with Lara at Agustín's house, Galileo 37 in Polanco.

94. Ramos, *Agustín Lara: Cien años, cien canciones,* p. 65–66.

95. Pedro Vargas would be the first to interpret the composition. Ruiz Rueda, *Agustín Lara: Vida y pasiones,* p. 229. Early the next year, Yucatecan musician Chucho Monge accused Lara of plagiarizing the song, saying it was the same as his "El Remero." *Revista de Revistas,* February 9, 1947. Later, Bing Crosby recorded a version that went on to sell thousands of copies. Testifying to the popularity of the song (and Félix herself), a Mexico City streetcar was for a time named "María bonita."

96. Carlos Monsiváis, "Agustín Lara: El harem ilusorio," in *Amor perdido,* p. 82.

97. *Revista de Revistas,* February 10, 1946. Elsewhere in the magazine she could be seen in an advertisement for Missunky face powder. Testifying to Félix's commercial appeal, a *Revista de Revistas* feature of the actress presented a photo and mention of "Doña Barbara" shampoo in the January 20, 1946 issue. A July 1946 issue of *Cinema Reporter* pictured billboards advertising Félix and the film in Buenos Aires.

98. Fernando de Fuentes made a name for himself as one of Mexico's first, and perhaps most important, directors with his Revolutionary Triology from the early 1930s and subsequent work with Lupe Vélez and Jorge Negrete.

99. Emilio García Riera figures the picture to be the best of la doña playing this particular kind of role. Emilio García Riera, *Historica documental del cine mexicano* (Guadalajara: Universidad de Guadalajara, vol. 4, 1993), p. 18. Fernando de Fuentes had directed *La mujer sin alma* with Félix in the lead role in October 1943.

100. *Cinema Reporter,* August 31, 1946.

101. *Cinema Reporter,* September 7, 14, 1946.

102. *Cinema Reporter,* September 7, 1946. The September 14 issue contains a short piece on *Enamorada,* while *Cinema Reporter* for October 5, 1946 covered Félix and Lara attending the premiere of *La Mujer de todas.*

103. *Cinema Reporter,* October 5, 1946.

104. The following year, María's film *La diosa arrodillada* would feature Lara's song "Revancha."

105. Riera, *Historia documental del cine mexicano,* pp. 115–17.

106. *Revista de Revistas,* September 7, 1947.

107. Revueltas quoted in Riera, *Historia documental del cine mexicano,* p. 117.

108. *Cinema Reporter,* November 16, 1946.

109. Valdés Peza was a costume designer active in Mexican cinema during the 1940s–1960s.

110. *Cinema Reporter,* November 2, 1946.

111. For an analysis of *La diosa arrodillada,* see Julia Tuñon Pablos, "Cuerpo y amor en el cine mexicano de la edad de oro: Los besos subversivos de *La diosa arrodillada,*" in Julia Tuñon Pablos (ed.), *Cuidado con el corazón: Los usos amorosos en el México moderno* (Mexico City: INAH, 1995), pp. 103–42.

112. *Cinema Reporter,* November 23, 1946.

113. *Revista de Revista* on December 29, 1946.
114. Mark Allen, "Destino de María Félix," *México Cinema*, January 1947.
115. Loaeza and Granados, *Mi novia, la tristeza*, pp. 161–62.
116. Pasquel was known for his big spending ways. At one point in the 1940s, he owned six Lincolns and had his own private haberdashery. www.baseball-reference.com/bullpen/ Jorge_Pasquel. On Pasquel see G. Richard McKelvey, *Mexican Raiders in the Major Leagues: The Pasquel Brothers vs. Organized Baseball, 1946* (Jefferson, NC: McFarland, 2006) as well as John Virtue, *South of the Color Barrier: How Jorge Pasquel and the Mexican League Pushed Baseball Toward Racial Integration* (Jefferson, NC: McFarland, 2008). For a fictional treatment of the brief romance between Pasquel and Félix played out amidst the Mexican winter baseball season, see Mark Winegardener, *The Veracruz Blues* (New York: Viking, 1996). Pasquel died in an airplane crash in San Luis Potosí in 1955.
117. Ramos, *Agustín Lara: Cien años, cien canciones*, p. 85.
118. García Riera, *Historia documental del cine mexicano*, p. 129.
119. For an overview of Sevilla's career and some entertaining photos see Fernando Muñoz Castillo, *Las reinas del tropico* (Mexico City: Grupo Azabache, 1993), pp. 162–206.
120. García Riera, *Historical documental del cine mexicano*, p. 130.
121. "Senora tentación" was first recorded by Lucha Guzmán for Peerless (833) in 1932.
122. García Riera, *Historia documental del cine mexicano*, pp. 149–50. The project was filmed starting in early August 1947 and debuted the following year in late April.
123. *Revista de Revistas*, November 10, 1946.
124. The fact that that some criticized the production for its portrayal of "bad Mexicans" generally added to the hype around the film. Mora, *Mexican Cinema*, pp. 79–80.
125. Ángel Garmendía, "Lara: espiritu y melodía," *México Cinema*, August 15, 1947.
126. Ayala, *Canciones y poemas de Agustín Lara*, p. 235.
127. "Agustín Lara murio en paz con el gran amor de su vida." Unidentified clipping, November 8, 1970, BLT.
128. Abaroa Martínez, *El flaco de oro*, p. 176. Loaeza and Granados suggest that a younger dancer, Clara Martínez, whom Lara began to court on the side may have inspired the 1947 composition "Pecadora." Loaeza and Granados, *Mi novia, la tristeza*, p. 356.
129. *Revista de Revistas*, September 28, 1947.
130. Félix, *Todas mis guerras*, p. 87; Agustín Lara, "La vida íntima de un gran músico," p. 58; Rueda, *Agustín Lara: Vida y pasiones*, p. 231.
131. *El Universal*, October 2, 1947.
132. Robert Browning, "El caballero Agustín Lara," *Cinema Reporter*, October 4, 1947, pp. 15–17.
133. *El Universal*, October 16, 1947.
134. *Cinelandia*, October 1947.
135. "Idilio roto: María y Agustín se separan," *El Universal*, October 25, 1947.
136. *El Universal*, October 24, 1947.
137. "Félix salió para L.A.," *El Universal*, October 26, 1947.
138. *El Universal*, October 27, 1947. Paco Pildora, "Revolviendo papeles," *Notiver*, no date, Fondo Francisco Rivera, AMV. Nevertheless, Lara would maintain that they had married and subsequently divorced. Agustín Lara, "La vida íntima de un gran músico," p. 58.
139. Translated as "May God forgive me." García Riera, *Historia documental del cine mexicano*, pp. 144, 168. See feature on *Que Dios me perdone* in *Cinema Reporter*, December 20, 1947, p. 20.
140. *Revista de Revistas*, October 26, 1947. The working title for the film was *Panama* and would later be changed to *Revancha*.
141. *Revista de Revistas*, November 2, 1947.

## Chapter 6

1. Quoted in Enrique Krauze, *Mexico: Biography of Power, A History of Modern Mexico, 1810–1996*, trans. Hank Heifetz (New York: Harper Collins, 1997), p. 543.
2. Peter H. Smith, "Mexico since 1946: Dynamics of an Authoritarian Regime," in Leslie Bethell (ed.), *Mexico since Independence*. (Cambridge: Cambridge University Press, 1991),

pp. 328–31; Centro de Estudios Económicos y Demográficos, El Colegio de México, *Dinámica de la Población de México* (Mexico City: El Colegio de México, 1970), p. 137. The city population would subsequently reach 1.6 million in 1940, 3.1 million in 1950, 5.4 million in 1960, 9.1 million in 1970, 13.9 million in 1980, and about 15.6 million in 1995, and then head upward to around 20 million more recently. See www.un.org/cyberschoolbus/habitat/profiles/mexico.asp. Rapid urban growth in Mexico City paralleled similar developments in many other cities worldwide.

3. Salvador Novo, *New Mexican Grandeur*, trans. Noel Lindsay (Mexico City: Petróleos Mexicanos, 1967). Novo's title references Bernardo de Balbuena's 1604 work *La grandeza mexicana* (Mexican Grandeur) which, in lyrical verse, described the colonial Spanish American city around the turn of the seventeenth century.

4. Novo's original 1946 title is *Nueva grandeza mexicana*. The chronicle, like much of modern Mexican history to this point, is divided by presidential sexenio starting with Lázaro Cárdenas and ending with incomplete works on the sexenios of Adolfo Ruiz Cortines and Adolfo López Mateos. José Emilio Pacheco assisted toward the end.

5. Oscar Lewis, *Children of Sánchez: Autobiography of a Mexican Family* (New York: Vintage, 1979).

6. On the Cristero conflict in Veracruz, see Andrew Grant Wood, "Adalberto Tejeda: Radicalism and Reaction in Revolutionary Veracruz," in William Beezley and Jurgen Buchenau (eds.), *State Governors of the Revolution 1910–1932: Portraits in Courage and Conflict* (Lanham, MD: SR Books/Rowman and Littlefield, 2009), pp 77–94.

7. Krauze, *Mexico*. This section draws on Krauze, pp. 535–49.

8. Krauze, *Mexico*, p. 543. On the economy during the conflict see John Womack, "The Mexican Economy," in William H. Beezley and Dirk Raat (eds.), *Twentieth Century Mexico* (Lincoln: University of Nebraska Press, 1986), pp. 73–83.

9. On development in Acapulco see Andrew Sackett, "The Two Faces of Acapulco," in Gilbert M. Joseph and Timothy J. Henderson (eds.), *The Mexico Reader: History, Culture, Politics* (Durham, NC: Duke University Press, 2002), pp. 500–10; Andrew Sackett, "Fun in Acapulco? The Politics of Development on the Mexican Riviera," in Dina Berger and Andrew Grant Wood, *Holiday in Mexico: Critical Reflections on Tourism and Tourist Encounters*. (Durham, NC: Duke University Press, 2010), pp. 161–182; and Alex Saragoza, "The Selling of Mexico: Tourism and the State, 1929–1952," in Gilbert M. Joseph, Anne Rubenstein, and Eric Zolov (eds.), *Fragments of a Golden Age: The Politics of Culture in Mexico since 1940* (Durham, NC: Duke University Press, 2001), pp. 91–115.

10. Lara later remembered meeting Alemán for the first time at the Teocali nightclub. "Como los conoci," Colección Juan Antonio Pérez Simon (JAPS), Archivo Agustín Lara.

11. Yolanda Moreno Rivas, *Historia de la música popular en Mexicana* (Mexico City: Alianza Editorial Mexicana, 1979, 1989), pp. 159–63. Personnel would change slightly over the years, with Chucho Navarro and Alfredo Gil nonetheless remaining constant. www.lospanchos.com/nuestra_historia.htm.

12. Information and video clips on Trío Los Panchos can be found at www.lastfm.es/music/Trio+Los+Panchos/+videos.

13. Celina Fernández, *Los Panchos: La historia de los embajadores de la canción romantica contada por su voz Rafael Basurto Lara* (Mexico City: Ediciones Martínez Roca, 2005), pp. 43–35.

14. Fernández, *Los Panchos*, pp. 27–35. On the requinto see also Jamie Rico Salazar, *Cien años de boleros* (Bogotá: Centro Editorial de Estudios Musicales, 1987), p. 97.

15. Salazar, *Cien años de boleros*, p. 97.

16. Fernández, *Los Panchos*, pp. 27–43.

17. Carlos Monsiváis, *Mexican Postcards*, trans. John Kraniauskas (London: Verso Press, 1997), p. 189.

18. Helio Orovio, *Cuban Music from A to Z* (Durham, NC: Duke University Press, 2004), p. 84.

19. For a discussion of cursilería in middle-class Spanish society see Noël Valis, *The Culture of Cursilélería: Bad Taste, Kitsch, and Class in Modern Spain* (Durham, NC: Duke University Press, 2002), p. 18.

20. Quoted in *Festival internacional Agustín Lara, nuestro flaco de oro* (Mexico City: Banco de Ideas/Gobierno del estado de Veracruz/Secretario de Educación y Cultura/Instituto Veracruzano de Cultura, 2001), p. 22.

21. Oscar LeBlanc, "Lara, el larismo y las mujeres," *El Illustrado*, Unidentified clipping, SLS, vol. 12.

22. José Alvarado, "Lara: revolución en lo cursi," *Excélsior*, October 28, 1970.

23. Alvarado, "Lara: revolución en lo cursi."

24. Guadalupe Loaeza and Pável Granados, *Mi novia, la tristeza* (Mexico City: Océano, 2008), p. 356.

25. Violinist Manuel Nuñez would soon also join the group and sometimes share booking duties with Carlos Águila. Gabriel Abaroa Martínez, *El flaco de oro* (Mexico City: Editorial Planeta, 1993), p. 174.

26. "Músico, compositor, romántico, larista de primera fila: Guillermo Salamanca," www.agustin-lara.com/txtfrente.thm. Adding to the uptick in Lara's career, the lyrics of selected Lara songs began to appear on packages of Tigres cigarettes.

27. "Aguilita" Carlos Águila, in Eugenio Méndez (ed.), *Agustín, rencuentro con lo sentimental* (Mexico City: Editorial Domés, 1980), pp. 290–91; Abaroa Martínez, *El flaco de oro*, pp. 170–72; Loaeza and Granados, *Mi novia, la tristeza*, pp. 356–57. A while later, Jesús "Cholito" or "Chucho" Ferrer and Félix Guerrero (who also worked for Andre Kostelanetz) would join as arrangers and sometimes stand-ins for Lara. Abaroa Martínez, *El flaco de oro*, pp. 172–74. Personnel changes occurred frequently, and unfortunately many of the details about all who played in Lara's orchestra may be lost. Alejandro Cardona played trumpet in the first years of the organization. Personal communication with Pablo Dueñas and Jesús Flores y Escalante, December 8, 2008.

28. Composer Alfonso Esparza Oteo led the initial organizing effort of the SMACEM in 1945. www.sacm.org.mx/archivos/conocenos.htm#

29. *Cinema Reporter*, October 23, 1948. The article also included a message from Mario "Cantinflas" Moreno urging him to make up with SMACEM members. See also *Jueves de Excelsior*, October 14, 1948. Today, Lara's music and legacy is proudly guarded by the (renamed in 1949) SACM. www.sacm.org.mx/archivos/biografias.asp?txtSocio=08017

30. Emilio García Riera, *Historia documental del cine mexicano* (Guadalajara: Universidad de Guadalajara, vol. 4, 1992-97), pp. 156-59. Interestingly, his entire section on 1948 films contains the subtitle "de la hacienda al cabaret."

31. On Barba see Fernando Muñoz Castillo, *Las reinas del tropico* (Mexico City: Grupo Azabache, 1993), pp. 64–123. García Riera briefly discusses *Cortesana* in his *Historical documental del cine mexicano*, vol. 4, pp. 152–53. Toña la Negra played a small part in *Cortesana*.

32. Roberto Ayala, *Canciones y poemas de Agustín Lara*. (Mexico City: Selecciónes Orfeón, 1969), p. 110.

33. "Revancha" accessed via *Agustín Lara: Serie 20 exitos*. RCA Victor/BMG, 1991.

34. Colección JAPS, Archivo Agustín Lara, undated comment (probably mid- to late 1950s), Carpeta #7 "Temas de Radioprograma." See also a brief interview with Paco Ignacio Taibo I titled "Lo que pensaba Lara del cine" in Paco Ignacio Taibo I, *La música de Agustín Lara en el cine*, (Mexico City: UNAM, 1984), pp. 63–68.

35. See promotions featuring Sevilla in *Cinema Reporter*, July 31 and August 7, 1948. The August 28 issue included a photo of Lara, Sevilla, Toña la Negra, and Pedro Vargas in a preview titled "Belleza y arte en *Revancha*" that offered a florid description of the film as an emotionally charged recreation of the musician-poet's romantic life. Subsequent September issues contained promotions featuring Lara and short, usually gushing, uncritical reviews.

36. Mario Arturo Ramos (ed.), *Agustín Lara: Cien años, cien canciones*, (Mexico City: Océano, 2000), p. 54.

37. Lara first recorded "Farolito" for Peerless in 1935. Pável Granados, *Agustín Lara: Canciones*. Veracruz/Mexico City: Gobierno de Veracruz/Océano, 2008, p. 195.

38. "Farolito" accessed via *Agustín Lara: Las número uno*. 2005 Sony/BMG, disc 1, track 7. This version was released on *Rosa: Agustín Lara*, MKL–1131 in 1956.

39. García Riera briefly discusses *Revancha* in his *Historical documental del cine mexicano*, vol. 4, pp. 211–13.

40. On the "model" family in Mexican cinema see, for example, Julia Tuñon, *Mujeres de luz y sombra en el cine mexicano, 1939–1959* (Mexico City: Colegio de México/Instituto mexicano de cinematografía, 1998) as well as Joanne Hershfield, *Mexican Cinema, Mexican Woman, 1940–1950* (Tucson: University of Arizona Press, 1996) and Sergio de la Mora, *Cinemachismo: Masculinities and Sexuality in Mexican Film* (Austin: University of Texas Press, 2006).

41. Ensuing promotion for the film included Lara pictured as a disheveled Rubén gracing the cover of *Cinema Reporter*'s July 30 issue. Lara's agenda for 1949 mentions production taking place largely in February 1949. Colección JAPS, Archivo Agustín Lara, Carpeta #1 "Documentos Personales." García Riera confirms this. *Historial documental del cine mexicano*, vol. 5, p. 30.

42. Director Fernando de Fuentes hastily made a film the same year titled *Hipólito de la Santa* that he intended as a sequel to *Santa*. Not surprisingly, it contains many of the same blind man character elements with José Luis Jiménez playing Hipólito. A column titled "Foro y melodía" in the August 7, 1948 issue of *Cinema Reporter* featured a picture of Lara as Hipólito with a brief discussion of the musician's affinity for the role. Generally, however, the film was panned.

43. Carl J. Mora, *Mexican Cinema: Reflections of a Society, 1896–1988* (Berkeley: University of California Press, 1982), pp. 83, 88, 101–21. On the cabaretera see Silvia Oroz, *Melodrama: el cine de lagrimas de América Latina* (Mexico City: UNAM, 1995), pp. 33, 56, 67,72–73, 94–95; Hershfield, *Mexican Cinema, Mexican Women, 1940–1950*, pp. 13–34, 77–99; María del Carmen de la Peza Casares, *El bolero y la educación sentimental en México* (Mexico City: Universidad Autónomia Metropolitana-Xochimilco, 2001), pp. 214–18; Debra A. Castillo, *Easy Women: Sex and Gender in Modern Mexican Fiction* (Minneapolis: University of Minnesota Press, 1998), pp. 37–62; Julia Tuñon, *Mujeres de luz y sombra en el cine mexicano: La construcción de una imagen, 1939–1952.*

44. García Riera, *Historia documental del cine mexicano*, vol. 5, pp. 111–13. Lara's agenda for 1949 mentions production starting August 11, 1949. Colección JAPS, Archivo Agustín Lara, Carpeta #1 "Documentos Personales."

45. *El Universal*, April 1, 1950.

46. *El Universal*, April 14, 1950. Meanwhile, María Félix continued to garner significant attention as one of Mexico's leading ladies. Articles in *Revista de Revistas* during the early 1950s informed the Mexican public that she earned approximately 40,000 pesos per film. *Doña Diabla* starring Félix premiered in late April 1950, and December 1952 in *El Universal* saw her appear with Jorge Negrete in a promotion campaign for Portrero Rum. In early February 1953 she was voted "star of the week" by *Revista de Revistas*. At some point Lara contacted her and they reconciled as friends. Allegedly, before he died, he sent María a small, mysterious box containing some undisclosed items and the instruction "Never Open." "Agustín Lara murio en paz con el gran amor de su vida," unidentified clipping, November 8, 1970, BLT.

47. Quoted in García Riera, *Historia documental del cine mexicano*, vol. 4, pp. 112–13.

48. Taibo, *La música de Agustín Lara en el cine*, p. 76; Riera, *Historia documental del cine mexicano*, vol. 5, pp. 178–80.

49. Lara's agenda for 1949 lists work on *Perdida* starting October 17, 1949. Colección JAPS, Archivo Agustín Lara, Carpeta #1 "Documentos Personales."

50. The next year Sevilla graced the cover of *Mexico Cinema* just as her new film *Sensualidad* premiered. The article inside praised the dynamic actress and reminded readers of Lara's penchant for celebrity women. "Al lado flaco de las estrellas," *Mexico Cinema*, July 15, 1951.

51. García Riera, *Historia documental del cine mexicano*, vol. 4, p. 137.

52. The Pygmalion story derives from the Greek myth of Pygmalion, a Cypriot sculptor who falls in love with a female figure he has carved out of ivory. See Ovid, *Metamorphoses*, trans. David Raeburn (New York: Penguin, 2004), especially book X.

53. See also Riera, *Historia documental del cine mexicano*, vol. 5, pp. 136–38.

54. Loaeza and Granados, *Mi novia, la tristeza*, pp. 281, 361.

55. Colección JAPS, Archivo Agustín Lara, Carpeta #1 "Documentos Personales."

56. Loaeza and Granados, *Mi novia, la tristeza*, pp. 357–58.

57. Rodríguez, loosely affiliated with XEW when Lara first met him in 1938, was hired by the musician-poet to help him keep track of all his personal business including monitoring his expenses, clothes, medicine, etc. (*Verdugo* in Spanish means "hangman.") He would remain Lara's assistant for the next thirty years. See testimony in *Agustín, rencuentro con lo sentimental*, pp. 307–12. Rodríguez tells that he met Lara in 1940 in his "Yo fui la sombra de Agustín Lara," in Guillermo Mendizábal and Eduardo Mejía (eds.), *Todo lo que quería saber sobre Agustín Lara* (Mexico City: Grijalbo, 1993), pp. 9–17.

58. Copyright 1948 Promotora Hispano Americana de Música (PHAM) S.A.

59. The Schottische derived originally from Bohemia and became popular throughout much of Europe and the Americas during the second half of the nineteenth century.

60. Loaeza and Granados, *Mi novia, la tristeza*, p. 360; Abaroa Martínez, *El flaco de oro*, pp. 176–81; Javier Ruiz Rueda, *Agustín Lara: Vida y pasiones* (Mexico City: Editorial Novaro, 1976), p. 232.

61. Loaeza and Granados, *Mi novia, la tristeza*, p. 362.

62. *El Universal*, April 8, 1950.

63. Loaeza and Granados, *Mi novia, la tristeza*, p. 361.

64. Fernández worked with Lara from 1950 to 1952. Jorge Fernández, in *Agustin: rencuentro con lo sentimental*, p. 330; "De la hora del aficionado a La Habana: Jorge Fernández el descubrimiento de Agustín Lara," www.agustin-lara.com/txtfrente.htm.

65. "Entrevista de una admiradora anónima," 2001 Festival de Agustín Lara, www.agustin-lara.com/txtembrador.htm.

66. Quoted in Abaroa Martínez, *El flaco de oro*, pp. 186–87.

67. While in Cuba, the ensemble paid a visit to composer Ernesto Lecuona at his ranch "La Comparsa." Agustín also had a chance to spend time with his friend the poet Luis Carbonell—with whom he once was photographed drinking from oversize cognac glasses. "En la poesía, Lara y Carbonell," www.agustin-lara.com/txtsisupieras.htm.

68. Carlos Águila, in *Agustín, rencuentro con lo sentimental*, pp. 292–93.

69. Abaroa Martínez, *El flaco de oro*, pp. 170–74; Ruiz Rueda, *Agustín Lara: Vida y pasiones*, pp. 245–46. No mention of this piece is to be found in Granados or Dueñas and Flores Escalante. Nevertheless, similar efforts titled "Bogotá," and "Lima" suggest "Brazil" may have simply been never recorded and/or lost. Granados, *Canciones*, p. 374.

70. Loaeza and Granados, *Mi novia, la tristeza*, p. 360.

71. Abaroa Martínez, *El flaco de oro*, pp. 184–85; Festival Internacional Agustín Lara, *Nuestro flaco de oro*, p. 39. Havana residents would later erect a statue of Lara in the city to honor the Mexican composer.

72. Loaeza and Granados, *Mi novia, la tristeza*, p. 363.

## Chapter 7

1. "Vivir con Agustín fue como un cuento." Yolanda Gasca, in *Agustín, rencuentro con lo sentimental* (Mexico City: Editorial Domés, 1980), p. 340.

2. "Que lindo es *mi* Veracruz"; "La vida íntima de un gran musico," *Life Magazine (en Español)*, January 15, 1968, p. 60.

3. Julia Tuñón, *Mujeres de luz y sombra en el cine mexicano: La construcción de una imagen, 1932–1952* (Mexico City: Colegio de México/Instituto Mexicano de Cinematografía, 1998), pp. 239–41. On the major stars of the cabareteras see also Fernando Muñoz Castillo, *Las reinas del tropico* (Mexico City: Grupo Azabache, 1993).

4. *El Universal*, February 15, 1953.

5. *El Universal*, March 8, 1953. Hoping to initiate a neighborhood reform campaign, Ruiz Cortines proposed in mid-March 1953 that "improvement committees" be established throughout the capital and in cities across the country. *El Universal*, March 10, 1953.

6. See articles and editorials in *El Universal*, January–February 1953.

7. *El Universal*, December 12, 1952, January 18, 20, 26, 1953.

8. Claudia Fernández and Andrew Paxman, *El Tigre: Emilio Azcárraga y su imperio Televisa* (Mexico City: Grijalbo, 2000), pp. 105–08 and passim. Carl Mora relates how Emilio

Azcárraga lost his Mexico City Alemeda theater and other movie houses after being pressured by William O. Jenkins and Manuel Espinoza Iglesias (Operadora de Teatros, S.A.). Carl Mora, *Mexican Cinema: Reflections of a Society, 1896–1988* (Berkeley: University of California Press, 1982), p. 77. He further insinuates that Jenkins and Azcárraga later teamed up together with the first television station owner in Mexico XHTV, Rómulo O'Farrill, to form the largest television station in Mexico. See also, Miguel Contreras Torres, *El libro negro del cine mexicano* (Mexico City: Editora Hispano-Continental Films, 1960).

9. Javier Ruiz Rueda, *Agustín Lara: Vida y pasiones* (Mexico City: Editorial Novaro, 1976), p. 247.

10. Guadalupe Loaeza and Pável Granados, *Mi novia, la tristeza* (Mexico City: Océano, 2008), p. 365.

11. On the Regis see Sergio H., Peralta Sandoval, *Hotel Regis: historia de una época* (Mexico City: Editorial Diana, 1996).

12. Gabriel Abaroa Martínez, *El flaco de oro* (Mexico City: Editorial Planeta, 1993), pp. 198–200. See also Gasca, in *Agustín, rencuentro con lo sentimental*, pp. 340–43; Loaeza and Granados, *Mi novia, la tristeza*, pp. 365–67.

13 See Roland Barthes, *A Lover's Discourse, Fragments*, trans. Richard Howard (New York: Hill and Wang, 1978).

14. Yiyi Gasca, *Para mi querido y admirable amigo Francisco Rivera* (Fondo Francisco Rivera, AMV no date). Loaeza and Granados refer to a 1992 publication by the Instituto Veracruzano de Cultura by Yolanda titled *Un poco de nuestra vida, Agustín y Yiyi*. This may be derived from the same text. Lara's recorded romantic musings during this time—along with other material such as his columns "Como los conoci" and some impressionistic radio program notes—are contained in three notebooks titled "Cuadernos." Colección JAPS, Archivo Agustín Lara.

15. "Yo sabía que era mujer, pero él me ensenó lo que si serlo y mi cuerpo lobró consciencia de si mismo, vivía a su lado satisfecha y tranquila; lo admiraba, lo quería." Yolanda Gasca quoted as part of photographic exposition for Agustín Lara festival, 2004, Instituto Veracruzano de Educación y Cultura (IVEC), Veracruz, Veracruz.

16. Gasca, in *Agustín, rencuentro con lo sentimental*, p. 340.

17. Some also identified the street as Edgar Allen Poe. Abaroa Martínez, *El flaco de oro*, p. 279.

18. Abaroa Martínez, *El flaco de oro*, pp. 200–02. See photos of Lara and Gasca dressed in tuxedo and wedding dress in Yolanda Gasca, *Para mi querido y admirable amigo*; Loaeza and Granados, *Mi novia, la tristeza*, p. 369–70. Loaeza and Granados suggest that Yolanda did not realize the unofficial, nonbinding nature of the ceremony. Southern Californians made Yiyi an honary cititizen of San Bernardino on March 30, 1990. Subsequently, the Mexican Symphony played Lara's music to a full house in Riverside, California on April 10, 1990. *Inland Empire Hispanic News*, April 11, 1990.

19. Abaroa Martínez, *El flaco de oro*, p. 217. Loaeza and Granados indicate that the operation occurred in early 1955. Loaeza and Granados, *Mi novia, la tristeza*, p. 379.

20. *El Universal*, October 13, 1953; *Cinema Reporter*, October 17, 1953; Abaroa Martínez, *El flaco de oro*, pp. 222–24; Rueda, *Agustín Lara: Vida y pasiones*, pp. 250–51; Loaeza and Granados, *Mi novia, la tristeza*, p. 375. Two days later, President Adolfo Ruiz Cortines met with Agustín in his office. During their conversation, the politician offered to pay for Lara and his ensemble to perform throughout Europe. For whatever reason, Ruiz Cortines's proposal was never realized.

21. Moré would return to Cuba by the end of the decade while Pérez Prado remained in Mexico.

22. At the time, Calle de los Estudiantes Street was changed to "Agustín Lara" in the musician's honor.

23. Paco Pildora, "Salutación," reprinted in *Notiver*, no date, Fondo Paco Pildora, file 4E, AMV.

24. Quoted in Loaeza and Granados, *Mi novia, la tristeza*, p. 377. "La casita blanca" was recorded by Toña la Negra in 1964 for Orfeón (lp-12-05). Lara recorded it for the same label but the exact date is unknown. Pável Granados, *Agustín Lara: Canciones* (Veracruz/Mexico City: Gobierno de Veracruz/Océano, 2008), p. 343.

25. See list of "buddies" in Abaroa Martínez, *El flaco de oro*, p. 216, and delicacies of the port on p. 217.

26. "Rebeca," not to be confused with the Mexican actress born in 1953.

27. Loaeza and Granados, *Mi novia, la tristeza*, p. 377.

28. Francisco Rivera, in *Agustín, rencuentro con lo sentimental*, p. 216.

29. "Gabriel Moreno: Una vida marcada por la música de Agustín Lara," www.agustin-lara.com/txtfrente.htm. Moreno's family had long been associated with the entertainment business in the port. Until 1939 they headed the Teatro Variedades orchestra. Subsequently, the family continued as some of the foremost proponents of Lara's music in Veracruz. Gaby Moreno formed his own orchestra in 1954 and played eight consecutive years at Carnival. They disbanded in 1974.

30. *Prensa Libre de Chicago*, February 1, 1964; Abaroa Martínez, *El flaco de oro*, p. 227; interview with Algara for 2002 Lara Festival, "Alejandro Algara: La voz de la Suite Española," www.agustin-lara.com/txtfrente,htm. See also photo of Lara in the Casita Blanca pictured with singer Alejandro Algara and the Ambassador of Mexico in Chicago. Before joining up with Lara, Algara had been performing alongside stars such as Libertad Lamarque and Los Hermanos Martínez Gil in Los Angeles.

31. Rey would eventually become known as the "last interpreter" of Lara.

32. Angelina Bruschetta, *Agustín Lara y yo: 1928–1938*. (Xalapa, Veracruz: Author's edition, 1979), pp. 111–13. Emilio Azcárraga sent a representative to the Casita Blanca to supervise the selection of songs for a forthcoming greatest hits collection titled "La Historia Musical de Agustín Lara." The project allegedly paid an advance on royalties of 300,000 pesos. Paco Pildora, "Revolviendo papeles," *Notiver*, no date, Fondo Paco Pildora, file 4E, AMV.

33. Carmela Rey subsequently began singing regularly with Lara in 1955. *Revista de Revistas*, 1990, p. 46.

34. Ricardo Garibay, "Agustín Lara: Retrato, balance, responso," *Excelsíor*, November 7, 1970.

35. Ruiz Rueda says that Clarita Martínez went on this trip. Rueda, *Agustín Lara: Vida y pasiones*, pp. 256, 259. See also Lara's "Mi España," in *Siempre*, October 20, 1954.

36. A small assortment of photographs from Lara's first visit to Spain is located in the Colección JAPS, Archivo Agustín Lara, Carpeta "Fotografias de los viajes de España."

37. Agustín Lara, "Mi España," *Siempre* October 20, 1954, p. 14. Various plaques and awards from Spain are on display at the Casa de Cultura in Tlacotalpan.

38. Loaeza and Granados, *Mi novia, la tristeza*, p. 372.

39. His bar was on Gran Vía near the corner of Alcalá.

40. "Biografía del compositor," unidentified clipping, Novermber 7, 1970, BLT.

41. "Agustín Lara y la fiesta brava," *Revista de Revistas*, 19, November 1990, pp. 60–61; Arreola in *Agustín, rencuentro con lo sentimental*, pp. 47–48.

42. Lara, "Mi España," p. 14, 16.

43. Lara, "Mi España," p. 16.

44. Abaroa Martínez, *El flaco de oro*, pp. 206–14; Ruiz Rueda, *Agustín Lara: Vida y pasiones*, pp. 255–59; Gasca, in *Agustín, rencuentro con lo sentimental*, p. 344.

45. La vida íntima de un gran músico," *Life en espanol*, January 15, 1968, p. 60.

46. Rueda, *Agustín Lara: Vida y pasiones*, pp. 259–60.

47. Loaeza and Granados, *Mi novia, la tristeza*, pp. 373–74. Loaeza and Granados suggest that the Caribbean tour was followed by a tribute to Lara at Bellas Artes in 1953, but this seems incongruous with Yolanda's account which describes being in the Dominican Republic shortly after returning from Spain.

48. Colección JAPS, Archivo Agustín Lara, "Como los conoci," See also handwritten originals in "Cuadernos."

49. Paco Ignacio Taibo, I, *La música de Agustín Lara en el cine* (Mexico City: UNAM, 1984), pp. 78–80.

50. Quoted in Eric Zolov, *Refried Elvis: The Rise of the Mexican Counterculture* (Berkeley: University of California Press, 1999), p. 42.

51. Zolov, *Refried Elvis*, pp. 42–46. On the controversy surrounding the screening of Presley's "King Creole" film see pp. 47–51.

52. Glenn C. Altschuler, *All Shook Up: How Rock 'N' Roll Changed America* (New York: Oxford University Press, 2003), p. 9.

53. Eric Zolov, "Rebeldismo in the Revolutionary Family: Rock 'n' Roll's Early Challenges to the State and Society in Mexico," *Journal of Latin American Cultural Studies*, Vol. 6, No. 2, 1997, pp. 201–16. See also Zolov, *Refried Elvis*, pp. 17–61. Lara's continued presence on the national entertainment scene was increasingly seen as anachronistic, even pathetic, according to Carlos Monsiváis. Carlos Monsiváis, "Agustín Lara: El harem ilusorio (Notas a partir de la memorización de la letra de 'Farolito')," in *Amor perdido* (Mexico City: Biblioteca Era, 1977), p. 86.

54. Loaeza and Granados, *Mi novia, la tristeza*, p. 379.

55. Taibo I, *La música de Agustín Lara en el cine*, pp. 78–80.

56. After being rejected for the role, Lara refused to allow the song "Granada" (with an arrangement by Manuel Esperón) to be used in the film because, he said, the accompanying scene had not been shot in the Spanish city. "Alejandro Algara: La voz de la Suite Española," www.agustin-lara.com/txtfrente.htm.

57. A glimpse of Lara's (however modest) income generated by the film can be gleaned from a monthly report for June 1959 from the production company stating they owed him just shy of 42,000 pesos. "Reporte Mensual de Ingresos (Monthly Income Report, June 24, 1959)," "La Vida de Agustín Lara," Tropical Films, C.A. Colección JAPS, Archivo Agustín Lara, Carpeta #1 "Documentos Personales." An ensuing November 30, 1959 receipt for the purchase of a Steinway grand piano, model S-negro series 359651 from "Sala Chopin" on Insurgentes Avenue #177 (for the price of 40,000 pesos, or somewhere in the $3,000–4,000 dollar range), nevertheless suggests a sufficiently handsome overall income generated by a number of sources.

58. In 1959 Lara composed a bolero for singer María Victoria titled "Tengo ganas de un beso." Other songs written at this time include "La Carmen de Chamberi" (added to his collection of Spanish songs), "Regalo de viaje" (honoring Yolanda after a short trip to Colombia), and "La Faraona."

59. Nat King Cole released "Cole Español" in 1958 on EMI.

60. Around this time Cole also performed duets with María Grever ("Te quiero, dijiste"), Bobby Capó ("Piel canela"), Alberto Dominguez ("Perfidia"), Rafael Hernández ("Capullito de ahelí"), and a classic bolero by Nilo Menéndez and Adolfo Utera ("Aquellos ojos verdes").

61. Rueda, *Agustín Lara: Vida y pasiones*, pp. 251–52; Agustín Lara, "La vida íntima de un gran músico," p. 59; Paco Pildora, "Revolviedo papeles," *Notiver*, no date, Fondo Francisco Rivera, file 4E, AMV.

62. Rueda, *Agustín Lara: Vida y pasiones*, pp. 263–67.

63. Photographs of Lara appearing in a special series in April 1960 with Consuelo Velázquez and Vicente Garrido in a program "Duelo de Pianos," as well as other shows from late 1961 and early 1962 titled "Un corazón en el tiempo" and various Nescafe-sponsored Broadcasts in 1964. Colecciíon JAPS, Archivo Agustín Lara, "Fotografias de Programas de Televisión." Selected television appearances have recently been packaged and included in DVD format on *Las Número Uno: Agustin Lara*. 2005 Sony BMG.

64. Yolanda Gasca, *Un poco de nuestra vida, Agustín y Yiyi* AMV.

65. Gasca, in *Agustín, rencuentro con lo sentimental*, p. 347.

66. Abaroa Martínez, *El flaco de oro*, pp. 239–40. In addition to his suffering from his breakup with Yolanda, Lara temporarily fell ill in the spring of 1961 as indicated by an article in *Excélsior* April 6, 1961 titled "Se recupera Agustín Lara satisfactoriamente." Colección JAPS, Archivo Agustín Lara, Carpeta "Impresos."

67. June Kay, *Las siete vidas de Agustín Lara*, trans. F. de Riba Millon (Mexico City: El Universal Gráfico, 1964), p. 90.

68. See his testimony in *Revista de Revistas*, October 1997, pp. 34–35.

69. "Entrevista a Vianey Lárraga," www.agustin-lara.com/envianey.htm. Despite appearances, Lara's previous marriage to Carmen Zozoya later discredited his apparent nuptials with Vianey.

70. Abaroa Martínez, *El flaco de oro*, pp. 243–47; Paco Pildora, "Revolviendo papeles," *Notiver*, no date. Fondo Francisco Rivera, file 4E, AMV.

71. Javier Ramos Malzárraga, "El último día feliz de Agustín Lara," in Guillermo Mendizábal and Eduardo Mejía (eds.), *Todo lo que quería saber sobre Agustín Lara* (Mexico City: Grijalbo, 1993), pp. 26–27; Rueda, *Agustín Lara: Vida y pasiones*, pp. 275–77.

72. Pildora, "Revolviendo papeles," *Notiver*, no date. Fondo Francisco Rivera, file 4E, AMV.

73. Pildora, "Revolviendo papeles."

74. José Natividad Rosales, "Mujer divina," interview conducted in February 1963 at the Casita Blanca. Reprinted in David Martin del Campo, *100 Entrevistas personajes* (Mexico City: Grupo Azabache, 1991), pp. 128–31.

75. Rocio Durán quoted in Loaeza and Granados, *Mi novia, la tristeza*, p. 388.

76. *El Nacional*, February 17, 1964; *El Siglo*, Bogotá, February 10, 1964; *El Comercio*, Lima, April 17, 18, 1964; *La Prensa*, Lima, April 18, 1964; Colección JAPS, Archivo Agustín Lara, Carpeta #10.

77. *La Cronica*, April 18, 1964; *El Comercio*, Lima, April 18, 1964. A smattering of positive follow-up articles then appeared following Lara's Lima television appearance.

78. Loaeza and Granados mention that Lara had apparently caught a glimpse of Franco in attendance at one of his performances while in Spain in 1954. *Mi novia, la tristeza*, p. 373.

79. *El Universal*, February 21, 1964; *Novedades*, March 3, 1964. Lara remembers the year being 1965. Lara, "La vida íntima de un gran músico," p. 60.

80. Paco Pildora, "Revolviendo papeles," *Notiver*, no date. Fondo Francisco Rivera, file 4E, AMV. A few rather insignificant clippings from Mexican magazines (principally *Siempre*) on Lara and Rocio's travels can be found in Carpeta #18, Colección JAPS, Archivo Agustín Lara.

81. "Agustín dirigió Madrid con la Banda Municipal," June 9, 1964, *Novedades*.

82. "Homenaje de la Sociedad de Autores de España al compositor Agustín Lara," *Excélsior*, June 8, 1964.

83. *El Nacional*, June 11, 12, 16, 1964; Abaroa Martínez, *El flaco de oro*, p. 267.

84. "Honraron a Agustín Lara en Granada," *Excélsior*, June 16, 1964 and "Llevó ya dos meses en España y seguiré aquí mientras me dura la plata. 'Vivas' a Mexico y a Granada en una ceremonia en honor de Lara," *Excélsior*, June 16, 1964. See also a cartoon of Lara and a woman titled "Granada" in *Excélsior* June 13, 1964. Another cartoon of the musician and Franco appeared in the same paper two days later.

85. See photos of the wedding in *El Universal*, July 7, 1964.

86. "Javier Gómez Lizardi, "Acordes de la Suite Española," in *Agustín, rencuentro con lo sentimental*, p. 165. There is a photo of Lara and Franco on display at the Casita Blanca in Veracruz.

87. Lara quoted in *Siempre*, November 4, 1964. Colección JAPS, Archivo Agustín Lara, Carpeta 10, "Notas periodicos."

88. *El Nacional*, June 26, 1964.

89. Paco Pildora writes that he and Dr. Horacio Díaz Cházaro watched home movie footage (probably Super 8) of the bullfights and other scenes from Spain once the couple was back in Mexico.

90. Ruiz Rueda talks about Lara patching things up with Cordoblés. Rueda, *Agustín Lara: Vida y pasiones*, pp. 282–83.

91. This material was most famously interpreted and recorded by Mexican singer Alejandro Algara. See Algara in *Revista de Revistas*, October 1997, p. 56–57.

92. Abaroa Martínez, *El flaco de oro*, pp. 252–71; Rueda, *Agustín Lara: Vida y pasiones*, pp. 281–86; Lizardi in *Agustín, rencuentro con lo sentimental*, pp. 166–68; Granados, *Canciones*, pp. 386–96.

93. "Filmarán Agustín Lara y Sarita Montiel también actuará en la cinta *El Cordoblés*," *Excélsior*, August 7, 1964. It could be that the project never came to completion as I found no mention of the film when reviewing either Lara's or Montiel's extensive filmographies. On Montiel see http://members.tripod.com/infomontiel.

94. Pildora, "Revolviendo papeles," *Notiver*, no date. Fondo Francisco Rivera, file 4E, AMV.

95. Abaroa Martínez, *El flaco de oro*, pp. 268–69.

96. Although seemingly excessive, the check made out to Lara—which he was required to share with the Sociedad Nacional de Autores—allegedly amounted to 160,000 pesos. Paco Pildora comments that the composer's union "operated in their usual mafia style." Pildora, "Revolviendo papeles," *Notiver*, no date, Fondo Francisco Rivera, file 4E, AMV.

97. *Excélsior*, October 9, 1964.

98. Cartoon in *Excélsior*, October 9, 1964.

99. Pildora, "Revolviendo papeles," *Notiver*, no date. Fondo Francisco Rivera, file 4E, AMV.
100. Dora Orea Maldonado, "Agustin Lara le canta a Tijuana," *Baja California*, December 2, 1964; "Alejandro Algara: La voz de la Suite Española," www.agustin-lara.com/txtfrente. htm; *El Nacional*, December 9, 1964.
101. Rueda, *Agustín Lara: Vida y pasiones*, p. 292.
102. Abaroa Martinez, *El flaco de oro*, p. 276.
103. "Los jarochos son mis amigos más queridos y probablemente los que más me quieren." Lara, "La vida íntima de un gran musico," p. 60.
104. Interview with María Rosario de Ochoa, March 16, 2005, Veracruz, Veracruz.
105. Félix even recorded (with her singing) four of Lara's songs ("Porque negar," "Escarcha," "Cada noche un amor," and "Solamente una vez") in 1964 for RCA Victor. Dueñas and Flores Escalante, *Discography*.
106. Abaroa Martínez, *El flaco de oro*, pp. 279–80. Technically, Carmen had remained married to Lara. Lara anonymously ceded royalties to her for many years; she left the money untouched. For many years, she worked for the National Lottery. She died in June 1992. Also mentioned by Abaroa Martínez is the fact that a floor of the Hospital Niños Héroes is named after Lara. Whether he donated money is unclear.
107. Colección JAPS, Archivo Agustín Lara, Carpeta #1 "Documentos Personales."
108. Guillermo Ochoa, "La casa en que la decepción enclaustro a Lara," *Excelsíor*, November 11, 1970; Abaroa Martínez, *El flaco de oro*, p. 285. Abaroa Martínez refers to the suburb as Tetelpan.
109. Lara, "La vida íntima de un gran músico," p. 60; "Biografía del compositor," unidentified clipping, November 7, 1970, BLT. "Quiero que mis cenizas, si es que llego a tener cenizas— porque quemar tantos huescos va a ser cosa tremenda—desaparezcan. Tengo muchos amigos pilotos y voy a pedirle a alguno de ellos que suelte mis cenizas sobre el mar. Devolverlas al mar es lo mejor. Porque a mi nada de serenatitas, ni de aqui está la guitarra; nada de tumultos, ni nade de nada. Por favor, que me dejen en paz. Y en cuanto a lo que produzcan— si acaso producen algo—mis pobres, mis tristes canciones, eso será para el Instituto de Cancerlogía de México. No puedo dar más Soy pobre, y quiero morir pobre, como nací."
110. Of course, Lara's actual place of birth had been the subject of earlier commentaries. At one point in the spring of 1965, Agustín wrote a letter to *El Dictamen* columnist Bartolomé Padilla declaring "I am a Veracruzan" and that "it is absolutely true that I was born under the silvery moon." *El Dictamen*, April 18, 1965. This article is framed and lay on Lara's desk in the Casita Blanca. Just days before his death in November 1970, close friends watched as journalist Jacobo Zabludovsky raised a copy of Lara's birth certificate documenting his birth in Mexico City on the program *24 Horas*. Some, including Pedro Vargas, were as surprised as anyone to find out that Lara indeed had not been born in Veracruz. Garmabella, *Pedro Vargas: "Una vez nada más"* (Mexico City: Ediciones de Comunicación, 1984), p. 101. José Pérez de León, "Remate Dominicial," unidentified clippings.
111. R. Delgado Lozano, "Muchas emociones para un solo día," *Life en español*, January 15, 1968 p. 59; Javier Ramos Malzárraga, "El último día feliz de Agustín Lara," in Mendizábal and Mejía, *Todo lo que quería saber sobre Agustín Lara*, pp. 20–22.
112. Rueda, *Agustín Lara: Vida y pasiones*, p. 296. Pinal and Guzmán were married for a time. One of their children is popular Mexican singer Alejandra Guzmán.
113. "La sensibilidad de un hombre de leyenda deje en sus canciones el testimonio de su propio vida," *El Nacional*, November 7, 1979.
114. Ramos Malzárraga, "El último día feliz de Agustín Lara," p. 28.
115. In the end Azcárraga allegedly paid all Lara's medical bills. Rueda, *Agustín Lara: Vida y pasiones*, p. 296.
116. Lara had also received a message from his friend Josephine Baker indicating that she would soon be in Mexico City. Josephine Baker to Agustín Lara, September 9, 1970. Colección JAPS, Archivo Agustín Lara, "Documentos Personales."
117. Abaroa Martínez, *El flaco de oro*, p. 290.
118. On alimony asked by Lárraga during this time and dispute between Rocío and Carmen Zozaya over estate see Abaroa Martínez, *El flaco de oro*, pp. 297–300. Amazingly, Lara's first wife Esther Rivas Elorriaga was also in the hospital.

119. Paco Pildora, "Cuando murio Agustín Lara," *Notiver*, November 1985, Fondo Francisco Rivera, file 4E, AMV.

120. Pildora, "Cuando murio Agustín Lara."

121. Juan Jaime Larios, "Pueblo y gobierno en el postrer homenaje," *El Universal*, November 8, 1970.

122. Larios, "Pueblo y gobierno en el postrer homenaje."

123. Larios, "Pueblo y gobierno en el postrer homenaje."

124. See, for example, Luis Fernando Lara, "Agustín Lara en la música mexicana," *Día*, November 10, 1970; Rafael Lara Cetina, "El pueblo llenó ayer de flores la tumba de Lara," *El Universal*, November 9, 1970.

125. "Mensajes de Díaz Ordaz y de Echeverría por la muerte de Lara," *Día*, November 7, 1970.

126. Pildora, "Revolviendo papeles," *Notiver*, no date. Fondo Paco Pildora, file 4E, AMV.

127. "La España que cantó esta de luto; Granada le hará un monumento," *Novedades*, November 8, 1970.

128. "La España que cantó esta de luto."

129. "El amor de Agustín Lara por España, lo convertió en música," *El Nacional*, October 9, 1977.

130. "Hay pesar en la América Latina por la muerte del músico veracruzano," *Novedades*, November 7, 1970.

131. "La España que cantó esta de luto; Granada le hará un monumento," *Novedades*, November 8, 1970.

132. Pildora, "Revolviendo papeles," *Notiver*, no date, Fondo Francisco Rivera, file 4E, AMV.

133. Pedro Vargas died on October 30, 1989. Toña la Negra died a few years earlier on December 16, 1982. Memorialized in the port of Veracruz, Paco Pildora wrote a decima titled "!Adios a Toña Peregrina." Paco Pildora, "!Una barrio, una mujer y una voz incomparable!" unidentified clipping, Fondo Francisco Rivera, file 1V, AMV.

134. Rueda, *Agustín Lara: Vida y pasiones*, pp. 313–14. Unfortunately, a May 2003 visit to the Centro de Documentacíon Musical de Andalucía unearthed virtually no material on Lara.

135. "El amor de Agustín Lara por España, lo convertió en música," *El Nacional*, October 9, 1977.

136. Enrique Loubet, "El recuerdo de Lara vuelve a Veracruz un día de Carnaval," *Excélsior*, November 7, 1974. Yet all was not well in regard to the musician-poet's legacy. "Mujer," one of his most beloved songs, was being used in a feminine hygiene commercial. A woman named Leticia Palma (allegedly an artist of some sort) had purchased La Casita Blanca and subsequently abandoned it. In no time, thieves had broken windows and stolen nearly everything, including electric fixtures and whatever furniture had remained. Before long, the building and its environs were shamefully in tatters. José Pérez de León, "Remate Dominical," clipping on display at Casita Blanca Museum; Paco Pildora, "El Agustín que you conocí," *Notiver*, no date, Fondo Francisco Rivera, file 4E, AMV.

137. "Agustín Lara, el día que nació una leyenda," *El Nacional*, October 30, 1997.

138. "Alejandro Algara: La voz de la Suite Española," www.agustin-lara.com/txtfrente.htm.

139. Javier Galindo Ulloa, "Hoy, centenario del natalico de Agustín Lara," *El Financiero*, October 30, 1997.

140. One of the most the most recent of these was an event I attended on a Sunday afternoon in October 2010 in the Mexico City Zócalo with a number of Cuban artists performing some of Lara's songs. Yolanda Gasca was in attendance. "Cuba le canta a Agustín Lara," *Milenio*, October 22, 2010; "La música de Lara sonará en el Zócalo," *La Jornada*, October 24, 2010; "Gran Concierto Baile: Solamente una vez," advertisement, *La Jornada*, October 24, 2010.

141. Conrado Zuckermann, "Agustín Lara," *El Universal*, November 22, 1970.

# REFERENCES

*Archives and Private Collections*

**MEXICO CITY**

Archivo Histórico del Distrito Federal
Archivo General de la Nación, Ramos Propiedad Artistica y Literaria, Presidentes, Gobernación
Biblioteca Miguel Lerdo de Tejada, Collection "Archivos Economicos"
Biblioteca Nacional de México
Biblioteca Nacional de México, Archivo Silvino González, Fondo Reservado
Biblioteca Instututo Mora
Colección Juan Antonio Pérez Simon, Archivo Agustín Lara
Instituto Nacional de Belles Artes Centro Nacional de Información y Promoción de la Literatura
    Consejo Nacional para la Cultura y las Artes
Instituto Nacional de Antropología e Historia, Fonoteca

**PORT OF VERACRUZ, VERACRUZ**

Casita Blanca de Agustín Lara, Boca del Río
Fondo Francisco Rivera, Archivo Municial del Puerto de Veracruz

**XALAPA, VERACRUZ**

Archivo General del Estado de Veracruz

**HAVANA, CUBA**

Museo de la Música

**MADRID, SPAIN**

Biblioteca Nacional de España

**GRANADA, SPAIN**

Centro de Documentación Musical de Andalucía

**BERKELEY, CALIFORNIA**

Bancroft Library

**AUSTIN, TEXAS**

Benson Collection

## Selected Newspapers

*El Dictamen,* Veracruz
*El Heraldo,* Ciudad Juárez
*El Hispano Americano,* Tijuana
*El Liberal Progresista,* Guatemala City
*El Mundo,* Havana, Cuba
*Notiver,* Veracruz
*El Paso Herald Post,* El Paso
*El Siglo,* Torreón, Coahuila
*El Sol,* Querétaro
*El Universal,* Mexico City
*El Viajante,* Monterrey
*Excélsior,* Mexico City
*La Noticia,* Managua, Nicaragua
*La Prensa,* San Salvador, El Salvador
*Los Angeles Times*
*New York Times*
*San Antonio Evening News*

## Selected Magazines and Journals

*Ases y Estrellas*
*Cinema Reporter*
*El Ilustrado*
*El Universal Gráfico*
*El Universal Gráfico*
*Jueves de Excélsior*
*Vida de Agustín Lara*
*México Cinema*
*México de Noche*
*Radiolandia*
*Revista de Revistas*
*Siempre*

## Discography

*Danzones del porfiriato y la revolución,* Mexico City: BMG, 1994.
*Danzón y más danzón: Grabaciones originales 1922–1940,* Mexico City: ICREM, 2000.
*The Cuban Danzón: Various Artists.* El Cerrito, CA, Arhoolie Recrods #7032, 1999.
*Orquesta Cuba: Charangas & Danzón,* Portland, OR, Nimbus Records #7058, 2000.
*Cuban Danzón: Its' Ancestors and Descendents.* Washington, D.C., Smithsonian Folkways #4086, 2010.
*Agustin Lara: Su voz, su piano y sus canciones,* Mexico City: Orfeon, n/d.
*Agustin Lara: 20 Exitos.* Mexico City: BMG, 1991.
*Agustín Lara a la cubana.* Havana, Cuba: EGREM, 2001.
*La voz y guitarra de Guty Cárdenas: El Ruiseñor Yucateco,* Mexico City: Discos Corasón, 1993.
Guty Cárdenas: *Grabaciones 1928–1930,* Mexico City: ICREM-003, 1999.
Pedro Vargas: *Época de oro de la radio, grabaciones de 1932 a 1935,* Mexico City: ICREM-01, 1996.
*Toña la Negra: La sensación jarocha,* Mexico City: Peerless, 1990.
*Inmortales de Toña la Negra,* Mexico City: Orfeon, n/d.
*Ana María González: Todas sus grabaciones vols. 1 & 2 (1948–1953),* Madrid: Rama Lama, 2004.
*Ana María González: Grabaciones 1950–51,* Mexico City: ICREM-014, 2000.

*México: Historia y música del siglo XX, vol. 1.* Mexico City: EMI, 2000.
*Rarezas discográficas Agustín Lara,* Included in Pável Granados, *Agustín Lara, Canciones,* Mexico City/Veracruz: Océano/Gobierno de Veracruz, 2008.
*Las Número Uno: Agustín Lara,* CD and DVD Sony/BMG, 2005.

## Dissertations and Theses

Baer, Miriam D., "Television and Political Control in Mexico." Ph D diss., Department of Communication, University of Michigan, 1991.
Berger, Dina Michelle, "Pyramids by Day, Martinis by Night: The Development and Promotion of Mexico's Tourist Industry, 1928–1946." PhD diss., Department of History, University of Arizona, 2002.
Hayes, Joy Elizabeth, "Radio Broadcasting and Nation-Building in Mexico and the United States, 1925–1945." PhD diss., Department of Communication, University of California, San Diego, 1994.
Renfro, Cole Norris, "A History of La Hora Nacional: Government Broadcasting via Privately Owned Radio Stations in Mexico." Ph D diss., Department of Speech and Theater, University of Michigan, 1963.
Sheehy, Daniel Edward, "The Son Jarocho': The History, Style, and Repertory of a Changing Mexican Musical Tradition," PhD diss., Department of Music, University of California, Los Angeles, 1979.

## Unpublished Materials

Dueñas, Pablo and Jesús Flores y Escalante, *Discografía de Agustín Lara.* November 2008.
Koegel, John, *A Provisional Listing of Some of Agustín Lara's Songs including Sheet Music, Recordings, and Copyright Information.* January 2006.

## Interviews/Personal Communication

Águila, Carlos, September 1999 Hostería de Santo Domingo Restaurant, Mexico City.
del Rosario del Ochoa, María, Various 1998–2006. Archivo Municipal, Port of Veracruz.
Granados, Pável, August 2006. Café La Blanca, Mexico City.
Magdaleno Cárdenas, María de los Ángeles. Various, Mexico City.
O'Farrill Márquez, Juan Pablo, June 29, 2006. XEW/Televisa Radio Studios, Tlalpan, Mexico City.
Pous, Armando, Various, 1999–2001. Mexico City.
Salamanca Herrera, Guillermo, June 24, 2006. Howard Johnson Hotel, Veracruz.
Dueñas Pablo, and Jesús Flores Escalante, November 2008. XEB radio station, Mexico City.

## Published Sources

Abaroa Martínez, Gabriel, *El flaco de oro.* Mexico City: Editorial Planeta, 1993.
Aguilar, Genaro Aguirre, *Los usos del espacio nocturno en el Puerto de Veracruz.* Veracruz: Colecíon Textos Universitarios/Universidad Cristóbal Colón, 2001.
Agustín, José, *Tragicomedia Mexicana: La vida en México de 1940 a 1970.* Mexico City: Planeta, 1990.
Alfaro, Francisco H. and Alejandro Ochoa, *La república de los cines.* Mexico City: Clío Editions, 1998.
Alonso, Enrique, *María Conesa.* Mexico City: Océano, 1987.
Altschuler, Glenn C., *All Shook Up: How Rock 'N' Roll Changed America.* New York: Oxford University Press, 2003.
*America Dances! 1897–1948: A Collector's Edition of Social Dance in Film.* Dancetime Publications, 2003.
*An American Ballroom Companion.* American Memory Project, United Status Library of Congress. http://memory.loc.gov/ammem/dihtml/dihome.html.

Anderson, Benedict, *Imagined Communities: Reflections on the Origin and Spread of Nationalism.* London: Verso Press, 1983, 2006.

Archivo Histórico del Distrito Federal/Universidad Autnónoma Metropolitana-Iztapalapa, *Gran Baile de Archivo Histórico del Distrito Federal, Pulgas en traje de charácter: Las diversiones públicas en la Ciudad de México del Siglo XIX.* Mexico City: Archivo Histórico del Distrito Federal/Universidad Autnónoma Metropolitana-Iztapalapa, 1999.

Ariel, Sigfredo, "La cumbancha cubana de Agustín Lara," in Bernardo García Díaz and Sergio Guerra Vilaboy (eds.), *La Habana/Veracruz, Veracruz/La Habana.* Veracruz/Habana: Universidad de Verarcruz/Universidad de La Habana, 2004, pp. 495–507.

Arreola, Juan José and Lilian Scheffler, *México: ¿quires tomarte una foto conmigo? Cien años de consumo.* Mexico City: Procuraduría Federal del Consumidor/Editorial Gustavo Casasola, 1996.

Aura, Alejandro, *La hora íntima de Agustín Lara.* Mexico City: Cal y Arena, 1990.

Ayala, Roberto (ed.), *Canciones y poemas de Agustín Lara: Colección completa.* Mexico City: Selecciónes Orfeón, 1969.

Barbour, Phillip L., "Commerical and Cultural Broadcasting in Mexico," *The Annals of the American Academy of Political and Social Sciences.* Philadelphia: March 1940.

Barrón Echauri, Mónica, *Álbum fotográfico de Agustín Lara.* Veracruz/Mexico City: Gobierno de Veracruz/Océano, 2008.

Barthes, Roland, *A Lover's Discourse, Fragments,* trans. Richard Howard. New York: Hill and Wang, 1978.

Bartra, Roger, *The Cage of Melancholy: Identity and Metamorphosis in the Mexican Character,* trans. Christopher J. Hall. New Brunswick: Rutgers University Press, 1992.

Bauer, Arnold J., *Goods, Power and History: Latin America's Material Culture.* Cambridge: Cambridge University Press, 2001.

Bauer, Arnold J. and Benjamin Orlove (eds.), *The Allure of the Foreign: Imported Goods in Postcolonial Latin America.* Ann Arbor: University of Michigan Press, 1997.

Bazán Bonfil, Rodrigo, *Y si vivo cien años: antología del bolero en México.* Mexico City: Fondo de Cultura Economica, 2001

Beezley William H., *Judas at the Jockey Club and Other Episodes in Porfirian Mexico.* Lincoln: University of Nebraska Press, 1987.

Beezley, William H. and Michael C. Meyer, *The Oxford History of Mexico.* Oxford: Oxford University Press, 2000.

Beezley, William H., Cheryl E. Martin, and William E. French (eds.) *Rituals of Rule, Rituals of Resistance: Public Celebrations and Popular Culture in Mexico.* Wilmington, DE: SR Books, 1994.

Beezley, William H. and Dirk Raat (eds.), *Twentieth Century Mexico.* Lincoln: University of Nebraska Press, 1986.

Beezley, William and Jurgen Buchenau (eds.), *Governors of the Revolution: Portraits in Courage and Conflict.* Lanham, MD: SR Books/Rowman and Littlefield, 2009.

Benitez-Rojo, Antonio, *The Repeating Island: The Caribbean and the Postmodern Perspective,* 2nd ed. trans. James E. Maraniss. Durham, NC: Duke University Press, 1996.

Benson, Susan Porter, *Counter Cultures: Saleswomen, Managers, and Customers in American Department Stores, 1890–1940.* Champaign: University of Illinois Press, 1986.

Berger, Dina and Andrew Grant Wood, *Holiday in Mexico: Critical Reflections on Tourism and Tourist Encounters.* Durham, NC: Duke University Press, 2010.

Bergero, Adriana J., *Intersecting Tango: Cultural Geographies of Buenos Aires, 1900–1930.* Pittsburgh: University of Pittsburgh Press, 2008.

Berman, Marshall, *All That is Solid Melts into Air: The Experience of Modernity.* New York: Simon and Schuster, 1982.

Bethell, Leslie (ed.), *A Cultural History of Latin America: Literature, Music and the Visual Arts in the 19th and 20th Centuries.* Cambridge: Cambridge University Press, 1998.

Bethell, Leslie (ed.), *Mexico Since Independence.* Cambridge: Cambridge University Press, 1991.

Bliss, Katherine Elaine, *Compromised Positions: Prostitution, Public Health and Gender Politics in Revolutionary Mexico City.* University Park: Pennsylvania State University Press, 2001.

Bourdieu, Pierre, *Distinction: A Social Critique of the Judgement of Taste,* trans. Richard Nice. Cambridge, MA: Harvard University Press, 1984.

Boym, Svetlana, *The Future of Nostalgia*. New York: Basic Books, 2001.

Bradbury, Malcolm and James McFarlane (eds.), *Modernism: 1890–1930*. New York: Pelican Books, 1976.

Brenner, Anita, *The Wind that Swept Mexico*. Austin: University of Texas Press, 1942.

Brenner, Anita, *Your Mexican Holiday: A Modern Guide*. New York: G.P. Putnam's Sons, 1932.

Brenner, Helmut, *Juventino Rosas: His Life, His Work, His Time*. Warren, MI: Harmonie Park Press, 2000.

Brock, Pope, *Charlatan: America's Most Dangerous Huckster, The Man Who Pursued Him and the Age of Flimflam*. New York: Crown Books, 2008.

Bronfman, Alejandra and Andrew Grant Wood (eds.), Media, Sound, and Culture in Latin America and the Caribbean. Pittsburgh: University of Pittsburgh Press, 2012.

Bruschetta, Angelina, *Agustín Lara y yo: 1928–1938*. Xalapa, Veracruz: Author's edition, 1979.

Buffington, Robert, "La 'Dancing' Mexicana: Danzón and the Transformation of Intimacy in Post-Revolutionary Mexico City." *Journal of Latin American Cultural Studies* 14, no. 1 (March 2005), pp. 87–108.

Bunker, Stephen B., "Consumers of Good Taste: Marketing Modernity in Northern Mexico, 1890–1910," *Mexican Studies / Estudios Mexicanos* 13, no. 2 (Summer 1997), pp. 227–69.

Bunker, Stephen B., Creating Mexican Consumer Culture in the Age of Porfirio Díaz. Albuquerque: University of New Mexico Press, 2012.

Butsch, Richard, "Introduction: Leisure and Hegemony," in Richard Butsch (ed.), *For Fun and Profit: The Transformation of Leisure into Consumption*. Philadelphia: Temple University Press, 1990, pp. 3–27.

Caistor, Nick (ed.) *Mexico City: A Cultural and Literary Companion*. New York: Interlink Books, 2000.

Carleton Millan, Verna, *Mexico Reborn*. Boston: Houghton Mifflin, 1939.

Carpentier, Alejo, *Music in Cuba*. Minneapolis: University of Minnesota Press, 2001. Timothy Brennan (ed.) trans. Alan West-Durán.

Castañeda, Daniel, *Balance de Agustín Lara*. Mexico City: Ediciones Libres, 1941.

Castillo, Debra A., *Easy Women: Sex and Gender in Modern Mexican Fiction*. Minneapolis: University of Minnesota Press, 1998.

Ceballos, Edgar, *La historia de México a través del teatro: Un siglo de contraste. la ópera, 1901–1925*. Mexico City: Consejo Nacional para la Cultura y las Artes/Escenología, 2002.

Centro de Estudios Económicos y Demográficos, El Colegio de México, *Dinámica de la población de México*. Mexico City: El Colegio de México, 1970.

Charosh, Paul, *Berliner Gramophone Records, American Issues, 1892–1900*. Westport, CT: Greenwood Press, 1995.

Chasteen, Charles, *National Rhythms, African Roots: The Deep History of Latin American Popular Dance*. Albuquerque: University of New Mexico Press, 2004.

Cirules, Enrique, *The Mafia in Havana: A Caribbean Mob Story*, trans. Douglas E. LaPrade. New York: Ocean Press, 2004.

Clark, Danae, *Negotiating Hollywood: The Cultural Politics of Actors' Labor*. Minneapolis: University of Minnesota Press, 1995.

Clague, Mark (ed.), *The Memoires of Alton Augustus Adams Sr.: The First Black Bandmaster of the United States Navy*. Berkeley: University of California Press, 2008.

Coatsworth, John, *Growth against Development: The Economic Impact of Railroads in Porfirian Mexico*. Dekalb: Northern Illinois University Press, 1981.

Collier, Simon, Artemis Cooper, María Susana Azzi and Richard Martin, *Tango!: The Dance, The Song, The Story*. London: Thames and Hudson, 1995.

Collier, Simon, *The Life, Times and Music of Carlos Gardel*. Pittsburgh: University of Pittsburgh Press, 1986.

Contreras Torres, Miguel, *El libro negro del cine mexicano*. Mexico City: Editora Hispano-Continental Films, 1960.

Córdova, Arnaldo, *En una época de crisis (1928–1934)*. Mexico City: Siglo XXI/Universidad Nacional Autónoma de México, 1980.

Cortés Rodríguez, Martha, "Bailes y carnaval en Veracruz, 1925." *Horizonte: Revista del Instituto Veracruzano de Cultura* (March–April, 1991).

Couture, Mark, "The Importance of Being Agustín Lara: Cursilería, Machismo and Modernity." *Studies in Latin American Popular Culture* vol. 20 (2000), pp. 69–80.

Dallal, Alberto, *La danza en México: El "dancing" mexicano*. Mexico City: Universidad Nacional Autónoma de México, 2000.

Dallal, Alberto, *La danza en México: La danza escénica popular, 1877–1930*. Mexico City: Universidad Nacional Autónoma de México, 1995.

De la Peza Casares, María del Carmen, *El bolero y la educación sentimental en Méxco*. Mexico City: Universidad Autónoma Metropolitana-Xochimilco, 2001.

De Los Reyes, Aurelio, *Cine y sociedad en México: Bajo el cielo de México 1920–1924*. Mexico City: Universidad Nacional Autónoma de México, 1993.

De Los Reyes, Aurelio, *Cine y sociedad en México: Vivir de sueños, 1896–1930*. Mexico City: Universidad Nacional Autónoma de México, 1981, 1996.

De María y Campos, Armando, *Las tandas del Principal*. Mexico City: Editorial Diana, 1989.

De Olavarría y Ferrari, Enrique, *Reseña histórica del teatro en México*. Mexico City: La Europa, 1895.

De Parodi, Enriqueta (Enriqueta Montaño Peralta), *Alfonso Ortiz Tirado: su vida en la ciencia y en el arte*. Mexico City: s.n., 1964

Del Campo, David Martin, *100 Entrevistas personajes*. Mexico City: Grupo Azabache, 1991.

Delpar, Helen, *The Enormous Vogue of Things Mexican: Cultural Relations between the United States and Mexico, 1920–1935*. Tuscaloosa: University of Alabama Press, 1992

Derbez, Alain, *El jazz en México: Datos para una historia*. Mexico City: Fondo de Cultura Económica, 2001.

Díaz-Ayala, Cristobal, *Encyclopedic Discography of Cuban Music. Díaz-Ayala Cuban and Latin American Popular Music Collection*, Florida International University. http://gislab.fiu.edu/smc/discography.htm.

Díaz Barriga, Carlos, *La calle de los sueños: Vida y obra de Mario Ruiz Armengol*. Veracruz, Veracruz: Instituto Veracruzano de la cultura, 2002.

Dickson, Jean, "¿Quién fue Carlos Curti?," *Heterofonía* 140 (January–June, 2009), pp. 61–75.

Dodd, Mead and Company, *The New International Year Book: A Compendium of the World's Progress*. New York: Dodd, Mead and Company, 1914.

Dregni, Michael, *Django: The Life and Music of a Gypsy Legend*. Oxford: Oxford University Press, 2004.

Dueñas, Pablo, *Bolero: Historia Ddocumental del bolero mexicano*. Mexico City: Asociación de Estudios Fonograficos, 1993.

Dueñas, Pablo, *Las divas en el teatro de revista mexicano*. Mexico City: Asociación Mexicana de Estudios Fonográficos/Dirección General de Culturas Populares, 1994.

Ellman, Richard and Charles Feidelson Jr. (eds.) *The Modern Tradition: Backgrounds of Modern Literature*. New York: Oxford University Press, 1965.

Erenberg, Lewis A., *Steppin' Out: New York Nightlife and the Transformation of American Culture*. Westport CT: Greenwood Press, 1981.

Ewen, Stuart, *Captains of Consciousness: Advertising and the Social Roots of the Consumer Culture*. New York: McGraw Hill, 1976.

Eyman, Scott, *The Speed of Sound: Hollywood and the Talkie Revolution, 1926–1930*. Baltimore: Johns Hopkins University Press, 1997.

Fajardo Estrada, Ramón, *Rita Montaner: Testimonio de una época*. Havana: Casa de las Americas, 1997.

Fass, Paula, *The Damned and the Beautiful: American Youth in the 1920s*. New York: Oxford University Press, 1977.

Fein, Seth, "Transnationalization and Cultural Collaboration: 'Mexican' Cinema and the Second World War," *Studies in Latin American Popular Culture* 17 (1998), pp. 105–28.

Félix, María, *Todas mis guerras*. Mexico City: Clío Editions, 1993.

Fernández, Celina, *Los Panchos: La historia de los embajadores de la canción romantica contada por su voz Rafael Basurto Lara*. Mexico City: Ediciones Martínez Roca, 2005.

Fernández, *Claudia and Andrew Paxman, El Tigre: Emilio Azcárraga y su imperio Televisa*. Mexico City: Grijalbo, 2000.

Festival Internacional Agustín Lara, *Nuestro flaco de oro*. Mexico City: Banco de Ideas/Gobierno del estado de Veracruz/Secretario de Educación y Cultura/Instituto Veracruzano de Cultura, 2001.

Flores y Escalante, Jesús, *Imagenes del danzón: Iconografía del danzón en México*. Mexico City: Asociación Mexicana de Estudios Fonograficos, 1994.

Flores y Escalante, Jesús, *Salón México: Historia documental y gráfica del danzón en México*. Mexico City: Asociación Mexicana de Estudios Fonográficos, 1993.

Foster, David William (ed.), *Mexican Literature: A History*. Austin: University of Texas Press, 1994.

Franco, Jean, *The Modern Culture of Latin America: Society and the Artist*. New York: Pelican Books, 1970.

Fraser, Valerie, *Building the New World: Studies in The Modern Architecture of Latin America, 1930–1960*. London: Verso Press, 2000.

French, William E. and Katherine Elaine Bliss. *Gender, Sexuality, and Power in Latin America since Independence*. Jaguar Books on Latin America Series. Lanham, MD: Rowman and Littlefield. 2007.

Fuentes, Carlos, *The Buried Mirror: Reflections on Spain and the New World*. Boston: Houghton Mifflin, 1992.

Galeano, Eduardo, *Memory of Fire: Century of the Wind*, trans. Cedric Belfrage. London: Quartet Books, 1989.

Gallo, Rubén, *Mexican Modernity: The Avant-Garde and the Technological Revolution*. Cambridge, MA: The MIT Press, 2005.

Gänzl, Kurt, *The Musical: A Concise History*. Freeport, MA: Northeastern Press, 1997.

García Canclini, Nestór, *Hybrid Cultures: Strategies for Entering and Leaving Modernity*, trans. Christopher L. Chiaparri and Silvia L. López. Minneapolis: University of Minneapolis Press, 1995.

García de León, Antonio, *El mar de los deseos: El Caribe hispano musical-Historia y contrapunto*. Mexico City: Siglo vientiuno editores, 2001.

García de Leon, Antonio, "Los patios danzoneros," *La Jornada Seminal*, #223, September 19, 1993.

García Diaz, Bernardo and Ricardo Pérez Montfort, *Veracruz y sus viajeros*. Xalapa, Veracruz: Estado de Veracruz/Grupo Sansco, 2001.

García Díaz, Bernardo and Sergio Guerra Vilaboy (eds.), *La Habana/Veracruz, Veracruz/La Habana: Las dos orillas*. Veracruz and Havana: Universidad de Veracruz, Universidad de Havana, 2002.

García Díaz, Bernardo, *Puerto de Veracruz: Veracruz: imágenes de su historia*. Xalapa: Veracruz: Archivo General del Estado de Veracruz, 1992.

García Riera, Emilio, *Historia documental del cine mexicano*. Guadalajara: Universidad de Guadalajara, 18 vols., 1992–97.

Garmabella, José Ramón, *Pedro Vargas: "Una vez nada más."* Mexico City: Ediciones de Comunicacíon, 1984.

Garrido, Felipe, *Luz y sombra: Los inicios del cine in la prensa de la ciudad de México*. Mexico City: Consejo Nacional para la Cultura y las Artes, 1997.

Garrido, Juan S., *Historia de la música popular en México. Mexico City, 1876–1973*: Editorial Extemporáneos S.A., 1974.

Gasca, Luis, *Cugat*. Madrid: Edicioned del imán, 1995.

Gerassi-Navarro, Nina, *Pirate Novels: Fictions of Nation Building in Spanish America*. Durham, NC: Duke University Press, 1999.

Giddens, Gary, *Bing Crosby: A Pocketful of Dreams: The Early Years, 1903–1940*. New York: Little, Brown, 2001.

Giddens, Gary, *Satchmo: The Genius of Louis Armstrong*. New York: DaCapo Press, 1988.

Giddens, Gary, *Visions of Jazz: The First Century*. New York: Oxford University Press, 1998.

Glickman, Lawrence B. (ed.), *Consumer Society in American History: A Reader*. Ithaca, NY: Cornell University Press, 1999.

Gioia, Ted, *The History of Jazz*. New York: Oxford University Press, 1997.

González, Ana María, *Mi voz y yo: memorias*. Madrid: Biblioteca Nueva, 1955.

Gonzáles, Michael J., *The Mexican Revolution: 1910–1940*. Albuquerque: University of New Mexico Press, 2002.

González Clavijo, Francisco, "Los colores interiors de la música Afrocubana," in Jesús Galindo Cáceres (ed.), *Entorno de miradaas*. Veracruz: Instituto Veracruzano de Cultura, 2003.

Gordon, Robert, *Can't be Satisfied: The Life and Times of Muddy Waters*. Boston: Little, Brown, 2002.

Granados, Pável, *Apague la luz . . . y escuche*. Mexico City: Biblioteca de ISSSTE, 1999.

Granados, Pável, *XEW: 70 años en el aire*. Mexico City: Editorial Clío, 2000.

Granados, Pável, *Agustín Lara: Canciones*. Veracruz/Mexico City: Gobierno de Veracruz/Océano, 2008.

Gutmann, Matthew C. (ed.), *Changing Men and Masculinities in Latin America*. Durham, NC: Duke University Press, 2003.

Gutmann, Matthew C., *The Meanings of Macho: Being a Man in Mexico City*. Berkeley: University of California Press, 1996.

Hamm, Charles, *Irving Berlin: Songs From the Melting Pot, the Formative Years, 1907–1914*. New York: Oxford University Press, 1997.

Hayes, Joy Elizabeth, *Radio Nation: Communication, Popular Culture, and Nationalism in Mexico, 1920–1950*. Tucson: University of Arizona Press, 2000.

Henríquez Ureña, Max, *Breve historia del modernismo*. México: Fondo de cultura económica, 1978.

Herf, Jeffrey, *Reactionary Modernism: Technology, Culture, and Politics in Weimar and the Third Reich*. Cambridge: Cambridge University Press, 1984.

Hermano, Vianna, *The Mystery of Samba: Popular Music and National Identity in Brazil*, trans. John Charles Chasteen. Chapel Hill: University of North Carolina Press, 1999.

Hershfield, Joanne, *Imagining la Chica Moderna: Women, Nation and Visual Culture in Mexico, 1917–1936*. Durham, NC: Duke University Press, 2007.

Hershfield, Joanne, *Mexican Cinema, Mexican Woman, 1940–1950*. Tucson: University of Arizona Press, 1996.

Hershfield, Joanne, *The Invention of Dolores del Río*. Minneapolis: University of Minnesota Press, 2000.

Hershfield, Joanne and David R. Maciel (eds.), *Mexico's Cinema: A Century of Film and Filmmakers*. Wilmington, DE: SR Books, 1999.

Hess, Carol A., "Silvestre Revueltas in Republican Spain: Music as a Political Utterance," *Latin American Music Review / Revista de Música Latinoamericana* 18, no. 2 (Autumn–Winter, 1997), pp. 278–96.

Huyssen, Andreas, *After the Great Divide: Modernism, Mass Culture and Postmodernism*. Bloomington: Indiana University Press, 1986.

Ignacio Taibo 1, Paco, *Agustín Lara*. Mexico City: Ediciones Jucar, 1985.

Ignacio Taibo 1, Paco, *La doña*. Mexico City: Planeta, 1985.

Ignacio Taibo 1, Paco, *La música de Agustín Lara en el cine*. Mexico City: Universidad Nacional Autónoma de México, 1984.

Irwin, Robert McKee, *Mexican Masculinities*. Minneapolis: University of Minnesota Press, 2003.

Jablonski, Edward, *Gershwin: A Biography*. New York: DaCapo Press, 1998.

Jackson, Jeffrey H., *Making Jazz French: Music and Modern Life in Interwar France*. Durham, NC: Duke University Press, 2003.

Jara Gámez, Simón, *Aurelio Rodríguez Yeyo and Antonio Zedillo Castillo, de Cuba con amor . . . el danzón en México*. Mexico City: Grupo Azabache/ Consejo Nacional para la Cultura y las Artes, 1994.

Jiménez, Armando, *Cabarets de antes y de ahora en la Ciudad de México*. Mexico City: Plaza y Janes, 1992.

Jiménez, Armando, *Lugares de gozo, retozo, ahogo y desahogo en la Ciudad de México*. Mexico City: Océano, 2000.

Jiménez, Armando, *Sitios de rompe y rasga en la Ciudad de México*. Mexico City: Océano, 1998.

Johns, Michael, *The City of Mexico in the Age of Díaz*. Austin: University of Texas Press, 1997.

Jones, John Bush, *Our Musicals, Ourselves: A Social History of the American Musical Theatre*. Lebanon, NH: Brandeis University Press, 2003.

Joseph, Gilbert, Anne Rubenstein, and Eric Zolov (eds.), *Fragments of a Golden Age: The Politics of Culture in Mexico since 1940*. Durham, NC: Duke University Press, 2001.

Kanellos, Nicolás and Claudio Esteva Fabregat (eds.), *Handbook of Hispanic Cultures in the United States*, Volumes 1–2. Houston: Arte Publico Press, 1994.

Kantor, Michael and Laurence Maslow, *Broadway: The American Musical*. New York: Bulfinch Press, 2004.

Katz, Mark, *Capturing Sound: How Technology has Changed Music*. Berkeley: University of California Press, 2004.

Kay, June, *Las siete vidas de Agustín Lara*, trans. F. de Riba Millon. Mexico City: El Universal Gráfico, 1964.

Kaye, Lenny, *You Call it Madness: The Sensuous Song of the Croon*. New York: Villard Books, 2004.

Kelly, Ian, *Casanova: Actor, Love, Priest, Spy*. New York: Penguin, 2011.

Kern, Steve, *The Culture of Time and Space, 1880–1918*. Cambridge: Cambridge University Press, 1983.

King, John, Ana M. López, and Manuel Alvarado (eds.), *Mediating Two Worlds: Cinematic Encounters in the Americas*. London: British Film Institute, 1993.

Kinney, William Howard, *Recorded Music in American Life: The Phonograph and Popular Memory, 1890–1945*. Oxford: Oxford University Press, 1999.

Kittler, Friedrich A., *Discourse Networks 1800/1900*. Palo Alto: Stanford University Press, 1990.

Kittler, Friedrich A., *Gramophone, Film, Typewriter*. Palo Alto: Stanford University Press, 1999.

Knight, Alan, "Popular Culture and the Revolutionary State in Mexico, 1910–1940," *Hispanic American Historical Review* 74, no. 3 (August 1994), pp. 393–444.

Knight, Alan, *The Mexican Revolution*. Lincoln: University of Nebraska Press, 2 Vols, 1986.

Koegel, John, "Mexican Musicians in California and the United States, 1910–50," *California History* 84, no. 1 (Fall 2006), pp. 6–29.

Koegel, John, "Crossing Borders; Mexicana, Tejena, and Chicana Musicians in the United States and Mexico," in Walter Aaron Clark (ed.), *From Tejano to Tango: Latin American Popular Music*. New York: Routledge, 2002, pp. 97–125.

Koegel, John, "Canciones del país: Mexican Musical Life in California after the Gold Rush," *California History* 78, no. 3 (Fall 1999), pp. 160–87, 215–19.

Koegel, John, "Compositores mexicanos y cubanos en Nueva York, c.1880–1920." *Historia Mexicana* LVI, núm. 2 (October–December 2006), pp. 533–612.

Koestenbaum, Wayne, *The Queen's Throat: Opera, Homosexuality and The Mystery of Desire*. New York: Da Capo Press, 1993.

Krauze, Enriue, *Mexico: Biography of Power: A History of Modern Mexico, 1810–1996*, trans. Hank Heifetz. New York: Harper Collins, 1997.

Lamb, Andrew, *150 Years of Popular Musical Theater*. New Haven, CT: Yale University Press, 2001.

Lapena, Alfonso and Fernando Reina, *Agustín Lara: El artista del amor y del recuerdo, novel biográfica*. Mexico City: Editorial Manila, 1943.

Lara, Agustín, "La vida íntima de un gran músico 'con alma de pirata,'" *Life en español*, January 15, 1968, pp. 50–60.

Lara, Juan Felipe, *Anales del cine en México, 1895–1911*, 10 volumes. Mexico City: Ediciones y Gráficos Eón, 2002.

Lara Chávez, Hugo, *Una ciudad inventada por el cine*. Mexico City: Consejo Nacional para la Cultura y las Artes/Cineteca Nacional/Nueva Era. México, 2006.

Lear, John, "Space and Class in the Porfirian Capital, 1884–1910," *Journal of Urban History* 22, no. 4 (May 1996): 444–92.

Lear, John, *Workers, Neighbors and Citizens: The Revolution in Mexico City*. Lincoln: University of Nebraska Press, 2001.

Lewis, Oscar, *Children of Sánchez: Autobiography of a Mexican Family*. New York: Vintage, 1961.

Lida, David, *First Stop In the New World: Mexico City, The Capital of the Twenty First Century*. New York: Riverhead, 2008.

Linares, María Teresa and Faustino Núñez, *La música entre Cuba y España*. Madrid: Fundación Autor, 1999.

Lipsitz, George, *Footsteps in the Dark: The Hidden Histories of Popular Music*. Minneapolis: University of Minneasota Press, 2007.

Loaeza, Guadalupe and Pável Granados, *Mi novia, la tristeza*. Mexico City: Océano, 2008.

Lomax, Alan, *Mr. Jelly Roll: The Fortunes of Jelly Roll Morton, New Orleans Creole and "Inventor of Jazz."* Berkeley: University of California Press, 1950.

López, Rick A., *Crafting Mexico: Intellectuals, Artisans and the State after the Revolution*. Durham, NC: Duke University Press, 2010.

López Sánchez, *Sergio and Julieta Rivas Guerrero, Esperanza Iris, la tiple de hierro: Escritos 1*. Mexico City: Instituto Nacional de Belles Artes Centro Nacional de Investigacíon Documentación e Información Teatral Rodolfo Usigli/Gobierno del Estado de Tabasco, Secretaría de Cultura, Recreación y Deporte, 2002.

Loyo, Jorge, "La vida íntima de Agustin Lara," *El Ilustrado*, April 26, 1934.

Loza, Steven, *Barrio Rhythm: Mexican American Music in Los Angeles*. Champaign: University of Illinois Press, 1993.

Lozano y Nathal, Gema (ed.), *Con el sello de agua: ensayos históricos sobre Tlacotalpan*. Veracruz: Instituto Veracruzano de Cultura, 1991.

Madrid, Alejandro, *Sounds of the Modern Nation: Music, Culture and Ideas in Post-Revolutionary Mexico*. Philadelphia: Temple University Press, 2009.

Malnig, Juli, *Dancing till Dawn: A Century of Exhibition Ballroom Dance*. New York: New York University Press, 1995.

Mancisidor Ortiz, Anselmo, *Jarochilandia*. Veracruz: Author's edition, 1971.

Manuel, Peter, *Caribbean Currents: Caribbean Music from Rumba to Reggae*. Philadelphia: Temple University Press, 1995.

Manuel, Peter, "Cuba: From Contradanza to Danzón," in Peter Manuel (ed.), *Creolizing Contradance in the Caribbean*. Philadelphia: Temple University Press, 2009, pp. 51–112.

Marchand, *Roland Advertising and the American Dream: Making Way for Modernity, 1920–1940*. Berkeley: University of California Press, 1985.

Marnham, Patrick, *Dreaming With His Eyes Open: A Life of Diego Rivera*. New York: Knopf, 1998.

May, Lary, *Screening Out the Past: The Birth of Mass Culture and the Motion Picture Industry*. New York: Oxford University Press, 1980.

McCracken, Allison, "'God's Gift to Us Girls': Crooning, Gender and the Re-Creation of American Popular Song, 1928–33," *American Music* 17, no. 4 (1999), pp. 365–95.

McCracken, Allison, "Real Men Don't Sing Ballads: The Radio Crooner in Hollywood, 1929–33," in Pamela Robertson Wojcik and Arthur Knight (eds.), *Sountrack Available: Essays on Film and Popular Music*. Durham, NC: Duke University Press, 2001, pp. 105–33.

McCann, Bryan, *Hello, Hello, Brazil: Popular Music in the Making of Modern Brazil*. Durham, NC: Duke University Press, 2004.

McGowan, Chris and Ricardo Pessanha, *The Brazilian Sound: Samba, Bossa Nova and the Popular Music of Brazil*. Philadelphia: Temple University Press, 1998.

Mejía Prieto, Jorge, *Historia de la radio y la televisión en México*. Mexico City: Editores Asociados, 1972.

Mejía, Eduardo, *Baúl de recuerdos: Sabores, aromas, miradas, sonidos y texturas de la Ciudad de México*. Mexico City: Océano, 2001.

Méndez, Eugenio (ed.), *Agustín, rencuentro con lo sentimental*. Mexico City: Editorial Domés, 1980.

Mendizábal, Guillermo and Eduardo Mejía (eds.), *Todo lo que quería saber sobre Agustín Lara*. Mexico City: Grijalbo, 1993.

Merlín, Socorro, *Vida y milagros de las carpas: La carpa en México: 1930–1950*. Mexico City: Instituto Nacional de Bellas Artes/Centro Nacional de Investigacón Teatral Rodolfo Usigli, 1995.

Miller, Michael B., *The Bon Marché: Bourgeois Culture and the Department Store, 1869–1920*. Princeton, NJ: Princeton University Press, 1981.

Miller, Nicola, *Reinventing Modernity in Latin America: Intellectuals Imagine the Future, 1900–1930*. New York: Palgrave/Macmillan, 2008.

Miguel, Ángel (ed.), *Placeres en imagen: fotografía y cine eróticos, 1900–1960*. Morelia: Universidad Autonóma del Estado de Morelos, 2009.

Miranda, Jorge (comp.), *Del rancho al Bataclán: Cancionero del teatro de revista 1900–1940*. Coyoacán, Mexico: Dirección General de Culturas Populares/SEP, 1984.

Miranda, Richard, *Manuel M. Ponce: Ensayo sobre su vida y obra*. Mexico City: Consejo Nacional para la Cultura y las Artes, 1998.

Miranda, Ricardo, "Los valses de Ricardo Castro: música de raro encantamiento," *Heterofonía*, 2007, pp. 9–26.

Monsiváis, Carlos, "Santa: el cine naturalista," *Anuario*, Departamento de Actividades Cinematográficas, Mexico, Universidad Nacional Autónoma de México, 1966.

Monsiváis, Carlos, "Yo te bendigo, vida: Amado Nervo: crónica de vida y obra". *Contenido*, November 1, 2003. http://www.revistas.unam.mx/index.php/rlm/article/view/28483.

Monsiváis, Carlos, *Celia Montalván (te brindas, voluptuosa e imprudente)*. Mexico City: Cultura/SEP, 1984.

Monsiváis, Carlos, *Amor Perdido*. Mexico City: Ediciones Era, 1977.

Monsiváis, Carlos, *Escenas de pudor y liviandad*. Mexico City: Editorial Grijalbo, 1992.

Monsiváis, Carlos, *Las tradiciones de la imagen*. Monterrey/Mexico City: Instituto Technológico y de Estudios, 2001.

Monsiváis, Carlos, *Mexican Postcards*, trans. John Kraniauskas. London: Verso Press, 1997.

Monsiváis, Carlos, *Rostros del cine mexicano*. Mexico City: Américo Arte Editors S.A., 1993.

Monsiváis, Carlos, *Salvador Novo: Lo marginal en el centro*. Mexico City: Ediciones Era, 2000.

Monsiváis, Carlos, *y sique siendo el rey: homenaje a José Alfredo Jiménez*. Mexico City: Museo Nacional de Culturas Populares, 1998.

Monsiváis, Carlos, *Aires de familia: Cultura y sociedad en América Latina*. Barcelona: Editorial Anagrama, 2000.

Moore, Robin, *Music and Revolution: Cultural Change in Socialist Cuba*. Berkeley: University of California Press, 2006.

Moore, Robin, *Nationalizing Blackness: Afrocubanismo and Artistic Revolution in Havana, 1920–1940*. Pittsburgh: University of Pittsburgh Press, 1997.

Moore, Robin, *Music in the Hispanic Caribbean: Experiencing Music, Expressing Culture*. Oxford: Oxford University Press 2010.

Mora, Carl, *Mexican Cinema: Reflections of a Society, 1896–1988*. Berkeley: University of California Press, 1982.

Morales, Ed, *The Latin Beat: The Rhythms and Roots of Latin Music from Bossa Nova to Salsa and Beyond*. New York: DaCapo Press, 2003.

Moreno Rivas, Yolanda, *Historia de la música popular mexicana*. Mexico City: Alianza Editorial Mexicana, 1979, 1989.

Moreno, Julio, *Yankee Don't Go Home: Mexican Nationalism, American Business Culture and the Shaping of Modern Mexico, 1920–1950*. Chapel Hill: University of North Carolina Press, 2003.

Mraz, John, *Looking for Mexico: Modern Visual Culture and National Identity*. Durham, NC: Duke University Press, 2009.

Muir, Peter C., *Long Lost Blues: Popular Blues in America, 1850–1920*. Champaign: University of Illinois Press, 2009.

Muñoz Castillo, Fernando, *Las Reinas del Tropico*. Mexico City: Grupo Azabache, 1993.

Museo Nacional de Culturas Populares, *El país de las tandas: Teatro de revista, 1910–1940*. Coyoacán, Mexico: Dirección General de Culturas Populares/SEP, 1984.

Novo, Salvador, *New Mexican Grandeur*, trans. Noel Lindsay. Mexico City: Petróleos Mexicanos, 1967.

Octavio Sosa, José and Mónica Escobedo, *Dos siglos de ópera en México*. Mexico City: SEP, 1988, 2 vols, 1988.

Ogren, Kathy J., *The Jazz Revolution: Twenties America and the Meaning of Jazz*. Oxford: Oxford University Press, 1989.

Olsen, Patrice Elizabeth, *Artifacts of Revolution: Architecture, Society and Politics in Mexico City, 1920–1940*. Lanham, MD: Rowman and Littlefield, 2008.

Oja, Carol J., *Making Music Modern: New York in the 1920s*. Oxford: Oxford University Press, 2000.

Olavarría y Ferrari, Enrique, *Reseña histórica del teatro en México, 1538–1911*, 3rd ed., 5 vols. Mexico City: Porrua, 1961.

Lina Odena Güemes H. (ed.), *Guía General del Archivo Histórico del Distrito Federal*. Mexico City: Gobierno del Distrito Federal, 2000.

Orovio, Helio, *El bolero latino*. Havana: Editorial Letras Cubanas, 1995.

Orovio, Helio, *Cuban Music from A to Z*. Durham, NC: Duke University Press, 2004.

Oroz, Silvia, *Melodrama: El cine de lagrimas de América Latina*. Mexico City: Universidad Nacional Autónoma de México, 1995.

Ortiz Garza, José Luis, *La guerra de las onda: Un libro que desmiente la historia "oficial" de la radio Mexicana*. Mexico City: Planeta, 1992.

Pacheco, Cristina, *Los dueños de la noche*. Mexico City: Plaza y Janés, 2001.

Palmer, Robert, *Deep Blues*. New York: Penguin Books, 1981.

Paranaguá, Paulo Antonio (ed.), *Mexican Cinema*. London: British Film Institute, 1995.

Paranaguá, Paulo Antonio, "María Félix: imagen, mito y enigma," *Archivos de la Filmoteca* no. 31 (February 1999), pp. 77–87.

Parker, David S., *The Idea of the Middle Class: White Collar Workers and Peruvian Society, 1900–1950*. University Park: Pennsylvania State University Press, 1998.

Pedelty, Mark, *Musical Ritual in Mexico City: From the Aztec to NAFTA*. Austin: University of Texas Press, 2004.

Peiss, Kathy, *Cheap Amusements: Working Women and Leisure in Turn-of-the-Century New York*. Philadelphia: Temple University Press, 1986.

Peña, Manuel, *The Mexican American Orquesta: Music, Culture, and the Dialectic of Conflict*. Austin: University of Texas Press, 1999.

Peña, Manuel, *The Texas-Mexican Conjunto: History of a Working-Class Music*. Austin: University of Texas Press, 1985.

Peña, Manuel, *Música Tejana: The Cutural Economy of Artistic Transformation*. College Station: Texas A&M Press, 1999.

Peralta Sandoval, Sergio H., *Hotel Regis: Historia de una época*. Mexico City: Editorial Diana, 1996.

Pérez Firmat, Gustavo, "Latunes: An Introduction." *Latin American Research Review*, 43, no. 2 (Spring 2008), pp. 180–203.

Pérez Montfort, Ricard, *Estampas de nacionalism popular mexicano: Ensayos sobre cultura popular y nacionalismo*. Mexico City: Centro de investigaciones y estudios superiores en anthropología social, 1994.

Pérez Montfort, Ricardo, *Expresiones populares y esterertipos culturales en México. Siglos XIX y XX. Diez ensayos*. Mexico City: CIESAS, 2007.

Piccato, Pablo, *City of Suspects: Crime in Mexico City, 1900–1931*. Durham, NC: Duke University Press, 2001.

Pilcher, Jeff, *Cantinflas and the Chaos of Mexican Modernity*. Lanham, MD: Rowman and Littlefield, 2001.

Pineda Franco, Adela, "The Cuban Bolero and Its Transculturation to Mexico: The Case of Agustín Lara." *Studies in Latin American Popular Culture* 15 (1996), pp. 119–30.

Pineda Franco. Adela. *Geopolíticas de la cutura finisecular en Buenos Aires, París y México: las revistas literarias y el modernismo*. Pittsburgh: Instituto Internacional de Literatura Iberoamericana, 2006.

Plaza, Antonio, *Album de corazón: Poesías completas de Antonio Plaza*. Mexico City: Casas Editoriales, 1899.

Ponce de León, Charles, *Self-Exposure: Human-Interest Journalism and the Emergence of Celebrity in America, 1890–1940*. Chapel Hill: University of North Carolina Press, 2002.

Pous, Armando, *Tlacotalpan: Veracruz, Patrimonio de la humanidad imágenes fotográficas, 1880–1950*. Mexico City: Author's edition, 1998.

Prieto, Jorge Mejía, *Historia de la radio y la televisión en México*. Mexico City: Editores Asociados, 1972.

Quiñones, Sam, *True Tales from Another Mexico*. Albuquerque: University of New Mexico Press, 2001.

Quintero Rivera, Angel G., *Salsa, sabor y control: Sociología de la música tropical*. Mexico City: Siglo vientiuno editores, 1998.

Quirarte, Vicente, *Elogio de la calle: Biografía literaria de la Ciudad de México, 1850–1992*. Mexico City: Cal y Arena, 2001.

Rashkin, Elissa, *The Stridentist Movement in Mexico: The Avant-Garde and Cultural Change in the 1920s*. Lanham, MD: Lexington Books, 2009.

Ramón, David, *Dolores del Río*. 3 vols. Mexico City: Clío editions, 1997.

Ramos, Mario Arturo (ed.), *Agustín Lara: Cien años, cien canciones*. Mexico City: Océano, 2000.

Roberts, John Storm, *Black Music of Two Worlds*: New York: William Morrow, 1972.

Roberts, John Storm, *Latin Jazz: The First of the Fusions, 1880s to Today*. New York: Shirmer Books, 1999.

Roberts, John Storm, *The Latin Tinge: The Impact of Latin American Music in the United States*. Oxford: Oxford University Press, 1999.

Rochfort, Desmond, *Mexican Muralists: Orozco, Rivera, Siqueiros*. San Francisco: Chronicle Books, 1993.

Rodrigo, Bazán Bonfil, *Y si vivo cien años: Antología del bolero en México*. Mexico City: Fondo de Cultura Económica, 2001

Rodríguez Kuri, Ariel, *La experiencia olvidada: El Ayuntamiento de México: pólitica y gobierno, 1876–1912*. Mexico City: Colegio de México/UAM Azcapotzalco, 1996.

Rodríguez, Victoria Eli, María de los Angeles Alfonso Rodríguez, and María Teresa Linares. *La música entre Cuba y España*. Madrid: Fundación Autor. 1999.

Rodriguez Lee, María Luisa, *María Grever: poeta y compositora*. Washington, DC: Scripa Humanistica, 1994.

Rubenstein, Anne, *Bad Language, Naked Ladies and Other Threats to the Nation*. Durham, NC: Duke University Press, 1998.

Ruiz Rueda, Javier, *Agustín Lara: Vida y pasiones*. Mexico City: Editorial Novaro, 1976.

Ryan, Alan (ed.), *The Reader's Companion to Mexico*. New York: Harcourt and Brace, 1995.

Salazar, Jaime Rico, *Cien años de boleros*. Bogotá: Centro Editorial de Estudios Musicales, 1987.

Salazar, Max, *Mambo Kingdom: Latin Music in New York*. New York: Schirmer Books, 2002.

Sánchez Fernández, José Roberto, *Bailes y sones deshonestos en la Nueva España*. Veracruz: Instituto Veracruzano de Cultura, 1998.

Sante, Luc, *Low Life: Lures and Snares of Old New York*. New York: Vintage, 1991.

Santos, John, *The Cuban Danzón and its Antecedents and Descendents*. Liner notes to Folkways FE 4066, 1982. http://media.smithsonianglobalsound.org/liner_notes/folkways/FW04066.pdf.

Savigliano, Marta E., *Tango and the Political Economy of Passion*. Boulder, CO: Westview Press, 1995.

Schneider, Luis Mario, *El estridentismo o una literatura de la estrategia*. Mexico City: Consejo Nacional para la Cultura y las Artes, 1997.

Schuller, Gunther, *Early Jazz: Its Roots and Musical Development*. New York: Oxford University Press, 1968.

Schwartz, Charles, *Cole Porter: A Biography*. New York: DaCapo Press, 1977.

Scott Eyman, *The Speed of Sound: Hollywood and the Talkie Revolution, 1926–1930*. Baltimore: Johns Hopkins University Press, 1977.

Serna, Enrique, *Jorge el bueno: La vida de Jorge Negrete*, 3 vols. Mexico City: Clío Editions, 1993.

Sevilla, Amparo *Los templos del buen bailar*. Mexico City: Consejo Nacional para la Cultura y las Artes, 2003.

Shubert, Adrian, *Death and Money in the Afternoon: A History of the Spanish Bullfight*. Oxford: Oxford University Press, 1997.

Simonett, Helena, *Banda: Mexican Musical Life Across Borders*. Middletown, CT: Wesleyan University Press, 2001.

Southern, Eileen, *The Music of Black Americans: A History*. New York: Norton, 1971.

Spottswood, Richard K., *Ethnic Music on Records: A Discography of Ethnic Recordings Produced in the United States, 1893–1942, volume 4: Spanish, Portuguese, Philippine, Basque*. Champaign: University of Illinois Press, 1990.

Stearns, Marshall, *The Story of Jazz*. New York: Oxford University Press, 1970.

Sterne, Jonathan, *The Audible Past: Cultural Origins of Sound Reproduction*. Durham, NC: Duke University Press, 2003.

Steward, Sue, *!Musica!: The Rhythm of Latin America, Salsa, Rumba, Merengue and More*. San Francisco: Chronicle Books, 1999.

Strasser, Susan, Charles McGovern and Matthias Judt, *Getting and Spending: European and American Consumer Societies in the Twentieth Century*. Washington, DC: German Historical Institute/New York: Cambridge University Press, 1994.

Sublette, Ned, *Cuba and its Music: From the First Drums to the Mambo*. Chicago: Chicago Review Press, 2004.

Taibo I, Paco Ignacio, *La Dona*. Mexico City, Planeta, 1985.

Taibo I, Paco Ignacio, *La música de Agustín Lara en el cine*. Mexico City: Universidad Nacional Autónoma de México, 1984.

Taibo I., Paco Ignacio, *Siempre Dolores*. Mexico City: Planeta, 1984.

Tamargo, Elena, et al., *Bolero: Clave del corozón*. Mexico City, 2004.

Tenorio Trillo, Mauricio, *Mexico at the World's Fairs: Crafting a Modern Nation*. Berkeley: University of California Press, 1996.

Terry, T. Philip, *Terry's Guide to Mexico*. Boston: Houghton Mifflin, 1935.

Thompson, Robert Farris, *Tango: The Art History of Love*. New York: Pantheon, 2005.

Toor, Frances, *A Treasury of Mexican Folkways*. New York: Bonanza Books, 1933.

Toor, Frances, *New Guide to Mexico*. New York: McBride, 1936.

Tuñon, Julia, *Mujeres de luz y sombra an el cine mexicano: La construcción de una imagen, 1939–1952*. Mexico City: El Colegio de México, 1998.

Valis, Noël, *The Culture of Cursilería: Bad Taste, Kitsch and Class in Modern Spain*. Durham, NC: Duke University Press, 2002

Vargas, Chavela, *Y si quieres saber de mi pasado*. Madrid: Aguilar/Santillana Ed., 2001.

Vega, Álvaro and Enrique Martin (eds.), *Guty Cárdenas: Cancionero*. Serie Cancioneros 2. Mérida, Yucatán: Instituto de Cultura de Yucatán, Centro Regional de Investigación, Documentación y Difusion Musicales "Geronimo Baqueiro Foster," 2006.

Vega Alfaro, Eduardo de la, *Arcady Boytler: Pioneros del cine sonoro II*. Guadalara, Mexico: Universidad de Guadalajara (Centro de Investigación y Estudios Cinematográficos), 1992.

Vera, Juan Carlos H. and Mauricio Sarabia Garrido (eds.), *El bolero en mi vida*. Mexico City: Dirección General de Culturas Populares, 1991.

Virtue, John, *South of the Color Barrier: How Jorge Pasquel and the Mexican League Pushed Baseball Toward Racial Integration*. Jefferson, NC: McFarland, 2008.

Von Eschen, Penny M., *Satchmo Blows up the World: Jazz Ambassadors Play the Cold War*. Cambridge, MA: Harvard University Press, 2004.

Wade, Peter, *Music, Race, and Nation: Música Tropical in Colombia*. Chicago: University of Chicago Press, 2000.

Wald, Elija, *Narcocorrido: A Journey into the World of Drugs, Guns and Guerrillas*. New York: Rayo Press, 2002.

Ward, Geoffrey C. and Ken Burns, *Jazz: A History of America's Music*. New York: Alfred A. Knopf, 2000.

Ward, Peter, *Mexico City*. New York: Wiley, 1990.

Waxer, Lise A., *The City of Musical Memory: Salsa, Record Grooves, and Popular Culture in Cali, Colombia*. Middletown, CT: Wesleyan University Press, 2002.

Waxer, Lise A., *The City of Musical Memory: Salsa, Record Grooves and Popular Culture in Cali, Colombia*. Middletown, CT: Wesleyan University Press, 2002.

Williams, Adriana, *Covarrubias*. Austin: University of Texas Press, 1994.

Williams, Martin, *The Jazz Tradition*. New York: Oxford University Press, 1970.

Williams, Roberto, *Yo nací con la luna de plata: antropología e historia de un puerto*. Mexico: Costa-Amic, 1980.

Winegardener, Mark, *The Veracruz Blues*. New York: Viking Press, 1996.

Wolfe, Bertram, *The Fabulous Life of Diego Rivera*. New York: Stein and Day, 1963.

Wood, Andrew Grant, "Blind Men and Fallen Women: Notes on Modernity and Golden Age Mexican Cinema," in *Post Identities* 3, no 1 (Summer 2001), pp. 11–24.

Wood, Andrew Grant, "María Félix and Agustín Lara: A Public Romance," in Jeffrey Pilcher, *The Human Tradition in Mexico*. Wilmington, DE: SR Books, 2003, pp. 185–97.

Wood, Andrew Grant, *Revolution in the Street: Women, Workers and Urban Protest in Veracruz, 1870–1927*. Wilmington, DE: SR Books, 2001.

Wood, Andrew Grant, "Modernity and Mobilization: Politics and Culture in the Port of Veracruz, Mexico, 1880–1930," in Johanna Von Grafenstein (ed.), *El Golfo-Caribe y sus puertos, siglos XVIII-XIX*, 2 vols. Mexico City: Instituto Mora/ Consejo Nacional de Ciencia y Tecnología, 2006, pp. 441–82.

Zacatecas, Bertha, *Vidas en al aire: Pioneros de la radio en México*. Mexico City: Editorial Diana, 1996.

Zolov, Eric, "Rebeldismo in the Revolutionary Family: Rock 'n' Roll's Early Challenges to the State and Society in Mexico." *Journal of Latin American Cultural Studies* 6, no. 2 (1997), pp. 201–16.

Zolov, Eric, *Refried Elvis:The Rise of The Mexican Counterculture*. Berkeley: University of California Press, 1999.

# CAST OF CHARACTERS

Águila, Esperanza, sister of Paz, singer, Lara interpreter
Águila, Paz, singer, Lara interpreter
Águila, Carlos, instrumentalist and arranger for Lara orchestra, brother of Paz and Esperanza
Aguirre del Pino, María, Lara's mother
Aguirre del Pino, Refugio, Lara's aunt
Algara, Alejandro, tenor, interpreter of Lara
Armengod, Ramón, singer, interpreter of Lara
Arvizu, Juan, singer, early collaborator with Lara
Azcárraga Vidaurreta, Emilio, XEW radio station owner
Beltri, Eva, revista theater dancer
Bruschetta, Angelina ("Bibi"), second wife of Lara
Bruschetta, Sofía, mother of Angelina
Campillo, Jose Luis, set designer for revista theaters
Campos, Dagoberto, Mexico City impresario, agent for Lara
Cárdenas, Guty, Yucatecan trovador, contemporary of Lara, shot in Salon Bach, 1934
Cházaro, Guillermo, Son de Maribu leader and Lara accompanist, husband of Toña la Negra
Conesa, María, actress in revista theater
Curiel, Gonzalo, composer, bandleader
del Moral, Jorge, contemporary of Lara, composer of popular songs
Derba, Mimí, actress in revista theater
Díaz de León, Raquel, girlfriend of Lara
Durán, Chabela, singer
Durán, Rocío, daughter of Chabela, wife of Lara
Fábregas, Virginia, actress and theater owner
Félix, María, actress and Lara girlfriend, common-law wife
Fernández Esperón, Ignacio ("Tata Nacho"), composer
Fernández, Ana María, singer, early interpreter of Lara
Fuentes, Luis, friend of Lara, introduced him to Angelina Bruschetta
Gamboa, Federico, author of novel *Santa*
González, Ana María, interpreter of Lara
Grever, María, composer
Guizar, Tito, (Federico Arturo Tolentino), singer and actor
Hipólito, blind piano player character in *Santa* and other films
Ibarra, José Nicolás ("Chino"), trumpeter, accompanist for Lara
Iris, Esperanza, revista theater owner, producer, actress
Lara Larraga, Agustín, adopted son of Lara

Lara, María Teresa, sister of Agustín
Lara, Salvador, uncle of Agustín
Lara Aparicio, Joaquín, Agustín's father
Larraga, Vianey, girlfriend of Lara
Lerdo de Tejeda, Miguel, composer, bandleader
López, Ricardo, XEW announcer
Marcué, Issa, actress-dancer in revista theater
Martínez, Clara, girlfriend of Lara
Marucha (also referred to as Estrella), prostitute who cut Lara's face
Mojica, José, tenor, later turned priest
Montalván, Celia, actress-dancer in revista theater
Moreno, Antonio, director of 1931 production of *Santa*
Muñoz Trumbull, Marco Antonio, Veracruz governor, bequeathed house to Lara
Negrete, Jorge, singer and actor
Nervo, Amado, *modernista* poet and writer
Novo, Salvador, Mexican writer
Ortiz Tirado, Alfonso, tenor and medical doctor, friend of Lara
Oteo Esparza, Alfonso, contemporary of Lara, composer of popular songs
Pagliai, Bruno, agent for Lara
Peregrino Álvarez, Manuel, brother of Toña la Negra, accompanist for Lara
Peregrino Álvarez, María Antonia (Toña la Negra), singer, interpreter of Lara
Pérez, Maruca, singer, early collaborator with Lara
Pierson, José, musical mentor to Pedro Vargas, Alfonzo Ortiz Tirado, Jorge Negrete, and José Mojica
Ponce, Manuel M., composer
Rangel, Rodolfo ("El Garbanzo"), musical mentor and collaborator of Lara
Ríos, Elvira, singer, interpreter of Lara
Rivas Elorriaga, Esther, Lara's first wife
Rivera Ávila, Francisco ("Paco Pildora"), friend of Lara, Veracruz poet and writer
Rodríguez, Raúl G. ("Raulito"), impresario, got Lara's "Imposible" recorded
Rodríguez, David ("Verduguillo"), personal assistant for Lara
Rosas, Juventino, composer
Sandoval, Rodolfo "El Chamaco," poet, lyricist, librettist, collaborator with Lara
Santacruz Gasca, Yolanda ("Yiyi") girlfriend (wife?) of Lara
Sevilla, Ninón, actress, film collaborator with Lara
Soto, Roberto "El Panzón," impresario, revista theater producer
Tabu, María, actress in revista theater
Talavera, Mario, composer, impresario, revista theater producer
Téllez Wood, Rosita, dancer and alleged inspiration for "Rosa"
Tovar, Lupita, lead actress in 1931 version of *Santa*
Trío Garnica Ascencio, early collaborators, touring partners with Lara
Trio Los Panchos, popular trio, interpreters of Lara
Uranga, Lauro, violinist, accompanist for Lara
Vargas, Pedro, singer, interpreter of Lara
Velázquez, Consuelo, popular composer
Walker, Aurora, singer, friend of Lara's
Zozaya, Carmen ("La Chata"), girlfriend, civil-law wife of Lara

## Selected Filmography

| Year | Film | Director | Songs |
|---|---|---|---|
| 1930 | Unknown | Arcady Boytler | Lara improvisations |
| 1931 | Santa | Antonio Moreno | *Santa and other songs* |
| 1936 | Novillero | Boris Maicon | *Novillero aka (El Novillero)* |
| 1936 | ¡Esos hombres! | Rolando Aguilar | *Noche de ronda* |
| 1937 | La gran cruz | Raphael J. Sevilla | Various Lara songs |
| 1937 | Adiós Nicanor | Rafael E. Portas | *Adiós Nicanor* |
| 1937 | Noches de gloria | Rolando Aguilar | Various Lara songs |
| 1938 | México lindo | Ramón Pereda | *El pregón de las flores; Xochimilco and other Lara songs* |
| 1938 | Padre de más de cuatro | Roberto O'Quigley | Various Lara songs |
| 1938 | Minetras México duerme | Alejandro Galindo | Various Lara songs |
| 1938 | El embrujo del trópico (Tropic Holiday) | Theodore Reed | Various Lara songs |
| 1939 | Mujeres y toros | Juan José Segura | Various Lara songs |
| 1939 | Carne de cabaret | Alfonso Patiño Gómez | Various Lara songs |
| 1941 | El capitán Centellas | Ramón Pereda | *El organillero* |
| 1941 | Virgen de medianoche | Alejandro Galindo | Various Lara songs |
| 1942 | La razón de la culpa | Juan José Ortega | *Bendita palabra* |
| 1942 | El circo | Miguel M. Delgado | Various Lara songs |
| 1942 | Noche de ronda | Ernesto Cortázar | *Noche de ronda; Señora tentación; Pervertida; Aventurera* |
| 1942 | Melodias de América | Eduardo Morera | Various Lara songs |

*(continued)*

| Year | Film | Director | Songs |
|---|---|---|---|
| 1943 | Santa | Norman Foster | *Santa* |
| 1943 | De Nueva York a Huipanguillo | Manuel Ojeda | *El cantar del regimiento* |
| 1943 | Distinto amanecer | Julio Bracho | *Cada noche un amor* |
| 1944 | Amok | Antonio Momplet | Various Lara songs and background music |
| 1944 | Los tres caballeros | Walt Disney | *Solamente una vez* |
| 1944 | Dos novias para un marino | Richard Thorpe | *Granada* |
| 1944 | Escuela de sirenas | George Sidney | *Granada* |
| 1945 | Palabras de mujer | José Díaz Morales | *Palabras de mujer* |
| 1945 | El hijo desobediente | Humberto Gómez Landero | Various Lara songs |
| 1945 | Pervertida | José Díaz Morales | *Pervertida* |
| 1946 | La devoradora | Fernando de Fuentes | Varous Lara songs |
| 1946 | Humo en los ojos | Alberto Gout | *Humo en los ojos; Palmeras y Veracruz* |
| 1946 | Lagrimas de sangre | Joaquín Pardavé | Various Lara songs |
| 1946 | Carita de cielo | José Díaz Morales | *Carita de cielo* |
| 1946 | Mujer | Chano Urueta | *Mujer* |
| 1947 | La diosa arrodillada | Roberto Gavaldón | *Revancha* |
| 1947 | Pecadora | José Díaz Morales | *Pecadora, María bonita; Te quiero; Tus pupilas* |

| Year | Title | Director | Songs |
| --- | --- | --- | --- |
| 1947 | Señora tentación | José Díaz Morales | Señora tentación; Solamente una vez |
| 1947 | Cortesana | Alberto Gout | Various Lara songs |
| 1948 | Revancha | Alberto Gout | Revancha; Oración Caribe; Rosa; Farolito; Rival; Imposible; Mía nomás |
| 1949 | Coqueta | Fernando A. Rivero | Noches de Veracruz; Siempre te vas; Oye la marimba; Escarcha; Noche de ronda; Madrid; Amor de mis amores |
| 1949 | Mujeres en mi vida | Fernando A. Rivero | María bonita y other Lara songs |
| 1949 | Perdida | Fernando A. Rivero | Oración Caribe; Talismán |
| 1949 | Aventurera | Alberto Gout | Aventurera |
| 1950 | Cabellera Blanca | José Díaz Morales | Caballera blanca |
| 1950 | La mujer que yo amé | Tito Davidson | Oración Caribe; Mujer; Por qué negarlo, Te vendes; A solas tú y yo; El cielo; el mar y tú; Si fueras una cualquiera. Mujer |
| 1950 | Victimas del pecado | Emilio Fernández | Pecadora |
| 1950 | Pobre corazón | José Díaz Morales | Azul, Solamente una vez |
| 1950 | El pecado de ser pobre | Fernando A. Rivero | Solamente una vez |
| 1950 | Burlada | Fernando A. Rivero | Te quiero |
| 1951 | La noche es nuestra | Fernando A. Rivero | Piénsalo bien |
| 1951 | Por qué peca la mujer | René Cardona | Azul; Mujer; Noche de ronda; Imposible; Siempre te vas; Mi rival; Te quiero |
| 1951 | El recuerdo del otro/ Mujeres sacrificadas | Alberto Gout | Mírame; Noche de ronda |
| 1951 | Mi campeón | Chano Urueta | Amor de mis amores, Pedadora |
| 1952 | Victimas del divorcio | Fernando A. Rivero | Oración Caribe; Tus pupilas; Palabras de mujer |

(continued)

| Year | Film | Director | Songs |
|---|---|---|---|
| 1952 | Ansiedad | Miguel Zacarías | *Farolito; Mujer; Noche criolla* |
| 1953 | Romance de fieras | Ismael Rodríguez | *Janitzio* and other Lara songs |
| 1953 | La perversa | Chano Urueta | *Te quiero* |
| 1953 | Solamenta una vez | Carlos Véjar | *Solamente una vez* |
| 1953 | Cantando nace el amor | Miguel M. Delgado | *Noche de ronda; Granada* |
| 1953 | Para siempre, amor mio | Tito Davidson | *Para siempre* |
| 1953 | ¿Por qué ya no me quieres? | Chano Urueta | *Te vendes; Cada noche un amor; Madrid; El coquero; Cuerdas de mi guitarra; Ven acá; Rosa; ¿Por qué ya no me quieres?* |
| 1953 | La duda | Alejandro Galindo | *Margot* |
| 1955 | Escuela de música | Miguel Zacarías | *Lamento jarocho; La cumbancha* |
| 1955 | Amor y pecado | Alfredo B. Crevenna | *Rival* |
| 1955 | Los tres amores de Lola | René Cardona | *Granada; Tus ojos; María bonita* |
| 1955 | La virtud desnuda | José Díaz Morales | Various Lara songs |
| 1955 | La Faraona | René Cardona | *La Faraona; Madrid; Cada noche un amor* |
| 1955 | Esposas infieles | José Díaz Morales | *Rival; Pervertida; Señora tentación* |
| 1955 | El jinete sin cabeza | Chano Urueta | *Aquel amor* |
| 1956 | El gran espéctaculo | Miguel Zacarías | *Janitzio* |
| 1956 | Besos prohibidos | Rafael Baledón | *¿Por qué ya no me quieres?; Mi novia es la tristeza; Oración Caribe; Arroyito* |
| 1956 | Los tres bohemios | Miguel Morayta | *Te quiero; Ayer, El organillo, Aquel amor* |
| 1956 | Música de siempre | Tito Davidson | *Granada* |

| 1956 | Locos por la televisión | Rafael Portillo | *Caritativamente* |
| 1956 | El teatro del crimen | Fernando Cortés | *¿Por qué ya no me quires?* |
| 1956 | Los chiflados del rock'n roll | José Díaz Morales | *Flor de Li, Rosa de Francia/Rapsodia en rosa* |
| 1956 | Un mundo nuevo | René Cardona | *Palmeras* |
| 1956 | Mujer en condominio | Rogelio A. González | *Arroyito; Si supieras; Compás de espera* |
| 1956 | Sueños de oro | Miguel Zacarías | *Veracruz* |
| 1956 | Tropicana | Juan J. Ortega | *Señora tentación* |
| 1957 | Mis padres se divorcian | Julián Soler | *Amor de mis amores* |
| 1958 | Una canción para recordar | Julio Bracho | *Madrid* |
| 1958 | Bolero inmortal | Rafael Portillo | *Palmeras; Por el triste camino* |
| 1958 | Nacida para amar | Rogelio A. González | *Nacida para amar* |
| 1958 | Mi mujer necesita marido | Rolando Aguilar | *Enamorada* |
| 1958 | La vida de Agustín Lara | Alejandro Galindo | *Pervertida; Imposible; Farolito; Santa; Escarcha; Señora tentación; Noche de ronda; Marimba; Aventurera; Noche criolla; Rosa; Mujer; Cautiva; Madrid; Palabras de mujer; María bonita; Rival; Solamente una vez; Hastío* |
| 1958 | La estrella vacía | Emilio Gómez Muriel | *María bonita; Cada noche un amor* |
| 1960 | Pepe | George Sidney | *Se escucha Concha nácar* |
| 1960 | El pecado de una madre | Alfonso Corona Blake | *Granada* |
| 1962 | Mi vida es una canción | Miguel M. Delgado | *Granada* |
| 1963 | Cri Cri, el grillito cantor | Tito Davidson | *Pelusa* |

*(continued)*

| Year | Film | Director | Songs |
|---|---|---|---|
| 1963 | La vida de Pedro Infante | Miguel Zacarías | Lamento jarocho y otros and other Lara songs |
| 1965 | Los que nunca amaron | José Díaz Morales | Various Lara songs |
| 1968 | Santa | Emilio Gómez Muriel | Santa |
| 1971 | Mi niño Tizoc | Ismael Rodríguez | Xochimilco |
| 1972 | La venida del rey Olmos | Julián Pastor | Aventurera |
| 1973 | Calzonzin inspector | Alfonso Arau | Aventurera |
| 1973 | La loca de los milagros | José María Fernández Unsáin | Arráncame la vida |
| 1974 | Tívoli | Alberto Issac | Noche de ronda |
| 1975 | El ministro y yo | Miguel M. Delgado | Madrid |
| 1975 | Chicano | Jaime Casillas | Silverio |
| 1976 | Las Poquianchis | Felipe Cazals | Santa |
| 1983 | El día que murió Pedro Infante | Claudio Isaac | Various Lara songs |
| 1983 | El diablo y la dama | Arial Zúñiga | Cabellera negra |
| 1991 | Danzón | María Novarro | Azul, Veracruz |

Source: Paco Ignacio Taibo I, la Música de Agustín Lara en el cine. (Mexico City: UNAM, 1984).

# INDEX